# Exploring
# DEVON

## INCLUDING THE DARTMOOR & EXMOOR NATIONAL PARKS

William Fricker

*gn, Fingle Bridge*

Ilfracombe
Mortehoe
Woolacombe
Croyde
Georgeham
Braunton
Berrynarbor
Combe Martin
Martinho
Kentisbury
Bittadon
Arlington
Shirwell
Bratton Fleming
Chivenor
Ashf
Goodleigh
Fremina
nstaple

**168**   **169**   **182**

Northam
Instow
Bishop's Tawton
Landkey
Swimbridge
Buck
Abbotsham
Bideford
Newton Tracey
Chittlehampton
Hartland
Clovelly
Littleham
Landcross
Weare Giffard
Alverdiscott
Atherington
George Nyr
Welcombe
Woolfardisworthy
Buckland Brewer
Frithelstock
Great Torrington
High Bickington
East Putford
West Putford
Little Torrington
Roborough
Burrington
Morwenstow
Bradworthy
Ne
S
Beaford
Ashreigney

**200**   **201**   **211**   **218**

Kilkhampton
Sutcombe
Milton Damerel
Buckland Filleigh
Dowland
Poughill
Thornbury
Bradford
Petrockstow
Winkleigh
Wem
Stratton
Pancrasweek
Cookbury
Highampton
Monk okehampton
Broadwoodk
Bude
Marhamchurch
Holsworthy
Hatherleigh
Bridgerule
Exbourne
Widemouth Bay
North Tamerton
Clawton
Halwill
Jacobstowe
Sampford Courtenay
Whitstone
Tetcott
Ashwater
Beaworthy
Inwardleigh
Jacobstow
Luffincott
Virginstow
Okehampton
Sticklepath
worthy
ater
Belstone
S

**120**   **121**   **124**   **125**

Broadwoodwidger
Clovelly
Sourton
Throwleigh
Gidleigh
Stowford
Bridestowe
Lifton
Lewtrenchard
Lydford
Launceston
Marystow
Brentor
Dartmoo
Lawhitton
Milton Abbot
Mary Tavy
Dunterton
Lamerton
Peter Tavy
W
in
Sydenham Damerel
Tavistock
Stoke
Sampford Spiney

**112**   **113**   **78**

Gunnislake
Horrabridge
Calstock
Yelverton
Bere Alston
Bere Ferrers
Bickleigh
Landulph
Tamerton Foliot
Cornwood
South E
Saltash
Plympton
Ivybridge
Plymouth
Ermington
ymstock

**102**   **72**

Holbeton
Wembury
Newton Ferrers
Kingston
Bigbury
Bigbury-on-Sea
Thurlestone
Malbo

**32**

THE SOUTH WEST

SOUTH HAMS

TORBAY

DARTMOOR

WEST DEVON

MID-DEVON

EAST DEVON

NORTH DEVON & EXMOOR

3

## ABBREVIATIONS IN TEXT

| | |
|---|---|
| C14 | 14th Century |
| Mar-Oct | 1 March to 31 October (inclusive) |
| NT | National Trust property |
| EH | English Heritage property |
| BHs | Bank Holidays |
| W/Es | Weekends |
| East | Easter |
| E/C | Early Closing |
| TIC | Tourist Information Centre |
| M | Monday |
| Tu | Tuesday |
| W | Wednesday |
| Th | Thursday |
| F | Friday |
| Sa | Saturday |
| Su | Sunday |
| SS | Supplied by Subject (reference illustrations) |
| WL | Wolsey Lodges |

## BEACH & SURFING ABBREVIATIONS

| | |
|---|---|
| HT | High Tide |
| HZ | Hazardous/Dangerous |
| Ls | Lefts (left turns) |
| LG | Lifeguard |
| LT | Low Tide |
| N | North |
| P | Parking |
| Rs | Rights (right turns) |
| S | South |
| S-B | Surfboard |
| SW | Southwest |
| WC | Toilets |

## CORRECT INFORMATION

The contents of this publication were believed to be correct and accurate at the time of printing. However, Goldeneye accepts no responsibility for any errors, omissions or changes in the details given, or for the consequences arising thereto, from the use of this book. However, the publishers would greatly appreciate your time in notifying us of any changes or new attractions (or places to eat, drink and stay) that you consider merit inclusion in the next edition. Your comments are most welcome, for we value the views and suggestions of our readers. Please write to: The Editor, Goldeneye, Broad Street, Penryn, Cornwall TR10 8JL.

*To Alice, my beloved Devon born daughter, bedridden for 7-years with Severe M.E. who with her worldly wisdom, free spirit and mental strength is an example to us all.*

Research and Text: William Fricker

Photography: William Fricker
(unless credited with an initial - see Acknowledgments)

Third & Extended Edition, 2022

First published in the United Kingdom, in 2007.

Goldeneye, Broad Street, Penryn, Cornwall TR10 8JL

goldeneyeguides.co.uk

Image Selection: William Fricker

Maps copyright © Goldeneye, 2022

Editor: Izy Fricker

Book design and layout: Phil Butcher @ Camouka
camouka.co.uk

A CIP catalogue record for this book is available from the British Library. EAN Number:

Printed in the Czech Republic

*With special thanks to my son Harry and the guys at Atlantic Longboards, and Surf South West, for checking our surfing details.*

"Hail thou, my native soil! Thou blessed plot,
Whose equal all the world affordeth not!
Show me who can so many crystal rills,
Such sweet clothed valleys, or aspiring hills;
Such woods, grand pastures, quarries, wealthy mines,
Such rocks in which the diamond fairly shines;
And, if the earth can show the like again,
Yet, will she fail in her sea-ruling men.
Time never can produce men to o'ertake
The fames of Grenville, Davies, Gilbert, Drake,
Or worthy Hawkins, or of thousands more,
That by their power made the Devonian shore
Mock the proud Tagus; for whose richest spoil
The boasting Spaniard left the Indian soil
Bankrupt of store, knowing it would quit cost
By winning this, though all the rest were lost."

William Brown of Tavistock 1590-1645

*Hartland Quay Rocks*

# PREFACE

Devon is an awesome County! I have always known this, from having produced Map-Guides, cycling and walking maps to North and South Devon, and from working on the previous edition of this book. But, having completely revised this book which was, in itself, a massive project. I have (again) under estimated the scale of my ambition. From the planning of the photography which rarely goes to plan given the precarious weather patterns, and then the research which reveals more than one can physically place in a book of 240 pages. Is a frustration one can live with because one can plan a further 32 pages, or more, in the next edition. This book, along with the others in the series, will be (so long as I am producing them) always a work in progress. How can I be ever satisfied with the final outcome? These guidebooks will be refined, year on year, and this allows you, the reader, to add your pennyworth of input, if you would be so kind.

The old adage reveals that "An army runs on its stomach" may be an obvious truism. But the habits of today reveals our interest and obsession with food and its producers. Nowhere in England is there such a rich vein of seafood, livestock and dairy produce, and this has been tapped into by the many environmentally conscious hotels, cafés, inns and restaurants thereby (hopefully) supporting low food miles.

The images in the following pages reveal my abiding interest in domestic farm animals and the fishes and crustacea of our rivers and sea, and I make no apologies for my love of pigs. They are such lovely warm and temperate animals with a friendliness akin to dogs. Though the fact that I still love a good sausage may seem a contradictiion given that I would never consider eating my adorable Salar (English Springer Spaniel) so you may well ask why a sausage? Devon is not Devon without its country characters and rambling farmsteads often to be found isolated at the end of pot-holed lanes. So get off the beaten track and wander along the country lanes. The best bits are to be found on the edges of Dartmoor and Exmoor, and on the peripheral borders of the county in East and West Devon.

More variance in budget options – As one doesn't always want a formal meal, or an expensive bed for the night. I have included more options, more variance such as Light Bites (cafés, fish and chips, burger bars, vegan eateries and fish mongers for self-caterers), and alternative places to stay, from a country house hotel (Hotel Endsleigh) to a Celtic Roundhouse (Upton Roundhouse), to country inn (Lamb Inn, Sandford), to glamping in yurts and gypsy caravans (Vintage Vardos). One can not ignore

airbnb either. A brilliant idea, but sometimes one worries about the fire risks involved, and you can not always be sure that breakfast is available.

Navigation & Clarity – For ease of use, Devon is split into seven regions. At the start of each is an area map followed by the respective guide text and illustrations. Each section is colour-coded and the area maps either overlap, or are juxtaposed, to allow easy navigation.

As always, the places included in this book are chosen on merit, and merit alone, and do not pay any kind of advertising fee. This allows me the freedom to choose only those places that I think are special enough to be part of this Guidebook, and I always pay my way. I would also like to point out that I rely on information provided by my team of friends and acquaintances. That I provide 85% of the images for the book has meant that I have visited the places of interest on more than one occasion; usually 6 times, or more. That I have holidayed, played cricket and cycled across the county, and lived in Devon for 14-years has given me a perspective, I believe, rarely matched.

But, what and where is Devon - somewhere in the south-west? There is no official Tourist Board to promote the county. Cornwall, Cumbria and Yorkshire have thriving boards. The promotion is fragmented and not co-ordinated. For there are two National Parks, two City Councils, five or six district councils... all competitively working to take your cash. It is up to a small publisher like Goldeneye to co-ordinate their efforts, and we do this without any sponsorship - not a penny.

I believe Devon (and Exmoor) to be a truly magical destination. Whether you are alone, or with friends and family. Whether you have a particular interest in beach combing, gardens and historic churches, or simple, hedonism. Take a deep breath of air, shrug off your working persona and live the life fantastic.

*William Fricker, Penryn April 2022*

*Challacombe*

# CONTENTS

# INTRODUCTION

Devon is a big county, England's third largest after Yorkshire and Lincolnshire. It has been described as the most beautiful county in England. A land of rich pastures; green fields, rivers and woodland encompassing two National Parks, and a coastline diverse in its ruggedness and endless charm. A landscape so achingly beautiful with beaches, coastal views, hedgerows, meadows and rivers unmatched elsewhere in England.

It is a county with a long and chequered history, producing men with big ideas; Drake, Hawkins, Raleigh who sailed the seas in tiny craft, in the name of Elizabeth 1, and England. These men were Soldiers, Privateers, Men of Letters, Scientists, Navigators, brave beyond measure. They brought great pride to Devon, and wealth to the merchants of Dartmouth, Plymouth and London, and power, to England.

It is a sobering thought to digest, that as we watch the divisions of race and class in the US, that arguably started with the Slave Trade, that Devon and England's wealth originated from this dastardly business. Although most of the commercial underwriting came from Bristol and London, it was to the Devon Privateers that these merchants looked to do their horrific deeds.

Devon was on the Front Line against the Spanish, Dutch and the Portugese. It was indeed the Wild West of its day, and it was to Devon Men that England sought to defend our trade routes and protect us from marauding Spaniards.

Life in the countryside was spare and unforgiving. The peasant's lot was not to be envied. The land was owned by a small number of families who came over from Normandy with William the Conqueror. Town life saw the upheavals of plague and fires. One-half of the clergy were wiped out in the plague of 1348.

It was not until the Railway Age that tourism took a foothold in the economy of the region. Shipbuilding has been a constant provider of work, precarious at times, for the yards of Devonport and Appledore.

Devon is now England's greenest county. The County Council is championing Sustainable Tourism to combat global warning. There are more green businesses and organic food producers here than anywhere in the UK. We have included many of the best farm shops, restaurants, hotels and gastro-pubs. Our selection has been severe. We expect them to use local produce, for Devon's larder is so abundant, there should be no excuses for providing less than excellent fare. We expect top quality. So look to feast on this green and pleasant land. Bon Appetit.

Devon has long been a favourite family holiday destination, and many who come, year on year, have second homes. South and East Devon has long been a last port-of-call for the genteel retired. North Devon has a growing reputation as Devon's surfing centre. The M5 stops at Exeter, and this creates two westbound routes that strike to the north, and south, of Dartmoor. Those Cornwall-bound press their foot down and leave behind a Devon foolishly unexplored and ignored. But before you, too, head off on a fast-flowing A-road, consider branching off onto an unbeaten track. Put your sat-nav aside and take time to wander aimlessly across the back reaches of Exmoor and Dartmoor, into the hidden depths of mid-Devon, and beyond. You may well find your Shangri-la.

*Saunton Sands*

*Surfing in Saunton*

**T**hese recommendations are in no order of preference.

Exmoor pony trip – there are many riding schools which organize daily or weekend rides. See the Exmoor Visitor newspaper.

Take a surf lesson in Croyde, Saunton or Woolacombe – two hour, or half-day lessons.

Hire a yawl from Salcombe and explore the estuary, or fish for bass and mackerel.

Evensong at Exeter Cathedral.

Dartmoor Tors Walk – bag five tors in a morning or afternoon.

*The Granite Way*

Tour the Blue Plaque buildings in Sidmouth.

Cycle a section of the Tarka Trail, the Granite Way or the Drake's Trail.

Take a trip to Lundy, and swim with the seals.

Treat yourself to a Dry Martini in the Art Deco setting of the Burgh Island Hotel.

Catch the Dart Valley Railway from Paignton to Kingswear.

*Vigilance, Brixham*

Take a boat trip up the River Dart from Dartmouth to Totnes, or vice versa.

Descend to the Teign Gorge from Castle Drogo.

Drive the coastal road from Porlock to Lynmouth.

Treat yourself to a Devon Cream Tea.

Lunch at an English Country House hotel; Gidleigh Park, Hotel Endsleigh or The Pig at Combe.

See the fan vaulting, St Mary's, Ottery St Mary.

Visit MAKE SouthWest, Bovey Tracey and then

Family bucket and spade beaches; Putsborough (North Devon), Hope Cove (South Hams), Blackpool Sands (South Hams).

Visit a Castle, Country House or Garden.

Visit Crow Point, Braunton and wonder at the light.

Try your hand at salmon or trout fishing on the rivers Lyd, Lyn, Taw, Torridge or Tamar.

Experience the wildness of Dartmoor by Camping Sauvage (wild).

*Salmon Fisherwoman, Arundell Arms ss*

see the Rood Screen in the Parish church. An opportunity to compare old and new craftsmanship.

Take a trip to Widecombe in the Moor. To reach it you will have had to cross the Moor. You must decide whether to go North, South, East or West to it or from it..

Aimlessly follow a South Hams country lane in Late May/Early June and marvel at the wild hedgerows.

*Saunton Sands*

*Tim Shaw, Dancer and Bull, Mild Steel, Broomhill Estate*

# WHICH REGION TO VISIT

You tell your friends you are off to Devon for the weekend. You may know where you are going because you have been there before. But do they? Perhaps they imagine Devon to be a land of cream teas, expansive beaches, rounded green hills dissected by lanes betwixt high hedges and red earth beset with misty, inhospitable mires and bogs akin to Sherlock Holmes and the Hound of the Baskerville's? Visit Devon is a newish body created to promote Devon's worth. It lacks, for example, the clout of the established Cornwall and Cumbria Tourist Boards for Devon is a fragmented whole. But, they are trying hard to put Devon on the Map. Bless them! With two city councils, two National Parks and various district councils all competitively promoting their charge for your patronage and cash. Below is a brief description of each area to provide you with an inkling of what you can expect:

## CITY OF EXETER

The great Cathedral city and county town of Devon, and a strategic settlement since the Romans arrived in 55 AD. An attractive city of smart streets, shops and restaurants. A University city, a Rugby city, a city of the Arts but one that is still dominated by its magnificent Cathedral.

## CITY OF PLYMOUTH

The greatest city in the South West. Famous for its swashbuckling and seafaring traditions. Arrive by sea and you will appreciate its true worth and magnificence. The Barbican, the old port area is where most visitors gather to be met with a plentiful supply of attractions and eateries.

## EAST DEVON

There is a gentility at work here. The patchwork fields and rolling hills, the Regency buildings of its coastal resorts, the craftsmanship of its magnificent churches. All appears well with the World.

## EXMOOR NATIONAL PARK

A small portion lies in Devon. The climate can be harsh with mist, cloud and rain but when the skies clear, the wild, wide beauty is unsurpassed. An undulating landscape divided by swift flowing streams which cut through the valleys. The only highland area of England overlooking the sea.

## SOUTH HAMS

A land of rolling hills covered with red-earthed fields, rocky coasts and beaches broken by the tidal estuaries of the Yealm, Erme and Avon with quiet creeks delving far inland. Up the creeks are affluent villages with well-tended gardens and village greens.

## MID-DEVON

Often by-passed and neglected. A shame for here is a tapestry of fields, narrow country lanes that create a rural idyll. The lack of sophisticated towns can be a charm in itself. Where time stands still.

## WEST DEVON

The Tamar Valley is the natural border between Devon and Cornwall fed by streams of the Lew and Lyd valleys. Not a place to hurry. Indeed, a place to savour and to enjoy the hospitality of its fine hotels and country pubs.

## TORBAY

This is the "Glorious Devon" of the old railway posters. The three contrasting towns of Torquay, Paignton and Brixham. The semi-tropical vegetation, the wide beaches and the awesome power of the sun shining down on the bowl of Torbay.

## NORTH DEVON

A rural landscape of small villages, rich pastures, secluded coves and long sandy beaches. The climate is warm and equable and favourable for family holidays, walking and surfing.

## DARTMOOR NATIONAL PARK

One of England's greater National Parks covering 365 square miles containing the highest ground in England south of the Peak District. On its desolate moorland tracks the wanderer can believe they are further from a public road than anywhere in the country, but on the fringes lush valleys lead down on every side to thick woodland and picturesque villages.

# WHICH BEACH TO VISIT

The North, South and East coastlines of Devon are peppered with beaches of indefinable beauty. In the North the Atlantic waves rage in to flatten the sands of Woolacombe and Saunton, and hidden behind rocky coves are havens of solitude. To the South are sheltered beaches hidden up estuaries, and to the East, the curious rock formations of the Jurassic Coast. All is in contrast and a delight for the beachophile.

## BIGBURY-ON-SEA

A fine sandy beach with rock pools and popular with families. The tractor that ferries you to Burgh Island and the Pilchard Inn is one to behold.

## PUTSBOROUGH SANDS

The access on bank holidays will stretch your patience. It is a flat beach given to water sports, particularly surfing, when the breaks are clean.

## BRANSCOMBE MOUTH

The chalk cliffs broken by landslips are noted for fossils and fossil hunting. It is a hard slog walking across the pebbles to Sherborne Rocks where you may find solitude.

## CROYDE

When the "surf is up" there is no better break for the experienced surfer. However, when flat and on calm summer days the beach is popular with the bucket and spade brigade.

## EXMOUTH

On a clear bright day the sea, the sky, the horizon flows off into infinity. A wide expanse of sand and pebbles popular with windsurfers and paddle-boarders.

### WOODY BAY

The access is via a steep, zig-zag lane protected by ancient trees bent double by the prevailing winds. A natural tidal pool of nature comes alive at low tide, as does the waterfall.

### SAUNTON SANDS

Once seen, never forgotten. A stunning view that goes on for 4-miles of extensive sands. Behind the beach, Braunton Burrows, a Nature Reserve and rabbit warren.

### BLACKPOOL SANDS

One of the cleanest beaches in Devon made possible by the parking charge. Set in a sheltered cove. No dogs.

### LEE BAY

An isolated hamlet with a beach of special marine biological interest. Low tide provides sand, rock pools and steps to Sandy Cove.

### WOOLACOMBE

One of England's purest beaches where the coastline is untouched by development. Two-miles of sands extend to Putsborough Sands. In high summer not a speckle of sand is visible due to its popularity as a family beach.

# ⛴ WHICH HARBOUR TO VISIT

The pages of Elizabethan history, the exploration into the New World, the defeat of the Spanish Armada, all originated from the two great Devon seaports; Dartmouth and Plymouth. It was from here that the great swashbuckling heroes of derring-do; Sir John Hawkins, Sir Humphrey Gilbert, Sir Francis Drake, Sir Walter Raleigh and Sir Richard Hawkins set forth on their great adventures. To represent England, and for the most part, Queen Elizabeth 1. Later, as one sees today, the deep estuaries of the South Coast, became safe ports-of-call for the yachtsman: Dartmouth, Salcombe and Plymouth. The North Coast has few such havens. Those that are host to the fisherman and yachtsmen are dependent on the tides and when visited are a pretty site, indeed: Clovelly, Lynmouth and Porlock Weir.

**BARNSTAPLE**

**CLOVELLY**

**BRIXHAM**

A timeless village of cobbled streets and quaint cottages descend steeply to the harbour and backdrop of rich blue sea. Popular with day-trippers. Take comfy footwear.

A harbour of great activity. A busy fishing industry together with the needs of tourism has made this historic harbour a popular destination. Fish restaurants are plentiful.

**APPLEDORE**

**DARTMOUTH**

A village of colour-washed cottages and inter-connecting streets reminiscent of a Greek Island. The centuries old tradition of shipbuilding continues but precariously here on the Torridge Estuary.

Set in deep water sheltered by steep hillsides. Few towns in Devon, or England, have had such an influence on our rich past. A place of great character and activity, and a popular port-of-call for yachtsmen.

### BARBICAN, PLYMOUTH

Plymouth's ancient harbour area and thankful survivor of the Luftwaffe's bombing raids of WW2. Home to many historic buildings, close to the boats of the thriving fishing industry and a haven of fish restaurants and fish'nchip shops.

### ILFRACOMBE

A place of high cliffs and rocky beaches, and a rare haven of safety on this North Devon coastline. The Damien Hirst sculpture Verity has brought much needed interest to this old Victorian resort.

### SALCOMBE

A haven for yachtsmen and those wishing to muck-about in boats. A pastoral backdrop of emerald green fields. Its sheltered position allows for the growth of sub-tropical plants & flowers.

### PORLOCK WEIR

One of the jewels of the Exmoor coastline. A mere hamlet overlooked by high cliffs, woodland and fisherman's cottages. A centre of fine cuisine.

### HARTLAND QUAY

Set in a wild and windswept corner of England and forever associated with smugglers of contraband, and a favourite landing for Sir Francis Drake and Sir Richard Grenville.

# THE VALUE & SURVIVAL OF HOSPITALITY

The Covid-19 Pandemic has been likened to a tsunami; b&bs, cafés, camp sites, hotels, inns/pubs, restaurants and self-catering businesses have been closed, some swept away for ever. Those with a will and an opportunity have sold take-away meals to ease their cash flow, and the Government has kept many businesses alive through the Furlough Scheme. But, this has all been for the short-term. The self-employed entrepreneur who has placed all their savings into their business will not wish to take on more debt and risk. A number of restaurateurs with a number of establishments have reduced them to one, or closed them for good. It is a hard game.

Indeed, the doyen, the original that created the genre of the English Country House Hotel, the Sharrow Bay in Cumbria went into administration. Covid-19 may not have been wholly responsible for its demise. Had it not addressed the new markets so steadfastly pursued by the likes of Burgh Island Hotel, Gidleigh Park and Lympstone Manor?

Today, these hotels need something extra, whether it be a brilliant chef or various hedonistic pleasures. They also need strong leadership, a passion and a vocation to serve. Others are hanging on by their fingertips in the hope that these months of Staycation will restore their livelihoods and we wish them every success and good luck.

It has not been an easy task to up-date this book. When we set out in February to up-date the Listings, what would we find? Who had closed down (with finality) and who was preparing to open for the season? Our policy has always been highly subjective. We like good manners, comfort, discretion, style and professional expertise. We like quirky personalities and value-for-money. We rarely include multiples. It is the Independent, free-spirited host/hostesses we are drawn to. So, we include the full gamut; the posh, country house hotel, the lively Inn With Rooms, the wacky rustic camp site...the delicious deli and coffee shop. It is a wide range. Those that do open again will require your patience and good faith. Many will have lost staff and will have had to train the new. Their financial frailties will have been tested, but one hopes they will find new vigour to welcome you! In the article below an idyllic hostelry (Inn With Rooms/Small Hotel) is described. Many generations of the same family have run this business. They provide comfort, good manners, wholesome food, a refuge from this crazy world. They have no debt, no bank manager giving them grief. They have independence from a brewery. They are chilled. How many like them do you know in the UK?

## AN EXTRACT FROM A WALKING MAN'S JOURNAL

Winter. For five months I had been tramping across Europe following paths, ancient tracks, canal and riverside paths. Where I could, I bought the local maps but very often I would just set my compass in a south-easterly bearing. Now I had reached a mountain range, and to cross a tricky col had decided to follow the old Pilgrim's path. I had heard it was way-marked and I needed an easy route down the mountain. Thing is, I missed it. A storm had come in. I had become disorientated and followed a parallel path that led me down into a valley where I had found refuge in a deserted barn.

For two or three days the storm raged. A helter-skelter of snow, hail and wind. I dined on packets of minestrone soup, chunks of brown bread, raisins, chorizo sausage and dark chocolate (always, chocolate in reserve).

On Saturday morning the day shone brightly. But, somehow I lost the path again, and found myself sliding down a rough track beside a torrent. Hopskipping over boulder to boulder, wet, cold, bedraggled, I slowly got off the mountain. By mid-afternoon I was pretty well beaten up and worried about where I could find refuge. A church bell woke me from my reverie. Through the mist I spied a mountain village. Entering the village a group were standing idly at the church's gate. Did they know of a local inn I could stay at?

Oh yes. The inn was in that direction. I couldn't miss it.

I smelt the wood smoke before I saw it. A solid stone built building with large chimney stacks at either end. Lights ablaze inside. The Inn stood on its own. A couple of vehicles were parked to the side, behind wood neatly stacked.

I entered through a heavy wooden door. A large, hairy bearded man stood inside slicing thin pieces of meat. Above him hanging from the ceiling were hams and sausages. On seeing me he stopped, quickly came around the bar and took my pack off me.

"Yes, we have been waiting for you. We spied you on the mountain this morning and

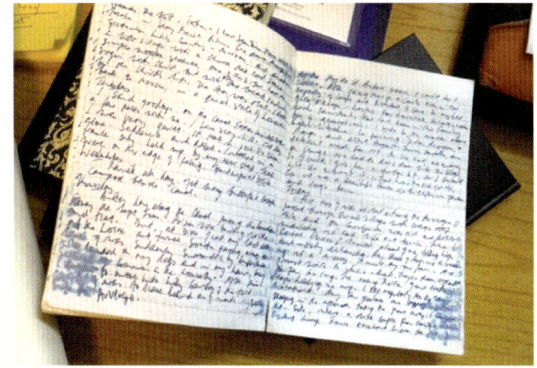

*Journal 1979*

wondered when you would arrive…come in, come in, settle yourself down over there by the fire and I'll bring you some water - you must be dehydrated - No worries, a room has been prepared for you." I slumped into a threadbare armchair beside the blazing fire and looked about me; low beams, wooden panels and oil paintings of hunting scenes, mountains and torrential rivers. Animals heads; foxes, badgers, deer stood out on plinths….a long, bruegellesque table was set ready for a busy repast.

I fell asleep.

I dreamt I was standing beneath a waterfall, my face burnished by cool running water…. "Wake up, wake up." I looked into the brown eyes of a massive hairy beast who was licking my face. A wolf hound. The hound was pulled away and two little girls stood in front of me. Behind them stood one of the most beautiful women I had ever seen. "Hello, don't mind Wolfie. It's her way of saying welcome. I am Francesca and this is Flora and Isabella. I have drawn you a bath and there are clean clothes, I hope not too large for you, Andrea's, and if you don't mind taking these off upstairs we can get them into the wash." I noticed my boots had been

pulled off me and my bare feet were being nibbled by Wolfie. My boots had been cleaned and polished and were sitting beside the fire. Laughter and the noise of people having a good time were somewhere in the distance.

While I was taking all this in Francesca continued: "We have been expecting you. A shepherd friend sighted you early this morning and warned us of your imminent arrival. You are to be our guest. No arguments. You remind us of Andrea who like you lost his way ten years ago and arrived unannounced and has never left…"

I'm not surprised I thought. Lucky man. She continued. "Today is our Saint's Day. You saw the Choir entering the church for St Teresa's Mass. And, here they are this evening for a celebratory supper and you are to be their special guest. So

no worries, enjoy your bath and come down in your own time."

The meal is all a hazy memory. I remember a thick broth followed by thinly sliced cold meats and cheeses, followed by a casserole….and pints of warm ale. I have no idea why but they all appeared very interested in my adventures and asked me endless questions. It was all very exhausting and I can't remember being taken to bed. It was a raucous and friendly evening…

I stayed for two more nights and earned my keep by helping Andrea chop wood, load his trailer and stack them around the Inn. Now that was quite a skill. It so happened the Inn had been in Francesca's family for six generations. For me it was a home from home. Their hospitality and kindness was natural and sincere, the food, simple country fare, and the decor resounded in history and comfort. One word, snug, describes the Inn. Of course, like all who stayed I fell in love with Francesca and Andrea and their children, and Wolfie. I was to return many times until the earthquake destroyed much of the village. Luckily, the Inn survived and by then the children had grown and left home, and their parents had leased the building whilst they sort new adventures in the City.

*Postcards 1979*

*Lympstone Manor ss*  *Broomhill Estate ss*

This is a selection to make choosing your place to stay an easy and quick process. We suggest you view their websites to find one that suits your tastes, expectations and budget. It is often the unexpected that will surprise you with a luxurious bathroom, an exquisite view or a quirky atmosphere that will draw you back again, and again.

## BOUTIQUE HOTELS

**Browns Hotel, 27-29 Victoria Road, Dartmouth.** 01803 832572 brownshoteldartmouth.co.uk

**Burgh Island Hotel.** 01548 810514 burghisland.com

**Hotel Du Vin Exeter, Magdalen Street, Exeter.** 01392 790120 hotelduvin.com/locations/exeter

**Orestone Manor, Rockhouse Lane, Torquay.** 01803 897511 orestonemanor.com

**South Sands Boutique Hotel, Salcombe.** 01548 845900 southsands.com

**Southernhay House Hotel, 36 Southernhay East, Exeter.** 01392 439000 southernhayhouse.com

## CAFÉ/RESTAURANT WITH ROOMS

**Anzac Street Bistro, Dartmouth.** 01803 835515 anzacstreetbistro.co.uk

**Bayards Cove Inn, Dartmouth.** 01803 839278 bayardscoveinn.co.uk

**Café Alf Resco, Dartmouth.** 01803 835880 cafealfresco.co.uk

**Café, Porlock Weir.** 01643 863300 thecafeporlockweir.co.uk

**Dartmoor Inn, Lydford.** 01822 820221 dartmoorinn.com

**Kentisbury Grange, Nr Barnstaple.** 01271 882 295 kentisburygrange.co.uk

**Plantation House Hotel, Ermington.** 01548 831100 plantationhousehotel.co.uk

**Salty Monk, Church Street, Sidford.** 01395 513174 saltymonk.co.uk

## CAMPING

**Orchard Village Camping, Croyde.** 07779 371195

**Ocean Pitch, Moor Lane, Croyde.** 07581 024348

**Incledon Farm, Georgeham.** 01271 890200 incledonfarm.co.uk

## COUNTRY HOUSE B & B

**Basket Factory, Weir Quay.** 01822 841455 weir-quay.com

**Dartmoor House B&B, Belstone.** 01837 840337 visitdartmoor.co.uk

**Larkbeare Grange.** 01404 822069 larkbeare.net

**South Hooe Captain's House, Nr Bere Alston.** 01822 840329 southhooecounthouse.com

## COUNTRY HOUSE HOTELS

**Arundell Arms, Lifton.** 01566 784666 thearundell.com

**Bovey Castle, Nr Moretonhampstead.** 01647 445000 boveycastle.com

**Gidleigh Park, Chagford.** 01647 432367 gidleigh.co.uk

**Hotel Endsleigh, Nr Milton Abbot.**
01822 870000 hotelendsleigh.com

**Lympstone Manor, Nr Exmouth.**
01395 202040 lympstonemanor.co.uk

**Mill End, Chagford.** 01647 432282
millendhotel.com

**Northcote Manor, Nr Burrington.**
01769 560501 northcotemanor.co.uk

**The Old Rectory Hotel, Martinhoe.**
01598 763368 oldrectoryhotel.co.uk

**The Pig at Combe, Gittisham, Nr Honiton.**
01404 540400 thepighotel.com

## FAMILY B & B

**Bridge Farm B&B, Croyde** 01271 890422

**Castle Hill Guest House, Lynton.**
01598 752291 castlehillguesthousedevon.co.uk

**Docton Mill Gardens & Tea Room, Nr
Hartland.** 01237 441369 doctonmill.co.uk

**Mount Tavy Cottage.** 01822 458354
mounttavy.co.uk

**Olive Branch Guest House, 50 Fore St.
Ilfracombe** 01271 879005

**Rosemary Cottage B&B, Knowstone.**
01398 341510 rosemary-cottage.co.uk

**2 Harton Manor B & B, Hartland.**
01237 441670 twohartonmanor.co.uk

**Silver Cottage B&B, Braunton.** 01271 814165
silvercottagebraunton.co.uk

## FAMILY HOTELS

**Thurlestone Hotel.** 01548 560382
thurlestone.co.uk

**Woolacombe Bay Hotel.** 01271 870388
woolacombe-bay-hotel.co.uk

## TOWN HOTELS

**Bedford Hotel, Tavistock.** 01822 613221
bedford-hotel.co.uk

**Hotel Riviera, The Esplanade, Sidmouth.**
01395 515201 hotelriviera.co.uk

**Kingswood Hotel, The Esplanade, Sidmouth.**
08000 481731 kingswoodsidmouth.co.uk

**Manor Hotel, The Beacon, Exmouth.**
01395 272549 manorexmouth.co.uk

**Royal Castle Hotel, The Quay, Dartmouth.**
01803 833033 royalcastle.co.uk

**St Olaves Hotel & Treasury Restaurant, Mary
Arches Street, Exeter.** 01392 217736

## FARM HOUSE B & B

**Combas Farm, Putsborough.** 01271 890398
combasfarm.co.uk

**Hele Farm, Nr Gulworthy.** 01822 833084
dartmoorbb.co.uk

**Higher Biddacott Farm, Chittlehampton.**
01769 540222 heavyhorsesnet.wordpress.com

**Hindon Organic Farm, Nr Minehead.**
01643 705244 hindonfarm.co.uk

**Lobhill Framhouse, Lewdown.** 01566 783542
lobhillbedandbreakfast.co.uk

**West Titchberry Farm, Nr Hartland.**
01237 441287 westtitchberryfarm.co.uk

## GLAMPING

**Big Sky Retreat, Hookhill Plantation.**
bigskydevon.uk

**Bulworthy Project, Rackenford.**
0759 4569441 bulworthyproject.org.uk

**Grey Willow Yurts, Knowle Farm, Nr
Hemyock.** 079666 17488 greywillowyurts.co.uk

**Owl Valley Glamping, Bideford.** 01237 721535
owl-valley.co.uk

**Treetops Treehouse, Fox & Hounds Hotel,
Eggesford.** 01769 580345
foxandhoundshotel.co.uk

**Upcott Roundhouse, Upcott Barton.**
01363 866182 upcottroundhouse.co.uk

**Vintage Vardos, Fisherton Farm,
Atherington.** 07977 535233 fishertonfarm.com

**Wagon With Faraway Views, Serstone Farm.**
01363 82366

## HOLIDAY COTTAGES/SELF-CATERING

**Church House Inn, Village Road, Marldon.**
01803 558279 churchhousemarldon.com

**Beara Farmhouse.** 01237 451666
bearafarmhouse.co.uk

**Frogmill Studio, Tedburn St Mary.**
01647 272727 frogmilstudio.co.uk

**Fursdon House**. 01392 860860 fursdon.co.uk

**Habit, Ilfracombe.** 01271 863272 habitilfracombe.co.uk

**Hollies Trout Farm, Slade Lane, Ottery St Mary**. 01404 841428 holliestroutfarm.co.uk

**Holne Chase Holiday Cottages.** 01548 202020 holne-chase.co.uk

**Lundy Island: Landmark Trust.** 01628 825925

**Pickwell Manor, Georgeham.** 01271 890110 pickwellmanor.co.uk

**Ruggelstone Inn, Widecombe-In-The-Moor.** 01364 621327 rugglestoneinn.co.uk

**Upcott Farm, Upcott.** 01271 816009 upcottfarm.com

## HOSTELS/ON A BUDGET/ ADVENTURES

**Adventure Okehampton (YHA), Klondyke Road, Okehampton**. 01837 53916 adventureokehampton.com

**Ocean Backpackers, Ilfracombe**. 01271 867835 oceanbackpackers.co.uk

**Skern Lodge, Nr Appledore.** 01237 475992 skernlodge.co.uk

## INNS WITH ROOMS

**Blue Ball Inn, Countisbury.** 01598 741263 blueballinn.com

**Bull Inn, Totnes.** 01803 640040 bullinntotnes.co.uk

**Bush Inn, Morwenstow.** 01288 331242 thebushinn-morwenstow.com

**Castle Inn, Lydford.** 01822 820242 castleinnlydford.com

**Chagford Inn.** 01647 433109 thechagfordinn.co.uk

**Cott Inn, Dartington.** 01803 863777 cottinn.co.uk

**Cricket Inn, Beesands.** 01548 580215 thecricketinn.com

**Cridford Inn, Trusham.** 01626 853694 thecridfordinn.co.uk

**Culm Valley Inn, Nr Wellington.** 01884 840354 theculmvalley.co.uk

**Drewe Arms, Drewsteignton.** 01647 281409

**Duke of York, Iddesleigh.** 01837 810253 dukeofyorkdevon.co.uk

**Elephant's Nest, Horndon.** 01822 810273 theelephantsnest.co.uk

**Exmoor Forest Inn, Simonsbath.** 01643 831341 exmoorforestinn.com

**Fortescue Inn, Salcombe.** 01548 842868 thefortsalcombe.co.uk

**George Hotel, Hatherleigh.** 01837 811755

**Hoops Inn & Country Hotel, Nr Clovelly.** 01237 451222 hotelsnorthdevon.co.uk

**Hunters Inn, Heddon Valley.** 01598 763230 thehuntersinnexmoor.co.uk

**Kings Arm, Tedburn St Mary.** 01647 61224 kingsarmsinn.co.uk

**Lamb Inn, Sandford.** 01363 773676 lambinnsandford.co.uk

**Maltsters' Arms, Bow Creek, Tuckenhay.** 01803 732350 the-maltsters.co.uk

**Masons Arms, Branscombe.** 01297 680300 masonsarms.co.uk

**Millbrook Inn, South Pool.** 01548 531581 millbrookinnsouthpool.co.uk

**New Inn, Coleford.** 01363 84242 thenewinncoleford.co.uk

**Nobody Inn, Doddiscombseigh.** 01647 252394 nobodyinn.co.uk

**Old Inn, Widecombe-In-The-Moor.** 01364 621207 theoldinnwidecombe.com

**Rams Head Inn, Dolton.** 01805 804255 theramsheadinn.co.uk

**Ring of Bells, Cheriton Fitzpaine.** 01363 860111 theringofbells.com

**Rock Inn, Haytor Vale.** 01364 661305 rock-inn.co.uk

**Royal Oak Inn at Luxborough.** 01984 641498 theroyaloakinnluxborough.co.uk

**Sea Trout Inn, Nr Dartington.** 01803 895395 seatroutinn.co.uk

**Sloop Inn, Bantham.** 01548 560489 thesloop.co.uk

**The Salutation Inn, 68 Fore Street, Topsham.** 01392 873060 salutationtopsham.co.uk

**Tally Ho! Country Inn, Hatherleigh.**
01837 810306 tallyhohatherleigh.co.uk

**Tarr Farm Inn, Tarr Steps.** 01643 851507
tarrfarm.co.uk

**The Thatch, Croyde.** 01271 890349
thethatchcroyde.com

**Three Crowns, Chagford.** 01647 433444
threecrowns-chagford.co.uk

**Tower Inn, Slapton.** 01548 580216

## LUXURIOUS B & B

**Agaric Rooms B&B, North Street,
Ashburton.** 07460 569125 agaricbnb.co.uk

**Bickleigh Castle.** 01884 855363
bickleighcastle.com

**Burnville House, Nr Brentor.** 01822 820443
burnville.co.uk

**Highcliffe House, Sinai Hill, Lynton.**
01598 752235 highcliffehouse.co.uk

**Tor Cottage, Chillaton.** 01822 860248
visitlaunceston.co.uk

**Westwood, Torrs Park, Ilfracombe.**
01271 867443 west-wood.co.uk

**White House, Chillington.** 01548 581748
thewhitehousedevon.com

## ROOM WITH A VIEW

**Hartland Quay Hotel.** 01237 441218
hartlandquayhotel.com

**Henley Hotel, Folly Hill, Salcombe.**
01548 810240 thehenleyhotel.co.uk

**Red Lion Hotel, Clovelly.** 01237 431237
redlion-clovelly.co.uk

**Soar Mill Cove Hotel.** 01548 561566
soarmillcove.co.uk

## SMALL HOTELS

**Crown Hotel, Exford.** 01643 831554
crownhotelexmoor.co.uk

**Dunkery Beacon Hotel.** 01643 841241
dunkerybeaconaccommodation.co.uk

**Edgemoor Country House Hotel.**
01626 832466 edgemoor.co.uk

**Fox & Hounds Hotel, Eggesford.**
01769 580345 foxandhoundshotel.co.uk

**Lydgate House, Postbridge.** 01822 880209
lydgatehouse.co.uk

**Luttrell Arms Hotel, Dunster.** 01643 821555
luttrellarms.co.uk

**Porlock Weir Hotel.** 01643 800400
porlockweirhotel.co.uk

**Prince Hall Hotel, Two Bridges.**
07541 421576 princehall.co.uk

## SPA STYLE

**Boringdon Hall Hotel & Spa, Plymton.**
01752 344455 boringdonhall.co.uk

**Dart Marina Hotel & Spa, Sandquay Road,
Dartmouth.** 01803 832580 dartmarina.com

**Salcombe Harbour Hotel & Spa.**
01548 844444 harbourhotels.co.uk/salcombe

*Treehouse, Eggesford*

*Luttrell Arms Hotel ss*

Devon has some of the most amazingly located places to eat and drink in the UK. Either by overlooking a golden beach or tucked away in a village overlooking a medieval church and village green. It also has a fast-growing café culture where you can buy some amazing bread and cakes. If you are worried about your waistline, why not get out onto the Coast Path, or bag a few Dartmoor Tors before Dinner. Many will choose a pub, or café, at the beginning, or end of a circular, or cliff top walk. I hope our selection below will make your life a little easier to plan. All entries are described in the following pages. Not all entries are listed below.

## CAFÉ CULTURE/DELIS

**Alder Vineyard & Coffee Bar/Kitchen, Lewdown.** 01566 783409 aldervineyard.co.uk

**Bakehouse Café Bar, Cullompton.** 01884 35222 thebakehousecullompton.co.uk

**Bayards Cove Inn, Dartmouth.** 01803 839278 bayardscoveinn.co.uk

**Brook Kitchen, 60 High Street Budleigh Salterton.** 01395 911313 brookkitchen.co

**Café du Parc, Burton Art Gallery, Bideford.** 01237 429317

**Café Alf Resco, Lower Street, Dartmouth.** 01803 835880 cafealfresco.co.uk

**Café-ode Dining, Shaldon.** 01626 873977 odetruefood.com

**Central Café, Moretonhampstead.** 01647 440520

**Charlie Friday's Coffee Shop, Church Steps, Lynton.** 07544 123324

**Corn Dolly, 115a East Street, South Molton.** corndollyteashop.co.uk

**Courtyard Café & Shop, Chagford.** 01647 432571

**Curator Café & Kitchen, The Plains, Totnes.** 01803 865570 thecurator.co.uk

**Duck & Bean, Fore Street, Tiverton.** 01884 798330 theduckandbean.co.uk

**Espresso Café Bar & Grill, 1 St James Place, Ilfracombe.** 01271 855485 seafoodrestaurantilfracombe.co.uk

**Exploding Bakery, Queen Street, Exeter.** 01392 829787 explodingbakery.com

**Fish Deli, 7 East Street. Ashburton.** 01364 654833 thefishdeli.co.uk

**Flying Pickle, 40 Gold Street, Tiverton.** 01884 242661 flyingpickledeli.co.uk

**Griffin's Yard, North Street, South Molton.** 01769 572372 griffinsyard.co.uk

**Higgler Coffee, South Street, Axminster.**

**Home Farm Café at Parke.** 01626 830016 homefarmcafe.co.uk

Hutong, Royal William Yard, Plymouth.

**John's Deli & Café, Appledore & Instow.** 01237 429065 johnsofinstow.co.uk

**Joshua's Harvest Store, Gosford Road, Ottery St Mary.** 01404 815473 joshuasltd.co.uk

**Liznojan Books & Coffee, Gold Street, Tiverton.** 01884 250183 liznojanbooks.co.uk

**Old Forge, Chagford.** 01647 433226 theoldforgechagford.co.uk

**Otterton Mill.** 01395 568521 ottertonmill.com

**River Cottage Kitchen, Trinity Hill, Axminster.** 01297 630300 rivercottage.net

**Rockets & Rascals, 7 The Parade,Barbican, Plymouth.** 01752 927555 rocketsandrascals.co.uk

**Port Espresso, Middle Street, Brixham.** 01803 411120 portespresso.com

**Salcombe Coffee Co. Salcombe.** 01548 842319 salcombecoffeecompany.com

**Sandleigh Tea Rooms, Moor Lane, Croyde.** 01271 890930

**Strawberry Fields Farm Shop & Café, Lifton.** 01566 784605 strawberryfieldslifton.com

**Temple Cornwall, Bude.** 01283 354739 templecornwall.com

**The Clipper, Shaldon.** 01626 873747 theclippershaldon.co.uk

**Toast Café & Patisserie, 155 High Street, Honiton.** 01404 598067 cafetoast.co.uk

**The Porthole, Woolacombe.** 07533 33396 theporthole.co.uk

**Vineyard Café, Sharpham Vineyard.** 01803 732203 sharpham.com

## INNS (DINING PUBS)

**Agricultural Inn, Bramford Speke.** 01392 841591 agriculturalinn.co.uk

**Beer Engine, Newton St Cyres.** 01392 851282 thebeerengine.co.uk

**Chagford Inn, Chagford.** 01647 433109 thechagfordinn.co.uk

**Cherub Inn, Dartmouth.** 01803 832571 the-cherub.co.uk

**Church House Inn, Marldon.** 01803 558279 churchhousemarldon.com

**Cornish Arms, West Street, Tavistock.** 01822 612145 thecornisharmstavistock.co.uk

**Culm Valley Inn, Culmstock.** 01884 840354 theculmvalley.co.uk

**Eversfield Organic Dartmoor Inn, Merrivale.** 01837 871400 eversfieldorganic.co.uk

**Farmers Arms, Woolsery.** 01237 439328 woolsery.com

**Fishermans Arms, Lambhay Stret, Plymouth.**

**Five Bells, Clyst Hydon.** 01884 277288 fivebells.uk.com

**Fortescue Inn, Union Street, Salcombe.** 01548 842868 thefortsalcombe.com

**Fox & Goose, Parracombe.** 01598 7633239

**Hanlons Brewery, Half Moon Village.** 01392 835116 hanlonsbrewery.com

*Thomas Carr, Ilfracombe ss*

*Culm Valley Inn ss*

*Old Exeter Inn, Ashburton ss*

**King's Arms, Georgeham**. 01271 890240
kingsarmsgeorgeham.co.uk

**Lamb Inn, Sandford**. 01363 773676
lambinnsandford.co.uk

**Horse Pub & Nosebag, Moretonhampstead**.
01647 440242 thehorsedartmoor.co.uk

**Hour Glass, 21 Melbourne Street, Exeter**.
01392 258722 hourglassexeter.co.uk

**London Inn, Molland**. 01769 550269
londoninnmolland.co.uk

**Masons Arms Inn, Knowstone**.
01398 341231 masonsarmsdevon.co.uk

**Millbrook Inn, South Pool**. 01548 531581
millbrookinnsouthpool.co.uk

**Nobody Inn, Doddiscombseigh**. 01647 252394
nobodyinn.co.uk

**Old Exeter Inn, West Street, Ashburton**.
01364 652013 oldexeterinn.com

**Rams Head Inn, Dolton**. 01805 804255
theramsheadinn.co.uk

**Rock Inn, Haytor Vale**. 01364 661305.
rock-inn.co.uk

**Royal Oak Inn at Luxborough**. 01984 641498
theroyaloakinnluxborough.co.uk

**Ruggelstone Inn. Widecombe-In-The-Moor**.
01364 621327 rugglestoneinn.co.uk

**Salutation Inn, 68 Fore Street, Topsham**.
01392 873060 salutationtopsham.co.uk

**Ship Inn, Noss Mayo**. 01752 872387
nossmayo.com

## LUNCH IN FORMAL SURROUNDINGS

**Arundell Arms, Lifton**. 01566 784666
thearundell.com

**Gidleigh Park, Chagford**. 01647 432367
gidleigh.co.uk

**Hotel Endsleigh, Nr Milton Abbot**.
01822 870000 hotelendsleigh.com

**Lympstone Manor, Exmouth**. 01395 202040
lympstonemanor.co.uk

**Pig at Combe, Gittisham, Nr Honiton**.
01404 540400 thepighotel.com

**Taylor's Restaurant, 8 The Quay, Dartmouth**.
01803 832748 taylorsrestaurant.co.uk

## RESTAURANT WITH ROOMS

**Dartmoor Inn, Lydford**. 01822 820221
dartmoorinn.com

**Locanda On The Weir, Porlock Weir**.
01643 863300 locandaontheweir.co.uk

## CAFÉS/RESTAURANTS/PUBS WITH A VIEW

**Beach House, Bigbury Bay**. 01548 561144
beachhousedevon.com

**Beachcomber Café, The Esplanade, Woolacombe**. 01271 871644

**Blue Ball Inn, Countisbury, Lynmouth**.
01598 741263 blueballinn.com

**Cricket Inn, Beesands**. 01548 580215
thecricketinn.com

**Dick and Wills, 42 Fore Street, Salcombe**.
01548 843408 dickandwills.co.uk

**Fremington Quay Café.** 01271 268720
fremingtonquaycafe.co.uk

**Pavilion Café, The Esplanade, Lynmouth.**
01598 753484

**South Sands Boutique Hotel, Salcombe.**
01548 845900  southsands.com

## SEAFOOD RESTAURANTS

**Crab Shed Seafood Restaurant, Fish Quay, Salcombe.**  01548 844280  crabshed.com

**Mor-shellfish-t-eat, 2 Rockleigh House, Mortehoe.** 01271 870633

**Oyster Shack, Milburn Orchard Farm, Aveton Gifford.**  01548 810876
oystershack.co.uk

**Salcombe Harbour Hotel & Spa, Salcombe.**
01548 844444  harbourhotels.co.uk/salcombe

**Seafood Restaurant, 33 Southside Street, Plymouth.**  01752 229345  piermasterhouse.com

**Start Bay Inn, Torcross.**  01548 580553
startbayinn.co.uk

**The Hook & Line, Royal William Yard.**
01752 265374  thehookandlineplymouth.co.uk

## RESTAURANTS

**Elephant Bar & Restaurant, 3-4 Beacon Terrace, Torquay.** 01803 200044
elephantrestaurant.co.uk

**Hathaways, Dunster.**  01643 821725

**Maiden Arch by Roberty Bryant, 14 Maiden St., Barnstaple.** 01271 523774  maidenarch.co.uk

**Noel Corston, South Street, Woolacombe.**
01271 871187  noelcorston.com

**Number 8, Allhalland Street, Bideford.**
01237 237589  onebideford.co.uk

*Broomhill ss*

**Pattards, Hartland.** 01237 441444
pattardsrestaurant.co.uk

**Reeves, High Street, Dunster.**

**Rendezvous Wine Bar & Restaurant, 38 Southernhay East, Exeter.** 01392 270222

**Rusty Pig, Yonder Street, Ottery St Mary.**
01404 815580  rustypig.co.uk

**Samphire21, The Beacon, Exmouth.**
01395 274477  samphire21.co.uk

**Spelt, 42 Broad Street, Bampton.** 01398 31044
speltbampton.co.uk

**The Angel, South Embankment, Dartmouth.**
01803 833488  theangeldartmouth.co.uk

**The Old Bank, Church Steps, Lynton.** 01598
751487  theoldbanklynton.co.uk

**Thomas Carr 1973, Fore St., Ilfracombe.**

**Woods Bar & Restaurant, 4 Bank Square, Dulverton.** 01398 324007  woodsdulverton.co.uk

**Yukisan, 51 Notte Street, Plymouth.**
01752 250240  yukisan.co.uk

*Crab Crumpet, Elephant Restaurant, Torquay ss*

*Chocolate Pudding, Dartmoor Inn, Lydford ss*

# SOUTH HAMS

Stretching from Plymouth to Salcombe and Start Point, and up the eastern coastline to Dartmouth. This curiously named area, based on the old English name "Hamme" meaning enclosed or sheltered place, is one of rocky coasts and beaches broken up by the tidal estuaries of the Yealm, Erme and Avon, and the lovely stretch of water below Kingsbridge with its quiet creeks delving far inland.

High cliffs mostly dominate the coastline, but here and there are attractive little villages of thatched cottages; Wembury, Bigbury, Inner and Outer Hope. Inland is a pastoral landscape of rolling hills and red-earthed fields bisected by twisty roads beneath high hedges - not a place for the traveller in a hurry.

Arriving from the north of the county one first descends on Totnes, the Jewel of the South Hams, which is bordered to the north eastern edge by the enchanting Dart Estuary and the well-tended villages on its shoreline; Cornworthy, Dittisham and Tuckenhay, all are worth a leisurely visit.

*Newton Ferrers*

## MODBURY

A hilltop town set in a deep hollow surrounded by the rolling, undulating hills of the South Hams and one of Devon's finest. The drive descending Church Street draws you to smart slate-hung houses built in the C18 and C19s. Walk left up Brownston Street to view more statuesque builds - see Kingsland House. In the Middle Ages the fortunes of the town were derived from wool. The affluent clothiers decorated the C14 church, and built some fine houses burnt down by the Parliamentarians in the Civil War battles of 1642 and 1643. Birthplace of Thomas Savery, business partner to Thomas Newcomen. St George's Fair. Walk down the street and on your right, a **Delicatessen**, then the **Aune Valley butchery** for pasties, pies and rolls, further on to **The Old Baker**y for their award-winning cakes, patisseries and coffee, open M-Sa 9-3. **The Modbury Inn** up on Brownston Street is your traditional inn offering ales and pub-grub 12-2, 6-8pm and

B&B: 01548 831230 themodburyinn.co.uk.

For fine dining and a bed, the **White Hart Hote**l on Church St, 01548 830652 (J2) whitehearthotelmodbury.co.uk

## TO VISIT…

**Brownston Gallery, 36 Church St**. Lively little gallery with an ever-changing venue for new and established artists, sculptures, ceramicists and West Country landscapes. Open M-Sa 10-5, W 10-1. 01548 831338 (J2) thebrownstongallery.co.uk

**Calancombe Vineyard.** A glorious new venture in South Hams - 60 acres with 23,000 vines and orchards with apples, damsons, mirabelles and thousands of blackcurrant bushes. All is sustainably grown and solar powered. To produce White, Rose and Sparkling wines, as well as sparkling cyders, cassis and more. Open Th-Su 11-5 for self-guided tours and tastings. Guided tours require pre-booking. Cellar Door Café open for lunch F-Su 11-5. (K1) 01548 830905 calancombe-estate.com

**Mr McAllister's Amazing Toy Soldier Emporium, Brownston St.,** Relive the battle of Rorke's Drift and many other battles of our forgotten Empire. Open Tu-Th 10-2, Sa 9-3. Call: 07957 597217 (J2)

**Parish Church of St George**. Viewed from afar, the tall, lofty medieval spire is unusual for a C14 church. Tombs of the Crusaders. Prideaux Arms. Carved pulpit. Jacobean chair. Note the differing styles of the exterior doors. (J2)

## SALCOMBE

No visitor can come to the South Hams without visiting Salcombe. The setting of the town beside the estuary with the pastoral backdrop of emerald green fields is simply stunning. Its sheltered position, and mild climate, encourages the growth of sub-tropical plants and flowers. The pockets of golden sand on either side of the estuary make for ideal family holidays. It is also a busy and popular location for learning to sail dinghies, and a favourite Port-of-Call for yachtsmen. In July and August the visitors outnumber the locals by 10 to 1. The abundance of second

400,000 bce
Acheulean hand axes deposited in Kent's Cavern.

250,000 bce
Hand axes deposited in Axe Valley.

homes is a sore issue for those Salcombe born and bred, who now have to look far and wide for affordable housing. The busy High Street and the narrow streets off it are brimming with mutiples' designer shops (Jack Wills, Fat Face, White Stuff, Musto etc) restaurants and gift shops. To get a real feel of Salcombe you either have to arrive via sail (or coastpath), or failing that by car. As you descend the steep hill follow the signs to the long term Creek Car Park on your left. Enter Gould Road into Island Street. This is old-time Salcombe with a bevy of interesting craftspeople and independent businesses. There is a wide choice of eateries and a number of boat hirers, too. The RNLI Lifeboat is one establishment that has no seasonal shortfall, and for all seafarers, the RNLI Museum is a worthy Port-of-Call. (M8)

## TO VISIT...

**Gallery Five, Island St.** This sweet little gallery features original paintings, ceramics, hand-painted furniture and unusual gifts. Open daily 10-5. 01548 288162 gallery5salcombe.co.uk

**Island Cruising Club, No 3 Boat Store**. Watersports, sailing centre; courses (residential and non-residential) and daily boat hire. Associated with The Egremont Trust. (M8) 01548 852405 islandcruisingclub.co.uk

**Jim Martins Sculptor, Thorning St.** Jim will design and carve a stone sculpture for you; your dog, a portrait. Open daily. jimmartins.co.uk

**Overbecks Museum & Gardens (NT)**. Elegant Edwardian house containing local photos, model boats, animals, birds and eggs, moths and butterflies, dolls and toys. Special interest for children. Museum open daily mid-Feb to Oct 11-5. (M9) 01548 842893 nationaltrust.org

**Rudds, Victoria Quay.** How many Welly makers have you met? Here, you can talk to the Man who knows his wellies, through quagmires, mud and rain. (M8) 01548 289041 ruddswellies.co.uk

**Salcombe Art Club, Victoria Quay**. Paintings, drawings and ceramics by local artists in large studio overlooking the Estuary. Tuition on painting, woodblock printmaking, Drawing and oil painting. Open dfaily 11-5. (M8) salcombeartclub.org.uk

**Salcombe Distilling Company, Island St.** You can visit the Distillery, learn the art of distilling in the Gin School and if your heart desires, taste the blessed nectar. Open Tu-Th 11-7, F-Sa 12-8 & Su 12-5. salcombedistilling.com

**Salcombe Maritime Museum, Market St.** Unique collection of antique paintings. Trading schooners. Shipwrecks, fishing and shipbuilding. Open daily Apr-Oct 10.30-12.30, 2.30-4.30. (M8) 01548 843080 salcombemuseum.org.uk

**Tonic Gallery, 30 Island St**. Large canvases of boatyards and memories of Salcombe by Greg Ramsden 07733 225662 (M8) tonicgallery.co.uk

**White Space Art, Coves Quay**. One of Salcombe's great attractions not to be missed; a bright and attractive gallery with a wide range of paintings and decorative art in all forms. Open daily Apr-Dec. (M8) 01548 844144 whitespaceart.com

**Will Bees Bespoke, Island St.** Handcrafted accesssories, personalised goods made in the finest fabrics and leather: bags, cushions, belts. Open daily. 01548 842119 willbeesbespoke.co.uk

## LIGHT BITES...

**From Creek Car Park** you can spy the **Crab Shed on Fish Quay**. Fish and crustacea: hand-dived scallops, crab and lobsters exclusively supplied by local boats. Seasonal vegetables. Open daily. (M8) 01548 844280 crabshed.com

On leaving head toward Island Street to the **Salcombe Dairy Ice Cream** store...then onto Fore St which has a fair selection of eateries. On your right is the **Salcombe Coffee Co, 73 Fore St**. A friendly little diner in centre of village. All day breakfast, high teas and supper. Some believe the best value food in town. Open all year. (M8) 01548 842319 salcombe.co.uk

Up the street across to the left is the **Salcombe Seafood Deli** at 11 Clifton Place for your Seafood boxes and crab sandwiches, 01548 84440. Next door, The **Salcombe Yawl** for salad boxes and sandwiches. Further up the street overlooking the Short Stay car park, **Captain Morgan's** for an all-day breakfast and take-aways. In need of breakfast, a seat, esoteric music and laid-back conversation where time stands still; **Time & Traveller at The Estuary Club**. Upstairs a Cocktail Bar and eclectic, luxurious accommodation. timeandtraveller.com

## TO VISIT...

**Ben's Farm Shop, Yealmpton.** It all started with a sausage. Ben Watson of Riverford Farm now has two farm shops and four other outlets in South Devon. Fresh organic meat and the full provison of agricultural produce on sale. Café. Open M-Sa 9-6, Su 10-5. (E2) bensfarmshop.co.uk

Next door you have:

**Yealmpton Chairs.** These are hand made by Jeremy Rowett, an ancient craft that developed and flourished in Yealmpton. The notable feature is the one piece of bent wood forms the arms and back. Open daily. 07977 098808 (E2) yealmptonchair.co.uk

**Flete.** Grade 1 listed building. Originally a Tudor manor house with C18 and C19 additions. Redesigned in late 1800s by Norman Shaw. Private residence with self-contained, private retirement apartments. No longer open. (G2)

**Flete Estate.** A selection of coastal holiday cottages to rent on this estate designated an Area of Oustanding Natural Beauty and a Site of Special Scientific Interest. All available to you as you walk the coastpath alive with wild flowers and wildlife. Glamping in six Bell Tents. (F/G4) 01752 830234 flete.co.uk

## EAT...DRINK...SLEEP...

**Burgh Island Hotel.** Art Deco meets Agatha Christie who wrote two novels whilst staying here. Indeed, a complete one-off in a sensational position on a private island overlooking Bigbury Bay. Evening Dress is the norm for Dinner in The Ballroom. (H6) 01548 810514 burghisland.com

**Henley Hotel, Folly Hill.** An Edwardian seaside villa with magical views over Bigbury Bay that has been converted into a small, cosy, cluttered, home-like hotel with 6-bedrooms. The Chef, Martyn, takes great care to prepare you feasts. (J5) 01548 810240 thehenleyhotel.co.uk

**Plantation House Hotel, Totnes Rd.** A highly praised boutique restaurant with rooms a short distance from Plymouth and the south coast. Added, an elegant dining experience to accommodate all foodie afficionados. (H2) 01548 831100. plantationhousehotel.co.uk

**Salcombe Harbour Hotel & Spa.** If you wish to be pampered, to enjoy some hedonism and to look and linger at a beautiful view, be sure to book a top-floor room with estuary views. Seafood

**8,500-5,500 bce**
Later Mesolithic deposits in Devon.

**3,500-2,500 bce**
Late Neolithic cultures in Devon.

restaurant. 01548 844444 [harbourhotels.co.uk](harbourhotels.co.uk)

**South Sands Boutique Hotel, Salcombe.** Bright, blue skies, a golden beach outside your light and airy bedroom, and all furnished in wood created by local craftsmen. Dog friendly. 01548 845900 [southsands.com](southsands.com)

**Thurlestone Hotel.** An established family hotel set beside the unspoilt and spectacular South Devon Coast. There are many leisure, sports and spa facilities including a 9-hole golf course and the Dolphin Children's Club. For more informality, the Village Inn, next door. (K6) 01548 560382 [thurlestone.co.uk](thurlestone.co.uk)

## EAT...DRINK...RELAX...

**Pilchard Inn, Burgh Island.** A glorious watering hole (since 1336) on a sunny day made famous by Tom Crocker whose ghost still haunts it. Fine ales and bar food. Cross via Sea tractor (cut off twice daily). (H6) 01548 810514 [burghisland.com](burghisland.com)

**The Ship Inn, Noss Mayo.** Light, airy and nautical waterside pub. Fresh fish, Devon lamb and salmon. Log fires and newspapers. What more could you wish for? (C4) 01752 872387 [nossmayo.com](nossmayo.com)

**The Sloop Inn, Bantham.** A former C14 pirates and smugglers' inn now offering fine fresh fish, shell fish and Devon beef and lamb dishes. 6-bedrooms. A good base from which to surf the local beach and walk the coastpath. (J6) 01548 560489. [thesloop.co.uk](thesloop.co.uk)

**Village Inn, Thurlestone.** C16 Inn belonging to the Grove family for over 100 years. Free house serving real ales and fresh seasonal food, seafood a speciality. Themed nights. Live music. Children and dogs welcome. Open daily from 11.30 for coffee and pastries. (K6) 01548 563525 [thurlestone.co.uk](thurlestone.co.uk)

## COASTAL FOOTPATH...

**Yealm Estuary to Erme Mouth;** 11 miles. From the far side of the ferry the path follows the left bank of the **Yealm** and rounds **Gara Point**, continuing along **Revelstoke Drive**, a scenic C19 carriageway. Up to **Blackstone Point** the coastline is owned by the National Trust. The path keeps close to the clifftops and there is access to a number of secluded coves. After **Stoke Point** comes the ascent of **Beacon Hill** and a succession of further climbs and descents. Approaching **Mothercombe** the route turns inland and there is a short stretch of road leading to the beach at the mouth of the **Erme**. There is no ferry and

*Burgh Island Hotel ss*

### LIGHT BITES...

**Beach House, Bigbury Bay.** What a great location: add the great food (fish, burgers, bfast butties, crab sarnies) and the chilled ambience and good weather, you have a combo made in...? Open from 11 M-F, 10 at W/Es (K7) 01548 561144 beachhousedevon.com

**Oyster Shack, Milburn Orchard Farm**. A seafood bistro of great renown and popularity; local oysters and fresh fish al fresco. Masterclass cookery classes on international seafood cooking. Open for breakfast, lunch and dinner. (K4) 01548 810876 oystershack.co.uk

**Venus Café, Bigbury On Sea**. Environmental award-winning café in stunning beach location. Breakfast, lunch and ice creams. Open daily East-Oct & winter W/Es 10-5. (J6) 01548 810141 venuscompany.co.uk

**Wembury Mill (NT).** Mill house on beach for breakfasts and cream teas. Open Apr-Oct 10.30-5. (B3) 01752 862314

the water can only be crossed one hour either side of low tide - otherwise a long detour is necessary.

**Erme Mouth to Bigbury**; 5 miles. The path continues near the cliff edge with fairly strenuous ups and downs. **Bigbury** is a small resort with modest amenities, from which **Burgh Island** can be visited.

**Bigbury to Hope Cove**; 7 miles. There is a ferry across the **Avon** on a limited summer schedule, but the river can also be crossed on foot at low tide. From **Bantham** is an easy cliffside walk skirting the golf course to **Thurlestone Sands** and along the shore to **Hope Cove**, an attractive fishing harbour.

**Hope Cove to Salcombe**; 9 miles. One of the most spectacular sections of the path - the whole stretch is owned by the National Trust. After ascending **Bolt Tail**, the route follows the cliff top all the way, with steep descents to **Soar Mill Cove** and **Starehole Bay.** After ascending **Sharp Tor** the path comes down past **Overbecks Gardens** to join the road to **Salcombe**.

### BEACHES...SURFING...

**Bovisand**. Sand and rocks. R/WC. (A3))

**Wembury**. Sand and rocks. R. (B4)

**Stoke**. Pebbly sand and rocks

*Hope Cove*

1/4 mile hike from P. (D5)

**Mothecombe**. Sand and low cliffs. 1/4 mile hike from P/WC/R. (G4)

**Bigbury-on-Sea.** Fine sandy beach popular with young families. Rock pools. One of Britain's best locations for windsurfing, canoeing and coastal walks. Beach cleaned daily in summer. Lifeguards May-Sept. Burgh Island and the Pilchard Inn accessible by the unique tractor, or by foot, at low tide. Check tractor times if looking to spend a day on the island. No dogs, May-Sept. Café/gift shops. (H6)

**Bantham**. Sand and safe bathing. Dogs in restricted areas. Gastrobus for hungry surfers. P/R/WC. (J6)

**Thurlestone.** Sand and safe bathing. Disabled access. Dogs permitted. Gastrobus. P/R/WC. (K7)

**Hope Cove.** Sand and safe bathing. Popular with young families. Shop. Inn. P/R/WC. (K8)

**Salcombe South Sands.** Fine golden sand. Safe bathing. Beach shop. Café and bar. Parking limited but can be accessed by ferry from Salcombe. R/WC. (M9)

**Salcombe North Sands.** Sand and safe bathing. Limited disabled access. Dogs permitted. P/R/WC. Winking Prawn Café. (M9)

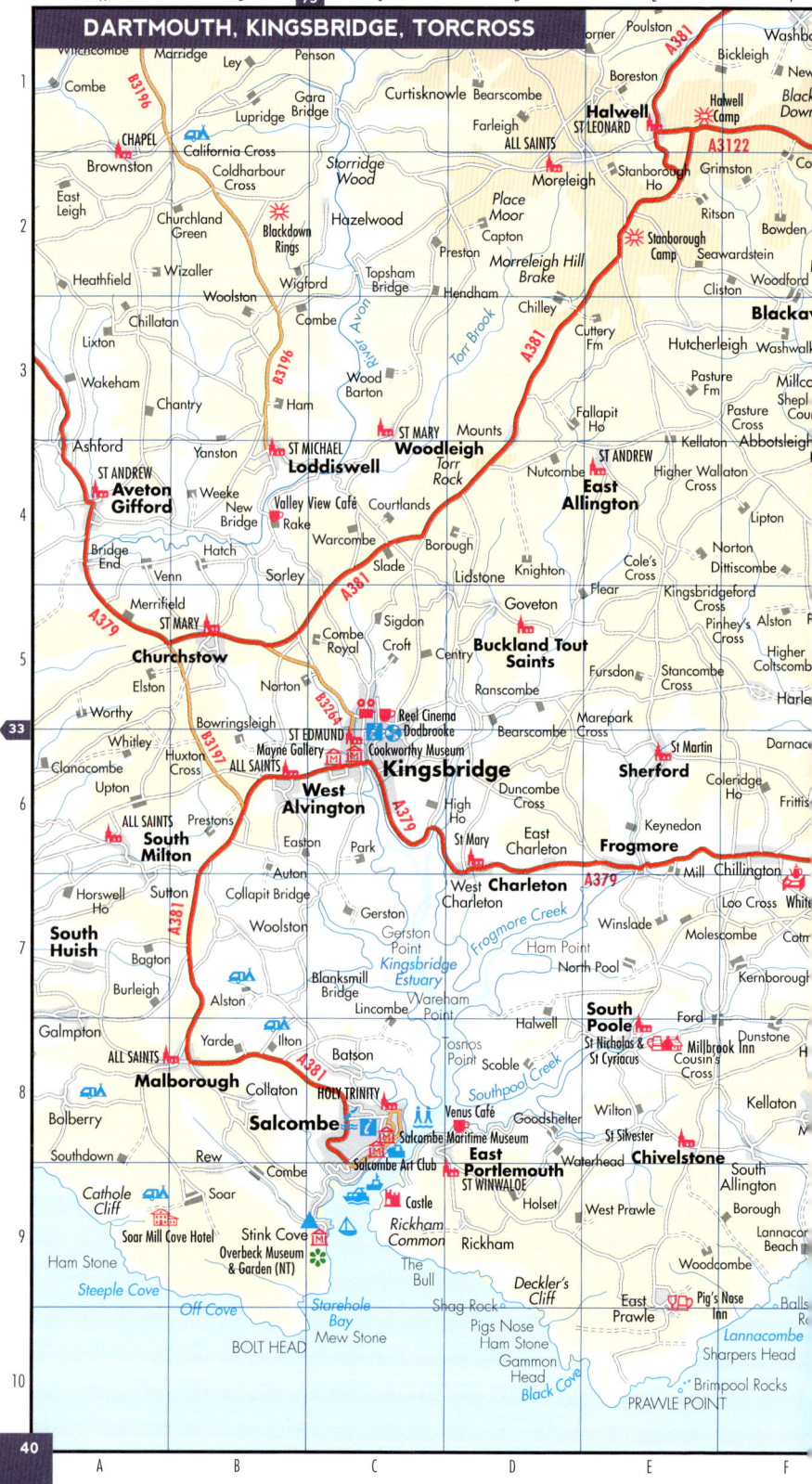

# DARTMOUTH, KINGSBRIDGE, TORCROSS

### DARTMOUTH

A rare gem. Magnificently situated harbour in deep water, sheltered by steep hillsides and a conduit for trade and pleasure boats sailing up and down the River Dart to Totnes. Few towns in Devon, or England, have had such an influence on the course of England's rich past. In the C12, the assemblage point for the second and third Crusades. The Elizabethan Age encouraged Devon men to explore the globe; to seek the North West Passage, the Straits of Magellan and the piratical waters of the Far East. Their boundless exploits on the High Seas, in the good name of Queen Elizabeth 1, and England, brought maritime supremacy and great bounty to this corner of England. Whether these men; Drake, Raleigh, Hawkins and Davis, be seen as adventurers, privateers or Her Majesty's Most Loyal Subjects, is open to debate. By the time of the Spanish Armada, Dartmouth was to be superseded by Plymouth as Devon's busiest port. The old warships would dock at Warfleet Creek, the smaller craft, largely smugglers, at Bayards Cove, now overlooked by some splendid C18 houses. Notably, the Custom House.

The town has great character and activity. Always a medley of locals and visitors. There is much to see; the finest building, The Butterwalk, enriched with eleven stone pillars. But take the riverside walk to the Castle and St Petrock's church, and look out across the water to smiling Kingswear, a feast of pastel-coloured houses, and junction for the Paignton Steam Railway, a marvellous site when in full steam charging up beside the river.

Behind, dominating the hillside stands the Brittania Royal Naval College, designed by Sir Aston Webb, architect of the V & A Museum. Opened by Edward V11, it is a most impressive building overlooking the Estuary, and the beckoning sea.

614    Battle at "Beandum", Bindon near Axmouth. Between the Saxons and Dumnonia.

680    St Boniface born in Crediton (approximate date).

*Bayards Cove, Dartmouth*

Always a popular port-of-call for yachtsmen, the Estuary has two marinas, and many cruisers plying their trade to show you the enchanting River Dart. The town has become something of a food and arts centre. Witness below the many arts and craft galleries, and the bountiful eating out emporia. Regatta time is a rewarding time to visit, the Estuary ablaze with sail and colour, and good times. (K2)

## ARTS & CRAFTS...

**Ainscough Contemporary Art, 16 Foss St**. An explosion of colour and large landscape paintings within ever-changing exhibitions on West Country themes. One of the regions finest galleries. Open daily. (K2) 01548 855732 acag.co.uk

**Andras Kaldor Gallery, 15 Newcomen Rd**. Drawings and paintings of architectural subjects, pots and amphorae. Originals and prints. Open daily. 01803 833874 (K2) kaldor.co.uk

**Coombe Gallery, 20 Foss St.** Exhibits some of the finest artists and craftsmen in the West Country with regular quarterly shows. Associated with Combe Farm Studios of Dittisham. Open daily. (K2) 01803 835820 coombegallery.com

**D'Art Gallery, 4 Lower St**. Paintings with a broad range of styles. Quarterly exhibitions display 70 + new works over 2-floors. Open daily from 10. (K2) 01803 834923 dart-gallery.com

## TO VISIT...

**Britania Museum, Royal Naval College.** The Royal Navy's Officer Training Establishment since 1905. Fine works of naval art. Museum with historic naval artefacts. Fully escorted tours in term time, M & W Details: 01803 677565 (K2) britanniaassociation.org.uk/tours

**Cherub Inn, 13 Higher St.** Claims to be Dartmouth's oldest surviving building dating from 1380 which was then close to the water's edge, and on Dartmouth's main street. A survivor of the 1864 fire and WW11 bombing. Restored in 1958. A cosy pub with log fire, beams, local ales and barfood. Restaurant open evenings. 01803 832571 (K2) the-cherub.co.uk

**Dartmouth Castle (EH),** Castle Road. Castle dating back

## LIGHT BITES...

The choice is bewildering. If you arrive via the **Kingswear Ferry** beside **Bayards Cove** pop into the charming C14 **Bayards Cove Inn** for coffee, breakfast, lunch…you may well wish to stay in one of their 7-bedrooms. Open from 8-10pm. 01803 839278 bayardscoveinn.co.uk

Continuing in to **Dartmouth**, on your left **Café Alf Resco, Lower St**. Yes? You could be forgiven for thinking this was an Italian Trattoria, in Italy. A family business always busy with a lively buzz. All-day breakfasts are a speciality. Coffees. Live music. A great place to meet up. Try their Marmalade flapjacks, just mouthwatering! B&B in Captain's Cabin. Open 7-2pm. (K2) 01803 835880 cafealfresco.co.uk

Just past the **Dartmouth Museum/Butterwalk**, on your rights **The Deli at Dartmouth**. They will make you up picnic hampers from their local cheeses, sourdough toasties and homemade mackerel pate. Bon Chance!

Then Right down Foss Street and Left for the French boulangerie, patisserie, chocolaterie **Saveurs, 4 Market St**. The pastries and cakes are to die for. A smile would be welcome, too. 01803 835852 saveurs.co.uk

You seek art, then head back into Foss Street, at its end, Bespoke Artisan Coffee for some refreshments.

*Dartmouth Museum*

to the late C15, stands guard over the Dart Estuary. Features include hands-on exhibitions and displays. Open daily 11-3. 01803 833588 (K2)

**Dartmouth Museum, The Butterwalk**. Housed in a group of C17 merchants' houses with fine panelled rooms. Notable ship models, paintings and rare books. Mayflower Pilgrims Exhibition. Open all year, Apr-Sept 10-4 (Su & M 1-4), Oct-Mar 1-3. 01803 832923 (K2) dartmouthmuseum.org

**Newcomen Engine House, Mayors Avenue.** Atmospheric beam engine on the unusual mechanical principle developed by Thomas Newcomen, 1664-1729, a native of the town, in 1725. Now electrically worked. Open Apr-Oct M-Sa 10-5, Su 10-2. Nov-Mar M-F 10-4.30 (W 10-1). (K2) 01803 834224 devonmuseums.net

**Parish Church of St Saviour**. In the centre of the town and worth a visit just for seeing its magnificent C15 rood and parclose screen. Multi-coloured Jacobean pulpit in stone. Fine ironwork to South doorway. (K2)

**St Petrock's Church.** Set within the Castle grounds and the last sacred site sailors would spy as they sailed off to new horizons. Rebuilt in the Gothic style. Fine brasses to wealthy merchants. Pulpit and Royal Arms. Norman font. (K2)

**The Flavel Centre, Flavel Place**. Multi-purpose arts and entertainment centre housing cinema, theatre and live music. Children's programmes, too. Bar with pre-show suppers. (K2) 01803 839530 theflavel.org.uk

## BOATING & RIVER FUN...

**Dartmouth Boat Hire Centre, North Embankment**. Self-drive cabin and open boats. Comprehensive safety brief. Competitive rates include, fuel, life jackets, river charts and info pack. Skippered boat trips available. (K2) 07545 518546 dartmouth-boat-hire.co.uk

**River Link, 5 Lower St.** Cruises on the beautiful River Dart departing from Dartmouth and Totnes. Bar, commentary, toilets. Day time and evening cruises from Apr-Oct, Nov-Mar by arrangement. Daily circular cruises from Dartmouth except M & F. (K2) 01803 555872 riverlink.co.uk

## EAT...DRINK...SLEEP...

**Anzac Street Bistro & Guesthouse, 2 Anzac St**. Bright, wood-panelled bistro/café serving locally caught seafood complemented with their home grown herbs and fruit. Contemporary, comfy double bedrooms. 01803 835515 (K2) anzacstreetbistro.co.uk

**Browns Hotel, 27-29 Victoria Rd.** Classy boutique hotel a short stroll from the harbour. Restaurant specialises in tapas, but this is not the limit of their culinary credentials, for the proprietor organises the local food festival. (K2) 01803 832572 brownshoteldartmouth.co.uk

*Ainscough Gallery, Dartmouth ss*

**Dart Marina Hotel & Spa, Sandquay Rd**. A relaxed and informal place to eat and drink (non-residents welcomed) with fabulous river views; Try Sushi or grilled fish for lunch, or more formal Dinner. Close to Health Spa (book in advance), Yacht Harbour, hotel and apartments (luxurious boutique-style). (K2) 01803 832580 dartmarina.com

**Royal Castle Hotel, The Quay.** Former C17 Coaching Inn within the heart of Dartmouth. Bright and colourful bedrooms, some with 4-posters and jacuzzis. Bargain Breaks. Dog friendly. (K2) 01803 833033 royalcastle.co.uk

### LUNCH...DINNER...

**Spice Bazaar, St Saviours Sq**. Simple style and relaxed atmosphere offering a fusion of authentic Indian cuisine suited to English tastes. Open 12-2, 6-11.30. (K2) 01803 832285.

**The Angel, 2 South Embankment.** They describe

*Cherub Inn, Dartmouth*

themselves as Taste Of Devon presumably the fish, meat and vegetables are Devon grown for what better larder in the UK is there than Devonshire? The wines, no. Loaded with mult-awards, the food will be preciously provided and an experience, no less. So Bon Appetit! Open W-Su. 01803 833488 theangeldartmouth.co.uk

**Taylor's Restaurant, 8 The Quay.** This more traditional restaurant affording spectacular views over the harbour will entice couples for a romantic lunch or dinner. (K2) 01803 832748 taylorsrestaurant.co.uk

## KINGSBRIDGE

An old established port at the head of a wide, landlocked estuary, now largely silted up but still active with small craft. The High Street ascends away from the river and is fronted by some attractive C18 and C19 buildings and is worth the climb for the shops are independent and worthy of your patronage. The Shambles (or Market Arcade) extends over the pavement with Elizabethan piers. Birthplace of William Cookworthy, discoverer of china clay. A centre for the "South Hams" district. St Edmund's church is C13 with C15 additions. Cruises to Salcombe and around the coast. E/C Th. (C6)

## TO VISIT...

**Cookworthy Museum, 108 Fore St.** Toys and dolls, farmhouse kitchen, rural trades, costumes, and local photos. Craft exhibs. "The Story of Kingsbridge." Conservation in farm gallery. Open Apr-Oct M-Sa 10.30-5. (C6) 01548 853235 kingsbridgemuseum.org.uk

### LIGHT BITES...

**The Harbour House** is a worthy destination, described below. Across the street is **Coasters Coffee Co., Abbots Quay.** Since it opened this café has been a great hit in **South Hams**. A full range of eats on offer from sandwiches to panini to delish cakes, and they know their coffee/hot chocs, too and have charm and comfy chairs. 01548 853004

Before climbing Fore Street take a left and spy the **Harbour Bookshop**, across from them is the **Duke Street Café-Deli** very popular with locals. Open M-Sa 8.30-3.30 for their coffee, cakes and savouries.

Now for some exploration. Ascending Fore Street you will soon reach the summit and be in need of sustenance. It has to be **Mangetout**, at No. 84, another delightful deli and café with splentiful seating, daily specials and nourishment. Opens Tu-Sa 8.30-5. mangetoutdeli.com

Bon Appetit!

*John Donaldson's Slapton Ley, Mayne Gallery, Kingsbridge ss*

878    Hubba landed at Appledore, to fight battle at Kenwith Castle before retreating to their ships off Northam

*Blackpool Sands*

**Harbour House, The Promenade.** A delightful space encompassing a centre for the Arts and Yoga. Indeed, a whole host of activities. The Vegetarian Café opens 10-3 for breakfast and lunch with teas, coffee and cakes, all day. The outside space is a delight. Recommended. 01548 854708 (C6) harbourhouse.org.uk

**Kings Cinema formerly The Reel Cinema, Fore St.** The former Town Hall and a building of some stature. A destination for cinema addicts with meal/bar deals on offer and the civilised right to drink while you watch the movie. (C6) 01548 856636 merlincinemas.co.uk

**Mayne Gallery, 14 Fore St.** Sculptures, etchings, watercolours of local, emerging and famous artists to match your lifestyle. Landscape a speciality. Open M-Sa 9.30-5. (C6) 01548 853848 maynegallery.com

**Rivermaid, Rivermaid Boatyard, Embankment Rd.** Kingsbridge to Salcombe ferry cruises, scenic creeks & coastal excursions, evening cruises. Light refreshments. May-Sept. (C6) 01548 853525/853607 kingsbridgesalcombeferry.co.uk

## TO VISIT...

**Blackpool Gardens.** Newly restored C19 sub-tropical garden. Open daily East-Oct. (J4) 01803 771801 blackpoolsands.co.uk

**Coleton Fishacre (NT).** Sheltered 18-acre garden in stream-fed valley. Uncommon trees and exotic shrubs. New plantings for year-round colour and interest. Set amid spectacular coastal scenery. Associations with D'Oyly Carte family. The house has Art Deco interiors that encapsulate the Jazz Era of the 1920s. Tearoom. Open daily Early Feb to Oct 10.30-5, Nov-Dec W/Es 11-4. (M3) 01803 842382 nationaltrust.org.uk

**Start Point Lighthouse.** Set on Devon's most southerly peninsula. Climb the Tower, hear of shipwrecks and lighthouse living. Explore the rugged coastline on each side, and or (if lucky) spy seals and dolphins below. Lighthouse cottages to rent. Open Feb 1/2 term, Apr-July, Sept-Oct, W, Su & BHs 12-5. Mid-July to Aug daily 11-5 except Sa, 12-dusk. (H9) 01803 771803 startpointdevon.co.uk

**Woodlands Leisure Park.** A unique combination; indoor and outdoor attractions and family rides from Watercoasters, Toboggan Run, Arctic Gliders to playzones for all ages. Awesome Avalanche, Polar Pilots, Dizzy Dune Buggies, Falconry Centre and Zoo Farm. Huge indoor venture zone, five floors of rides and slides. Big Fun Farm. Award-winning camping site. Open daily mid-Mar to early Nov, winter W/Es & school hols, 9.30-5. (G2) 01803 712598 woodlandspark.com

## TO STAY...TO SLEEP...

**Soar Mill Cove Hotel.** In a quite superb position overlooking one of England's prettiest coves. Unusual in that this family-friendly hotel is on one level with all the necessities to unwind; saunas, indoor and outdoor pools. West Country produce supplies the kitchen's delicous creations. And, Three self-catering properties on hand. (A9) 01548 561566 soarmillcove.co.uk

**The White House, Chillington.** This is a boutique B&B of high quality, style and comfort. The handmade beds are enormous and you won't wish to leave them, or the cosy bar downstairs for your pre-prandials. Your South Devon home away from home, rather than spending every weekend doing up an old wreck, Better here m'lud! Minimum 2-night stay. Dog friendly. (F6) 01548 580505 whitehousedevon.com

## EAT...DRINK...RELAX...

**Millbrook Inn, South Pool.** A touch of Gallic brilliance in the kitchen coupled with a jug or two of English ale, and top-notch bedroom facilities within a boutique apartment. Esprit de Corps lives on! (E8) 01548 531581 millbrookinnsouthpool.co.uk

**Pig's Nose Inn, East Prawle.** Jolly atmosphere and fine hostelry for walkers and birdwatchers. Children and dogs welcome. Tempting ales. Camping nearby in Stephen's Field and Little Holloway. (E9) 01548 511209 pigsnoseinn.co.uk

**Start Bay Inn, Torcross.** C14 thatched inn noted for its wealth of seafood; John Dory, bass, skate, cod, sole (Dover and lemon) caught off the beach. Dog and child friendly. (G7) 01548 580553 startbayinn.co.uk

**The Cricket Inn, Beesands.** One place you could sit for hours, with pint in hand to watch the world come to you, and to watch the sun go down. Old hang out of the youthful Mick Jagger and Keith Richard. 7-bedrooms decorated in the New England style. B&B. (G8)

*Newton Ferrers*

01548 580215
thecricketinn.com

**Tower Inn, Slapton.** C14 coaching inn hidden away beside the Chantry Tower. Fresh local produce prepared for lunch and dinner by an anglicized Frenchman. B&B. (G5) 01548 580216
thetowerinn.com

## EAT...DRINK...RELAX...

**Venus Café, Blackpool Sands Beach**. Alfresco dining; breakfast lunch and ice creams. Organic foods. Open daily from 10. (J4) 01803 770209
venuscompany.co.uk

**The Venus Café, Ferry Steps, East Portlemouth**. Overlooks Salcombe's best beaches. Specialises in organic and local produce. Open daily East-Oct. (C8) 01548 843558
venuscompany.co.uk

## B & BS – A SELECTION...

**Blackawton - Woodside Cottage** 01803 898164 (F2)
woodsidedartmouth.co.uk

**Dartmouth - Hill View House, 76 Victoria Rd**. 01803 839372 (K2)
hillviewdartmouth.co.uk

**East Allington - Lower Norton Farmhouse, Coles Cross**. 01548 521246 (E4)

**High Nature Centre, East Portlemouth.** Herewith, eco-tourism that the family will love with 5-yurts in a large field that are cosy and decorated with unusual textiles and furnishings. Solid oak frame beds. high-nature.co.uk

**Kingswear - Nonsuch House, Church Hill.** 01803 752829 (K2)

## COASTAL FOOTPATH...

**Salcombe to Start Point**; 9 miles. There is a frequent ferry service to East Portlemouth throughout the year. The path traverses National Trust land for the first 5 miles and continues along an increasingly rugged coast, with some isolated beaches, and spectacular views around Prawle Point. Walking is moderately strenuous. Start Point has witnessed many wrecks over the years. The lighthouse can be visited and the area is noted for birds and butterflies.

**Start Point to Torcross**; 5 miles. After the descent to Hallsands the path follows an almost level shore.

**Torcross to Dartmouth**; 10 miles. For the first 6 miles the path follows the main road alongside Slapton Ley and on to Stoke Fleming. At the NT car park a mile beyond the village the path diverges round the coast and commands some fine views. The road is regained after Dartmouth Castle.

## BEACHES...

**Mill Bay.** Fine golden sands and rock pools. Limited parking. Access is via the ferry from Salcombe, or on foot from East Portlemouth. Considered to be one of the finest sand castle beaches in England. (C8)

**East Portlemouth.** Fine golden sand and rock pools popular with young families. Dogs permitted. Dinghy sailing centre. (C8)

**Venerick's Cove.** Access is from the car park at Prawle Point. Walk west along the coast path for a mile, plus then down a steep path to an isolated silver beach for wild swimming. (E10)

**Lannacombe.** Small sandy beach accessed via the Coast Path. (F10)

**Beesands.** Shingle. Safe bathing. Boating pool. Disabled access. Dogs permitted. P/R/WC. (G8)

**Torcross.** Sand and shingle. Disabled access. Dogs permitted. P/R/WC. (G7)

**Blackpool Sands.** The most popular family beach on this stretch of coastline. Set in a sheltered cove. The sands (shingle) are cleaned daily in summer. Lifeguards on duty May-Sept. Fine location for water sports; swimming, sailing and scuba diving. Hire of kayaks, paddleboards and surfboards. No dogs permitted. Café serves scallops and chorizo. You could be in the Med. Shop. Parking charge. WC. (J4)

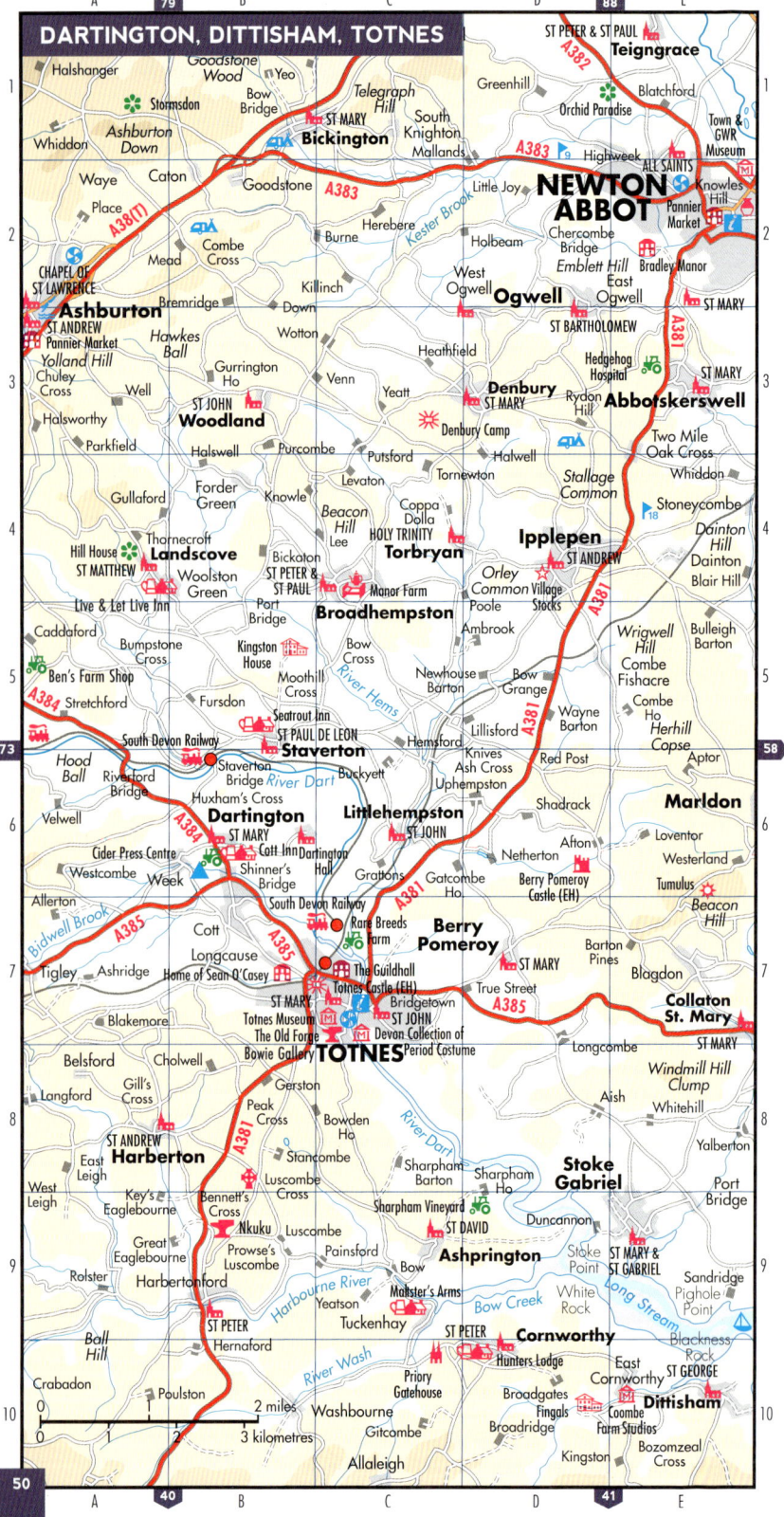

## TOTNES

"The Jewel of the South Hams," so they say, and who would argue with them. If music be the food of your love, and art your divine mistress, then Totnes is the town for you. The close proximity to Dartington and the well-heeled villages of the Dart Estuary has given Totnes an artiness and comfort level rarely seen outside London. It is the "Boho" look, mix of bohemian and affluence, you see here. The many health shops, cafés and restaurants, busy all year, lend the town an affluence unique to Devon. It is a colourful place to people watch, best seated from the many cafés above East Gate, the medieval arch. The shops are unusual and independent, festooned with colour, a welcome relief from the samey, dull, dreariness of many British High Streets.

The town is split into two parts connected by the ascending Fore Street. The lower end, beside the River Dart, has open spaces and riverside walks overlooked by yacht marinas and former warehouses converted into prestigious flats. It is here you can hop on a boat to Dartmouth. The ascending Fore Street which becomes the High Street above the medieval arch is one of Devon's and England's most historic and interesting thoroughfares leading to the Castle and Guildhall, passing by Elizabethan and Jacobean houses fronted by more modern exteriors.

According to legend, Totnes was discovered by Aeneas (Brutus), who had left Troy encouraged by a prophecy from the Goddess Diana. He sailed up the Dart, landing here, to discover Albion. He rid the land of giants and serpents, and created The Britons. The Brutus stone on Fore Street commemorates this unlikely tale.

Totnes is the second oldest borough in England, minted coins in 979, and was granted a Charter by King John in 1206, authorising the Merchant's Guild. The export of tin and wool enriched the town's medieval merchants who also imported wines from France. Defoe noted that in 1740 "the town has more gentlemen in it than tradesmen of note." A truism of today? The history of the town can be discovered in the castle, church and museums.

And when next you climb the draughty High Street think of William Wills, born 1834 in Totnes, the first white man to cross Australia, south to north (Melbourne to the Gulf of Carpentaria), who finally succumbed to starvation at Cooper's Creek in 1861, missing out on the £2,000 prize money. (C7)

### TO VISIT…

**Bowie Gallery, 54b Fore St.** Contemporary art in all its finery and creativity; paintings, sculptures and ceramics. Open Tu-Sa 10-4. (C7) 01803 865054
thebowiegallery.co.uk

*Totnes River*

## LIGHT BITES...AND, A BIT MORE...

Totnes is spoilt for choice. If you start from the bottom of the **High St** below William Wills' house is **The Curator Café & Kitchen, The Plains**. An Italian café serving coffee sourced from the supplier - traditional wood (oak) roasted beans. Rustic, Italian food in the evenings. Seating outside. 01803 865570 italianfoodheroes.com

Continue along the street to **Eversfield Organic,** café, butchery and cocktailbar sellin their organic produce direct from their farm: butter, milk, cream, cheeses and meats. Open 9.30-5.30. eversfieldorganic.co.uk

Around the corner is **Annies Fruit Shop, Ticklemore St** for your organic fruit and veg, cheeses and Juice Bar. 01803 867265 anniesorganics.co.uk

Ascend **Fore St** through the **East Gate** arch, and on your left **Rumour Kitchen & Bar**, a convivial and laid back eatery, always popular for their daily specials and cocktails. Continue climbing to **No. 50, Ben's Wine and Tapas**, for a glass of chilled Prosecco, or marinated pork skewers or Spanish tortilla, a slice of the **Riverford Farm** empire on 01803 840853. Soon on your left the popular café **Seeds 2, 53 Fore St**. Much is gluten free with Vegetarian and Vegan options but they also cater for carnivores. It's a pretty hip place to hang out. 01803 864829. Across the road their health food shop with tasty sandwiches, fritattas, et al.

Another good choice would be **The Green Café** for your veggie, vegan and traditional dishes, you keep going up the street rounding the corner to **Willows Vegetarian & Vegan Restaurant**, many a smart persons favourite dive where you can enjoy their garden out back.  Open M-Sa 11-5, F & Sa 6.30-10. But, if it's a pint of ale and some fine organic food, enter **The Bull Inn B&B, Rotherfold Square.** There's a homely, airy ambience to this ethically minded pub and hotel. A charm all its own; eclecticity, sustainablility, charm and good food drives this busines. Open from 8am for breakfast, lunch and dinner.  01803 640040 bullinntotnes.co.uk

**Dart Valley Cycleway (NCN2).** Totnes lies in the middle of this route and you can cycle/walk north to Hood Manor via Dartington (7km/4miles), or south to Ashprington via Sharpham (8km/5miles). Terrain is mostly off-road except through Totnes and near Sharpham. Park in Totnes Station or Dartington. (C7)

**Fashion & Textiles Museum, 43 High St.** A Tudor merchant's house hpuses the Devonshire Collection of Period Costume. Costumes from the mid-C18, onwards. New themed

Dartington.Estate

| 1018 | Benedictine abbey of Buckfast founded by Danish king. Cnut. | 1068 | Exeter besieged by William the Conqueror, Rougemont Castle built. |

*Sharpham Vineyard ss*

exhibition each year. Open mid-July to late Sept Tu-F 11-4. More details: totftm.org

**The Guildhall, 5 Ramparts Walk**. Originally the Rectory of 1088 Benedictine Priory. Rebuilt as meeting place of Merchant Guild in 1553. From 1624-1974 used as Magistrates Court and Town Gaol until 1887. Now Mayor's Parlour with historic prints, documents and artefacts. Open as advertised.

**Image Bank, Town Mill.** Photographic archive of the town. View 60,000 images on a computer database. Heritage exhibition describing the history of Totnes. Open Tu & F 10-4. (C7) totnesimagebank.info

**Rare Breeds Farm**. View the rare breeds, cuddle and fuss the friendly animals, walk and brush the donkeys, see the owls. Refreshments. Open daily East-Oct 10-5. 01803 840387 totnesrarebreeds.co.uk

**Totnes Castle (EH)**. Norman motte and bailey castle probably built about 1100.

Open daily Apr-Sept 10-6, Oct daily 10-5, Nov-Mar W/Es 10-4, closed 1-2 in winter. 01803 864406 english-heritage.org.uk

**Totnes (Elizabethan House &) Museum, 70 Fore St**. Period furniture, toys, exhibition on Charles Babbage and computing. Artisans Kitchen and grocer's shop. Children can dress up in old clothes of bygone days. Open Apr-Oct, M-F 10.30-5. (B7) 01803 863821 totnesmuseum.org

**Whitespace Art, 72 Fore St.** Exhibits emerging British contemporary artists at affordable prices. Situated just before the Clock Tower. Open Tu-Sa 10-5. (B7) 01803 864088 whitespaceart.com

## TO VISIT OUTSIDE TOTNES…

**Berry Pomeroy Castle.** Late C15 stone quadrangular fortress and stone Elizabethan mansion. Open daily Apr-Oct 10-6, W/Es in winter from 10-

dusk. (D6) 01803 866618 english-heritage.org.uk

**Bradley Manor (NT).** A small roughcast C15 manor house that is still a home. Great Hall, screens passage, buttery. Perpendicular chapel. Decorated with medieval stencils and paintings. One of the oldest inhabited houses in Devon. Open Apr-Sept Tu-Th 11-5. (E2) 01626 354513.

## TO VISIT IN SOUTH HAMS…

**Blacksmith South Devon, Brewery Cottages, Old Rd**. Spencer Larcombe forges artistic metalwork designs in amazing shapes; chairs, candelabra and gates. Commissions undertaken. Open M-F 9-5. 07762 198169 spencerfieldlarcombe.com

**Coombe Farm Studios, Dittisham**. A dynamic oeuvre of creativty that will unlock a burst of magic from within. Tutors and students come back from all over the world. Courses on

1086  Domesday Book compiled. About 20,000 persons out of a total Devon population of some 70,000 accounted for.

53

*Rood Screem Harberton*

ceramics, watercolours and oils, drawing in many forms. Accommodation here and nearby. Book on: 01803 722352 (E10) coombefarmstudios.com

**Hedgehog Hospital & Prickly Ball Farm, Dentbury Rd.** Cares for sick and injured hedgehogs, rears baby hoglets. Also, an open farm - lots of "hands on" fun with many animals. Café. Open daily 10-5. (D3) 01626 362319 pricklyballfarm.co.uk

**Hill House Nursery & Garden**. Construction of over 18,000 sq ft of glass-houses, open to the public with a large range of plants for sale. You are invited to relax in the Garden. Tea Room (Mar-Sept) overlooking water garden. Open daily, all year 11-5. (A4) 01803 762273 hillhousenursery.co.uk

**Nkuku Lifestyle Store & Café, Brockhills Barns.** An Aladdin's cave of handmade home and lifestyle products from artisans throughout the world. Open daily 9-6, for brunch 9-12, lunch 12-3.30. (B9)01803 866847 nkuku.com

**Sharpham Vineyard & Cheese Dairy**. Farm set in 500-acres of vineyard, meadows & wooded slopes. Vineyard & riverside trails. Shop offers full range of wines & cheeses. The Vineyard Café serves fish and crustacea. Opens Mar M-Sa 10-5, Apr-Sept daily 10-5, Oct-Dec M-Sa 10-3. (C8) 01803 732203 sharpham.com

## TO STAY...TO SLEEP...

**Fingals.** A complete one-off, in style and attitude. Richard Johnston has created a refuge from our mad, mad world where you can relax, meet old and make new friends in a laid back, comfortable environment. Art is ubiquitous. Fleet of wooden boats moored nearby. 5-apartments for self-catering. (D9) 01803 722398 fingals.co.uk

**Kingston House**. Rare survivor of C18 architecture. Lovingly restored to former glory with fabrics and furniture true to period. Magnificent 4-poster beds. Candlelit gourmet dinners. Swimming, spa, sauna and steam room for your holistic pampering. Self-catering cottages. A popular wedding venue. (B5) 01803 762235 kingston-estate.co.uk

**Dartington Hall Trust.** 1,000-acre estate bought in the 1920s by Leonard Elmhirst and his wife, American heiress, Dorothy Whitney as a base to try new methods of farming and forestry, and rural construction. It has developed into an international centre for the generation and application of new ideas in the arts, ecology and social justice. C14 mediaeval courtyard. Music and Literature Festivals. International summer school. Cinema. Small hotel. One of the great independent institutions in Britain that realizes it has had to change its direction. The University School of Drama and Music has moved to Falmouth, and now the Trust is returning to its roots. I quote:

"To seek a new long-term vision for Dartington as a laboratory for living and learning with the purpose of pioneering deep personal and societal change. This is inspired by the Elmhirsts' original Dartington Experiment, their concept of expressing a 'many-sided life' and their ethos of openness, creativity and 'learning by doing'." (B6)
01803 847100 dartington.org

## SPECIAL ATTRACTIONS AT DARTINGTON...

**Cider Press Centre.**
A complex of shops and restaurants in a picturesque cluster of C16/C17 stone buildings; bookshop (arts and crafts), Dartington Crystal, jewellery, pottery, farm foods, toys, kitchenware. Open daily M-Sa 9.30-5.30, & Su East-Xmas 10.30-5.30.
01803 847500 dartington.org

**High Cross House.** A superb Modernist house designed by William Lescaze in 1932. Period furniture, Art exhibited (Ben Nicholson and Christopher Wood) and material derived from The Dartington Hall Trust and its beginnings. Plans are to restore this building for a range of creative and experimental activities. It is closed for the foreseeable future. (B6)

**More Café Restaurant.**
Within the Cider Press Centre, serves breakfast, brunch and lunch, and Devon cream teas. Why not try the Dartington Mushroom burgers? Open M-Sa 9.30-5.30, Su 10.30-5.30. (B6)
01803 847524
dartingtonciderpress.co.uk

**White Hart Inn, Dartington Hall**. Great value food. Extremely popular with the locals. Relaxed attitude and booking advised. (B6)
01803 847111.

## EAT...DRINK...SLEEP...

**Hunters Lodge Inn, Cornworthy**. A local that has been reborn offering a fine range of ales. Fish and shellfish feature strongly. Children and dogs welcome. (D9)
01803 732204
hunterslodgeinn.com

**Maltsters' Arms, Bow Creek.** C18 inn accessed via boat, car or foot with many small, bright rooms. Serious selection of ales and wines, cider too. Wholesome food. Child friendly. B&B. A former hostelry of the infamous, mischievous and sadly, late Keith Floyd. 01803 732350. (C9)
tuckenhay.com

**Sea Trout Inn**. A 400-year old inn that has had considerable modernisation. Head for the Stable Bar for old settles, log fire and the historic seatrout. Mix of cosy and spacious rooms. Accommodation. 6-rods for fly fishing. (B5)
01803 762274 seatroutinn.co.uk

**The Cott Inn, Dartington**. Very much your chocolate-boxy and cream tea Devon pub. With thatched roof, interior beams and comfortable bedrooms. The draw is the dining experience: the local fish and the well-hung Devon Ruby steaks that melt in your mouth. Live Music Night on W & Su evenings. (B6)
01803 863777 cottinn.co.uk

*High Cross House*

1196    Torre Abbey founded.

1205    First mayor of Exeter recorded – second only to  Winchester in provincial cities.

55

# TORBAY

**T**his is the "Glorious Devon" of the old railway posters. Centred on the wide bay made popular in Napoleonic times as an important naval base. The mild climate and fine coastal scenery attracted the naval officers to set up their domestic quarters, the foundation of present-day Torquay.

Around the Bay, the three contrasting towns of Torquay, Paignton and Brixham, providing amenities for differing tastes; Torquay with its fine situation, imposing buildings and lush semi-tropical vegetation, the wide beaches and traditional seaside diversions of Paignton, and the old-world charm of the fishing port of Brixham.

To the north, beside the beautiful Teign Estuary lie the smaller resorts of Shaldon and Teignmouth,  set just to the south of the bright red sandstone cliffs so characteristic of this part of Devon. Brunel's Great Western Railway hugs the coast, perhaps forming a barrier to local visitors but providing a magnificent introduction to Devon for generations of rail travellers.

*Torquay Marina*

*Brixham Fleet*

## BRIXHAM

One of the oldest fishing ports in Britain manages to combine the balance of a busy fishing industry with the demands of modern tourism. In the last few years new builds are aplenty: note the Marina and the Fish Market. Colour-washed cottages on the hillside front narrow, winding streets that overlook the harbour and rows of colourful craft. The prettiest of the three Torbay towns, popular with artists and writers. Robert Graves, Flora Thompson and Francis Brett Young, all made Brixham their home, for a short while. Prominent in the war against the Spanish Armada, and later, the landing place of William of Orange, for his rebellion to rid England of the Stuart dynasty and Catholicism, although he had the indignity of being piggy-backed off his stranded ship by a local fisherman. Church of All Saints' vicar Henry Lyte wrote the hymn "Abide With Me" which rings out daily at 18.00 hours. An oasis for all lovers of seafood. You may need to book a full 2-days sojourn to take full advantage of the food on offer. Annual Trawler Race in June. (D9)

## TO VISIT...

**Berry Head National Nature Reserve.** Within a half-hour walk of Brixham; an old Napoleonic fort on the headland with lighthouse, Café and Visitor Centre open Apr-Sept. Live TV link to bird colonies below. Park open all year. (E9) 01803 882619 countryside-trust.org.uk/berryhead

**Browse Seafood, The Quay.** Wholesale crab business with wet fish shop, crab sandwiches and café. Supplies top hotels in Devon. (D9)

**Brixham Heritage Museum, The Old Police Station.** Local maritime and social history, boat building and navigation. Scale model of Brixham Station as in 1947. Open Apr-Oct Tu-F & BH Ms 10-4, Sa 10-1 (C9) 01803 856267 brixhamheritage.org.uk

**Fish Market Tours, Brixham Fish Market.** £25 million of fish is annually landed at Brixham to provide local fishmongers and restaurants. 50% is exported worldwide. Book a tour to start at 6.00am and you can view 40 species of fish auctioned to be followed by a hearty breakfast. Book early: bfmt2014@gmail.com (D9) 07973 297620

**Shoalstone Sea Water Pool.** This is a stunning 'Art Deco' icon of the south-west's coastline. Originally buiilt in 1896, with alterations in 1926, 1946, storm damage in 1979, Torbay Council involvement in 2004, and finally in 2012 some action to restore it. The fund raising goes on, and on... the Friends work tirelessly to make it live for another

*Mussels & Cockles, Brixham*

### LIGHT BITES...

If you seek seafood in all its simple and Arthropodic (crustacean) forms you have come to the right place. Beside the quay are huts selling cockles, mussels, whelks, prawns...to reach the harbour you will have passed by many an emporium selling fishn'chips. You can also sit in a comfortable restaurant, order a cool glass of Chablis or Meursault and partake of a glorified feast of fresh fish, come Dinner. **Beamers, 19-20 The Quay** is a notable restaurant open from 6pm W-M.

For better or worse, try **Rockfish, Harbourside** for freshly caught cod, haddock and hake. 01803 850872 therockfish.co.uk Robert's Fisheries (Merchants) own **Simply Fish** 01803 883858 robertsfisheries.com

You seek Breakfast, Brunch, a coffee? It has to be **Port Espresso on Middle Street**. Their Hash is divine. Open M-Sa 9-3. portespresso.com

In need of ale, a Gin? Turn L, then L again and ascend to the oldest pub in Brixham, **The Manor at 28 Higher Street** host to music nights, real ales and fun. No food. themanorpub.com

Another treat in store, lunch at: **Albero, New Quay Lane** in the Harbour's corner. Food is served all year, a fusion of mediterranean and British cuisine: Lobster Linguine, Monkfish, Oven backed Hake and their Seafood Platter. 01803 882753 alberobrixham.co.uk

day, season...to wild swim. shoalstoneseawaterpool.co.uk

**Strand Art Gallery, 2 The Strand**. Working studio and large gallery of original paintings. Open daily 10-5. 01803 854762 strandartgallery.com

**Vigilance of Brixham**. One of the last four restored 78-foot sailing ketches crewed by three men and a boy in existence available for charter and afternoon/evening trips. Built for strength and speed they were unique in British waters and they were able to tow heavy trawl gear and capable of getting fish to market on time. Half-day sailings from Easter. (E9) 07764 845353 vigilanceofbrixham.co.uk

### WHERE TO STAY AFLOAT...

**Faithful, Brixham Marina.** Ideal for 2-Romantics who seek

a retreat afloat. The double-cabin has a King-size bed and a fully equipped galley. To be welcomed by fresh flowers and delish pastries. (D9)
07939 850680

## Newton Abbot

A busy market town dating back to Roman times. The Great Western Railway moved their locomotive and carriage repairs here in the 1800s, and this made it a centre of rail transportation. In the 1960's the specialist Canal and Rail publisher David & Charles opened their offices bringing succour to all transport enththusiasts with their range of books. C17 Forde House, now Council Offices, and one-mile to the south, Bradley Manor. Racecourse open from April to early September for Flat racing. Air Fusion Festival. Merrymaker's Day in May. Cheese and Onion Fair in September. E/C Th. (A2)

## TO VISIT...

**Burnham Nurseries Orchid Paradise, Forches Cross.**
Herwith a rare and exotic orchid specialist for 60-years. Mail order. Open daily 10-4. (A1)
01626 352233 orchids.org.uk

**Plant World, St Marychurch Rd.** Outstanding collection of rare and exotic plants from around the world. 4-acres of landscaped gardens. Large cottage garden. Mediterranean garden. Seeds from rare plants are offered for sale through mail order catalogue. Open daily Apr-Oct 9.30-5. (A2)
01803 872939
plant-world-seeds.com

**Newton Abbot Town & GWR Museum, 2a St Paul's Rd.**
History of the GWR and the people who operated it. Working signal box, Aller Vale Art Pottery Collection, John Lethbridge's diving machine automaton, and the magnificent Sandford Orleigh Overmantle, a highly carved 1534 floor to ceiling fire

surround. Open Apr-Oct M-Th 10-4, F 10-12, (Town Museum Sa 2-4). (A2) 01626 201121
museum-newtonabbot.co.uk

## Paignton

Often overlooked given its proximity to Torquay, and as a family resort has had to struggle against the cheap Mediterranean and Far Eastern resorts. It has a little harbour, a flat, extensive beach and a number of interesting attractions described below. An affordable place to live for those who work and socialise in nearby Totnes and Torquay. Theatre and cinema. June carnival. E/C W. (B7)

## TO VISIT...

**Kirkham House (EH), Kirkham St.** Small C14 merchant's house somewhat hidden among back streets. Display of furniture, pottery, and fabrics. Open BHs Good F-Aug, & all Su July/Aug 2-5. (B7) 0370 3331181

*Brixham Harbour*

**1307**  Introduction of Stannary Towns for the administration of tin mines; Tavistock, Ashburton, and Chagford. Later, Plympton was added in 1327.

**61**

*Net Fishermen, Shaldon*

**Occombe Farm, Preston Down Rd**. Here you are invited to engage in the whole organic process; the food, farming and wildlife (as well as butchers and bakers). Cookery School & café. Open 9-5.30. (B6) 01803 520022 occombe.org.uk

**Oldway Mansion, Torquay Rd**. Building planned by Isaac Merritt Singer, 1811-1875 (of Singer sewing machines) in 1873 in the style of the Palace of Versailles. Remodelled 1904. Marble staircase, ballroom, ornamented painted ceilings and extensive gardens. Open M-Sa 9-5, also Su in summer 2-5. Grounds open daily. No charge. Café open in summer. (B6) 01803 207933 torquay.com/listings/oldway-mansion

**Dart Valley Railway**. Relive the "Great Age of Steam" on the Nations Holiday Line along the spectacular Torbay coastline to Kingswear for Dartmouth and the fascinating River Dart Estuary. Steam trains run East BH, selected days in Apr, May & Oct. Daily June-Sept. The Timetable is complex and I can't get it. Santa Specials in Dec. 01803 555872 dartmouthrailriver.co.uk

**Paignton Pier**. All visitors to this town must, just must visit this iconic build. A few years ago there was a £1,000,000 rebuild to part of the pier. Pier head includes trampolines, mega slide & kiddies cars, all in wonderful colour and razzamatazz. Open Mar-Oct 9-late. Nov-Feb 10-6/8. (C6) 01803 522139 paigntonpier.co.uk

**Paignton Zoo, Totnes Rd**. Whatever your reserves about zoos this one's raison d'etre is about conservation and education. In 80-acres

1318 Tavistock Abbey rebuilt (to fall into disrepair in 1539)

1328 Chagford made a Stannary Town (until 1790)

there are 2,000 animals: Giraffes, Gorillas, lions, tigers, gibbon islands. Birds flying freely. Tropical plants. Rhino House. Family activity centre. Miniature railway (East-Sept). Open daily summer 10-6, winter 10-5. (B7) 01803 697500 paigntonzoo.org.uk

**Splashdown Waterpark, Goodrington Sands**. Outdoor waterpark with 8-slides and pool, go-karts, bumper boats, shops etc. Open daily from 10. (B7) 01803 555550 splashdownquaywest.co.uk

### SHALDON
A seafaring community of long standing that has made its livelihood from fishing, boat trips and water sports. Connected since the C13 by foot ferry to Teignmouth. A thriving village with an immaculate Village Green used for the game of Bowls. Georgian and earlier buildings. Lively pubs and creative cafés afford this village to be a desirable destination. June Festival attracts world-class musicians. (D2)

## TO VISIT...
**Shaldon Wildlife Trust, Ness Drive.** Collection of small, rare, and unusual mammals, birds reptiles and invertebrates born here in a woodland setting. Open daily East-Sept 10-5, winter 10-4. (D2) 01626 872234 shaldonwildlifetrust.org.uk

### TEIGNMOUTH
A seaside resort of long standing that is in the process of reinventing itself, big time. There are new restaurants and cafés springing up, and folk are realizing it's a cheaper place to live than Exeter, and not so far away, either. The band Muse

were brought up here, and every so often they play to the town's rock lovers. The harbour and estuary side is always a busy and attractive sight with fine views across to Shaldon. The town centre still needs a lot of paint and care. The Den, an area of open space and early C19 buildings overlooks the sea front. Sea and river excursions. August carnival and regatta. (E1)

## TO VISIT...
**Brodequin Shoemakers, 42 Teign St**. Handmade colourful shoes, boots and sandals for men and women, plus satchels, bags & other leather goods. Open M-Sa 10.30-4. (D1) 01626 776341 handcraftedshoes.co.uk

**Teignmouth & Shaldon Museum, 27 French St.** The story of sea and land, war and peace, of interactions with far off places and developments of domestic industries. Open all year Tu-Sa from 10. (E1)

01626 777041 teignheritage.org.uk

## EAT... DRINK...RELAX...
**The Owl and Pussycat Restaurant, 3 Teign St.** You will dance to the light of the moon after sampling this fine Devon cuisine and friendly service. Live Jazz on Mondays. Open M-F 6-9, Sa 12-2, 5.30-9.30. (D1) 01626 775321 theowlandthepussycat.co.uk

## LIGHT BITES...
If you fancy some shellfish for lunch or dinner move along the beach to **Crabshack On The Beach, 3 Queen St** where you can start with Crab soup or parfait, or oysters followed by Seafood Platter, a whole lobster or crab or simple fish and chips. Child's portions available. 01626 777956 crabshackonthebeach.co.uk

*Dart Valley Railway ss*

## TORQUAY

Devon's "Queen of Resorts" occupying a magnificent natural setting on the north side of Tor Bay where the mild climate encourages sub-tropical vegetation and all-year-round visitors. There are twenty-two miles of attractive cliff paths stretching around to Babbacombe, and beyond. Well provided with a comprehensive shopping centre, numerous hotels, entertainments and a thriving nightlife.

There was an early Premonstra-tension house at Torre Abbey in the C12 but it was not until the Napoleonic Wars that Torquay expanded so. During the C17 and C18s the Navy would seek shelter here from all but the East and South Easterly winds. More often in preference to Plymouth Sound. The Napoleonic Wars attracted the wives and families of the Naval officers to Torquay, to be near their loved ones. The difficulties of travel on the Continent also brought new visitors, and physicians would recommend their consumptive patients to come here for the clear skies and sea air for towns and cities were often ridden with smog and damp conditions. The C19 saw an explosion of new villas and terraces set amidst woodland drives. Much in evidence today. It can best be described as a genteel resort that has had to change some of its old-fashioned ways to meet the demands of today. Some of the larger hotels have realised they must improve their interior design, service and cuisine, and to go upmarket, returning to their origins. One wonders who fills all the beds in the other mediocre hotels and guesthouses. It can't all be coach parties and businessmen attending the numerous conferences held in the Riviera Centre. A name taken from the marketing men's slogan, "The English Riviera." A poor cousin when compared to the original, and a misleading description. Better to wax lyrical about the mild, temperate climate, the shimmering sea, the miles of footpaths leading up and down

*Torquay Pedestrian Bridge*

to numerous beaches, the English civility, the fine terraces and tree-lined avenues. And, if you should tire of this oasis, and wish for action and company, strike to the harbour, a haven of coffee shops, bars and restaurants, and if you still have your sea legs, take a boat trip to Brixham, or further afield, to Dartmouth and Totnes, pleasing towns very different from your hostess. (C5)

### TO VISIT…

**Dinosaur World, 3 Victoria Parade.** For those rainy days when your children need some Jurassic excitement, and you wish they were fossilised. Open daily East to mid-Sept 11-3, winter Tu W & W/Es 11-3. (C6)

**Kents Caverns, Ilsham Road.** Two million years in the making. Let your imagination and senses be challenged as you travel back to the realm of bears, cavemen and beyond. Visitor Centre, Rock & Fossil shop. Café. Open all year from 10. Cave tours from 11, 12.30, 2 & 3.30. (D5) 01803 215136
kents-cavern.co.uk

**Living Coasts Zoo & Aquarium, Beacon Quay.** Aquatic visitor attraction; penguins, seals, puffins. Reconstructed beaches, cliff-faces and an estuary. Gift shop. Café with panoramic sun terrace serving child-size portions. Open daily 10-dusk. (D6) 01803 202470
livingcoasts.org.uk

**Torbay Quad Centre, Moles Lane.** Bikes for all ages 5yrs+, beginners welcome, supervised instruction track. Open 9.30-5.30 W/Es & School Hols. (C5) 01803 615660
torbayquadcentre.co.uk

**Torquay Museum, Babbacombe Rd.** Animal remains from Kent's Cavern. Fairytale Exhibition, Pictorial records, Victoriana, rural Devon, pottery, archaeology, Agatha Christie Gallery, world jewellery and adornment. Gift shop & Tea room. Open M-Sa 10-4 all year (Su in school hols). (C5) 01803 293975
torquaymuseum.org

**Torre Abbey & Gallery, Kings Drive.** Torquay's oldest historic building. Art gallery specialising in maritime paintings and landscapes by local artists. Devon miniatures, antiques, Torquay terracotta & sculpture. Open W-Sa 10-4. (C5) 01803 293593
torre-abbey.org.uk

**Waves Leisure Pool, Riviera Centre.** Giant inflatable, paddling pool, sloping beach, indoor soft play area, gym, sun beds, sauna, steam room & jacuzzi, beauty suite & aerobics. Café diner. (C5) 01803 299992
rivieracentre.co.uk

### EAT…DRINK…RELAX…

**Elephant Bar & Restaurant, 3-4 Beacon Terrace.** Award-winning restaurant considered one of the most stylish places to eat in the South West. Sources their pork, lamb, chicken, turkeys and vegetables from their South Devon farm. Michelin Star in 2016. Open M-Sa for lunch and dinner. (C5) 01803 200044
elephantrestaurant.co.uk

**No 7 Fish Bistro, 7 Beacon Terrace.** Simply cooked fish just off the boats. Specials; lobster, Dover sole, oysters. Warm and efficient service. (C5) 01803 295055 no7-fish.com

**The Hole in the Wall, Park Lane.** By all accounts Torquay's oldest Inn since c.1540. This fact alone brings it much trade; smugglers fisherfolk and traders have drunk and dined here as you can on their seafood, steaks and bar meals. Live Music W/Es, Tu & Th. 01803 200755
holeonthewalltorquay.co.uk

1356 Watercourse, or leat (clean water for cleanliness and health) provided for the inhabitants of Cullompton by the Abbot of "Bokland".

65

## TO VISIT...

**Babbacombe Model Village, Hampton Avenue.** 4-acres of gardens with miniature landscapes and 413 buildings to scale of 1 inch to 1 foot. Model railway. Open daily. (D4) 01803 315315

**Bishopsteignton Museum of Rural Life, Shute Hill.** Displays ranging through geology, occupations, dress, village and school life. Open East-Sept Su & BHs 2.30-4.30. (C1) 01626 775308 devonmuseums.net

**Bygones, St Marychurch.** Nostalgic look at a life-size Victorian Street of shops. Giant Model Railway and Railwayana Collection. Militaria from Waterloo to WW1, WW11 & The Gulf War. Open daily all year. (C4) 01803 326108 bygones.co.uk

**Cockington Court.** Set amidst a traditional Devon material village there are 20+ Craft studios which makes this a destination for all creatives. Café. Wedding Venue. Open daily from 10. (B5) 01803 607230 cockingtoncourt.org

**Compton Castle (NT).** C14 manor. Great hall, Solar, Chapel, Rose Garden and kitchen. Open Apr-Oct Tu W & Th 10.30-4.30. 01803 661906 nationaltrust.org

**Greenway (NT).** Birthplace of Sir Humphrey Gilbert in 1539. The beautiful woodland garden slopes down to the River Dart. Now famous as the former home of Agatha Christie with new features about her life. Unique bath and boathouse. Café. Try visiting by river transport aboard the Greenway ferry from Dartmouth. The NT operates a traffic management system. Open daily mid-Feb to Dec 10.30-5, W/Es 11-4 Nov/Dec.(A9) 01803 842382 nationaltrust.org.uk

## EAT...DRINK....SLEEP...

**Imperial Hotel, Park Hill Rd.** What impressed me were the high imperious ceilings and the sense of Victorian grandeur and space, so reminiscent of the lunch scene in Visconti's *Death In Venice*. It is packaged for the Wedding Party, Conference, Spa treatments, A Room With A View of the sea.Established in 1886, the facade has changed, surprisingly. (D4) 01803 294301 theimperialtorquay.co.uk

**Orestone Manor, Rockhouse Lane.** A mix of the Mediterranean and English Country House/boutique style pervades this well appointed, friendly small manor overlooking Lyme Bay, and beyond. 14 Spacious bedrooms. Fine cuisine. Non residents are welcome to try their cream teas. You may then decide to stay further. Associations with I. K. Brunel. 01803 897511 (D3) orestonemanor.com

## EAT...DRINK...RELAX...

**Church House Inn, Village Rd, Marldon.** A large C14 inn with stunning Gothic-style windows and steps leading up to the front door, no doubt originally designed for horsemen. A popular inn noted for fine ales, and honest-good fare. Flagstone floors and fireplaces add to the rustic scene. Pretty garden. Dogs and children welcome. Two cottages to let. (A5) 01803 558279 churchhousemarldon.com

*Greenway Boat & Bath House ss*

1390 Exeter Cathedral's great East Window is rebuilt by Robert Lyen. 1403 Plymouth burned by Breton raiders.

## BEACHES...
## SWIMMIMG...

**St Mary's Bay, Brixham**. Sand and shingle. Safe bathing. Access tricky at the bottom of cliffs. Panoramic views from the coast path above. Dogs permitted. P. (D9)

**Churston Cove, Brixham**. Sand and shingle. Safe bathing. Dogs permitted. P. (D8)

**Fishcombe Cove, Churston Ferrers**. Sand and shingle. Safe bathing. Dogs permitted. P/R/WC. (C8)

**Elberry Cove, Churston Ferrers**. Shingle. Safe bathing. Dogs permitted. P. (C8)

**Preston, Paignton**. Popular sandy beach lined with colourful beach huts. Restricted parking. Deckchairs. (B6)

**Goodrington Sands, Paignton.** Expansive, wide beach with red sand. Safe bathing. Rock pools at LT. Deckchairs. Disabled access. Dogs permitted in restricted areas. P/R/WC. (B7)

**Central Paignton, Paignton**. Extensive, flat sands attract young families wishing to paddle, and water sports. Pedaloes/boats for hire. D/R/WC. (B6)

**Corbyn Head Beach, Torquay.** Shingly sand and rocky pools. Beach huts. Disabled facilities. Boating pool. No dogs in summer. D/R. (C6)

**Torre Abbey Sands, Torquay.** Main beach for Torquay and traditional family beach with flat sand. No dogs in summer. D/R. (C5)

**Beacon Cove, Torquay.** Sheltered position makes for a warm, sunny spot. Pebbles and rocks. Short walk from the harbour. D/R/WC. (C5)

**Meadfoot, Torquay**. Shingle. Safe bathing. Beach huts. Paddle boats. Café. Dogs permitted in restrictive areas. P/R/WC. (D6)

**Ansteys Cove, Torquay**. Shingle and rocks. Set between high cliffs and wooded hillside. Steep path leads down from P. D/R/WC. (D5)

**Babbacombe, Babbacombe Bay.** Sand and shingle with safe bathing. Local sailing club. Steep walk down, or take the short railway ride. Spectacular views from above. Dogs permitted. P/R/WC. (D4)

**Oddicombe, Babbacombe Bay.** Shingly sand. Steep path descends to beach or take the cliff lift. Café. Paddle boats. Disabled facilities. D/R/WC. (D4)

**Watcombe, Babbacombe Bay**. Sand. Short, difficult access from parking down steep path. Café. D/WC. (D4)

**Maidencombe, Babbacombe Bay**. Sand and rocks. Short hike from parking, steep in places. Café. D/R/WC. (D3)

**Shaldon, Babbacombe Bay.** Sand and cliffs. Cliff access. D/WC. (D2)

*The Lounge, Imperial Hotel*

## COASTAL FOOTPATH...

**Kingswear to Brixham**; 10 miles. A fairly arduous stretch with some fine scenery. The first few miles traverse National Trust land. The path gives access to sandy beaches at Scabbacombe and Man Sands, later rounding Sharkham Point and Berry Head.

**Brixham to Godrington Sands**; 5 Miles. An easy semi-urbanised stretch passing some pleasant beaches. From Godrington the route passes through Paignton and Torquay, and there is no path as such.

**Meadfoot Beach to Teignmouth;** 10 miles. The route follows the Marine Drive past Thatcher Point and round Hope Nose. The path branches off at Hope Cove and runs for the most part close to the cliff edge with a series of ups and downs. Beyond Maidencombe, sea views tend to be obstructed by thick hedges. After passing Ness Headland, Teignmouth is reached by ferry from Shaldon.

# DARTMOOR

One of England's greater National Parks; the Forest of Dartmoor covers 365 square miles and contains the highest ground in England south of the Peak District. On its desolate moorland tracks the wanderer can believe they are further from a public road than anywhere in the country, but on the fringes lush valleys lead down on every side to thick woodland, green vegetation and picturesque villages.

Geologically, Dartmoor was formed by the up swelling millions of years ago of a vast mass of molten granite, bursting through the earth and forming a group of colossal and terrifying mountains. Softened and rounded through time, their summits cracked in pieces by the elements of snow and ice. All that remains are the "tors," piles of rock, often in uncanny shapes, which surmount the present day flattened landscape.

The main mass of Dartmoor is to a large extent a desolate peat bog, a challenge to the experienced walker, but to the east, where the rivers Teign and Dart carve their way tortuously through the rocks in deep gorges, is a more friendly landscape of grassy uplands with easily accessible viewpoints - Hound Tor, Haytor and Bonehill Down.

Dartmoor is well known for its attractive herds of ponies with their varied colouring - apparently wild but in fact individually owned. Every year they are rounded up and branded with the owner's mark. Feeding them is strictly prohibited, and in the interest of the animals who have plenty to eat, they must not be tempted to wander towards you across the roads.

Other wildlife includes foxes, badgers and otters - also the occasional adder. Fallow, roe and Sitka deer can often be seen, but the red deer of Exmoor have never penetrated the area. Buzzards, kestrels and various Birds of Prey are frequently seen, as well as the wheatear, while crows, ravens and the skylark are fairly commonplace. A variety of insects inhabit the Moor, and the interesting insect-eating sundew plant can often be identified. Heather, bracken and whortleberries grow in profusion in the drier areas, and in the woodland there is much to interest the student of mosses and lichens. These can often be seen covering the roadside stonewalls.

The Moor abounds in prehistoric remains. There are also many deserted medieval villages with remains of the traditional "longhouse" buildings. For centuries tin mining has been an important activity and there is much to interest the industrial archaeologist, including abandoned tramways and railways of more recent times - notably the Princetown Railway, once the highest railway line in England, now a moderately easy mountain bike track.

Many historic legends surround the Moor. Conan Doyle's "Hound of the Baskervilles" is based reputedly on Fox Tor.

*Scorhill Circle*

## THE TORS

Highest on the Moor are Yes Tor and High Willhays (2038 ft) in the north. To the east, are the fine viewpoints of Kes Tor and Hay Tor, the easily recognised shapes of Hound Tor and Bowerman's Nose, and Buckland Beacon with the Ten Commandments carved in the rock by a religious dissident. Near Tavistock are the westward-looking viewpoints of Pew Tor and Vixen Tor, and the isolated church-crowned summit of Brent Tor.

## THE VALLEYS

The River Dart rises in the Moor and crosses its centre. At Postbridge there is a fine clapper bridge, and lower down is Dartmeet, a famous beauty spot. On the eastern fringe the Teign flows for many miles through deep wooded valleys, while on the Tavistock side is the Tavy with its spectacular gorge. Smaller rivers draining the Moor are the Okement, and on the south side the Plym, Avon and Erme, each deeply cleaved into the landscape.

## CROCKEN TOR

Once the meeting place of the Stannary Court, arbiters of the tin industry in the Middle Ages. Nearby is Wistman's Wood, a grove of gnarled and twisted trees, the surviving remains of primeval forest. Around here can  also be seen parts of the Devonport Leat, an ancient water supply. In the most desolate part of the Moor is Cranmere Pool, a sinister bog and site of the first of the Dartmoor Postboxes (the custom being for visitors to leave a card and note the lapse of time before the next visitor came to collect and post it).

## WALKING ON DARTMOOR

Dartmoor offers opportunities for every kind of walker from the easy family stroll through woodland and over grassy hillsides to the long distance endurance test for those who prefer to make their own way across trackless country by map, compass and GPS. Most of the Moor is common land with free access to unfenced country, but there are restricted military training areas in the north-west. These are usually accessible at weekends and school holidays - enquiries should be made locally. A comprehensive programme of guided walks, ranging from 1 1/2 to 6 hours duration is available, through summer starting from a variety of centres. For those who would rather go it alone there are many detailed books available - the following are just a few suggestions. The Ordnance Survey 1:25,000 Explorer series are recommended for use on the Moor.

The Moor is crossed by several ancient trackways which can still be traced. The Lych Way from Bellever to Lydford was used for funeral processions.

## SHORT WALKS
### UP TO 3 HOURS

1.  Sheepstor from Burrator Reservoir.
2.  Black Tor & the Meavy Valley from the Princetown-Yelverton road.
3.  Birch Tor & Vitifer Mine from Warren House.
4.  Dr Blackall's Drive.
5.  Vixen, Henwood & Pew Tors from Merrivale.
6.  Bench Tor from Venford Reservoir.
7.  Grimspound & Hamelton Tor.
8.  Great Hound & Grae Tors.
9.  Hay Tor & the Granite Tramway.
10. Belstone Tor from Belstone.
11. Bonehill & Honeybag Tors.

## LONGER WALKS
### UP TO 6 HOURS

1.  Staldon from Cornwood.
2.  Ditsworthy, Eylesburrow & Nuns Cross from Burrator.
3.  Duckspool from Whiteworks.
4.  Ryders Hill from Holne.
5.  Cranmere Pool from Okehampton Military Rd.
6.  Shiel Top from Cornwood.
7.  Doe & Great Links Tor from Lydford.

Walks for the experienced are better left for individual planning, but there are two historic routes which can be traced; the Abbot's Way (Buckfast-Princetown) and the Lych Way (Bellever-Lydford). A complete traverse of the Moor can be made up the Erme Valley from Ivybridge, past Childe's Tomb to Two Bridges, thence north via Cut Hill to Cranmere Pool and down to Okehampton.

The Two Moors Way provides a 100 mile walk from Ivybridge to Lynton, skirting the fringes of Dartmoor and continuing through pastoral mid-Devon, and across Exmoor.

*Spinster's Rock, Nr Sandypark*

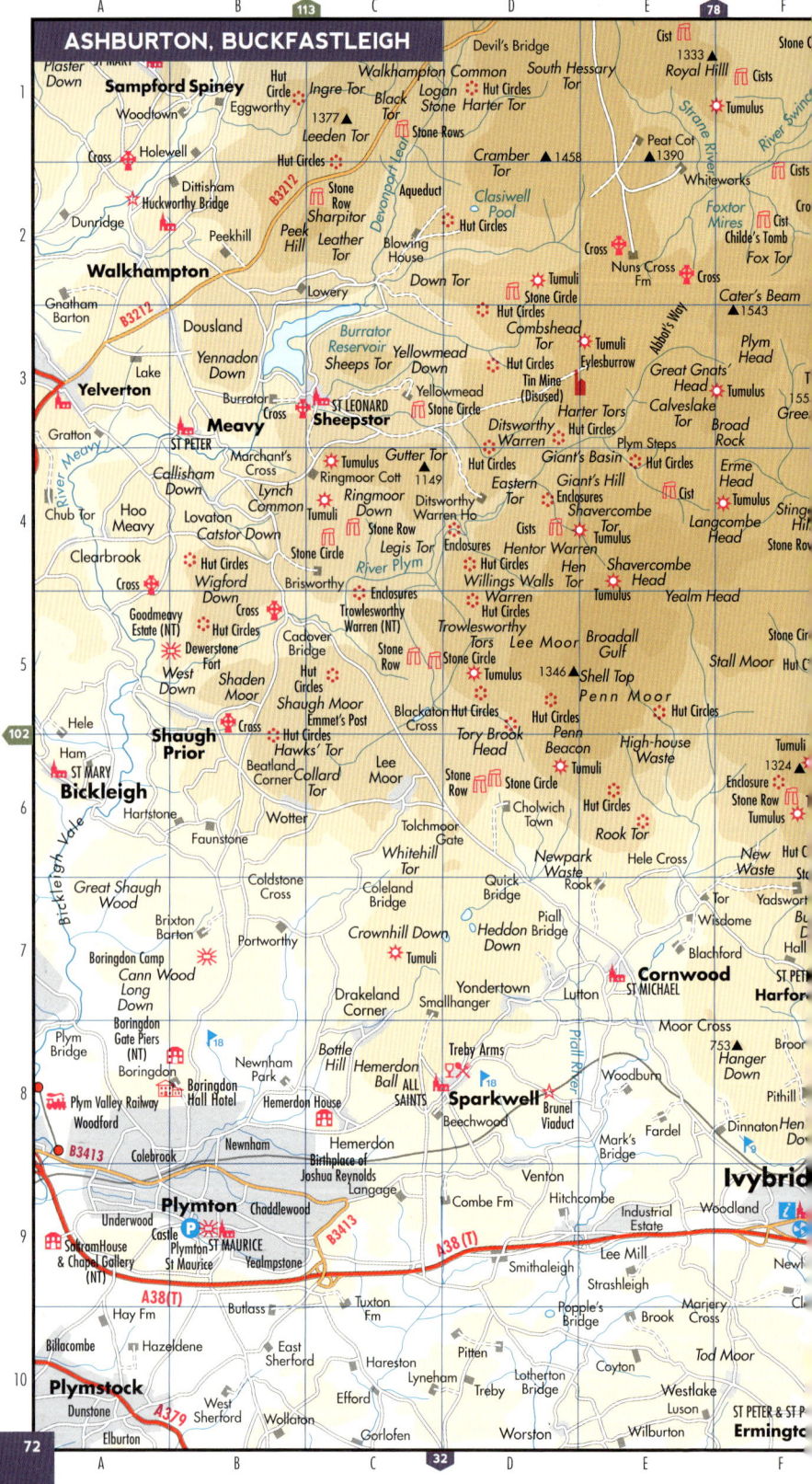

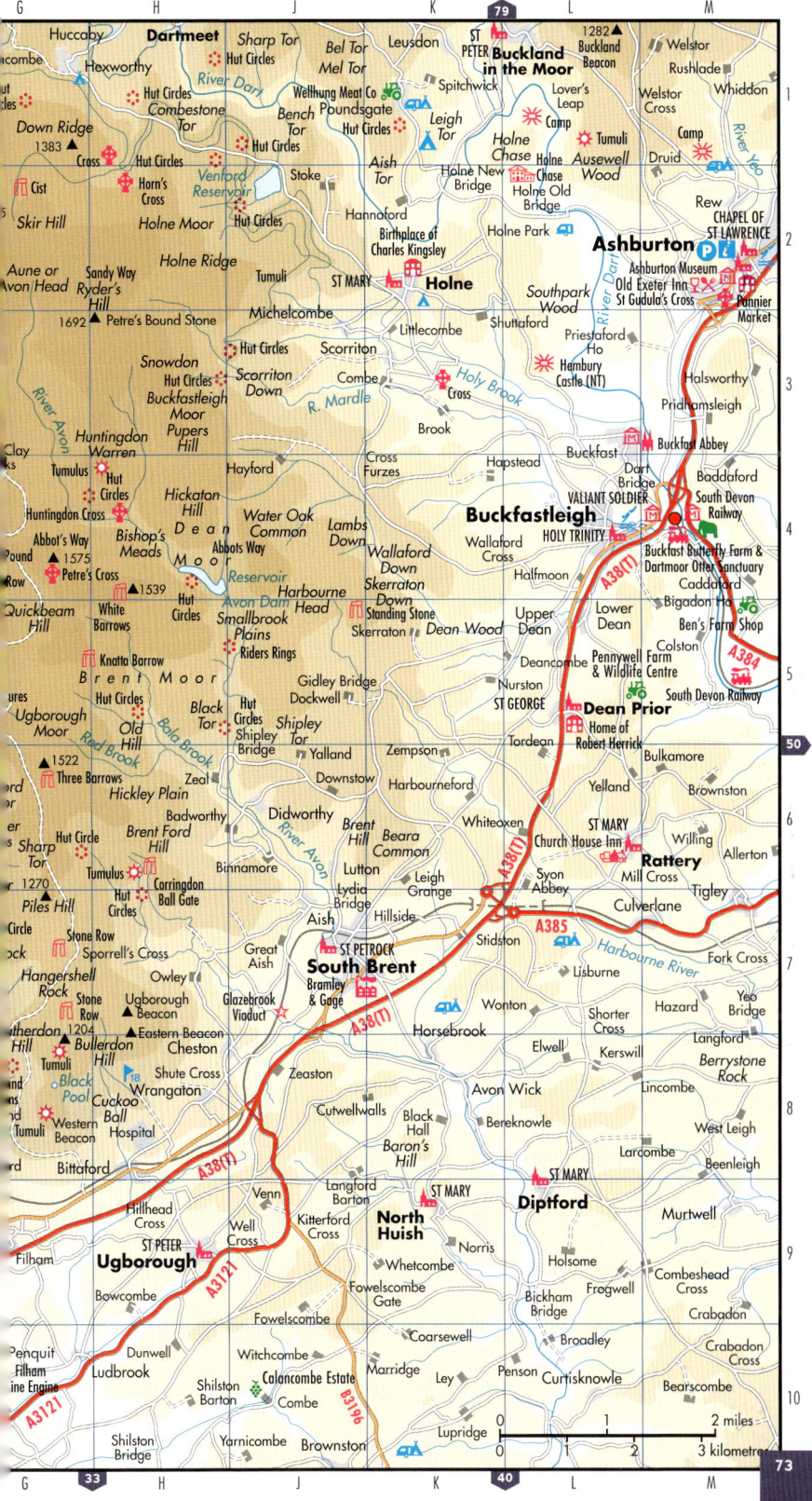

## ASHBURTON

A charming town just off the A38, and well placed to explore Dartmoor and the South Hams. An ancient borough and "Stannary Town" considered by Anthony Trollope, to be the fairest corner of England. There is a gracious air and steady civility here, and pleasing architecture of slate carved roofs and oriel windows. Now a centre for good eating and antiques. There must be in excess of 6 antique emporia. The Post Office is the first in the UK to house a Public Library. Brilliant! Just outside town on the industrial estate, Big Peaks, bike shop. (M2)

## TO VISIT...

**Ashburton Museum, The Bull Ring.** History and geology of Dartmoor. Tin and woollen industries. Red Indian collection. Open May-Sept Tu Th & F 2-4, Sa 10-12. (M2) 08081 203865 oldexeterinn.net

**Old Exeter Inn, 26 West St.** An Inn since 1130 a.d., a historic build (with a recent restoration of exceptional integrity and panache) where Sir Walter Raleigh was arrested for treason July 19, 1603, to be imprisoned in the Tower of London, later beheaded on October 29, 1618. An Old Worlde ambience pervades...

cosy and comfortable to be nourished by fine ales and homely pub-grub. Table reservations: 01364 652013 oldexeterinn.com

**Parish Church of St Andrew.** C15 creation with cradle roof and fine bosses. Herbert Read's sculptures fill three niches over the west door. (M2)

**Reuben Lenkiewicz Fine Art Gallery, 6 North St.** Herewith, a range of original paintings and prints by Robert Lenkiewicz, the redoubtable Plymouth artist. Other Landscape and Figurative artists, too. On site, a coffee garden serving cream teas and cakes. Events galore -

## LIGHT BITES...

On North Street is the **Asburton Delicatessen**. I always visit this store for their amazing sausage rolls and Bakewell tarts, and cheeses for filling rolls.

Across the street for a conventional tea drinking experience amongst period antiques and soft furishings, **Tea at Taylors** open from 9.30. In need of seafood? **The Fish Deli, 7 East St**. Fresh fish sourced from local boats, and Isles of Scilly lobster. Fish cooked on premises for home consumption. Deli for olive oils and tapas. Books and organic wines. Open M-Sa 9-5. (M2) 01364 654833 thefishdeli.co.uk

And finally, should you wish for a mediterranean cuisine, walk into **West Street** to **Cojan** for tapas, grilled lamb with spinach and wondrous oils and balsamic vinegars. 01364 654011

For a pint of ale? It has to be the **Old Exeter Inn** opposite the Church - see above for details.

Now for something completely different: **Creamo's!** Crafted ice cream like you have never tasted before. Down past the Post Office on St Lawrence Lane. Open F 12-5, Sa 10-5, Su 10-4. Delish!!!

*Buckfast Abbey*

writing and music courses, chess evenings. 07464 631671 lenkiewiczart.com

## BUCKFASTLEIGH

Worth a detour to visit this pretty, well-groomed village with a one-way High Street. Swimming pool and museum, below. (L4)

**The Valiant Soldier, Fore Street.** A village inn for two centuries where time was never called, and now a museum showing furniture, pub artefacts of the 40s and 50s. Open as localy advertised.

## TO VISIT...

**Ben's Farm Shop, Wash Barn**. Home to their award-winning organic restaurant, the Riverford Kitchen, and where they organize organic vegetables from the farm to table. Their vegetable box scheme allows you to choose from a range of box sizes, the contents of the box will be different each week. Open M-Sa 9-6, Su 10-5. (M5) 01803 762851 bensfarmshop.co.uk

**Buckfast Abbey**. Benedictine Abbey church built by personal labour of the community of monks during the years 1903-38, on site of the former medieval Cistercian abbey. Finely decorated interior. Chapel of the Blessed Sacrament added in 1966 with the colourful mosaic window. Exhibition of monastic history, vestments and plate in C15 Guest Hall. The community produce honey, wine and other artefacts for sale. These, they sell onto the visitors who come in charabancs and coaches, in their teeming hundreds. Their commercial acumen has had the locals decrying the place as "Fastbuckleigh." Bookshop. Grange Restaurant. Open daily. (L3) buckfast.org.uk

**Buckfast Butterfly Farm & Dartmoor Otter Sanctuary**. Butterflies from all over the world in tropical landscaped garden. Otters in underwater viewing areas. Open daily Mar-Oct 10-5 (dusk). 01364 642916 ottersandbutterflies.co.uk

**1538** Dissolution of the monasteries begins in Devon with priories in Barnstaple, Cornworthy, Exeter, Frithelstock and Pilton.

75

**South Devon Railway, The Station**. The SDR is a 7-mile Great Western heritage steam railway (built in 1872) from Buckfastleigh to Totnes beside the picturesque River Dart. Buckfastleigh Station, with free car parking, beside the A38 Devon Expressway. Totnes Station beside Mainline Station. (M4) 01364 644370 southdevonrailway.co.uk

**Dean Court Farm Shop & Café, Lower Dean.** A farm shop that supports local farmers by selling their produce. Butchery and Café. Open daily 9-4. 01364 642199 (L5) deancourtfarmshop.co.uk

**Dean Prior, Church of St George.** For all lovers of English poetry, and considered by some scholars to be our finest poet, the home of Robert Herrick, Cavalier Poet and acolyte to Ben Johnson. It was here he wrote his great Hesperides, a lengthy manuscript on Celibacy, Marriage, Ritual and Sexual Politics. Appointed vicar by Charles 1 in 1629, he took a long, long time to understand his flock, eventually to be driven out by Puritans, to return fifteen years later after the Restoration. It is a little church, on a fast road, with parking. The East Window is his Memorial. Herrick lies outside in an unmarked grave. (L5)

**Hemerdon House**. Georgian family house. Collection of West Country paintings and prints, furniture and library. Open Day Tours May to Aug at 2.30. Details on website. (B8) 07704 708416 hemerdonhouse.co.uk

**Lukesland Gardens, Harford Rd**. 24-acres of flowering shrubs, trees and wild flowers by a Dartmoor stream. Open mid-Mar to mid-June Su W & BHs 11-5. In the Autumn Su & W early Oct to mid-Nov. (F8) 01752 691749 lukesland.co.uk

**Pennywell Farm & Wildlife Centre**. 80-acres to roam, with activities every half-hour. Farm & British wild animals. Owl and Falconry Centre. Pets corners. Special Events. Open daily Feb half-term for lambing, to end Oct 9-6. (L5) 01364 642023 pennywellfarm.co.uk

**Rattery.** Village with one of the oldest inns c.1028 in Devon and beyond - if you believe the tall stories told here in **The Church Inn.** Where you can feast on Rattery Beef, Dartmoor Venison and Roasted Cornish scallops helped down with some fine local ales. 01364 642220 thechurchhouseinn.co.uk.

Next door is the **Church of St Mary.** A C13-C15 church beside the village green. Norman font and C15 oak screen restored in the C20 are of interest. Further along a rambling old mill with leaded windows. (L6)

**Treby Arms, Sparkwell**. For that Special Occasion unless your pockets are lined with gold. A rustic country pub that serves Michelin starred, style of cuisine. So in short, it's more of a precious restaurant within

*South Devon Railway*

1549 Crediton occupied by 10,000 Catholic insurgents demonstrating against The Reformation.

*Holne Bridge*

a pub build. (D8) 01752 837363
thetrebyarms.co.uk

## DARTMOOR SPECIAL PLACES TO VISIT…

**Childe's Tomb.** A stone cross marks the site of the tragedy of the Lord of the Manor of Plymstock. Caught in a blizzard, he killed his horse and climbed inside to keep warm but still froze to death. He left a will leaving his estate to those who would find and bury him. The monks of Tavistock did so, and thus, claimed his land. (F2)

**Dewerstone Rocks.** Granite outcrop 300 feet high, packed with legend and known as the Devil's stone. Fine views to be had over Goodameavy, the River Meavy and beyond. (B5)

**Holne Bridge**. A beauty spot, especially colourful in Spring and late Autumn on either side of this fine old bridge. (L2)

## EAT…DRINK..SLEEP…

**Agaric Rooms B&B, 36 North St**., **Ashburton.** Former restaurateurs now provide luxurious B&B in their Georgian Townhouse with two double rooms accompanied by supreme breakfasts. (M2) 07460 563125 agaricnbnb.com

**Ashburton Luxury Lets, North St.** Three sites available; The Meeting House, The School House and The Upper School House all within walking distance of the village centre. 01364 653189 ashburtonluxurylets.com

**Boringdon Hall Hotel & Spa**. An Elizabethan manor house, formerly a National Trust property, combines antique furnishings, superb fireplaces and 4-poster bedrooms coupled with jacuzzis, spa treatments and mod-cons on tape to usher you to a stress-free weekend. Yoga Breaks. (B8) 01752 344455 boringdonhall.co.uk

**Holne Chase Holiday Cottages.** A former hunting lodge for the Abbots of Buckfast Abbey set amidst a nature reserve. A centre that specialises in fly fishing, riding and shooting. There is the Carriage House that sleeps 8, the Grooms Cottage sleeps 5 and the Fishermans Flat for 2. Dogs welcome. (L2) 01548 202020 holne-chase.co.uk

**Okehampton Hamlets**

Black Down  
Rough Tor  
Red-a-ven Brook  
Scarey Tor  
Belstone Common  
Belstone Tor  
Foxes' Holt  
Hut Circles  
East Week  
Whiddon Dov  
Gooseford  

West Mill Tor Beacon  
East Okement Fm  
Winter Tor  
Higher Tor  
River Taw  
Tumuli  
Cawsand Hill  
Stone Row  
Cawsand Beacon  
South Tawton Common  
Clannaborough  
East Ash  

Okehampton Common  
New Bridge  
Tumulus  
Small Brook  
White Hill  
▲1505  
Hut Circles  
Throwleigh  
ST MARY  
Blackaton Brook  

Yes Tor ▲2028  
East Mill Tor  
▲1684 Beacon  
Taw Marsh  
Danger Area  
Oke Tor  
Metherall Hill  
Tumulus  
Little Hound Tor  
Rayborrow Pool  
Throwleigh Common  
Higher Shilstone  
Langston  
Wonson  

Tumuli  
Danger Area  
▲1504 Beacon  
White Moor Stone  
Kennon Hill  
▲1570  
Ensworthy  
Moortown  
Chapple  

High Wilhays ▲2039  
Hound Tor  
Hut Circles  
Gidleigh Castle  
HOLY TRINITY  
St. Jc  

Fordsland Ledge  
Danger Area  
Steeperton Tor ▲1739  
Knack Mine  
Ruelake Pit  
Stone Circle  
Buttern Hill  
Gidleigh  
Murchir  

Dinger Tor  
OAKHAMPTON RANGE  
Wild Tor ▲1741  
Gidleigh Common  
Hut Circles  
Gidleigh Park  

Lints Tor  
Okement Hill ▲1857  
Walla Brook  
Scorhill Circle  
Teigncombe  
Leig  
Th  

Kneeset Nose  
Watern Tor  
Batworthy  
Hut Circles  
Waye C  
Barton  

Amicombe Hill  
Great Kneeset  
Tumulus  
Taw Head ▲1984  
Hangingstone Hill  
Hew Down  
Triple Circle  
Chagford Common  
Stone Avenue  
Frenchbeer  
Hole  

Danger Area  
Black Ridge  
Cranmere Pool  
Dart Head  
▲1974  
Tumulus  
Shovel Down  
Stonetor Hill  
Long Stone  
Yardworthy  

Whitehorse Hill  
▲1917  
Manga Hill  
Great Varracombe  
North Teign River  
Thornworthy Tor  
Hut Circles  

Little Kneeset ▲1694  
Teign Head  
Teignhead Fm  
Fernworthy Reservoir  
Stone Avenue  

Hut Circle  
Danger Area  
Quintin's Man  
Little Varracombe  
Stone Circles  
Hemstone Rocks  
Fernworthy Forest  
Metherall Heath Stone  

▲1877 Fur Tor  
▲1981 Cut Hill  
Danger Area  
Sittaford Tor ▲1764  
Grey Wethers  
Hut Circles  
Chagford Common  
Hut Circles  

**D A R T M O O R**

Tavy Head  
Walkham Head  
White Stone Row Ridge ▲1654  
Assycombe Hill  
Stone Row  
Hurston Ridge  
Water Hill  
Bush Down  
Bennett's Cross  
Wart  
Vit Bir Tin He  

**Dartmoor Forest**  
Hut Circles  
Beehive Hut  
Stannon Tor ▲1517  
Stone Row  
Tumulus  
Warren House Inn  
Merripit Hill  

Danger Area  
Cowsic Head  
Broad Down  
Hartland Tor  
Hut Circles  
Hut Circles  
West Webu  

Maiden Hill  
Devil's Tor ▲1791  
Rough Tor  
Beardown Man  
Hut Circles  
Hut Circles  
Tumuli  
Soussons Down  

Conies Down Tor  
Crow Tor  
Lower White Tor  
Cist  
Archerton  
ST GABRIEL  
Runnage  
Stone Circle  
Sousso  

Rich Way  
Hut Circles  
Higher White Tor ▲1712  
Arch Tor  
Clapper Bridge  
Postbridge  
Piswell  

Hut Circles  
Blackbrook Head  
Lydford Tor  
Stone Row  
Longford Tor  
Hut Circles  
Lakehead Hill  
Lydgate House  
Dury  
Cator Common  

▲1615 Black Dunghill  
Danger Area  
Cowsic River  
Beardown Tors ▲1680  
Hut Circles  
Bellever Forest  
Clapper Bridge  
Hut Circles  
Cator Court  

Danger Area  
Holming Beam  
Wistman's Wood  
Littaford Tors  
Powder Mill Pottery  
Clapper Bridge  
Hut Circles  
Bellever  
Riddon Ridge  
Lowe Cato  

Prison Leat  
Devonport Leat  
Beardown Hill  
Hut Circles  
Bellever Tor ▲1456  
Hut Circles  
Laughter Hole  

Crockern Tor  
Parson's Cottage  
Smith Hill  
Cist  
Laughter Tor  

Blackbrook River  
Beardown  
B3357  
B3357  
Menhir  
Dunnabridge Pound  
Babeny  
Shalla  

Rundlestone  
Hollow Tor  
Two Bridges  
Prince Hall Hotel  
Prince Hall  
West Dart River  
Hut Circle  
Huccaby Rings  
Hut Circles  
Yar Tor  
Hut Circ  
Co  

HM Prison  
**Princetown**  
ST MICHAEL  
Cist  
Hut Circles  
Hut Circle  
Huccaby Tor  
**Dartmeet**  

High Moorland Visitor Centre  
B3212  
Fox Tor Café  
Tor Royal  
Cist  
Moorlands  
Sherberton  
Stone Circle  
Huccaby  
Clapper Bridge

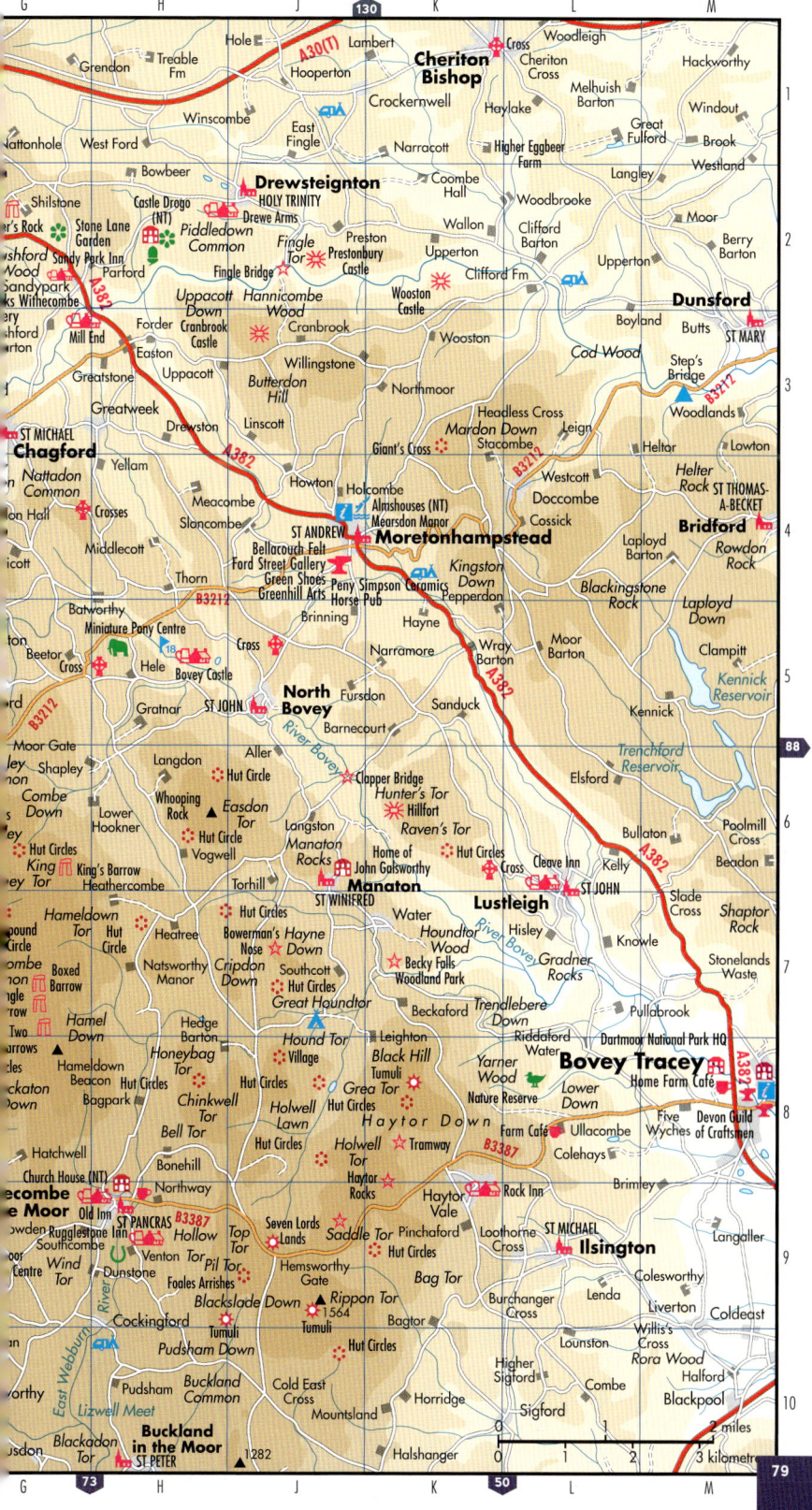

*Chagford Churchyard*

## CHAGFORD

One of the four "Stannary Towns" given to manage the medieval tin industry and thereafter an affluent little town for many years until the Agricultural Depressions of the 1870s and 80s. The far-thinking vicar of the time organised a modern sewage system to encourage tourism. This endeavour moved George Haynes to introduce electric lights, the first town west of London to do so. The town, and surrounding hamlets are popular with the Retired, although there are always young persons enjoying the health shops and al fresco drinking. Has one of the few ironmongers (stores that sell every device known to man) left in the country. The surrounding hamlets and farms abound with sturdy, Dartmoor architecture, especially those north of Chagford. The Devon Longhouse is much in evidence; the vernacular design, of a long house usually built by a farmer in an L-shape within a courtyard. A comparable design would be a Cotswold house of similar proportions, and magnitude. Chagford is always a pleasant place to visit. Not a happy place in 1642 for the young poet Sydney Godolphin who was slaughtered in the porch by Cromwell's troops whilst defending the King's name. He returns to curse pub bores. (G3) visitchagford.com

## TO VISIT…

**Church of St Michael the Archangel**. A stone's throw from the aforementioned inn. For yet another poor soul met a sticky end; Mary Whiddon was shot dead by a jealous suitor beside the church steps on her Wedding Day in 1641. Some scholars believe her sad end inspired the tale of Lorna Doone. Inside the church some fine creations; a parclose screen, carved pulpit and roof bosses of rabbits and hares. (G3)

**Ludgate Fine Art, 20 The Square**. This gallery is a showcase of Eleanor's work; Nature in all its differing forms, from watercolours, to oils and pastels. Open daily except Tu & Su from 10. 01647 433287 paintingsofprovence.com

**Monks Withecombe Gallery**. An amazing space given to changing exhibitions of contemporary West Country artists in a light and airy studio overlooking the National Park. Open daily 9-6. (G2) 01647 432858 monkswithecombegallery.co.uk

**Stone Lane Garden Sculpture Exhibition**. 5-acre arboretum presenting an annual sculpture exhibition. National Collections of Birch and Alder trees in a landscaped water and woodland setting. Open daily 10-6. (G2) 01647 231311 stonelanegardens.com

## MORETONHAMPSTEAD

A busy town, beware of the tricky road junction as you enter. Like many a Dartmoor town it profited from the medieval wool industry but has little to show for it save the Church and the handsome almshouses built in 1637, for a great fire in 1845 destroyed all but a few of the medieval and Tudor buildings. Today, a centre for many craftsmen and

1571   Crediton hit by the Plague with 540 deaths.

1575   The first county map of Devon produced by Christopher Saxton.

## LIGHT BITES...HEAVY BITES...

There is quite a choice; **The Three Crowns** is a comfortable hostelry recently refurbished where you can take morning coffee, lunch and dinner, or stay the night. 01647 433444 threecrowns-chagford.co.uk.

For a relaxed pint and the best Sunday lunch it has to be **The Chagford Inn B&B**, on Mill St. A butchery on hand to supply the finest beef. Scrubbed pine tables, artworks and three bedrooms endears one to rest here, awhile. 01647 433109 thechagfordinn.com

If in need of society continue down this street to **Folklore B&B**, a wee café, child friendly, music nights,treats and workshops. Open Tu-Sa 9-3, Su 10-5. F & Sa eves 6-11.30. folkorekitchenandsocial.co.uk

You are self-catering head back to The Square to **Jaded Palates** for some fine wines. In need of a picnic, sandwich and cheeses, try **Blacks Deli**. Their home-made quiches are yummy. Coffee, a cream tea, down the hill to **The Old Forge**. Serves lunches of Shepherd's Pie, Tuna and mozzarela fishcakes, English Rabbit. 01647 433226 theoldforgechagford.co.uk

Across the street for organic fare, the farm shop and café **The Beehive.** A fabulous selection of fresh vegetables and delicious cakes, homemade soups, salads etc. 01647 432571

For the full Main Course it has to be: **Gidleigh Park**. One could describe this hotel as a Restaurant With Rooms. For it is to the restaurant that the guest is bidden to share an experience to succour and tell tales over the campfire. The build is mock Tudor, black and white timber-framed overlooking the river Teign. One wonders if the course of the river has been re-directed? A luxurious double-room and dinner for two will set you back between £500 to £1,000. There will be 8+ courses, and 2-nights might appease your appetite. On the third morning you may well seek a Spa for some colonnic irrigation? Lunch is not so demanding and is thus a popular choice for many. 01647 432367 (F3) gidleigh.co.uk

a convenient place from which to explore the Moor and to stop for some refreshment, be you walking or on two-wheels. (K4)

## TO VISIT...

**Bellacouch Felt, The Unitarian Chapel.** Dartmoor's best wool is used to make felted and hand-made items, all naturally dyed. Open M-F 10-5. (J4)  07763 935897 bellacouche.com

**Ford St Gallery**. A poppet of a gallery displaying fine art and sculpture from local artists. Open daily. (J4) 01647 440362 fordstreetgallery.co.uk

**Green Shoes, 26A Cross St**. Ever hankered for home-made, artisan shoes, sandals and boots. Choose your colour, sole, style, width and Last.

Workshops, too. Open M-F 9.15-5, Sa 10-4. (J4) 01647 440735 greenshoes.co.uk

**Greenhill Arts, Fore St.** Art Gallery with a full-range of arts and crafts.  Open daily 10-4 (East-Sept Th-Sa). (J4) 01647 440775 greenhillarts.co.uk

**Motor Museum, Court St.** Herewith a private collection of 150+ vintage and classic cars, motorcycles and light commercials from the pre-1920s to the 1990s. Open Apr-Oct Tu-Th & W/Es 11.30-4.30. (J4) 01647 440636 moretonmotormuseum.co.uk

*Motor Museum*

**Penny Simpson Ceramics, 44A Court St**. Penny makes domestic stoneware for the kitchen in lively colours, and pots for plants and flowers. Open M-Sa 10-5. (J4) 01647 440708 pennysimpsonceramics.co.uk

### PRINCETOWN

You may wish to visit this isolated village out of curiosity and wonder at the misguided souls who have thrown their lives away to be incarcerated in this dark and dismal place. It is eerie and is penalised by the full force of weather, from the north and east. And you may thank god for your good

**LIGHT BITES...**

On a fine day you will see people (often cyclists) sitting outside the **Central Café,** in **The Square**. Here you can order an early breakfast, paninis and toasties, or simple tea and coffees. Opposite, **The Horse Pub & Nosebag** (great name) where you can order fine ales and wine, or sit, in comfort and order a special Pizza, Tapas, fresh fish, all cooked under the eye of Frenchman, Christoff. 01647 440242 thehorsedartmoor.co.uk

If you are a fan of Italian food and pizzas it has to be **Berto's** on Cross Street - opens evenings. 01647 441240 bertospizzeria.com

On the edge of the Square, **Baskervilles** coffee shop and ice cream parlour. Open for breakfast, soups, cream teas. Family friendly. Perhaps some good-value pub-grub is in order? **The Union Inn** is a fair bet.

fortune and freedom and move on to warmer climes. The prison was built in 1808 by French and American prisoners of war. There are always plans to close the prison. What will be done with the building is uncertain. The Officers' Mess is an impressive building now a Dartmoor National Park Centre. An easy off-road cycling route along the old railway tracks starts from here heading in an easterly direction. Should you seek outdoor gear for an adventure on Dartmoor and beyond head to: Ice-Warrior Basecamp, Tavistock Rd. These guys organize trips to the Polar Ice Cap and know about gear. 01822 890338. (A10) ice-warrior.com

### WIDECOMBE IN THE MOOR

Set in a bowl of a valley surrounded by rugged country. Journey in from the Haytor road and what impresses is the perfect shape of the church, "The Cathedral of the Moor," and the isolation of the village, originally built by tin miners. The village is famous for the song about Widecombe Fair, held on the second Tuesday of September. Be advised, arrive early. And learn your lines, thus:

*Tom Pearce, Tom Pearce, lend me thy grey mare,*

*All along, down along, out along, lee-*

*For I want to go to Widecombe Fair,*

**1580**    Sep 26. The Golden Hinde sailed into Plymouth after Sir Francis Drake's three year voyage round the world.

*Widecombe Landscape*

Wi' Bill Brewer, Jan Stewer, Peter Gurney, Peter Davy,

Dan'l Whiddon, Harry Hawk,

Old Uncle Tom Cobleigh and all,

Chorus - Old Uncle Cobleigh and all.

## TO VISIT...

**Parish Church of St Pancras.** The striking tower rises to 120 feet. It is a pinnacled battlement design. The interior shows two aisles with 6 bays and a painted screen. In 1638 a thunderstorm struck, killing four of the congregation, an event commemorated by a poem:-
"Some had their skin all over scorcht, yet no harm in their cloaths." (H9)

**Widecombe Church House (NT).** C16 brewhouse, later a village school. Incorporates Sexton's Cottage, now the National Trust shop. Open daily, all year 10.30-4.30 (H9) 01364 621321
nationaltrust.org.uk

**Becky Falls**. 50-acre estate of woodland, rivers and waterfalls plus nature reserve and walking trails with special interest to woodland ecology; mosses and lichens. Visitors in the past have included **Bronze** Age man, and the writers Rupert Brooke and Virginia Woolf. Café. Open daily Mid-Feb to - end Oct 10-5. (K7) 01647 221259
beckyfalls.com
nationaltrust.org.uk

**Dartmoor Prison Museum, Princetown**. Contains part of the famous prison built between 1805 and 1808. Discover the lives of the French and American prisoners of war held here. Open M-Th & Sa, 9.30-4.30. F & Su 9.30-4. Phone before visiting. (A10) 01822 322130
dartmoor-prison.co.uk

**Gidleigh Castle**. Ruined Norman keep, with church adjoining. Not open but visible from the road. (E3)

**Powder Mill Pottery, Nr Postbridge.** Hand-made, glazed pots using the local clays found on Dartmoor. Shop selling Dartmoor arts and crafts. Cream teas. Open daily. (C8) 01822 880263
powdermillspottery.com

## LIGHT BITES...

**Fox Tor Café & Bunkhouse.** There's an all-day breakfast, vegatarian option, sandwiches, baguettes, toasties, burgers and cream teas. Open W-Su from 9. The Bunkhouse sleeps up to 12 persons in 3 rooms. (A10) 01822 890238 foxtorcafe.com

**The Miniature Pony Stud & Farm.** Interact with miniature mares and their foals, tiny donkeys and a whole host of other friendly animals. Play areas, miniature farm, shops, restaurants and walks. Open Apr-Oct 10.30-4.30. (H5) 01647 432400 miniatureponycentre.com

**Ullacombe Farm Café & Shop.** A passion for locally sourced produce drives this café and gift shop which all started in a chicken shed! A great stopover for the family, for there's a Tractor Shed, Children's play area and animals to chat to. Open daily 9-5. (L8) 01364 661341 ullacombefarm.co.uk

## DARTMOOR ATTRACTIONS...

**Bowerman's Nose.** The word is a corruption of bowman, archer or huntsman. So the legend goes that Bowerman was a mighty hunter afraid of no man or beast and dismissive of crones. One day he disturbed a group of witches/crones, and in their disgust they turned him to stone. Access is via a short ascent from the road. Climbing is forbidden. (J7)

**Cranbrook Castle, Prestonbury Castle & Wooston Castle.** These three Iron Age forts near Drewsteignton were designed to protect families and their livestock from raiding parties. (J3/J4/K2)

**Cranmere Pool.** The first Letterbox site set up by James Perrott of Chagford in 1854. It can be a bleak, wet and boggy place. Quite a challenge in foul weather. Easier access now the Military road is open. (B4)

**Dartmeet Bridge.** Remains of C13 clapper bridge. A popular picnic spot, best avoided on bank holidays, and former gathering site for gypsies. Tea rooms at Badgers Holt. (E10)

**Fingle Bridge.** A popular beauty spot beside the River Teign. Waymarked walks lead off in all directions. There's a pub/tearoom to assuage your thirst, if need be. Steep lane descends from Drewsteignton, so beware of other traffic. (J2)

**Haytor Rocks.** The most visited rock formation on Dartmoor. It is easily accessed with car parking close to, but best seen at dawn or sunset when the molten granite appears to change colour and shape. At 1,499 feet with two granitee outcrops, it has been classified as an "Avenue Tor" due to the erosion of the central section. (J8)

**Hound Tor.** Associated with the legend of Bowerman's Nose, for his hounds were too, turned to stone by the witches, and here they lie, scattered and forlorn. It also inspired Conan Doyle's The Hound of the Baskervilles. Some refuse to visit believing it is haunted and a dangerous place. It can be. In 1995, a 500-ton boulder came crashing down. Popular with rock climbers. (J8)

**Grey Wethers Stone Circle.** Two granite circles excavated in 1898, and restored in 1909. The northern circle has 20 stones and is 107 ft diameter, the southern has 29 with a diameter of approximately 115 feet. All the stones are about 4.5 feet. (D6)

1583   June. The Golden Hind sails from Plymouth with five vessels for the New World. Sir Humphrey Gilbert lands at St John's Newfoundland and founds the first British colony.

**Grimspound.** Bronze Age village hut circle overlooked by Hookney Tor. A walled enclosure of about 4-acres, and as its situation is not strategically sound was most probably a farm. (G7)

**Postbridge Clapper Bridge.** One of Dartmoor's most visited beauty spots built in the C13 and C14. (D8)

**Scorhill Circle.** A Bronze Age circle with about 35 stones remaining from the original 70. Local legend has it that horses cannot be ridden through the circle. Try it. Waymarked access via Batworthy or Gidleigh. (E3)

**Spinster's Rock.** A Neolithic Dolmen surmounted by a capstone in an isolated field close to the A382, often populated with sheep. (G2)

**Wistman's Wood**. According to legend, planted some 600 years ago by Isabella de Fortibus, Countess of Devon. What remains is a unique collection of stunted, gnarled and weatherbeaten oaks curiously interspersed amongst granite boulders. A sacred place populated by adders. Best advised not to take your dog. A 40-minute walk beside the wall from Two Bridges. Not to be undertaken in mist, or fog. (B9

## INNS SERVING FOOD…

**The Cleave, Lustleigh.** C15 thatched pub with inglenook fireplaces and thick cob walls that has had a recent renovation. Cosy and comfortable. Daily specials. Fine ales. Dogs, children, cyclists and walkers made welcome. (L6) 01647 277223 thecleavelustleigh.co.uk

**Drewe Arms B&B, Drewsteignton**. Lovely old furnishings and photos, simple decor and wholesome food. Formerly run by Mabel Mudge for 75 years, retiring at 99 in 1996. Her memory lives on. Children and dogs welcome. Bunk Rooms for walkers and families. 01647 281409. (J2)

*Clapper Bridge , Postbridge*

(Sir Humphrey later drowns on return voyage aboard the Squirrel off the Azores.)

*The Cleave, Lustleigh*

**Rock Inn B&B, Haytor Vale**. A long-standing favourite of mine. Never know who you might sit next to; Ex-Cabinet Ministers or a UN Ambassador. Friendly atmosphere and good, honest food. Log fires. Large garden. 01364 661305. (K9) rock-inn.co.uk

**Sandy Park Inn.** A charming historic thatched inn serving rustic pub-grub with three local real ales on tap. Cosy, welcoming and dog friendly. Cheers! 01647 432114 (G2)

**Warren House Inn, Nr Postbridge.** Welcome site on a bleak and blustery day. Third highest Inn in England since 1845. Home cooked fare. Simple decor suits the Dartmoor landscape. (F6) 01822 880208 warrenhouseinn.co.uk

## EAT...DRINK...SLEEP...

**Bovey Castle.** Perhaps a little over the top, the refurbishment exudes the luxury, elegance and excitement of the 1920s. With castle staterooms, health and beauty spa, sporting activities including golf and 24-miles of trout and salmon fishing, cocktail bars, Art Deco dining and facilities for children. (H5) 01647 445000 boveycastle.com

**Edgemoor Country House Hotel, Haytor Rd.** Set in beautiful gardens on the edge of Dartmoor. The owners claim "Elegance without Pretension," and provide clean and neat decor. (M8) 01626 832466 edgemoor.co.uk

**Lydgate House, Postbridge**. Set in the heart of Dartmoor. Ideal for walking, pony trekking and golf. Home-cooked evening meal using local produce. Bedrooms have luxurious goose down duvets and pillows. Dogs welcome. No children under 12. (E8) 01822 880209 lydgatehouse.co.uk

**Mill End.** A small and comfortable hotel with old-style charm and notable restaurant. A fine walking and sportsman's base from which to explore the National Park. Private salmon and trout fishing. Dogs welcome. (G3) 01647 432282 millendhotel.com

**Prince Hall Hotel,** Two Bridges. In the heart of Dartmoor and fine centre for walking, fishing, touring, relaxing. French style cuisine using local produce. Bedrooms with all facilities. Dogs welcome. (C10) 07545 1421576 princehall.co.uk

**White Hart Hotel, Moretonhampstead.** I have a fascination for maps and here you have two in Reception; One, an enormous ancient map of Devon, and secondly a rarity, a map that describes a dastardly deed. The murder of Mr Jonathan May of July 16, 1835. This ancient Posting Inn of 300 years is comfortable, recently up-dated and dog friendly, for dogs are considered as important as humans. (J4) 01647 440500 whitehartdartmoor.co.uk

1585   War with Spain declared. Plymouth became Naval Base.

1585   Sir Richard Grenville departs Bideford for the New World, to colonize Virginia.

**CASTLE DROGO (NT)**. Granite castle built by Lutyens between 1910 and 1930 for Julius Drewe, the founder of Home and Colonial Stores. Varied collection of furniture and paintings. Terraced gardens and croquet lawn. Superb views over the Teign Gorge. Castle open daily Early Mar to Oct & Nov to mid-Dec W/Es 11-5.30. Garden, VC Café, shop & Estate open all year. (H2) 01647 433306 nationaltrust.org.uk/castle-drogo

*Vault Ceiling, Castle Drogo nt*

*Drawing Room, Castle Drogo nt*

*Drewsteignton Landscape in frost*

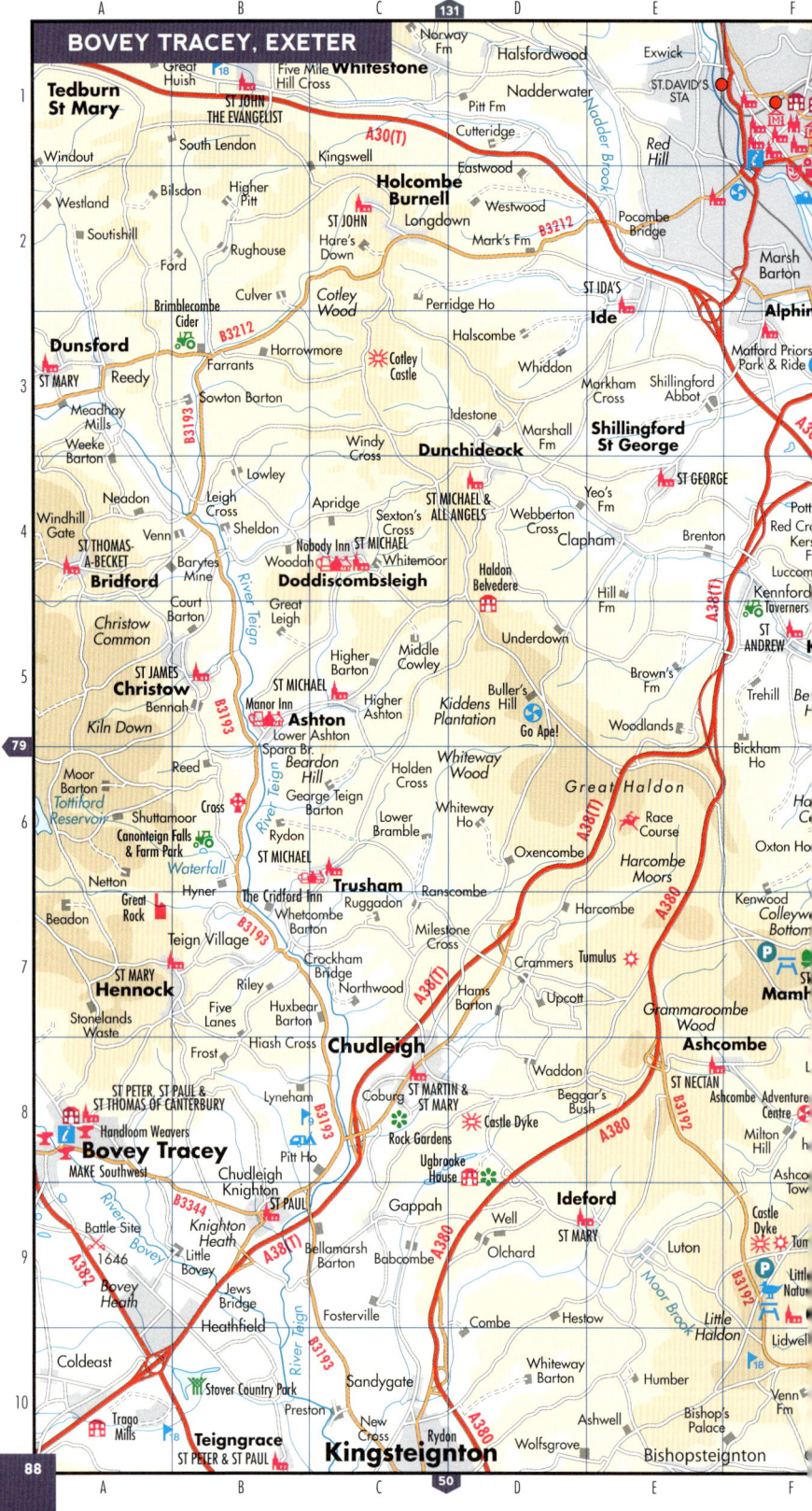

# BOVEY TRACEY, EXETER

Tedburn
St Mary

Great
Huish

Five Mile
Hill Cross

Norway
Fm

Halsfordwood

Exwick

ST.DAVID'S
STA

Whitestone

ST JOHN
THE EVANGELIST

A30(T)

Nadderwater

Red
Hill

Windout

South Lendon

Kingswell

Cutteridge

Pitt Fm

Eastwood

Bilsdon

Higher
Pitt

Holcombe
Burnell

Westwood

Pocombe
Bridge

Marsh
Barton

Westland

ST JOHN

Longdown

Mark's Fm

B3212

Soutishill

Hare's
Down

Alphir

Ford

Rughouse

Culver

Cotley
Wood

Perridge Ho

ST IDA'S

Ide

Matford Priors
Park & Ride

Dunsford
ST MARY

Brimblecombe
Cider

B3212

Horrowmore

Halscombe

Whiddon

Markham
Cross

Shillingford
Abbot

Reedy

Farrants

Cotley
Castle

Shillingford
St George

Meadhay
Mills

Sowton Barton

Idestone

Marshall
Fm

Weeke
Barton

Windy
Cross

Dunchideock

ST GEORGE

Neadon

Lowley

Apridge

Sexton's
Cross

ST MICHAEL &
ALL ANGELS

Webberton
Cross

Yeo's
Fm

Windhill
Gate

Leigh
Cross

Sheldon

Nobody Inn

ST MICHAEL

Clapham

Brenton

ST THOMAS-
A-BECKET

Venn

Barytes
Mine

Woodah

Whitemoor

Haldon
Belvedere

Hill
Fm

Bridford

Court
Barton

Doddiscombsleigh

Christow
Common

Great
Leigh

Underdown

Brown's
Fm

Trehill

ST JAMES
Christow

ST MICHAEL

Higher
Barton

Middle
Cowley

Kiddens
Plantation

Buller's
Hill

Go Ape!

Woodlands

Bickham
Ho

Manor Inn

Ashton

Higher
Ashton

Bennah

Kiln Down

B3193

Lower Ashton

Spara Br.

Beardon
Hill

Whiteway
Wood

Great Haldon

Moor
Barton

Reed

George Teign
Barton

Holden
Cross

Whiteway
Ho

Race
Course

Tottiford
Reservoir

Shuttamoor

Cross

Rydon

Lower
Bramble

Oxencombe

Harcombe
Moors

Kenwood
Colley
Bottom

Canonteign Falls
& Farm Park

ST MICHAEL

Ranscombe

Harcombe

Netton

Waterfall

Hyner

The Cridford Inn

Trusham

Ruggadon

Milestone
Cross

Crammers

Tumulus

Upcott

Grammaroombe
Wood

Mamh

Great
Rock

Whetcombe
Barton

Hams
Barton

Ashcombe

Beadon

Teign Village

B3193

Crockham
Bridge

Northwood

A38(T)

ST NECTAR

Ashcombe Adventure
Centre

ST MARY
Hennock

Riley

Huxbear
Barton

Chudleigh

Waddon

Beggar's
Bush

Milton
Hill

Stonelands
Waste

Five
Lanes

Hiash Cross

Lyneham

Coburg

ST MARTIN &
ST MARY

Castle Dyke

Ashco
Tow

Frost

ST PETER, ST PAUL &
ST THOMAS OF CANTERBURY

Pitt Ho

Rock Gardens

Ugbrooke
House

Ideford
ST MARY

Luton

Castle
Dyke

Handloom Weavers

Bovey Tracey

Chudleigh
Knighton

ST PAUL

Gappah

Well

Little
Natu

MAKE Southwest

B3344

Knighton
Heath

A38(T)

Bellamarsh
Barton

Babcombe

Olchard

Lidwel

Battle Site
1646

Little
Bovey

Jews
Bridge

Fosterville

Combe

Hestow

Little
Haldon

A382

Bovey
Heath

Heathfield

Whiteway
Barton

Humber

Venn
Fm

Coldeast

Stover Country Park

Sandygate

Ashwell

Bishop's
Palace

Trago
Mills

Preston

New
Cross

Rydon

Wolfsgrove

Bishopsteignton

Teigngrace
ST PETER & ST PAUL

Kingsteignton

50

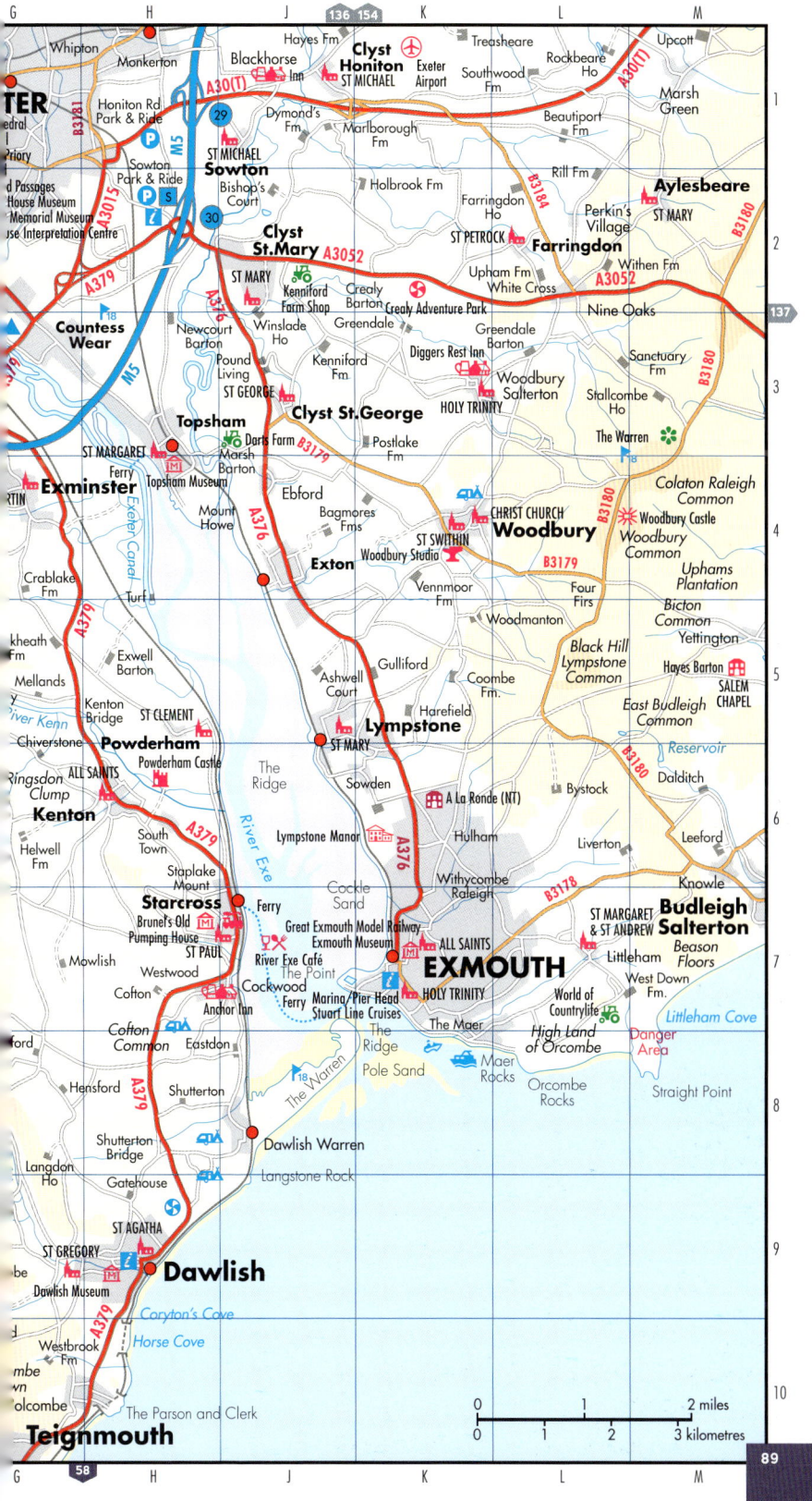

### EXETER

The great Cathedral city and county town of Devon, has been a strategic settlement since the Romans came here in 55 AD. Later, developed by Alfred the Great, and followed by the Normans who strengthened the town with City Walls. The magnificent Cathedral can be seen from the M5, where it dominates the view. There are medieval churches and the City Walls to discover, a circuit will take one-and-a-half hours. The City centre was badly damaged during the Second World War but luckily most of the ancient buildings escaped, including the Guildhall, St Nicholas Priory and Tucker's Hall. The city had a busy time of it during the Civil War, changing sides on numerous occasions. Outside the City walls, on the east side, the gracious avenue of C18 buildings, Southernhay, was where hangings took place, and agitators aired their views. John Wesley preached here. It is today the home of lawyers and estate agents, and a convenient place to park if visiting the Cathedral. It is also the address of a fine hotel and restaurant - see below.

When the celebrated traveller Celia Fiennes visited Exeter in 1698 she noted that for twenty miles around, all the villages, farms and country folk were in some way involved in the production of serge cloth. Exeter made more money in a week than any other town in England. This all halted during the Napoleonic Wars, and production moved north to Yorkshire and Lancashire.

The new buildings replacing those destroyed in the Second World War have not had a good press. The High Street has been described as dull. The new Priceeshay Shopping Centre has fine views of the Cathedral from many angles and as part of the City fathers and planners massive reconstruction programme has been an undoubted success amongst the thousands who shop and eat here.

The visitor will naturally first progress to the Cathedral and its spacious Close where there are cafés and smart shops, and the devastation that was once the Royal Clarence Hotel burnt down on 29 October, 2016. Then, onto the Quay, where you can also eat and drink well, and take up some exercise by foot, cycle or paddle, and if this is not to your pleasure, aimlessly visit the many antique and bric-a-brac emporia. For those who seek independent shops head to Fore Street. Here you will discover a rich vein of wacky and creative retailers, as well as some splendid places to Light Bite.

For more retail therapy, a short distance north-west from the Quay you will come to shopping outlets represented by TK Maxx and others.

The Devon County show is in May, and the Exeter Festival in June. (G1)

### TO VISIT …

**Custom House Visitor Centre, Quayside.** Earliest surviving brick building in Exeter, used by HM Customs until 1989. Exhibits an audio-visual presentation, "Exeter – 2,000 Years of History," highlighting Exeter, from Roman times to the present day. Open daily. 01392 271611 (F2) visitexeter.com

**Guildhall, High St.** One of the oldest municipal buildings in England dating back to 1330. (F1)

*Exeter Canal*

**Royal Albert Memorial Museum, Queen St.** Largest Museum in South West; Prehistory and Roman Gallery, natural history, archaeology, Exeter silver, clocks and watches, pottery, world cultures and paintings by British artists, especially of Devon. Café. Gift shop. Open Tu-Su 10-5. Free. (F1) 01392 265858 rammuseums.org.uk

**The Quayside Exeter**. Apart from the Cathedral and its surrounds, this is where the action takes place in Exeter. Wander down from the Cathedral (and car park) and admire the boats and swans, the old warehouse buildings. You have Antique emporia, nightclubs, craft shops, the Custom House Visitor Centre. If you fancy a cycle or a paddle on the river, visit **Saddles & Paddles**. For food and drink, a varied selection. **The Prospect Inn** serves Devon ales and pub-grub cooked with local produce. Next door, **Mango's** for breakfast, great coffees smoothies, light meals and for people watching. Open 9-6. (F1) cafemangos.co.uk

Fancy a steak, burger and puddings? Cross the footbridge to **Samuel Jones,** part of the St Austell's Brewery.

**Underground Passages, c/o Visitor Information Centre, Dix's Field.** Guided tours of medieval vaulted passageways from the C14 and C15 stretching under the City's streets. Open as locally advertised. (F1) 01392 665887

**University Gardens**. 300-acres of grounds, award winning landscaped gardens, sculptures. Open daily, free admission. (G1) 01392 215566

*The House That Moved*

1591    Men of Bideford  fight fifteen French galleons off Flores, for fifteen hours.

91

# CATHEDRAL CHURCH OF ST PETER

One of the finest English cathedrals, and Devon's most magnificent building. Statuesque with twin Norman Towers. Bishop Marshall in the C13 started this great project. However, it was Bishop John Grandisson, 1327-1365, in the C14 who moved the construction forward with greater panache and fortitude, greatly encouraged by Pope John XX11. He organised the construction up to the Nave, largely his own creation. The truly magnificent (and it is difficult not to be over awed by this) rib-vaulting of the Nave extends to over 300 feet, and is quite unique. The carved misericords, 1230-1270, were the first in England. But surely what strikes the visitor, time and again, is the great West Front.

Sit outside in the Close with your coffee and admire the frontage. The large window filled with intricate tracery, Grandisson's work, and the lower wall, filled with sculptured images, eighty-eight in all, of warriors, angels, kings and saints. The effect is unforgettable, truly astounding. In recent years, some have crumbled and have been restored. Defoe claimed it took four hundred years to build, and yet it appears as one whole. No patchwork lines to spy. The interior has more to succour; colourful roof bosses, C14 Choir screen and Bishop's Throne, Lady Chapel, East Window with medieval glass. The C14 Window with modern glass. Sir John Speke's C16 Chantry, The C15 Astronomical Clock and Minstrels' Gallery.

One can't not mention Herbert Read, who did so much to restore the Cathedral following the bombing of 1942. We must give thanks to his memory, for his tireless and patient work. Café/Shop. Open M-Sa 9-5, Su 11.30-4.(F1) 01392 255573 exeter-cathedral.org.uk

*Lady Doderidge, Exeter Cathedral*

*Hugh Oldham, Exeter Cathedral*

*West Front, Exeter Cathedral*

*The Nave, Exeter Cathedral*

## ART, CINEMA, CRAFTS, MUSIC...

**Bill Douglas Cinema Museum, The Old Library, Prince of Wales Rd**. Museum housing a unique collection of items relating to cinema history, tracing its roots in earlier forms of entertainment. Explore the Victorian world of animated toys, dioramas, panoramas and magic lanterns, or follow British and Hollywood cinema through the C20. Guided tours. Open daily 10-5. (G1) 01392 724321 bdcmuseum.org.uk

**Cygnet Theatre, Friars Gate**. A school of drama influenced by their Patron, Peter Brook. There are regular performances by the students, many of whom go on to star on stage and screen, in the 100-seat theatre. 01392 277189 cygnettheatre.co.uk

**Exeter Phoenix, Gandy St**. Arts and media centre with daily programme of events; music, drama, dance, film, visual arts. A centre of student life in Exeter. Café/Bar. Open M-Sa from 10 til late. (G1)

Box Office: 01392 667080 exeterphoenix.org.uk

**Fore Street**. An extension of the High Street descends to bring you all manner of entrepreneurial, independent and creatives from **The Belt Makers & Friends** to **The Glorious Art House,** a wacky café and art gallery, to cross the road to **The Press House** at 132, a letterpress printer and café, further exploration will find you in **McCoys Arcade,** to the guitar shop, to **Bookbag,** an independent bookseller and to **Sacred Grounds**, the 100% vegan café. A veritable hub of hidden treasures.

**Northcott Theatre, Stocker Rd**. Exeter's premier theatre produces quality plays, opera, dance, comedy and family theatre often before, and after, the West End. 01392 726363 exeternorthcott.co.uk

**Polka Dot Gallery, 12 Martins Lane**. Attractive gallery just down from the Cathedral brimming with ceramics, glass, jewellery, paintings, photography, sculpture and textiles. Open daily M-Sa. 01392 276500 polkadotgallery.com

## TOUR, CANOE, CYCLE...

**Exeter Red Coat Guided Tours**. Departing from the West Front of the Cathedral these are free entertaining guided walking tours of 90-minutes that reveal Exeter's fascinating history and hidden treasures. No booking required and choice of 17-tours. Open daily, all year. See Notice Board for Start Times. (F1) 01392 265203 exeter.gov.uk

**Saddles & Paddles, 4, Kings Wharf, The Quay**. Single and double kayaks (with child seats) or Canadian canoes hired out to explore the wildlife beside the River Exe and canal. Drop in on the two pubs en route. Buoyancy aids provided. Or, on bikes explore 7-miles of flat, easy traffic-free routes. Large selection of mountain bikes and hybrids, plus child seats and trailers for under-5s. Open daily 9.30-5.30 (closed W Nov-Apr). 01392 424241 sadpad.com

*Mol's Coffee House, Cathedral Close*

1593   Sir Richard Hawkins departs Plymouth for South America, and ultimate disaster off Chile.

*The Guildhall, High Street*

## LIGHT BITES...

Arriving from **Central Station** onto **Queen St** on your right is the **Exploding Bakery**. The cakes and savouries are mouth-wateringly delicious. Open M-F 8-4, Sa 9-4. A great place to start your journey.

Then onto the **High St**. Up to your left is **Artigiano** with yellow chairs on pavement. All-day coffees, cakes and much more. On leaving turn right down the **High St** into **Fore St**. Soon to come to **McCoys Arcade** and **Sacred Grounds** for that very special vegan cuppa, toastie, waffles, smoothies, hanging plants and worldly enthusiasm.

Returning to ascend **Fore St** and right into **John St** to the **Fat Pig**. A distillery, brewery and smokehouse. Indeed, a proper pub with all manner of decor. The food is  wholesome pub-grub. Open W-F 5-late, W/Es from 12. 01392 437217 fatpigexeter.co.uk

Perhaps, in need of a Confessor after all this over indulgence. We are heading for **Cathedral Green**. Beside the fire damaged hotel is the **Cote Brasserie** where you can ponder life's ills and draw hope from Devon's most magnificent building. In the corner, **Eat On The Green** where you can sit outside, down your breakfast, all day and enjoy the throng of passersby. If in need of shade, retreat to an alley toward the High Street to **Drakes Coffee House & Bistro f**or a cosy and crazy atmoshphere. Craft beers, veggie breakfast and gluten-free options. Now, if you or your children feel in need of something different take the path to the left of the **Cathedral** onto **Southernhay**, and strike right into the corner to the **Cosy Club**. Here the wacky walls and full-on decor will keep them amused should conversation be muted. Burgers, pizzas and the like on offer. 01392 848744 cosyclub.co.uk

## EAT... DRINK...SLEEP...

**Hotel du Vin, Magdalen St**. A feast of chic, spare designs, at times bright and dazzling in this former Eye Hospital. An off-beat venue  to meet friends, chat and have coffee, and admire the design features. Cocktail bar, Kino.  Restaurant for lunch and dinner. (F1) 01392 790120 hotelduvin.com/locations/exeter

**St Olaves Hotel & Treasury Restaurant, Mary Arches St**. Set in the heart of the city close to the cathedral. Intimate C19 Georgian house with stunning Spiral Staircase. Walled garden or Conservatory for light lunches and teas. Fine restaurant.  01392 217736. (F1)

**Southernhay House Hotel, 36 Southernhay East**. Perhaps, the Exeter Boutique hotel you have been seeking?  With 10-bedrooms, all individually created and a spacious bar and al fresco terrace for cocktails, all within a short walk of the Cathedral and City Centre. 01392 439000 southernhayhouse.com

## EAT...DRINK...RELAX...

**Michael Caines Academy @34 Restaurant, Laurence Building, Exeter College.** The students will cook you lunch daily (M-F 12-2) and supper two evenings (W & Th 7-9) per week. A 5-course table d'hote menu. Their passion and expertise will surprise you, and it's great value, too. 01392 400334
exe-coll.ac.uk

**Rendezvous Wine Bar & Restaurant, 38 Southernhay East.** This venue is smart, casual and friendly. The wines are extensive and the food is classic English fare from Devon's rich larder of fresh seafood and pastoral meadows. Two-course set lunch. Open M-Sa 12 - late. 01392 270222
winebarlo.co.uk

**Steaks n Sushi, 23 North St.** Their imaginative cuisine has got Exeter folk rushing to their doors. Traditional Japanese food, all freshly made to order. Takeaways, too. Open M-Sa 12-3, 5-9. 01392 250414
steaksnsushi-exeter.co.uk

**The Hour Glass, 21 Melbourne St**. Just up from the Quay. This is a proper pub since 1848 with atmosphere and fine ales, an assortment of old chairs, newspapers, books, wooden panelling and dark red paintwork. The food is good, pub grub. Basement restaurant. Open 12-3, 5-11. (F1) 01392 258722
hourglassexeter.co.uk

**The Old Firehouse, 50 New North Rd.** This is a popular haunt of students and locals keen to hear live music, enjoy real ales and start a romance on their candlelit tables.
01392 277279
oldfirehouseexeter.co.uk

### BOVEY TRACEY

A quiet, elongated town noted for its exquisite church (and Beckett associations) and the Devon Guild of Craftsmen, the finest craft gallery in Devon (and the South-West). The town's wealth was built from china clay deposits, or Bovey Clay, established in 1772. The results can be seen on Bottle Road, statuesque, old kilns. In the C18 and C19, Haytor quarries carried granite on tramways to Bovey for onward transport to the Dart Valley. These were used in

*Bovey Tracey Churchyard*

following the road over the bridge takes you to the little High Street. The magnificent C12 Church is at the top of the town where there is parking available. (A8)

## TO VISIT...

**Bovey Tracey Heritage Trust, The Old Railway Station.**
The Trust is a registered charity which researches and preserves the history of the town and area. Open East-Oct M-F 10-4, Sa 10-12. (A8) TIC 01626 835078
devonmuseums.net

**MAKE Southwest Craft.**
The largest contemporary craft centre in the South West exhibiting work by artists of national and international renown in the converted grade 11 listed Riverside Mill, in a beautiful location. Shop selling their Makers' crafts. Open W-Sa 11-5. (A8) 01626 832223
crafts.org.uk

**Parish Church of St Peter, St Paul & Thomas of Canterbury**. Catholic guilt hath no bounds with William de Tracey, one of the four knights who carried out Henry 11's dastardly command "Who will rid me of this meddlesome priest"? Hacking to death Thomas a Beckett on the High Altar of Canterbury Cathedral, in 1170. For his penance, he built this church. Later additions in the C14, and a C15 Tower with pinnacled battlements and the C15 rood screen, considered the town's greatest treasure, and one of Devon's finest, has an exquisite panel of carved sculptures of the 31 apostles. And a medieval stone, carved pulpit and old wood bosses. (A8)

**House of Marbles, Pottery Rd**. Museum of glass, games, marbles, and Bovey Pottery. Coffee shop. Open M-Sa 9-5, Su 10-5. (A8) 01626 835285
houseofmarbles.com

the construction of London Bridge and the pillars for the British Museum. In the Second World War lignite (peat and coal mix) was mined for a short time. Park beside the bridge and the Information Centre (hut),

## LIGHT BITES...

A little to the north of **Bovey** is **Home Farm Café** at **Parke**, the National Park HQ. Mouthwatering seriously delicious fare on offer. Where they claim the local produce is made with love and enthusiasm. Open daily from 10. Evenings Th-Sa from 7 (booking essential). 01626 830016
homefarmcafe.co.uk

*Powderham Castle ss*

**1620** Sep 16. The Pilgrim Fathers set sail in the Mayflower from Plymouth for New England.

**1625** The Earl of Totnes created by Charles 1, and awarded to George Carew.

97

## DAWLISH

A modest resort compared to its neighbours. Yet recognised in literature as the birthplace of Dickens' Nicholas Nickleby, and as a pleasing place in Jane Austen's Sense and Sensibility. IK Brunel's railway cut a swathe through the red cliffs, a brilliant feat of Victorian engineering. Troubled today by heavy seas, an eroding coastline and the controversy following the devastation of the Line after a storm. To the north of the town, a row of pretty cottages, then onto Dawlish Warren, a naturalist's feast and the reason for a visit (H9)

## TO VISIT IN DAWLISH...

**Dawlish Museum, The Knowle**. Victorian rooms, military and railway with unique collection of photos of Dawlish. Open daily. (H9) 01626 888557 devonmuseums.net

**Dawlish Warren**. A spit of land at the mouth of the Exe Estuary, its shape, best appreciated from a bird's eye. On the seaward side, an extensive beach noted for shells. Inland, the mudflats are teeming with birdlife, especially autumn and winter migrants. The botanist will be excited with the Rare Crocus in spring, and the Ladies Tresses Orchid, in summer. Guided walks. No dogs. (J8) 01392 279244 devonwildlifetrust.org

## TO VISIT...

**Canonteign Falls**. Dramatic waterfalls, featuring the highest (manmade waterfall) in England, lakes and ancient woodland, in private 100-acre park. Assault course, children's play areas. Restaurant/Tea room. Open daily Mar to Nov 10 - dusk. (B6 ) 01647 252434 canonteignfalls.com

**Exe Estuary**. You can pick up leaflets that describe the cycleways, ferries, history, walkways, watersports, wildlife and all manner of activities associated with this little corner of Devon. The Estuary invites a multitude of fun-packed days. exe-estuary.org

**Go Ape, Haldon Forest Park**. Treetop adventures via two zip wires that fly you from hilltop to hilltop. Awesome fun! Book at: 01603 895500 or: goape.co.uk (D4)

**Haldon Belvedere**. A monument to Major General Stringer Lawrence, built in 1788 by Sir Robert Park. Restored in 1994. Superb viewpoint. Also called Lawrence Castle. Closed to public viewing. 01392 833846 (D4) haldonbelvedere.co.uk

**Powderham Castle**. Built in 1390 by Sir Philip Courtenay whose descendants, the Earls of Devon, have lived here ever since. Restored and altered in C18 and C19. Fine interiors including music room by Wyatt. Furniture, paintings, tapestries, china and plasterwork. Newly restored C18 Woodland Garden. Formal garden and well stocked deer park with fine views. Diary of Events. Open daily Apr-Oct 10-5.30. (H6) 01626 890243 powderham.co.uk

**Powderham Country Store**. Produce from the estate; with butchery, bakery, delicatessen

and food hall. A great day out. Open M-F 9.30-5, Sa 9-5, Su 10-4. (H6) 01626 891883 powderhamfarmshop.co.uk

**Taverner's Farm**. The 5th generation of a 500-acre farm are the makers of Orange Elephant ice cream named after the herds of Devon cattle (of long ago) because of their enormous size. 18-different flavours to savour. Open in season. (F4) 01392 833766 tavernersfarm.co.uk

**Ugbrooke House & Gardens**. Medieval House redesigned by Robert Adam. Home of the Clifford family. Fine furniture and paintings, embroideries, uniforms and costumes. Library. Marble St Cyprian's Chapel, of 1830, the oldest Catholic Parish Church in the south-west. Cardinal's 4-poster bed. Gardens and grounds by Capability Brown. Open June to July M - Th 12-5. Orangery tearoom opens at 12. (D8) 01626 852179 ugbrooke.co.uk

## INNS SERVING FOOD

**Anchor Inn, Cockwood.** C16 Inn with superb estuary views and an enthusiastic nautical flavour, as well as a fine range of beers. Bar and restaurant menu. Dog/child friendly. (J7) 01626 890203 anchorinncockwood.com

**Cridford Inn B&B, Trusham.** Step back in history to the oldest pub in Devon. Certainly one of the best preserved with evidence ranging from the original floor (under glass) to medieval glass, to Inglenook fireplaces, to Gothic doorways. A cob and thatch build worthy of your patronage. The food is British with a fusion of Asian delights. Four ensuite bedrooms to rest and enliven your senses. (C6) 01626 853694 thecridfordinn.co.uk

**Manor Inn, Lower Ashton**. Fine country pub loaded with ambience. Range of fine ales. Large portions. Open Tu-Su. (B5) 01647 252304 manorinn.co.uk

**Nobody Inn B&B, Doddiscombsleigh**. C17 Inn provides jolly atmosphere and supreme service. Serious wine and whisky list. Local ales. Lunch M-Sa 12-2.30, dinner Su-Th 6-9. 5-luxury bedrooms. (C4) 01647 252394 nobodyinn.co.uk

*Dawlish Warren*

**1643**   Sep 5. Articles of surrender were signed and the Royalists took control of Exeter after a siege.

99

# WEST DEVON

**T**his corner of England invites exploration. Lying between the western reaches of Dartmoor and the River Tamar of the Cornish border and, to the south, the urban expanse of Plymouth, to the north, the fast-burning A30. Within this triangle an enchanting array of small rivers, wooded valleys and a bevy of hamlets and villages connected by slow lanes.

Not a place to hurry. Be advised to carry a compass, for disorientation is the norm in the Lew and Lyd Valleys. Road signs are, at times, confusing, and your mapping skills will be sorely tested. For you may wish to take advantage of the many fine hostelries within this domain.

Often the edges of a county are the most interesting. It is our habit to rush to the centre, and then to explore outwards. But, if you look to the natural border, in this instance, the Tamar Valley, and its feeding lines there are sweet names to conjure with; Sydenham Damerel, Horsebridge, Bere Ferrers, Weir Quay, Lopwell...Into these conduits great ships passed by with their tonnage. Visit Morwellham Quay and you will experience our rich, industrial past.

Explore this area and you will be forgiven a hearty appetite. For it is here that Tavistock was judged a worthy centre of fine produce and cuisine.  And, not too far distant are hotels noted for their fine cuisine and sporting endeavours; Hotel Endsleigh, Arundell Arms and Lewtrenchard Manor. Added to this list, the supreme Restaurant With Rooms, the Dartmoor Inn, and the country pubs, the Elephant's Nest and Peter Tavy Inn will nourish and tender your gastronomic desires.  So, Bon Appetit, and a safe journey home.

*View from the Granite Way*

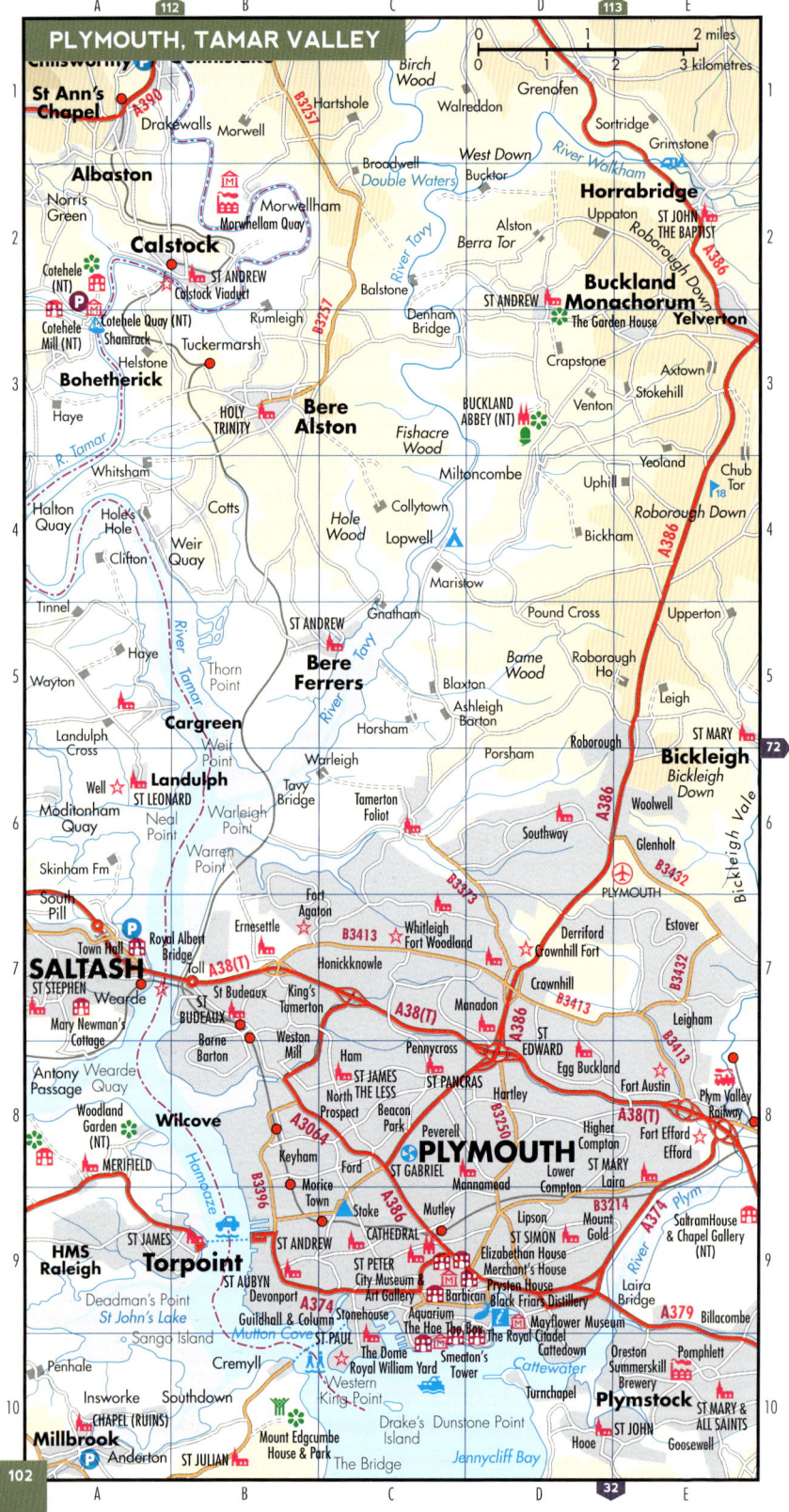

# PLYMOUTH, TAMAR VALLEY

*Sutton Pool, The Barbican*

## PLYMOUTH

The largest city in Devon, and the most well known, for Plymouth men have exported their birthplace's name to forty other towns and cities across the world. It is the greatest city in the South West, and lies between the rivers Tamar and Plym which form the estuaries of the Hamoaze and Cattewater, making a fine natural harbour. It is a city of its own making with a swashbuckling, seafaring tradition, and although the men who made Plymouth great were Devon men; Drake, Frobisher, Gilbert and Raleigh, their initial loyalty was to their Queen, Elizabeth 1 and to England. They sailed under the Queen's flag, for England, and their own, self-interest, and were party to England's maritime supremacy in the Elizabethan era, and thereafter. In 1585, it became a Naval Base, and at the time of the Armada in 1588,

Plymouth had superseded Dartmouth as the principal port of Devon. Sutton Pool was the location for the original port set beside the fishing quays of today's Barbican.

In 1691, William III established the Royal Naval Dockyard at Devonport in five acres, by 1765 it had expanded to a sprawling, 74 acres. Plymouth Dock was renamed Devonport in 1824. Much of the land is today in private hands, the remainder is known as the Plymouth Naval Base where one of their duties is to maintain and refuel the Vanguard Class of nuclear ballistic missile submarines.

The city suffered terrible losses and destruction during the Second World War. The whole centre of the city was virtually obliterated with over 1,200 civilian mortalities, unknown service losses, 10,000 houses destroyed and more damaged. Utter destruction. These lost

souls are remembered in the memorial at Charles Church, built 1641-1708 in the Gothic style. It, too, suffered untold destruction, now a mere shell of its former glory. So it is a fitting tribute that the Men of Plymouth saw fit to leave this "much talked about" monument in the centre of the Charles Cross roundabout, in front of the new shopping development, to be seen by all who drive into the city centre along the A374.

Following the Second World War, the rebuilding of the city centre was not considered a great success from an aesthetic or planning point of view, and the hideous Drake's Circus has been demolished to make way for the new £200 million Drake's Circus Shopping Centre, which opened to much fanfare on the 5th October, 2006. The City fathers and planners have drawn up ambitious plans

for regenerating the City; "A Vision for Plymouth." We are already seeing progress. The Royal William Dockyard at Stonehouse, the former Victualling Yard (storage of food etc) has been developed into £1,000,000 apartments and prestigious offices attended by art galleries and restaurants - see overleaf.

The Barbican is where most visitors (who are not interested in retail therapy) progress to. It is Plymouth's old harbour area and fortuitously avoided the Luftwaffe's bombing raids. A place of character and activity, close to the fishing boats of the thriving fishing industry. The fish market trades from 4.00 am and supplies the great wholesale markets of Billingsgate and

Birmingham, as well as the countless restaurants of the south-west, and beyond. There are ancient buildings, including Prysten House, the Elizabethan House, and the Merchant's House. Nearby is the Mayflower Stone from where the Pilgrim Fathers set forth aboard the Mayflower. All about you is life and activity, there are coffee shops, pubs and restaurants, and within view, the National Marine Aquarium.

With the sea to your left you ascend to the Hoe passing the Royal Citadel on your right. It is a fine, open space, given to kite flying and dog walking, and memories, dreams, reflections (apologies, dear Carl Jung). There are impressive memorials; Armada Memorial, the Naval

War Memorial, Soldiers of Plymouth, Royal Marines Memorial and Smeaton's Tower, which appears to be leaning.

Plymouth is not the city to typify the characteristics of Devon; thatch, cream teas and pastoral bliss. It is out on its own. And like Venice, best approached from the sea. Although, today, most of us arrive by train, or car via unattractive ring roads cutting between dull housing and equally poor industrial estates. Don't let these negatives put you off. One feels tremendous energy emanating from all this activity and new birth. It is a city to explore and grow to like, if not love. It has a future, and if you tire of it, Dartmoor is but a stone's throw away.

1646  Fairfax defeated Lord Hopton at Great Torrington.    1646  Jan. John Fairfax captures Dartmouth.

*Royal Albert Bridge*

## LIGHT BITES...IN THE BARBICAN

You are spoilt for choice. There are a number of street vendors selling food and drinks. **Cap'n Jaspers** is popular with motorcyclists, whilst those on the other two-wheel experience should visit the bike shop and café **Rockets & Rascals, 7 The Parade**.   A seriously good café opening at 8 for breakfast til 12, lunch 12-4. Great atmosphere, great food and great meeting place. 01752 927555 rocketsandrascals.com

For all who love to sew and make stuff walk a hundred yards north towards **Sutton Harbour** to **Make** at 140 Vauxhall Street. It's a coffee shop and Makery with workshop where you can learn to sew, stitch, cut fabrics, crochet...have lunch. 07776 757300 makeat140.co.uk

Returning to the Barbican, cross into **South St** to the **Jacka Bakery**. Here since time began. An artisan bakery, plus small café. Open daily.

For more substantial fare there is: **Monty's Coffee Shop, 13 The Barbican**. All-day breakfasts, and a fine selection of coffees. Burgers and steak sarnis, fishcakes. A comfortable and friendly place to hang out. Open daily from 9. 01752 252877 montyscafeplymouth.co.uk

**Quay 33, 33 Southside St.** The original; the oldest seafood eatery in the City set opposite the old fish market. Full blackboard menu. Open daily for lunch, 12-2, and dinner 5-late. 01752 229345 piermastersrestaurant.com

**Yukisan, 51 Notte St**. The first Japanese restaurant in Devon! You can eat on three floors, on chairs or in the authentic manner, on cushions. Whichever, you choose, you are in for a Sushi feast. Open daily 12-2.30, 5 til late. 01752 250240 yukisan.co.uk

**1660**  General George Monck (later Duke of Albermarle) of Great Potheridge, near Great Torrington organizes (The Restoration) the return of Charles II from exile.

105

## ALE & PUB-GRUB...IN THE BARBICAN

If you seek a full range of ales and some local colour: pirates, smugglers, fishermen with tall stories hold out at **The Dolphin**, 14 The Barbican. If you seek a civilised sanctuary and some fine pub-grub make you way up the steps to **The Fishermans Arms** at 31 Lambhay Street. 01752 268243. Not the easiest Inn to find but a well-known landmark here since 1740.

## VEGAN CHOICES...

**Cosmic Kitchen,** Sir John Hawkins Square. A family-run vegan bistro run by twin sisters Gabriella and Lucia. A lovely place to eat, dream and relax. All recipes have something extra originating from their Cypriot heritage. Open M, W & Th 12-9pm, F  12-12am, Sa 12-1am, Su 12-4pm. 01752 229955 cosmickitchen.co.uk

**Samphire Brasserie,** 111 Mayflower St. Herewith another family business, this time influenced by American cuisine. All meals made to order. Cakes, wines and juices. Open Tu-Sa 5-9pm. 01752 263116 samphirebrasserie.com

## TO VISIT IN PLYMOUTH...

**Crownhill Fort.** A quite extraordinary building, on a hill overlooking the northern outskirts of Plymouth. Well worth a visit to see its unique design. It was a Victorian fort built in the 1860s to defend Plymouth, from what one may wonder, given its isolation. Open for visitors to explore the earth ramparts, gun emplacements and tunnels. Open 10-5  Apr-Oct Su-F. 01752 793754 landmarktrust. org.uk

**Drake's Trail.** This is a 21-mile cycling and walking route between Plymouth and Tavistock. It is part of the National Cycle Route 27 (Devon Coast-to-Coast). It follows the western edge

*Elizabethan House*

1682    Aug 14. Three Bideford women tried for witchcraft at Exeter were convicted and sentenced to death.

*National Marine Aquarium*

of Dartmoor beside and through spectacular scenery, passing through tunnels and over bridges. A shared path, ideal for families with pushchairs and dogs, or those in wheelchairs. Marsh Mills and Plymbridge Woods are good start-off points for short excursions. drakestrail.co.uk

**Elizabethan House, 32 New St., The Barbican.** Memories and tales of old come to life: merchants, fishermen and wig makers share their stories in sight, sound and smells. A unique "Immersive Experience." Open Tu-Su & BH Ms 10-5. ehouseplymouth.com

**Mayflower Museum, 3-5 The Barbican.** Experience the "Story and Journey" aboard the Mayflower to the New World. A tale of great adversity and courage, and the significance of their role in America's history.

Open Apr-Oct M-Sa 9-5, Su 10-4. Nov-Mar M-F 9-5, Sa 10-4. 01752 306330 visitplymouth.co.uk

**National Marine Aquarium, The Barbican.** Britain's biggest, Europe's deepest Aquarium; specimens mainly from local waters. Octopi, crabs, lobsters, starfish, conger eels. Open daily 10-6 (-5 in winter). 08448 9317938 national-aquarium.co.uk

**Plymouth Arts Cinema, Tavistock Place.** An Independent cinema for the Enthusiast. An everchanging showcase of European, Asian and Contemporary movie-makers. Open Tu, Th & F 5-8.30pm, W 1-8.30pm & Sa 10-8pm. 01752 206114 plymouthartscinema.org

**Plymouth Gin, Black Friars Distillery, 60 Southside St.** "Spirit of Plymouth" exhibition

- history of the city and its world famous gin. Brasserie, Cocktail Lounge and Shop selling their produce. Open daily 10-5, Su 11-5. Party bookings by arrangement. 01752 66529 plymouthdistillery.com

**Royal William Yard.** Designed by the architect and engineer Sir John Rennie as the major victualling depot for the Royal Navy. Named after King William IV. Built between 1824 and 1835 using locally sourced Stonehouse limestone and Cornish, Penryn granite. 250 men were employed plus Officers and Officials. For one hundred years the yard was in use. It survived the Blitz in 1941 but was closed in 1985. In 2004 the City Council started a regeneration programme. What you see today are luxurious apartments and enterprising businesses;

**1685** The Devonshire Regiment raised in Bristol as the Duke of Beaufort's Musketeers to help crush Monmouth's Rebellion.

107

restaurants, a flourishing café culture at play and one of Plymouth's fab destinations. Beside the entrance is **The Hutong Café** who specialise in bagels made fresh on-site, daily. (C10)

### The Box, Tavistock Place.

This is Plymouth's newest and most spectular visitor attraction costing £47m. An eclectic mixture of maritime history and the Arts in eight galleries, seven exhibition spaces, six national collections and two million artefacts. Open Tu-Su & BH Ms 10-5. (C9) 01752 304774 theboxplymouth.com

### TO VISIT OUTSIDE PLYMOUTH..

**Antony Woodland Gardens.** Privately owned by the Carew Pole Garden Trust has 100 acres of woodland with 300 types of camellias bordering the Lynher River. Open Tu, W, Th & W/Es Mar-Oct 11-5.30. (A8)

**Antony House & Gardens (NT)**. Built for Sir William Carew from 1711-1721 and considered the most distinguished example of early C18 architecture in Cornwall. Colonnades, panelled rooms and family portraits. Open 4 Apr-31 Oct Tu, W, Th & BH M's 12-5 (also Su June-Aug). (A8)

**Buckland Abbey (NT).** C13 Cistercian abbey bought by the grandfather of Sir Richard Grenville, and later the home of Sir Francis Drake. Now houses period rooms and museum of Drake relics including Drake's Drum, 3 1/2 acre shrub and herb garden and fine tithe barn. Estate walks. Craft workshops. Holiday family activities. Open daily mid-Feb to Dec from 10. Jan to early Feb W/Es. Shop and Refreshments. (D3) 01822 853607

**1685** Judge Jeffreys Bloody Assizes sent many West Country men to horrific executions – their bodies quartered before family and friends.

*Views of Royal William Victualling Yard*

**1686** James 11 visits the West Country and pardons the dissenters. Later to grant freedom of worship with his Declaration of Indulgence.

*Smeaton's Tower, The Hoe*

**Calstock Viaduct.** 12 arch viaduct built to carry railway wagons from local mines to Calstock Quay where the wagons were raised and lowered in a lift. (B3)

**Cotehele Gallery, The Quay.** Showcasing professional artists and makers from the South West in seven exhibitions annually. Open daily 11-4. (A3)

**Cotehele House (NT).** Medieval house of grey granite (built 1485-1627) in romantic position overlooking the River Tamar and Devon beyond. For centuries, the Edgcumbe family home containing original furniture, C17 tapestries, armour and needlework. The gardens lie on several levels. Medieval dovecote. Ancient clock in chapel. Refreshment and shop. House open daily mid-Mar to Dec 11-4. Gardens & Estate open all year dawn-dusk. (A2)

**Cotehele Mill (NT).** Picturesque C18 and C19 buildings beside the River Tamar. A small outstation of the National Maritime Museum and berth for the restored Tamar sailing barge.

'Shamrock'. Museum and the Edgcumbe tea room selling light lunches and cream teas. Open daily from 11. (A3)

**Garden House, Buckland Monachorum.** Breathtaking terraced walled garden surrounding ruins of medieval vicarage. Innovative with stunning colours. Tearoom and plant sales. Open daily Apr-Oct 10.30-5, Nov-Feb 10.30-3.30. 01822 854769 (D3) thegardenhouse.org.uk

**Mary Newman's Cottage, 48 Culver St.** C15 Cottage of Mary Newman, first wife of Sir Francis Drake. Furniture supplied by the Victoria and Albert Museum. Open Apr-Sept W Th & W/Es, 12-4. (A7)

**Morwellham Quay.** Reconstruction of the busy C19 river port serving copper and arsenic mines, and its associated canals and railways. Workshops, Victorian Village, Edwardian Farm with animals, Folk in period costumes. Open as locally advertised. Tearoom, shop and campsite. (B2) 01822 832766 morwellham-quay.co.uk

**Mount Edgcumbe House & Park.** Sensitively restored Tudor mansion in beautiful landscaped parkland. Formal English, French and Italian Gardens. National Camellia Collection. Park and gardens open daily all year. House and Earl's Garden open Apr-Sept Tu-Th & Su 11-4.30, winter Oct-Mar Su 11-4.30. (B10)

**Royal Albert Bridge.** An iron single-track railway bridge built by I.K. Brunel in 1859, his last great feat of engineering. (B7)

**Saltram House (NT).** Largest country house in Devon, dating from the mid C18 with Tudor remnants. Mirror Room, Library, Chinese Chippendale bedroom. Furniture, plaster and woodwork. Pictures include 14 Reynolds portraits. Great Kitchen and stables. Garden with Orangery, shrubs and trees. Landscaped park. Open daily Mar-Dec 11-4.30 (winter - 3.30). Garden, Café & Shop open 10-5 all year. Park dawn til dusk. (E9) 01752 336546

**Tamar Valley Donkey Park.** Donkey sanctuary, Eeyore's Souvenir Store, woodland walk, café. Open daily Apr-Sept 10.30-5, W/Es Feb, Mar, Nov, Dec. (A2) 01822 834072 donkeypark.com

**1688** Nov 11. Prince William of Orange entered Exeter with swords drawn, colours flying and drums beating.

## TOWNS TO VISIT..

**Calstock.** Attractive old river port on the Tamar. Steep wooded riverbank and the abundance of fruit growing provide a splendid sight in spring, 12 arch viaduct. Numerous disused mining chimneys and engine houses haunt the landscape. (B3)

**Devonport.** The Royal Naval Dockyard was located here in the late C17. It is now known as HMNB Devonport the largest naval base in Western Europe, and the sole nuclear repair and refuelling facility for the Royal Navy. Home to the Naval barracks, HMS Drake, the Royal Marines base, RM Tamar and the HQ for 1 Assault Group Royal Marines. Within the town, sadly neglected by Devon visitors, you have the Regency Guildhall and Column. Within the Guildhall, the Column Bakehouse, a café serving fresh bread and cakes M-Sa 10-4 beside a funky art gallery. All visitors must climb the Column. Built between 1821-27 it rises to 124 ft providing panoramic views. Open M-F 9-5, Sa 10-4. devonportguildhall.org

**Saltash.** Attractive river port with steep streets running down to Tamar estuary. C18 Guildhall. May Fair - 1st week. Regatta - June 3rd week. (A7)

## EAT...DRINK...IN THE OUTER REACHES...

**Jolly Jacks, Mayflower Marina, Richmond Walk**. On the Western side of the City overlooking a mass of sail and plastic (hulls). Very much a family friendly bistro serving seafood, burgers, sunday roasts and little sailor mini meals. Open daily 9am-10pm, Su 9am-6pm. 01752 500008 jollyjacks.co.uk

**The Hook and Line, Royal William Yard**. A seafood bar and café, for all the seafood is caught by a hand-line from their boats. You get the full works: scallop shack, grilled octopus, fish tacos, fresh fix boxes. Endless choice. Open daily 12-9. (C10) 01752 265374 thehookandlineplymouth.co.uk

## B&BS...UP THE TAMAR...

**South Hooe Captain's House, Holes Hole, Nr Bere Alston.** Quite a find. A rural idyll set in ten acres of woodland overlooking the Tamar. Free range eggs, home-grown vegetables and your own private jetty, and log fires in winter. Too much. Writers' workshops. 01822 840329. (A4) southhooecourthouse.com

**The Basket Factory, Weir Quay**. A comfortable house proving B&B set within a large garden overlooks the Tamar. Children and dogs by arrangement. 01822 841455 (A4)

*Cotehele House nt*

1688   Nov 5. Prince William of Orange lands at Brixham, and then makes a triumphant entrance into Exeter on Nov 9th.

111

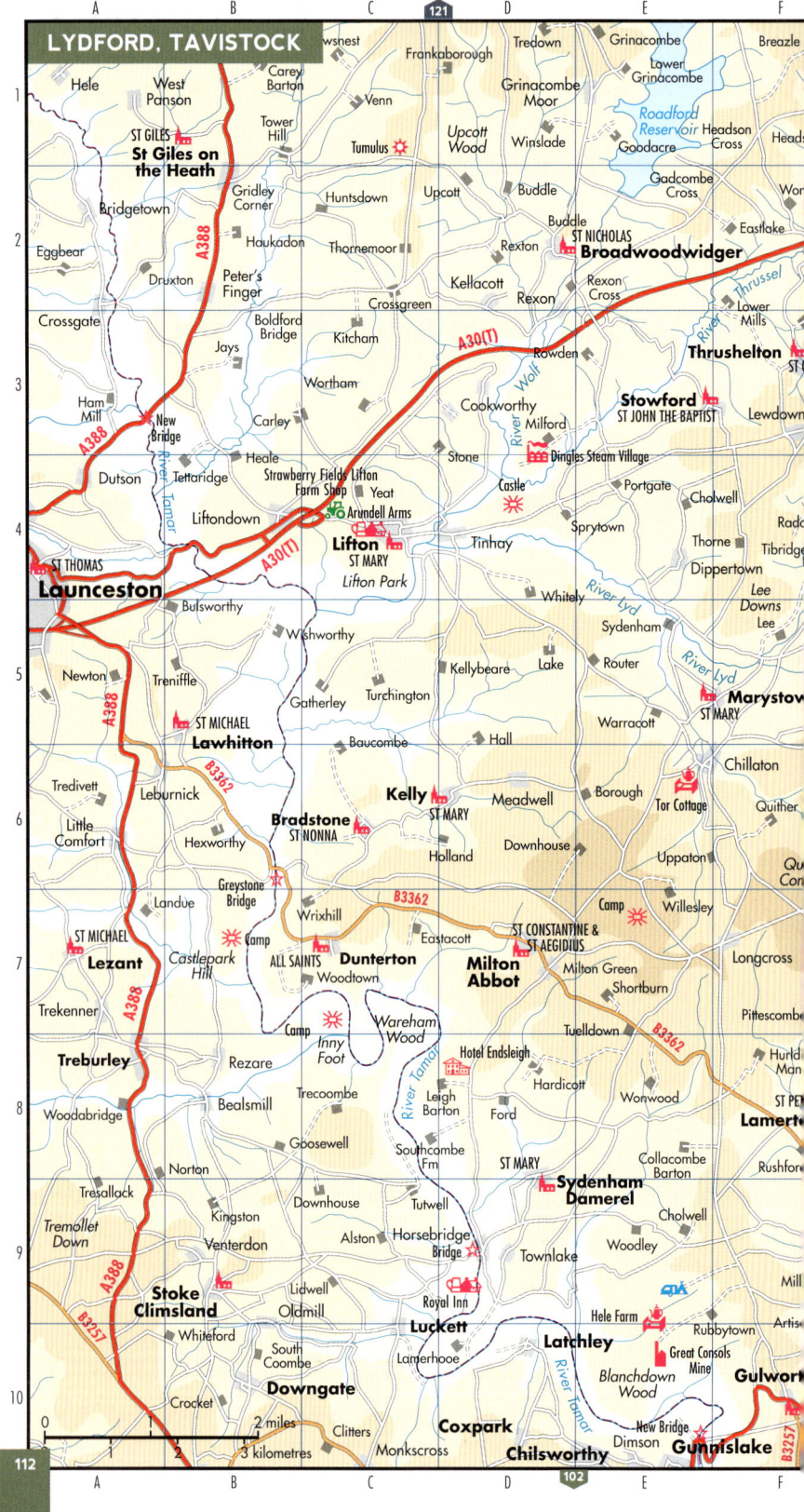

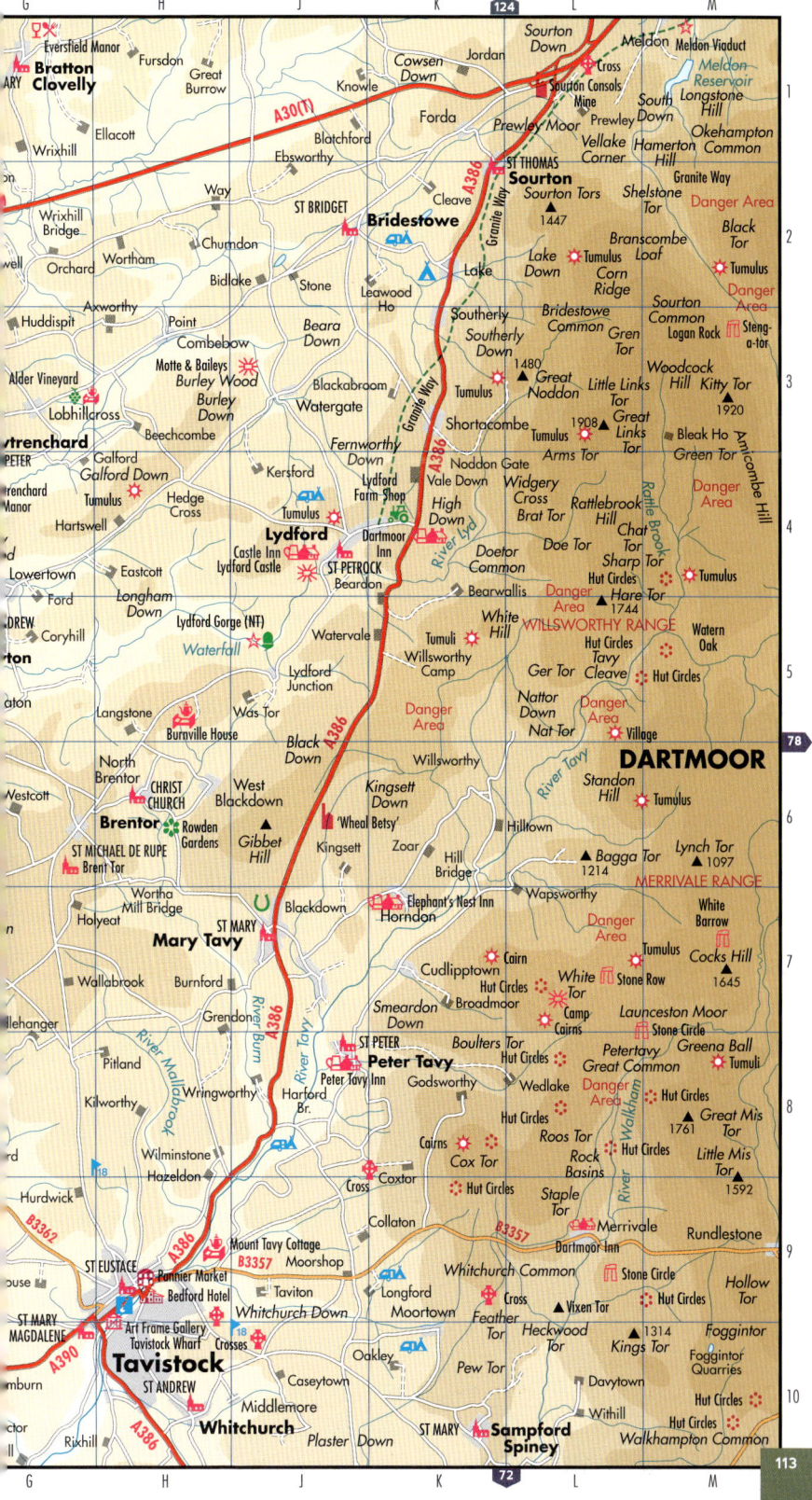

## TAVISTOCK

One of the four "Stannary Towns," established to control the production and distribution of tin from Dartmoor, and birthplace of Sir Francis Drake in 1542 at Crowndale Farm (now no more), south of the town. Later, developed by the Dukes of Bedford who lived in what is now the Bedford Hotel, and in the summer for six weeks at Endsleigh House (hotel) near Milton Abbot. The Bedfords were formidable, forward thinking town planners of their day, the early C19, and the impressive buildings have great dignity; the Town Hall and Pannier Market, and the long avenues were to their choosing. Drake's statue stands at the west end of the town's entrance, whilst at the end of the same road, stands a statue of Bedford. The Parish Church of St Eustace is formidable, too, and the Abbey, founded in 974, destroyed by Henry V111 in 1539 has a few surviving walls beside the riverbank. Tavistock is an attractive town, and a popular one to live in. It has plenty of smart, independent shops, good schools and a lively food culture. The area is noted for its abundance of smart hotels, restaurants and gastro-pubs. To offset your indulgences, Dartmoor is a few steps to the east. Plymouth is within commuting distance, and the Cornish border not too distant, either. (H10)

### TO VISIT..

**Artframe Gallery, 17 Duke St**. Broad range of paintings, ceramics bronzes and studio glass. Original art, limited editions. Open M-Sa 9.30-5. (H10) 01822 611091 tavistockgalleries.com

**Drake's Trail**. This is a 21-mile cycling and walking route linking Tavistock with Plymouth. Ideal for family and elderly cyclists keen to enjoy fresh air, fine views and free of traffic. It is part of the NCN Route 27, the "Devon Coast to Coast." It travels through tunnels and over bridges, and a viaduct. Just a couple of short road sections to be aware of. (H10) drakestrail.co.uk

**Pannier Market**. Purpose built in the 1850s. Markets held daily Tu-Sa 9-4. Crafts and antiques Tu, Mixed Tu & W, Fresh produce F, All sorts on Sa. Dukes Coffee House. (H10)

**Parish Church of St Eustace**. A fine, C15 construction with pinnacle tower and wide nave. A roof of carved beams and bosses, bench ends and C16 font. Tomb monuments to many local dignitaries; Sir John Glanville and John Fitz. William Morris stained glass in the north-east Chantry window and a clear reflection of the wealth created by the wool and tin merchants of west Devon. (H9)

**Tavistock Wharf, The Wharf.** Tavistock's art centre featuring cinema, live music, theatre and an art gallery. Bar and coffee shop. Open daily. (H9) 01822 611166 tavistockwharf.com

**Teddy's Dolls House, Village Shopping Arcade, Brook St**. Collection of dolls and teddies. Dolls & Teddies Hospital. (H10) 01822 612128

### LIFTON

The new A30 by-passes this charming old settlement founded by the Saxons as an admin centre. The C15 church with C12 and C14 origins is particularly fine, and the countryside around to the East is a gem. And, popular with fishers of men (and their ladies). (C4)

## TO VISIT…

**Alder Vineyard & Coffee Bar/ Kitchen.** Relax in their Kitchen Café and soak up the pastoral view. Perhaps, take a Vineyard Tour (bring boots), wallow in the mud, enjoy a glass of their nectar and breakfast on eggs benedict muffins, later stay for lunch. Life's a breeze. Open W-Su 9-5 (BHs 10-4). (G3) 01566 783409 aldervineyard.uk

**Strawberry Fields Farm Shop.** Always busy, popular with locals and day-visitors to the restaurant, bakery, fruit and veg stalls, and the butchery. A great family breakfast stop for those coming to and from Devon or Cornwall. (C4) 01566 784605 strawberryfieldslifton.co.uk

### LYDFORD

From the C9 when Lydford was laid out in a grid system, visible today, where it has been an important centre on the Western reaches of Dartmoor. Today, it is well located for visiting Dartmoor and the beautiful pastoral countryside of the Devon/Cornwall border. Off the beaten track and credited with country inns and charming places to stay. (J4)

**Lydford Castle (EH)**. A C13 Tower remains above the C12 predecessor built during the Saxon and Medieval period when Lydford was an important centre of the tin trade and administrative centre for the forest of Dartmoor. From the Middle Ages to the C18 the Castle became a prison for those who disobeyed the Stannary laws. Open daily. (J4)

**Lydford Gorge (NT).** The beautiful woodland walk leads you down the deep wooded ravine 1.5 miles long carved out by the River Lyd as it plunges into the 'Devil's Cauldron.' The White Lady Waterfall is quite spectacular at 90 ft high. Open daily Apr-Oct from 10. Refreshments. Admission charge. Waterfall only rest of year 10.30-3. Tea room. (J5) 01822 820320 nationaltrust.org.uk

**Merrivale Stone Circle.** Remains from one of the earliest settlements in Devon. Clearly visible are boulders from Hut Circles, square dwellings, and Stone Rows from funeral burials. Two of the standing stones have markings indicating an A and a T, as an early road sign for crossing the Moor. A stream of pure water crosses the area. Park in car park. (L9)

**Rowden Gardens, Brentor.** World famous for their range of rare aquatic plants, especially irises. Consultancy service available. (H6) 01822 810275 gardenscentral.co.uk

**Wheal Betsy.** Former tin mine in the care of the National Trust. You can spy the mine from the main road. (J6

## CHURCHES TO VISIT…

**St Mary, Bratton Clovelly.** C15 with many attactive Norman features. (G1)

**St Michael De Rupe, Brent Tor.** Built by the monks of

*Merrivale Stone Circle*

**1690** Devonshire Regiment fight with King William III at the Battle of the Boyne.

115

Tavistock Abbey in the C14, and romantically poised on an extinct volcano at 1130 feet. Like Glastonbury Tor, a favourite with children to clamber up, and witness the fine views across to Dartmoor, and west to Brown Willy, on Bodmin Moor. (G6)

## TO STAY...TO SLEEP...

**April Cottage, 12 Mount Tavy Rd, Tavistock**. Friendly accommodation overlooks the River Tavy. All bedrooms with bathroom. Easy walking distance to town centre. (H10) 01822 613280

**Burnville House, Nr Brentor.** Large, comfortable Georgian house with views across to Dartmoor offers solitude and farmhouse cuisine. B&B room. Three self-catering cottages. (H5) 01822 820443
burnville.co.uk

**Hele Farm, Nr Gulworthy**. Grade 11 listed farmhouse with organic dairy dating back to 1780. Somewhat old fashioned décor. Steeped in history of mining – see Great Consols Mine. Nature walks down to Tamar. Self catering, too. (E9) 01822 833084
dartmoorbb.co.uk

**Lobhill Farmhouse B&B.** Set in lovely grounds close to the family's Alder Vineyard. The four bedrooms are lovingly tended in varying colour schemes. Self catering cottage available. (H3) 01566 783542
lobhillbedandbreakfast.co.uk

**Mount Tavy Cottage.** Lovely old gardener's cottage just ten minutes walk from Tavistock. Family room and 4-poster bedroom with bathrooms. Organic breakfasts. All set within 10 acres of paradise. Self

catering, too. (H9) 01822 458354
mounttavy.co.uk

**Tor Cottage, Chillaton**. A rural retreat in their own private valley with over 18 acres of wildlife to explore and get lost in. Elegant and spacious rooms. Outdoor pool. (E6) 01822 860248
charmingsmallhotels.co.uk

## INNS TO EAT...DRINK... SLEEP...

**Castle Inn B&B, Lydford**. A C16 Inn with an ancient history modernised with style; Lydford Pennies, Lydford Mint, Ghosts of Sherlock Holmes, all with open fires, settles, pub-grub and a beer garden. Storage for bikes. (J4) 01822 820242
castleinnlydford.co.uk

**Elephant's Nest B&B, Horndon.** Always a favourite. Nothing better than sitting out

1698   Samuel Darker sets up first permanent printing press in Exeter.

1698   Thomas Newcomen of Dartmouth invents atmospheric steam pumping engine.

in their garden on a summer's evening with a pint in hand. (K7) 01822 810273
[elephantsnest.co.uk](elephantsnest.co.uk)

**Eversfield Organic Dartmoor Inn B&B, Merrivale.** A carnivores feast! The grass-fed beef cattle are a mere 15-miles away. Expect delicious steaks and burgers, organic ales and wines. Open for breakfast, lunch and dinner reservations. Beside this **The Little Farm Shed Café**, a haven for walkers and cyclists. (L9) 01837 871400
[eversfieldorganic.co.uk](eversfieldorganic.co.uk)

**Peter Tavy Inn.** Popular with all the foodie guides, for you have low beams, slate floors and large cosy fireplaces, plus an ambience conducive to children and dogs. Fine start off point for Dartmoor walks. (J8) 01822 810348
[petertavyinn.co.uk](petertavyinn.co.uk)

*The Granite Way*

**Royal Inn, Horsebridge.** A C15 Inn with Gothic windows, beams and log fires overlooks the Tamar. A no-nonsense attitude to good pub-grub with ingredients sourced locally. Meals 12-2, 6-9. 01822 870214
[royalinn.co.uk](royalinn.co.uk)

## EAT...DRINK...SLEEP...

**Arundell Arms, Lifton.** One of England's premier fishing and shooting hotels offering 22-miles of Salmon, Sea Trout and Brown Trout fishing in the Tamar and Lyd valleys. Tuition and ghillieing on-hand. The Arundell is comfortable, unpretentious and relaxed. The Restaurant's cuisine is heightened by local, seasonal and sustainable produce. New onsite deli sells fresh produce and personally approved wines. Tesla supercharger points. (C4) 01566 784666 [thearundell.com](thearundell.com)

**Bedford Hotel, Tavistock.** An imposing, town hotel offering traditional comforts and elegant charm. Quite a pile. It's a former Benedictine Abbey and residence of the Dukes of Bedford. Special Breaks. Serves food all day (the best Minute Steak I have ever tasted!), and if you have been rushed off your feet, a large armchair awaits you. "A Scotch or Pot of Tea, Your Grace..." (H9) 01822 613221 [bedford-hotel.co.uk](bedford-hotel.co.uk)

**Dartmoor Inn.** More a Restaurant with (3) Rooms than country inn. The beautifully designed pieces of artwork set the scene for great cuisine, a genial atmosphere in the three cosy dining rooms and small bar with log fire. Regular art exhibitions. Classy bedrooms. With being a short distance from the Moor and Gorge, walkers, dogs and

their grubby boots (please leave by the front door) are encouraged to venture here. Lunch & dinner served W-Su 12-4, 6.30-9 also Su lunch. (K4) 01822 820221
[dartmoorinn.com](dartmoorinn.com)

**Hotel Endsleigh.** Olga Polizzi's hotel blends a fusion of country house styles with contemporary boutique and manages to pull it off. A former fishing lodge set high above the Tamar Valley of indescribable beauty. Offset with ornamental gardens; a Fairy Dell, Rock Gardens and Grotto and an Arboretum. After a summer's lunch there's bound to be a tree to rest under, to dream of Shangri-Las in this hideaway overlooking the Tamar. 2-rods for hire. (D8) 01822 870000
[hotelendsleigh.com](hotelendsleigh.com)

**Lewtrenchard Manor.** A C17 manor house that became the home of the Victorian squire and parson, Sabine Baring-Gould. He inherited the estate in 1872 comprising 3,000 acres and the gift of a living at Lew Trenchard Parish. In 1865 he published his hymn *Onward Christian Soldiers* with music composed by Arthur Sullivan. Nearby is Galford the site in the C9 of a battle involving the West Welsh and the Defnas tribes. Today, the house is a country house hotel in the grand style. Old Masters line the oak panelled walls, a log burns in the hearth of a large fireplace, sofas invite relaxation and calm. It is a fine place to be. The Ball Room is exquisite and will play host to many a Wedding Feast. You can enjoy afternoon tea and the full complement. (G4) 01566 783222
[lewtrenchard.co.uk](lewtrenchard.co.uk)

**1698** Traveller and chronicler, Celia Fiennes visits Exeter, and marvels at the immense output of serge cloth. The most commercially productive area of Britain.

117

This stretch of country belongs to a Devon often neglected and forgotten. An undulating, pastoral landscape lying between the coastal resorts and medieval trade routes of North Devon, and to the south, the great expanse of Dartmoor.

Here are isolated villages and hamlets, sometimes made up of a single or secondary homestead originally built from the local earth, commonly known as cob. Connected by narrow country lanes set between high hedgerows, that with time, have grown in height and width. Built up by peasant farmers long since dead, who cleared the stone from the fields, a tapestry of a thousand natural colours; greens, reds, oranges and mauves.

Is this the rural idyll of an England long forgotten, and sought for, in glossy magazines? Not if you live and work here. The 45 parishes that surround Holsworthy and Hatherleigh have created the brand "Ruby Country" to market their towns following the disastrous foot n' mouth epidemic of 2001. The name is taken from the indigenous breed of cattle, Ruby Red Devon; a handsome beast, given to fine cuts of meat.

It was this Devon, in isolation, that so attracted the poet, Ted Hughes. He lived the last third of his life in the parish of North Tawton. Close to nature, he wrote about the natural world, as he saw it, and fished the upper reaches of the Taw and Torridge, for salmon and sea trout.

These communities have witnessed a great change since the development of the A30 and A36, now largely inhabited by commuters from Exeter and Taunton. Yet, despite this, there are still those whose lifestyle remains unchanged, where the major social event of the week is Market Day, or the village cricket match. The church, pub and village store continue to be the focal points of village life.

Mid Devon can be a charming place to visit. You will find that people have more time for you. Just watch the locals of Hatherleigh walk about their daily business, forever stopping to talk with their friends and acquaintances. You too will come across friendly pubs and churches offering solitude and fine craftsmanship.

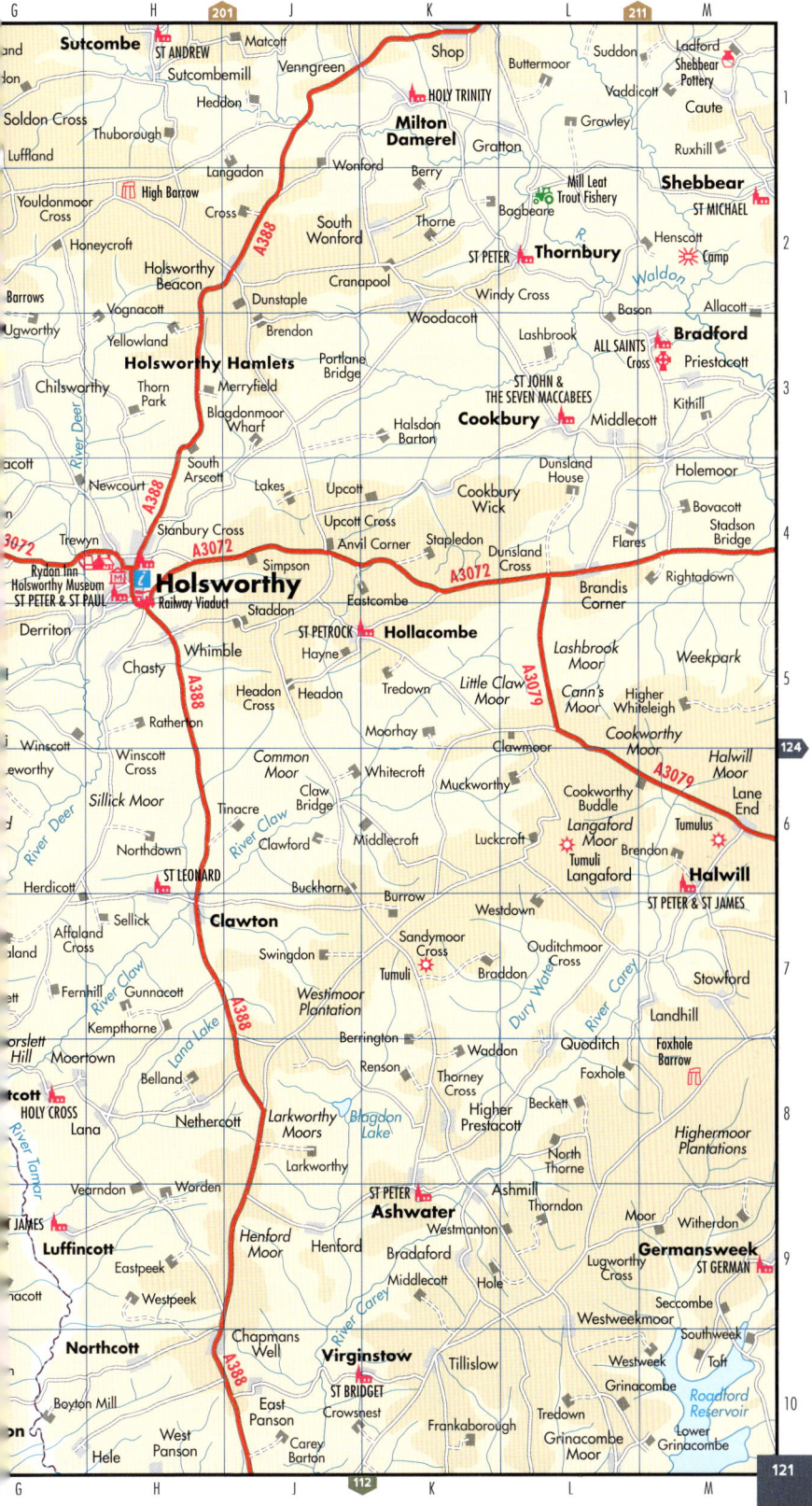

## Holsworthy

The area was once the centre of cattle rearing, especially Red Rubies, a native breed originating in the West Country. A rural idyll of scattered farms and hamlets, rolling, green pastures unintimidated by our crazy world. Hence, a Market town with a thriving cattle market, and Pannier Market every Wednesday in the Market Square. Be sure to visit "St Peter's Fair" in early July to catch the crowning of the "Pretty Maid." Hereabouts is real Devon for you. Unsophisticated, quiet, miles from the nearest motorway. A haven of peace. In need of a rustic breakfast, a posh brunch, coffee, a cream tea? **Posh Totties** will provide. (H4) redrubydevon.co.uk

### TO VISIT...

**Holsworthy Museum, Manor Offices.** Housed in a C17 Parsonage. Themed rooms feature the area's heritage, memories, traditions and bygones of rural life. Open East-Nov M-F 11-1, (W to 4). (H4) 01409 259337 holsworthymuseum.co.uk

**Mill Leat Trout Fishery.** Fresh and smoked trout. Children's fishing ('Catch your own') in two lakes and 1/2 mile of River Waldron 9-5.30, (dusk fly fishing). Three self-catering cottages. (L2) 01409 261426 millleat.co.uk

**Shebbear Pottery.** Clive Bowen is one of the country's leading ceramicists. He studied painting and etching before taking up an apprenticeship. He makes (often large) wood-fired earthenware pots in a variety of colours and styles. (M1) 01409 281271 clivebowen.co.uk

**Tamar Lakes.** Reservoirs in remote country near Tamar's source. Sailing, canoeing, lakeside walks and windsurfing. Fly fishing in upper lake. Lower lake has coarse fishing, bird sanctuary and hide. Camping. Shop and refreshments. (F1) 01288 321712 swlakestrust.org.uk/tamar

### EAT...DRINK...RELAX..

**The Rydon Inn, Rydon Hill.** Take the Bude Road out of Holsworthy. Inside, the barn-like wood construction based on a Devon longhouse glows with warmth. You can lunch or dine overlooking the lake and nourish yourself with better than average pub grub. They claim it's a dining-pub. It's certainly the place to eat, hereabouts. (G4) 01409 259444 rydon-inn.com

### BUDE

A seaside resort first developed by the Victorians that has witnessed, of late, much resurgence in no small part due to the popularity of surfing and beach activities. The long extensive beaches just a short walk from the town centre and those to the south and north of the town are breathtaking.

The coastline has been the scene of many shipwrecks - 80 ships were foundered or wrecked between 1824-74. The town abounds with surf shops, hostels, countless coffee shops and when the Low Pressure

*Sandy Mouth Beach*

| 1700 | Exeter build a poor house and establish a Corporation for the Poor. | 1700 | At least 200 Devon ships trade with Newfoundland. |

is in force the beaches are populated with black shadows, in summer and winter. It is the most accessible of Cornish surf resorts and is host to many surf schools. Canal, carnival and fete - August (third week). 'Blessing of the Sea' - Aug. E/C Th. (A3)
bude.co.uk visitbude.info

## WHAT TO SEE & VISIT...

**Launcells Church.** Fortunate to be the only Cornish church not tampered with by the Victorians. Wall painting and 60 carved bench ends shown off in the light interior. Monument. Fine wagon roof. A haven of solitude beside the little stream in a wooded valley. Magical. (C3)

**Old Canal.** Built in 1819-26 at a length of 43 miles (61km). For 60 years used to transport coal and lime inland, and to export grain and slate. Killed off by the railways. Best sections are at Marhamchurch, Hobbacott Down and Werrington. (A3)
bude-canal.co.uk

**The Castle Bude.** Museum celebrates the heritage of Bude and Stratton with a tableaux of interactive displays and exhibits: Canal, shipwrecks, lifeboats and railways. New "Gurney" exhibition of Bude's Forgotten Genius, Sir Goldsworth Gurney. **Café Limelight** open daily, all year 10-4. (A3) 01288 357300
thecastlebude.org.uk

## EAT...DRINK...RELAX...

**Temple Cornwall, Granville Terrace.** An obsession with design and the delicacies of life are what drives this new eatery and emporium. It has to be organic and there will a choice of vegan/vegetarian, as well

*Lone Surfer, Bude*

as brunch, chicken and meat dishes. Opens at 10 for brunch. Open evenings, too. (A3) 01288 354739
templecornwall.com

**Life's A Beach, Summerleaze Beach.** Bistro restaurant offers all types of food from locally caught sea bass, to burgers, and pizzas. A great place to watch the sunset and to relax after a day in the surf. Open daily in season. (A3) 01285 355222
lifesabeach.info

## STRATTON

A pretty village with a long and fascinating history. Now very much a suburb of Bude. C15 church. Battle of Stamford Hill, 1643. (B3)

## XTREME SPORTS...

**Big Blue Surf School, Summerleaze Beach.** Learn, improve, excel at one of Europe's top schools with National Team coach, Jon Price. Open to all, no matter your age, size and ability. Open all year. (A3) 01288 331764
bigbluesurfschool.com

**Bude Surfing Experience, Summerleaze Crescent.** Surf and SUP lessons, board hire & private lessons. (A3) 07779 117746
budesurfingexperience.co.uk

**OA Surf Club, Atlantic Court.** Family and group activity centre for body boarding, coasteering and surfing for all ages and experience with plentiful accommodation for up to 40 persons. Tuition. (A6) 01288 362900 oasurfclub.co.uk

**Raven Surf School**. Mike Raven is a former surf champion whose school caters for all levels; from beginners' groups to 1 to 1 tuition. Groups out of season. (A3) 07860 465499 ravensurf.co.uk

1715 Construction of the Exeter Canal completed.

1727 John Gay's Beggar's Opera runs for 62 nights in London – a resounding success.

123

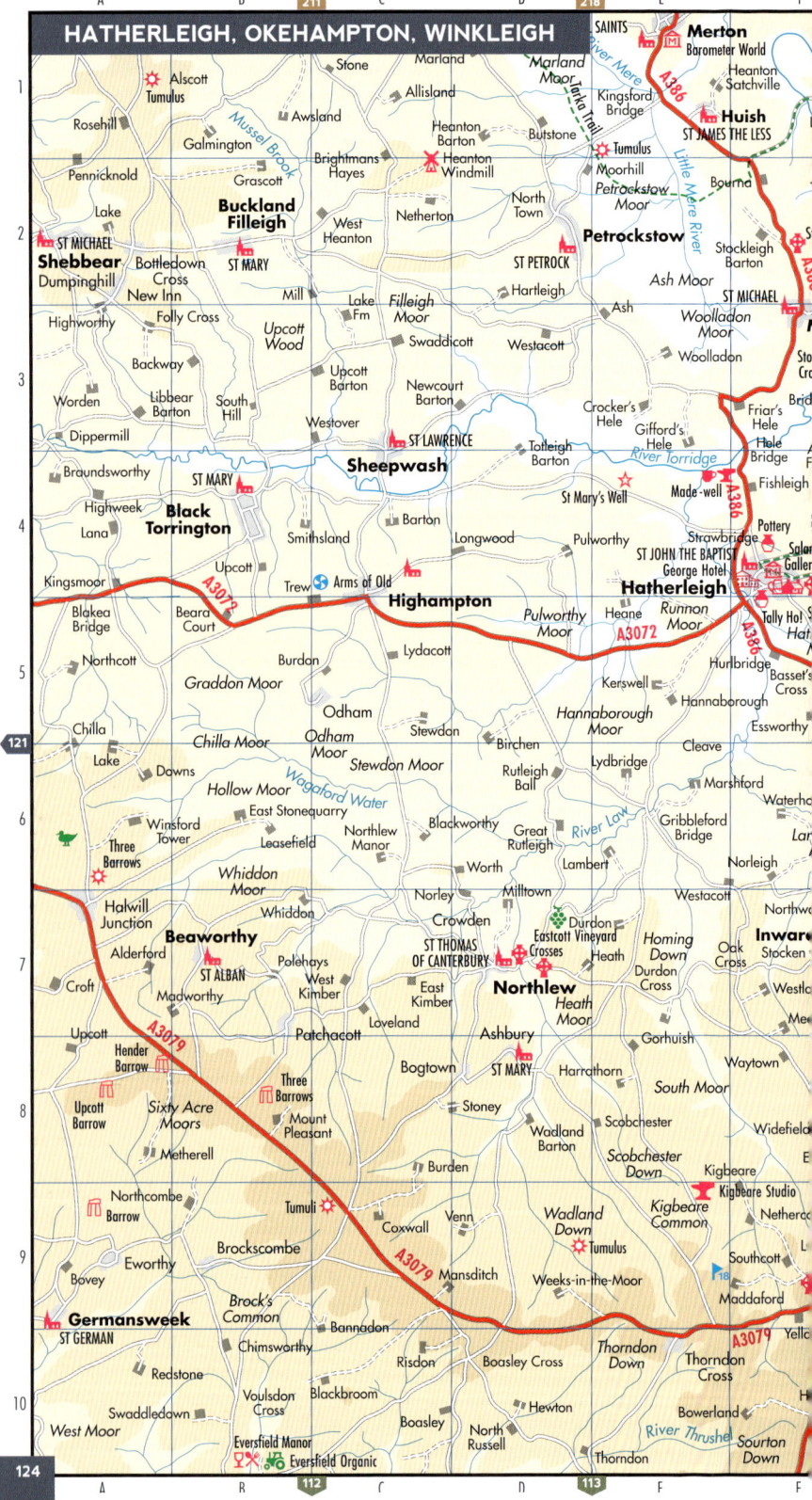

A3079

A3072

A386

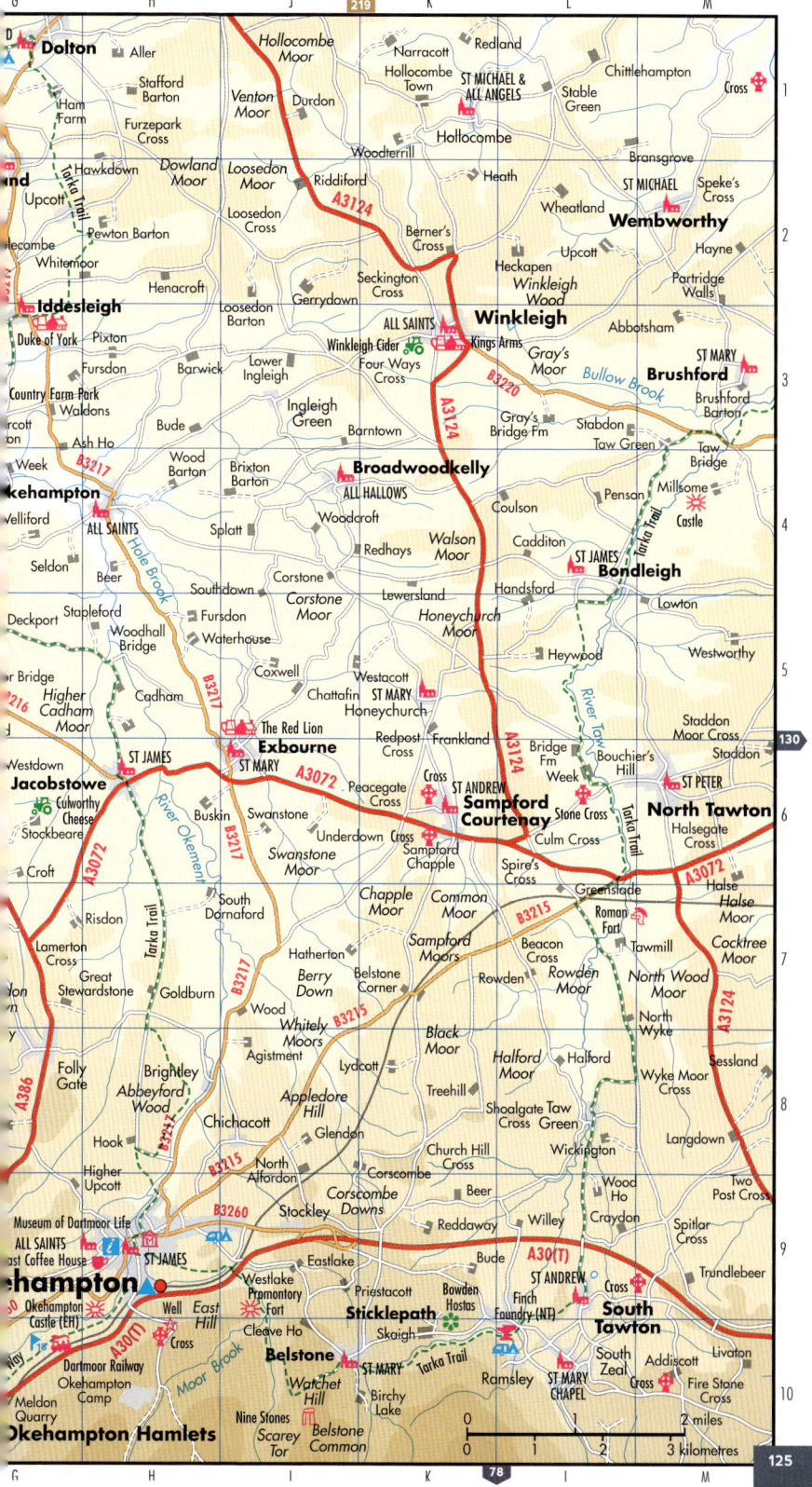

### HATHERLEIGH

An ancient market town of thatched and cob cottages nestling in a rural landscape shaped by a thousand years of settlers and farming. This must be one of the most delightful little towns in Devon. The local community realize the privilege of living here and are always active in promoting regular events, from the Arts Festival in July to the Carnival in November. Artwork is exhibited about the town. The Livestock Market is famous. (E4) hatherleigh.net

### SPECIAL PLACES TO VISIT IN AND AROUND HATHERLEIGH…

**Arms of Old, Trew.** The ancient profession of Archery is laid bare here where you can learn to use an English Longbow and a modern bow under qualified tuition. Families and groups welcome. Call to book. (B4) 01409 231171 armsofold.co.uk

**Hatherleigh Market.** This is quite an attraction, from the Monday auction of ewes and lambs to the sales of live poultry (and furniture) on Tuesdays. Monthly horse sales. Café. Phone for details: 01837 810496 (E4) vickshatherleighmarket.co.uk

**Hatherleigh Methodist Chapel, High St.** The beautiful stained glass was supplied by the monks of Buckfast Abbey. (F4)

**Hatherleigh Pottery, 20 Market St.** A working pottery for 25-years with showroom displaying the work of Jane Payne and Michael Taylor, plus textiles and original prints from local craftsmen. Open Easter to New Year Tu-Sa 10-5. (F4) 01837 810624 hatherleighpottery.co.uk

**Made-Well, West Fishleigh Farm.** A Community Interest Co with garden café and shop selling fresh vegetables, herbs and plants. Play area. Family/ dog friendly. Open daily. (E4) 01837 810584 made-well.co.uk

**Salar Gallery, 18/20 Bridge St.** The Devon landscape and its occupants provide a never-ending source of inspiration for the painters, sculptors, photographers and craftspeople who show their work here. Regular exhibitions. Open Tu-Sa 10-1, 2-5. Closed W. (F4) 01837 810940 salargallery.co.uk

**St John the Baptist.** Built at the top of the High Street its fine position provides splendid views. Early Norman church with C15 additions. In 1990 the medieval wooden spire collapsed during a great storm causing extensive damage and gaining national press coverage. Some interesting churchyard monuments. (F4)

**War Horse Country Farm Park, Parsonage Farm.** It was this valley and surrounding countryside that inspired Michael Morpurgo to write

*Ruby Reds*

*The George, Hatherleigh*

his book and play. WW1 Horse Exhibitions, Farm Trail, Kids Play Area. A History of Farming 100 years ago. Cream teas. Open daily Apr-Sept 2-6. (G3) 01837 810318 warhorsevalley.co.uk

## EAT...DRINK...SLEEP...

**Tally Ho! Country Inn B&B, 14 Market St**. Traditional pub with oak beams and log fires serving home cooked food and real ales. Micro-Brewery. Beer garden. Open all day. (F4) 01837 810306

**The George Hotel, Market St**. A medieval C15 Inn that had been a sanctuary for monks, a brewery, law court and coaching inn that was burnt down a few years ago. What we now see is an extraordinary resurrection to its former glory. A hostelry of the old-school. One can imagine coaches coming through the Arch to the Inner Courtyard. It is an Inn and a comfortable hotel. Coffees, bar food and Daily Specials. (F4) 01837 811755 thegeorgeinnhatherleigh.com

## NORTH TAWTON

Interesting little town formerly the home of the poet, the late Ted Hughes where he had a farm nearby. More recently its claim to fame, as the setting for the TV series "Jam and Jerusalem." An elaborate clock stands in the Town Square to mark the 1877 jubilee. Interesting church, closed when I visited but there are remains of a Saxon or Roman cross, lovely bench ends and some C15 stained glass to look at if you have the opportunity. (M6)

## EAT...DRINK...SLEEP...

**Duke of York, Iddesleigh.** A friendly welcome awaits you in this C15 Devon Longhouse. Old photos, bank notes, low ceilings, small rooms and a large fireplace provide a fine ambience. Simple, honest food can be eaten in the bar or Dining Room and a selection of real ales to succour the palate. "The War Horse" story has its origins from tales told in front of the fire by Wilfred Ellis to Michael Morpurgo. B&B. (G3)

01837 810253 dukeofyorkdevon.co.uk

**Red Lion Inn, Exbourne**. A traditional real ale pub of C16 origins where a sincere welcome greets you. Inded, popular as a diversion off the Tarka Trail for cyclists and walkers. Basic pub-grub. (J6) 01837 851551 theredlionexbourne.co.uk

## OKEHAMPTON

A finely situated town on the northern edge of Dartmoor, and well situated for exploring the "High Tors" and West Devon. The buildings are statuesque and remind one of the bygone Victorian age of steam and engineering excellence. Of late, has become a centre for family cycling and mountain biking on Dartmoor. The Granite Way starts off from the Railway Station and YHA (Adventure Okehampton) and was extended in 2013 to expand the route to 18km of traffic-free cycling. Ideal for small families, or jaded city dwellers in search of peace and solitude. The

*Trees, Honeychurch*

arrival of Waitrose (that must surely serve a vast hinterland) brought amazement and great joy to the local chattering classes. However, it has been the opening of the Dartmoor Line, the Great Western Railways connection with Exeter that has and will have lasting new developments for Okehampton. Estate Agents are seeing a rush of prospective commuters coming to town. (H9)

## LIGHT BITES...

Okehampton has many venues offering you a cuppa. First head to the sisters at **ImageOke Coffee-Bar-Bakery**, 6 The Arcade to sample their superb baking, banter, cakes and joie de vivre. 01837 53765

Does your bike need some maintenance? **Cycleworks** around the corner will repair your bike and offer you a coffee and more.

Cross the High Street to **Toast Coffee House on 2-4 Market Street** for your coffees, smoothies and ciabattas, as well as the Dish of the Day. Free wifi. Open M-Sa 9.30-5. (H9) 01837 54494 eattoast.co.uk

## TO VISIT...

**Adventure Okehampton (YHA), Klondyke Rd.** You can try 15 different adventure activities suitable for all ages from 5; Archery to Climbing to Kayaking to Orienteering to Raft Building, and more. Ideal for families, groups, hen and stag parties, and individuals. Accommodation. Bike hire with E-Bike and Disabled three-wheelers. (H9) 01837 53916 adventureokehampton.com

**Granite Way.** This is a family trail and walkway for 18km/11 miles otherwise known as National Cycle Network Route 27/Coast to Coast. The trail follows the former Okehampton to Lydford railway line and affords superb views of Dartmoor and the West Devon countryside. It crosses two spectacular viaducts at Meldon and Lake. Cycle hire is available at Okehampton Station from the YHA 01837 53916 **Adventure Okehampton (YHA)** and **Devon Cycle Hire** at Sourton Down, 01837 861141 where there is ample parking space. Refreshments (pubs) at Sourton Down, Bearslake and Lydford. Recommend you carry a picnic/provisions and water. (H9)

**Museum of Dartmoor Life, 3 West St.** Fascinating interactive displays on 3-floors illustrates the lives, work and beliefs of Dartmoor's people across time. Tearoom, gift and craft shops. TIC. Open Mar-Dec 10-4. (H9) 01837 52295 dartmoorlife.org.uk

**Okehampton Castle (EH)**. Ruins of the largest castle in Devon built in the C11. The square Norman Keep is all that remains of a seat of once great power in the hands of the Courtenays,

Lords of Devon before Henry Courtenay upset Henry VIII, and subsequently lost his head. Its strategic position is in effect, questionable. Open daily Apr-Oct 10-dusk. (G9) 01837 52844 english-heritage.org.uk

## TO VISIT…OUTSIDE OKEHAMPTON…

**Bowden Hostas.** The National Collection of over 1,000 hybrid Hostas in a 1-acre garden for 30-years. Chelseas RHS Gold Medal winners. Plant sales. Open Days. Visitors welcome. (K10) Cleave House, Sticklepath 01837 840989 bowdenhostas.com

**Finch Foundry (NT).** The last (C19) water powered-edge forge in England. 3 working water-wheels. Giant trip hammer and shears. Demonstrations of working machinery. Open daily Apr-Oct 11-5. (L9) 01837 840046 nationaltrust.org.uk

**Kigbeare Studio & Gallery.** A creative retreat hidden away down a long, bumpy lane. A selection of makers exhibit their work. Mainly ceramicists. Courses in glazing. Cottage to rent. Gallery open Tu-Sa 10.30-5. (F9) 01837 53787 kigbeare.co.uk

*Museum of Dartmoor Life*

**Winkleigh Cider Co., Hatherleigh Rd.** Traditional cider pressed here since 1916. The apples collected from local orchards are fermented, and matured, in giant oak vats. Shop sells a range of ciders. Open M-Sa 9-5. (K3) 01837 835560 winkleighcider.co.uk

## COUNTRYSIDE INTERESTS…

**Curworthy Cheese, Stockbeare Farm.** For 25-years hand-made cheeses in many varieties have been made here. Milk sourced from the local farms. Beware of rough pot-holed track. (G6)

01837 810587 curworthycheese.co.uk

**Eastcott Vineyard.** A small 6-acre winery that has achieved remarkable success with their Sparkling and White Wines. 2-hour tours of the vineyard. Shop. Open June-Sept & 1/2 terms Tu-Sa, Oct-May Th-Sa, 9.30-5. Winter by appoint. (D7) eastcottvineyard.co.uk

**Eversfield Organic.** 850-acre estate producing award-winning Aberdeen Angus beef, lamb, pork and chicken plus wild venison and game reared in the woods. (B10) 01837 871400 eversfieldorganic.co.uk

*Okehampton Castle*

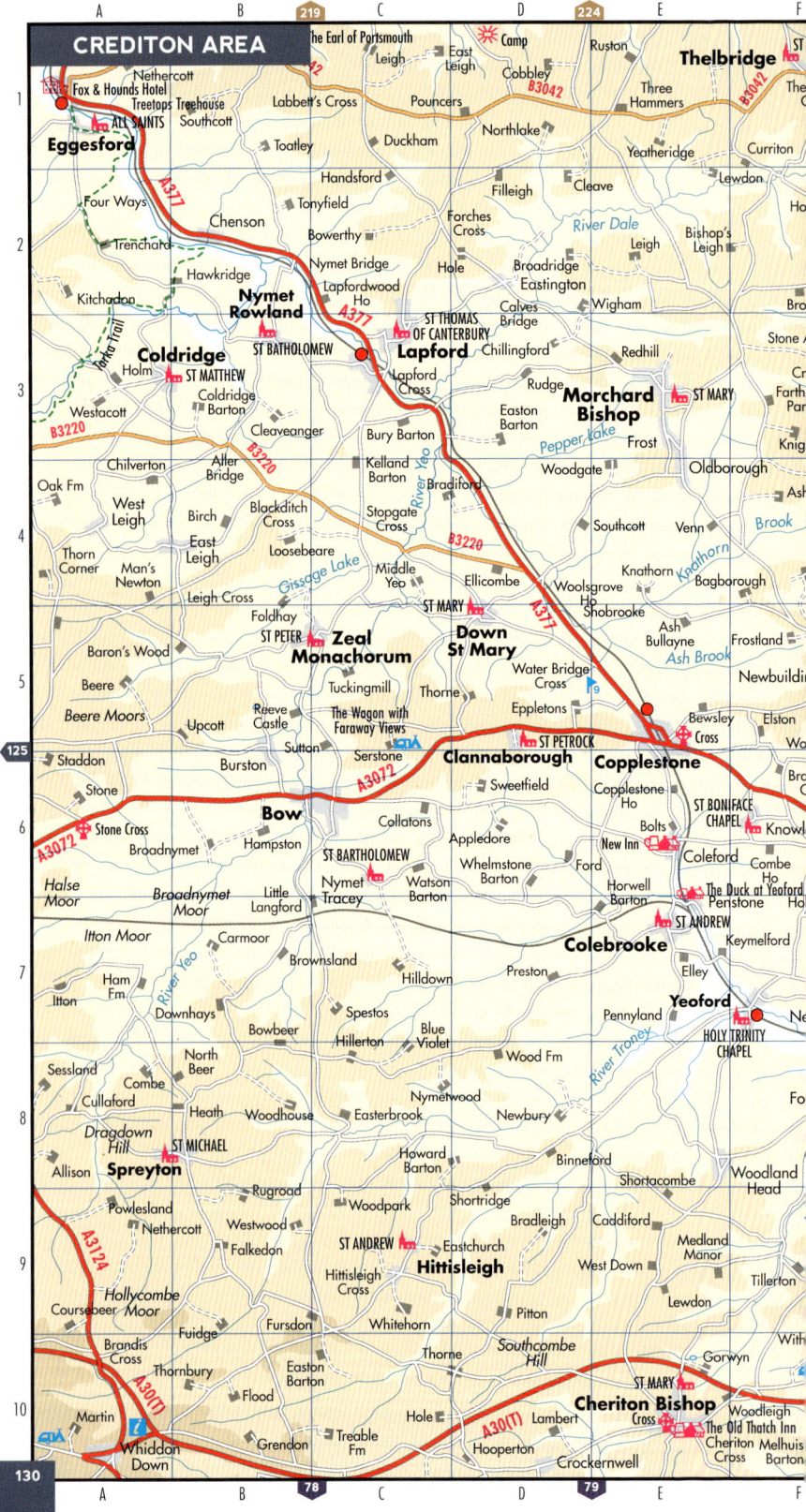

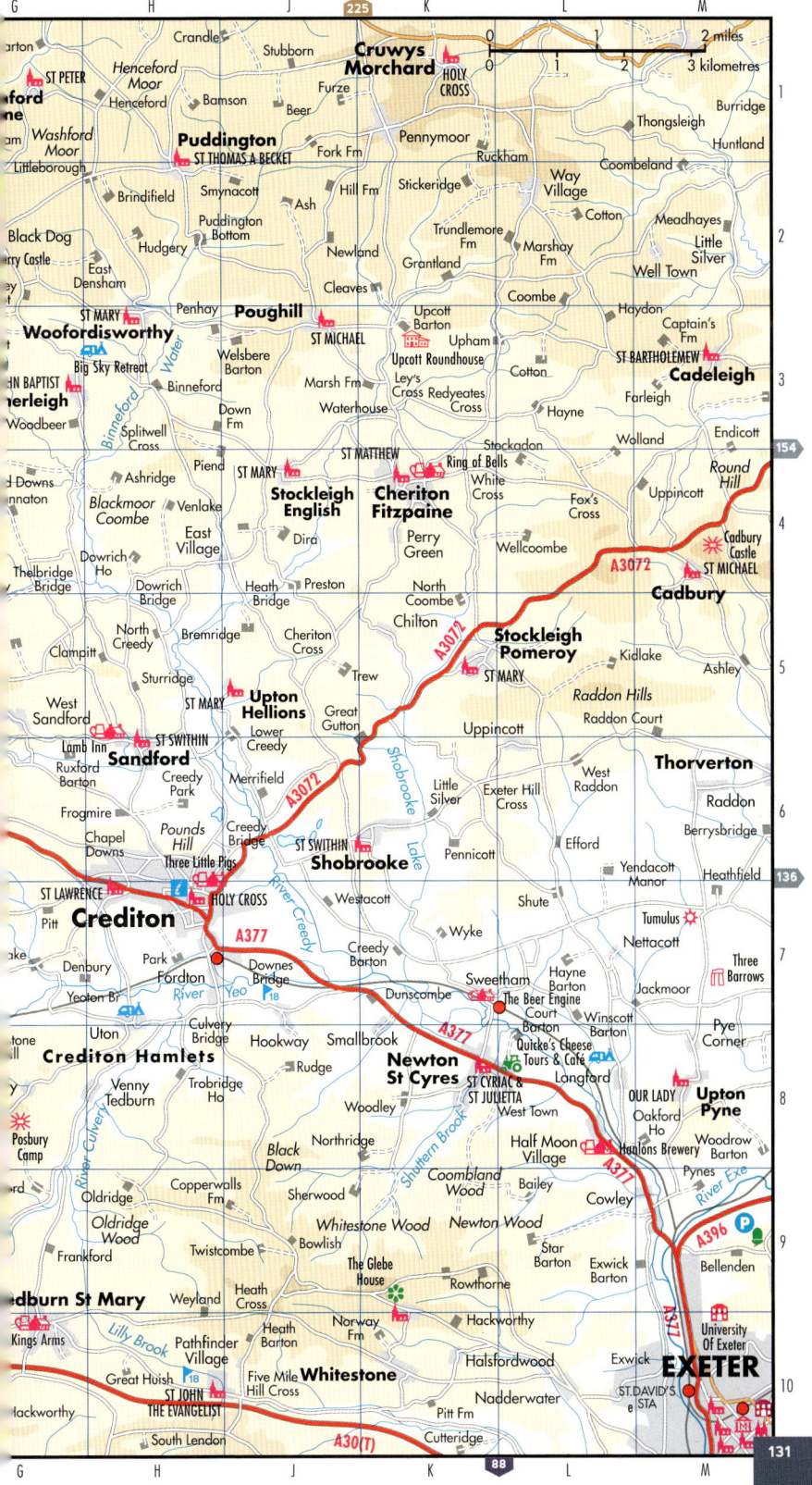

*Church of the Holy Cross*

## CREDITON

The proximity to Exeter has created a resurgence and new dynamism in the town. Delis and eateries, as well as new galleries have recently opened. There is a welcome buzz about the town.

The ecclesiastical capital of the west before Exeter, and birthplace of St Boniface (Winfrith). There is a magnificent medieval church, but few other buildings survive due to disastrous fires. In 1743 all but a few of the C16 buildings were destroyed, also bringing ruin to many of the cloth makers and their looms. The woollen cloth industry was the major employer in the C16. Crediton serge was exported worldwide, and was very much a family industry; the children combing and carding the cloth, the mother spinning and the father weaving. In the C19, the cloth industry declined, and tanning leather became the staple industry of the town. The fertile countryside has affected the commercial output of the town. Smaller industries have thrived, and a number of trading estates are to be found on the outskirts. The soil is red, at times, crimson, and the cob walls on the farms bears witness to this phenomenen. A town trail is available to those seeking more information. (H7) crediton.co.uk

## TO VISIT…

**Church of the Holy Cross.** The grandest feature of this country town. A red, sandstone building dating from the 1130s. There was a church here before but it would have been made of wood, and was probably some short distance from this site. The birth of St Boniface in 680 together with records dating back to the C10 proves that a monastery was built here. As a Norman Collegiate Church it was the ecclesiastical centre of Devon until the Bishop's throne was removed to Exeter in 1050 under the command of Leofric. Apparently Exeter was easier to defend against the marauding Danes. Fine monuments survive, Tuckfield, Periam and others, and notable stained glass. The Chancel Roof, restored by John Hayward over 40 years in the Victorian Era is very fine. Small museum. St Boniface has been described as the first European. He took Christianity to Germany and the Netherlands, and is their Patron saint. He was martyred with 52 of his followers in 754 at Dokkum in Friesland which today is a place of pilgrimage and prosperity. (H7) creditonparishchurch.org.uk

**Quicke's Cheeses, Newton St Cyres.** 14 generations have ploughed and sown these fields, milked the cows, crafting and maturing their cheeses for you to enjoy. Shop open M-F 10-4. Café. (K8) 01392 851000 quickes.co.uk

1759   John Smeaton completes the third lighthouse on Eddystone Rock.

1760   Ramillies frigate wrecked off Bolt Head with loss of 500 lives.

## EAT...DRINK...SLEEP...

**Beer Engine, Newton St Cyres.** Said to be Devon's oldest working brew pub within a C19 coaching inn. At last count eleven beers; Piston, Old Iron Horse, Rail Ale... names to conjur with. Added is solid pub-grub to hearten a hungry soul. (K7) 01392 851282 thebeerengine.co.uk

**Duck at Yeoford, The.** A boutique-style country pub offering lunch, dinner, a whole host of ales and wines, and top-nosh food. Perhaps, more a restaurant within a pub. Lovely garden, too. (F7) 01363 85273 theduckatyeoford.co.uk

**Hanlons Brewery, Half Moon Village.** There is the family brewery who delight in producing craft beers of mouth-watering intent. Brewery tours are arranged on irregular Friday nights -see their website. For sustenance the Beer Factory & Kitchen provide rustic comfort food where you can take supper in an atmosphere of fellowship and good cheer. Open Th 4-10pm, F & Sa 12 to 10. (L8) 01392 8351160 hanlonsbrewery.com

**Kings Arms B&B, Tedburn St Mary.** A traditional and substantial C16 inn offering hospitality with 4-poster beds, open fireplaces, beams and a riotous history of ill-repute. (G10) 01647 61224 kingsarmsinn.co.uk

**Lamb Inn B&B, Sandford.** This still remains a country pub (hostelry) despite its fine cuisine, par excellence, one of the finest in Devon that has garnered awards, galore. Lunch, dinner, a pint, or two, snacks, and a garden to linger in, or chew your baccy. Cinema every F & W/Es. (H6) 01363 773676 lambinnsandford.co.uk

**New Inn B&B, Coleford.** A C13 whitewashed cob pub in thatched village of great beauty. Good pub-grub and craft beers. (E6) 01363 84242 thenewinncoleford.co.uk

**Old Thatch, Cheriton Bishop.** This inn typifies a picture postcard scene of an English pub. It's a Free House serving Devon ales and homespun pub-grub and perfectly located as a stopover just off the A30. 01647 24204 theoldthatchinn.co.uk

**Ring of Bells B&B, Cheriton Fitzpaine.** Stunning thatched Grade 11 listed Inn provides good, Devon food, simply cooked. Regular events: Cider & Beer Festival, Meat & Malbec Nights. 01363 860111 theringofbells.com

## TO STAY...TO SLEEP...

**Big Sky Retreat, Hookhill Plantation.** A hand-crafted wooden yurt affording 180 degree views. Secluded in a former stone quarry, on a former grass farm. (H3) 01363 866146 bigskydevon.uk

**The Wagon With Faraway Views, Serstone Farm.** As the name suggests the horizon and immediate views are stunning from this luxurious wagon. Sleeps 4-persons and a dog. Wood burner and more comforts.(C5) 01363 82366 uniquehideaways.com

**Upcott Roundhouse, Upcott Barton.** Your chance to live like a Celtic King of the Dumnoni Tribe in C21 luxury. A quite magnificent thatched cob simulation of a Saxon/Viking homestead. Sleeps 9. (K3) 01363 866182 upcottroundhouse.co.uk

### LIGHT BITES...

Enter from the Exeter road and one lights upon **Union Road Moto Velo**, an oasis for all two-wheel enthusiasts, with or without a motor. Coffee shop, cakes, twin or single en-suite rooms available. Harley Davidson and Indian Motorcycles for sale. 01363 777299 unionroadmotovelo.com

Now head for **Parliament Square**. For that cuppa to clear the head (and bowels?) it has to be the **Crediton Coffee Company.** They roast the (rubica) beans on the premises. On hand, an insight into the Exeter Chiefs for all Rugby enthusiasts. creditoncoffee.co.uk

Next door, **Baobab Café**, a feast of Mediteranean cuisine, a cocktail of Persian, Turkish, Israeli recipes - every day is different. Family friendly. Just across the Square you can spy the **Three Little Pigs** inn and this is more a museum of bric-a-brac and an attic turn-out. Unbelievable collection of memorabilia. If at a loss for conversation, or a loss of appetite, just look and wonder. Real Ales and pub grub. (H6) 01363 774587.

If you seek more coffee and fab cakes head to **Coco's Devon** 6 High Street where a friendly welcome and comfy chair awaits you. Opens at 8. cocosdevon.co.uk

# EAST DEVON

To the east of the Exe is a stretch of coastline where for the most part sand gives place to shingle interspersed with high cliffs; Devon Red to start with, but changing to White Chalk towards the Dorset border.

Along the coast, the busy port of Exmouth, the genteel town of Budleigh Salterton, the elegant Regency buildings of Sidmouth, and Seaton with its attractive neighbouring village of Beer. Inland, the market town of Honiton, renowned for lace, and Ottery St Mary, with its magnificent church. All around is a beautiful landscape of patchwork fields and rolling hills, where Devon meets Somerset. It is a countryside worthy of exploration and best suited to those with time on their hands. Best to leave the A-roads and to wander aimlessly from village to village.

Explore the Farway Valley and you may imagine you are lost in time, or if you are lost on a foreign shore, dreaming of England's green pastures and smooth hillsides,  it is this valley that may come to mind; a bowl of aching beauty, bidden with villages of thatch and little churches. Climb out of this valley, and you will find yourself on a plateau with stupendous views, to west and east.

But if architecture, or to be more specific, church art and craftsmanship, interests you,  then this corner of England will hold your attention for hours. You will be entranced by the magnificent churches of Broadclyst, Colyton, Cullompton and Ottery St Mary, and the smaller, no less charming ones, of Branscombe, East Budleigh, Northleigh, Shute, Southleigh and Uplyme ... the list goes on.

*Ladram Bay Stacks*

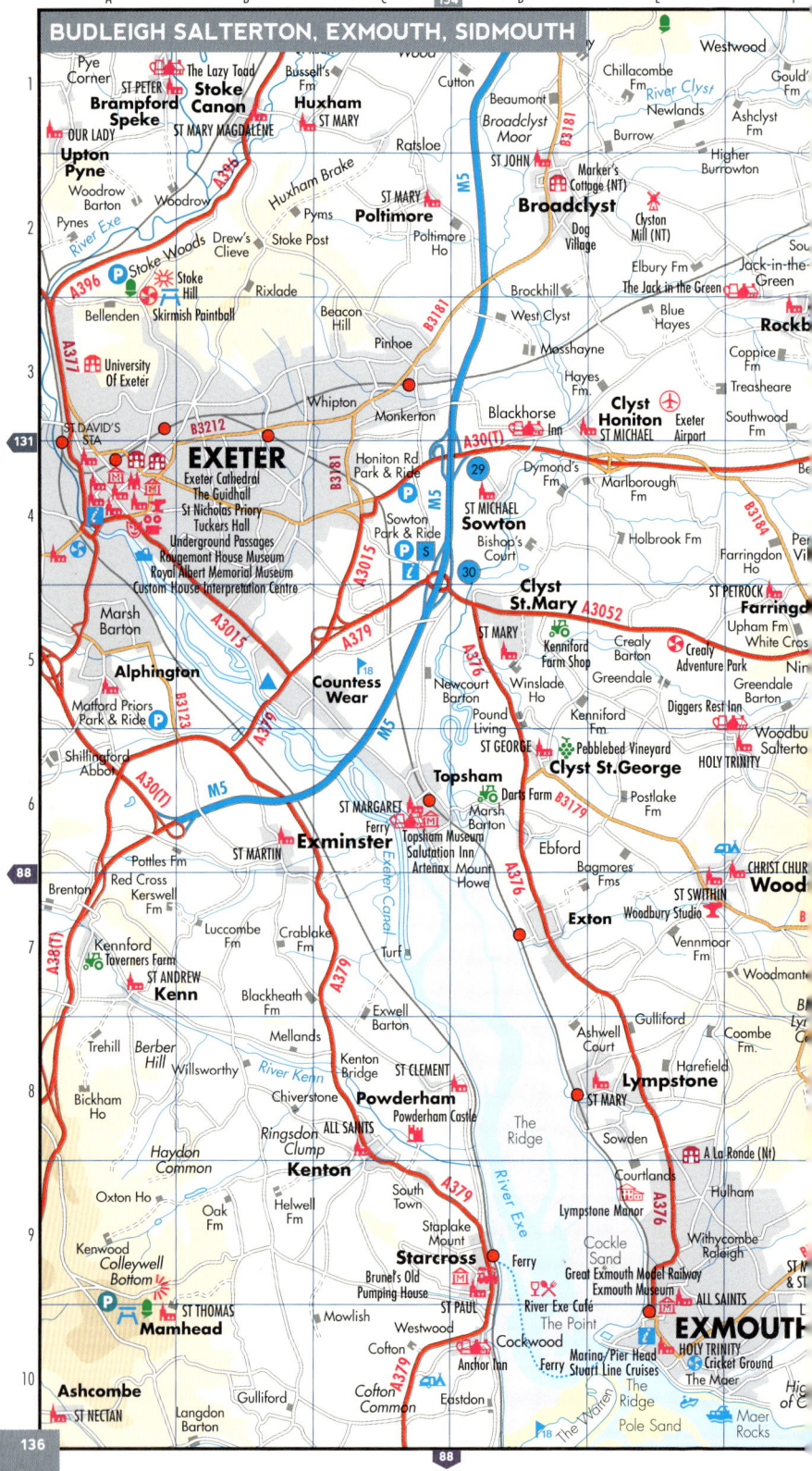

# BUDLEIGH SALTERTON, EXMOUTH, SIDMOUTH

## BUDLEIGH SALTERTON

A genteel town favoured by the retired, especially elderly Ladies of Means. The shelving, oval pebbled beach festooned with fishermen's boats used not to attract day visitors or families, like nearby Exmouth and Sidmouth. But, today those "In The Know" realize it to be a heaven-sent suntrap. The High Street has greatly improved of late wth new cafés, delis, galleries and restaurants. The climate, mild, sheltered and well suited for the frail and weary. The high point of one's visit may be the conversation. The wisdom gained from meeting a lonely soul. It is possible to strike up an easy conversation with the residents who are often over-blessed with charm and manners, but they will frankly inform you that they would prefer to keep the town to themselves, than be overrun by outsiders. But, things are a changing. Late April invites the Jazz Festival for 3-days, budleighjazzfestival.org, and when the sun shines, come summer, Naturists are to be found desporting their hides on the western fringes of the beach!

If you seek fresh seafood look for the Skull & Crossbones flag on the beach.

There are some attractive, little Regency and Georgian houses. Sir John Millais lived here and painted "The Boyhood of Raleigh." The Fairlynch Museum is an interesting building. Of more interest, East Budleigh to the north with its fine church, and monuments to Sir Walter Raleigh. Also, Otterton Mill and the gardens of Bicton. (H9)

## TO VISIT...

**Brook Gallery, Station Rd.** An energetic and open space given over to West Country artists, ceramicists and sculptors. Open daily. Associated with Brook Contemporary Art, a fine art consultancy. 01395 443003 brookgallery.co.uk

**Fairlynch Arts Centre & Museum, 27 Fore St.** Interestingly shaped building designed in 1811 with costumes, geology and lace making exhibits plus demonstrations. Open Tu-Su 11.30-4.30. (H9) 01395 442666 fairlynchmuseum.uk

### LIGHT BITES...

At the top of the High Street is **Brook Kitchen** at No 60. A beautiful space for food, more akin to being a place for art. Indeed, they call it a Licensed Art Café. The Art Gallery is next door. Full breakfasts, brunch and daily specials. Every Friday Tapas 6-10pm. Live Music Nights. 01395 911313 brookkitchen.co No need for anywhere else...

1769   William Cookworthy set up the first British porcelain factory in Plymouth.

1786   Final meeting of the tinners Great Court held at Dunnabridge.

*Fortfield Terrace, Sidmouth*

*Exmouth Lifeboat Station*

## EXMOUTH

The oldest seaside resort in Devon, and the fourth largest populated town in Devon. It is a town with two sides; on the one, the commercial port and marina development, on the other eastern side, the sweeping sands of the seaside resort meet the cliff wall of the World Heritage Site. It is here standing still overlooking the beach the sea, sky  and sun meet to create a space of enormity. Few beaches in the West Country have this power of expanse. The town's beaches developed as a recreation area

---

### LIGHT BITES...

We now come down to earth...On the **Exeter Rd** at **No. 57** is **Krispies Fish and Chips**. Tim and Kelly Barnes have won garlands galore for their fry ups, and raised hundreds of pounds for charities.  Open daily 12-8.30. 01395 278823 krispies.co.uk

Moving into town heading toward the **Pier/Quay** you must drop in to the **Grapevine Brew House** on **2 Victoria Rd** for one of Ruby's burgers and their home brewed beer. My children cried when they closed in Exeter! Succulent burgers that drip down your chin with delight. Yum yum. 01395 222208 thegrapevineexmouth.com

To the **Pier and Quay** we must go! A delight is in store....splice the main brace...prepare yourself for a seaward passage, to the **River Exe Café**. How did they do it? It's a custom built barge that floats in the centre of the channel. Access is via a Puffin Water Taxi from **Exmouth Pier Head/ Marina**. Tricky to concentrate on your food when the views are 180 degrees. You have 3-hours to enjoy your booking on this floating gastro shed. 07761116103 riverexecafe.com

Returning to terra firma, there is **The Point** for grilled steaks and ciabatta sarnis, and shelter. 01395 227145  thepointbarandgrill.com

Now if you are still are in need of fresh fish you will be able to spy **The Rockfish** on your right. 01395 272100 therockfish.co.uk

Now for Exmouth's best kept secret, **The Hut Café and Pavilion Bar** overlooking the Cricket Ground, a sward of English turf. Open daily April to September.

---

**1787**   The ships Friendship and Charlotte depart Plymouth with convicts bound for Australia.

**139**

*Exmouth Beach*

for Exeter folk in the early C18 before the upper classes came here during the Napoleonic Wars when barred from Continental travel. Thus the demand for civilised housing was acute which prompted the building of The Beacon in 1792, a fine Regency Terrace and the finest piece of architecture in the town. The numbers 6 and 19, were to become homes for the widows of Nelson and Byron. There are a multitude of recreational activities to be gained from visiting Exmouth; deep sea fishing, watersports, donkey rides and an idyllic cricket ground used for Minor County and Devon Youth Cricket. The new Marina and Pier Head are interesting spots to while away the time. Just to the north of the town the fascinating property, A La Ronde and across the road the Michael Caines creation, Lympstone Manor. (E10)

## TO VISIT...

**A La Ronde (NT), Summer Lane**. Unique 16-sided house designed in 1795 by two ladies on returning from the 'Grand Tour' combining the features of a rustic cottage with the style of the Basilica at Ravenna. Inside are Gothic grottoes, the Shell Gallery, and the Feather Frieze and Dado. 12 acres of parkland with fine views. Shop & tea room. Open daily Feb-Oct from 10. (E8) 01395 265514

**Bicton College Gardens, via Sidmouth Lodge.** Monkey puzzle avenue, walled garden, herbaceous borders, rock garden and arboretum. Open daily 10-4.30. (H7) 01395 562353 bicton.ac.uk

**Bicton Park**. 60-acres of glorious gardens and parkland spanning 300-years of horticultural history. Specialist greenhouses. Tropical & Palm House. Bird Garden, children's

fun world, 'Fabulous Forest' indoor activity for under teens. Restaurant, gift and plant shop. Disabled facilities. Open daily 10-6 (-4.30 winter). (J7) 01395 568465 bictongardens.co.uk

**Crealy Adventure Park, Sidmouth Rd**. Animal and working dairy farm in 100-acres to explore with viewing galleries, milk a cow - hands on adventures for children, and over 60 rides and attractions. Accommodation in glamping tents and hot tub lodges. Restaurant. Open daily from 10. (E5) 01395 233200 crealy.co.uk

**Darts Farm**. Award-winning farm shop and independent gift retailer with food hall, restaurant (child friendly), bakers/deli, fish shed, plant centre, Aga, Fired Earth, Cotswold Outdoor, contemporary art and much

1788  Devonshire ports have 707 registered ships, employing 4,500 men (despite small skiffs and barges not included in register).

*Bicton Park Palm House ss*

more. Open daily from 8. (D6) 01392 878200 dartsfarm.co.uk

**Jurassic Coast.** This is a Natural World Heritage Site, and the only one in England. It runs from Exmouth along the coast to Swanage in Dorset. From Exmouth to Lyme Regis the rock is of the Triassic Period - 250 and 230 million years ago. Red rocks formed in a Triassic desert, would you believe in the time of dinosaurs and giant marine reptiles? The local Information Centres have details of the guided walks. jurassiccoast.org

**Stuart Line Cruises, Exmouth Pier.** Boat trips to cruise the River Exe, Jurassic Coast, a day cruise to Brixham/ Torquay, or Sidmouth. All year in all weathers. 01395 222144 stuartlinecruises.co.uk

**Wildwood Escot**. East Devon's conservation and wildlife branch of the Wildwood Trust. In 200+ acres of parkland; Birds of Prey, otters, red squirrels, wild boar and lynx. Coach House restaurant, arts & crafts, and a Saxon Village. Open daily Apr-Sept from 10. (J1) 01404 822188 devon.wildwoodtrust.org

**World of Country Life**. All-weather family attraction with falconry displays (except Sa), farm museum, playgrounds and petting farm, vintage cars - Hall of Transport, 'Victorian' street, lots of stuff to exhaust kids. Open daily mid-Mar to Oct 10-5 & half-terms. (G10) 01395 274533 worldofcountrylife.co.uk

**Otterton Mill.** 1,000 years of baking on this site! There's a working water mill, bakery and shop selling local produce, restaurant, and art and crafts gallery. Live music most Th eves. Award-winning café-restaurant. Open daily from 9.30. (J8) 01395 568521 ottertonmill.com

**Tim Andrews Gallery, Woodbury.** Tim's raku ceramics, and pieces by other well-known contemporary ceramicists. Summmer Garden exhibition in May/June and Annual Ceramics Exhibition in mid September. Open M-F 10-6, Sa 10-1. (F7) Please phone out of season to check times. 01395 233475 timandrewsceramics.co.uk

**Larkbeare Grange**. A large house set in idyllic country close to Exeter and the Jurassic Coast. The beds are Vi-Spring, the bathrooms are luxurious, the breakfast will set you up for the day, and you have all the mod-cons available to deal with this crazy world. Also, on site

1792  Fashionable houses built on the beacon in Exmouth.

1793  Jan 11. The radical Tom Paine's effigy burnt in Exeter.

141

luxury self-catering in The Granary. (H2) 01404 822069 larkbeare.net

**Lympstone Manor**. The realisation of Michael Caines, to create an English Country House hotel for the twenty-first century. The exterior is white and formal, the landscaped gardens are sparse, a sward of English turf planted with vines. All sweep down to the glittering Exe Estuary. The sumptuous bedrooms are named after the indigenous birds and the walls are beautifully painted by local artist Rachel Troll. The bar is swanky and the parallel lounge is comfortable. The ambience is relaxed, informal but it is for the cuisine the visitor has made this journey. Caines, the patron/chef has his many disciples and you know the cuisine will be a one-off, exceptional, experience. Dinner recently cost 4-couples a mere £800.00. A special Restaurant With Rooms. (E9) 01395 202040 lympstonemanor.co.uk

**Manor Hotel, The Beacon.** The most prestigious address in town located on Exmouth's historic promenade. A seaside, family-run hotel exuding friendly hospitality. There is a welcome freshness and sincerity at play here backed up by the openness of the light and the expansive sea views. The decor is of bright posters and maps (which as a publisher of maps, we heartily approve of), the beds are sumptuous. A real find! (E10) 01395 272549 manorexmouth.co.uk

1793    Plymouth Gin is first distilled by Coates.     1796    Bread riots in Exeter.

## LIGHT BITES...

I suspect your first thought is the **Seafront**. **Dukes** has a loyal, local following and entertains Al fresco wining and dining. A seaside café/restaurant with rooms. 01395 513321 dukessidmouth.co.uk

On the corner overlooking the sea is **Mocha** where you can sit and watch the world come to you. Going west you will soon come to **Pea Green Boat**. A rustic-style bistro offering imaginative med-style cuisine. Open daily 12-2 lunch, dinner 5-8.30. (L7) 01395 514152 thepeagreenboat.com

Perhaps, you seek a no fancy tea and cake, or English breakfast with a view, then stroll along to the **Promenade** to **The Clock Tower Café**, **Jacob's Ladder, Seafront.** 01395 515319 clocktowercafesidmouth.co.uk

Heading back to town? Then seek out the Church and below is a little, cute tearoom **Someday Something** for a nice cuppa and cake and light conversation, or for something a little wacky and colourful **Selley's** on York St for homemade soups and crusty granary.

*Lympstone Manor ss*

Next door the restaurant **Samphire21.** A chic, new eatery and creative addition to the locals restaurants. What we hear is favourable and positive. Open for Brunch, Lunch, Dinner and Bar Snacks
01395 274477  samphire21.co.uk

## SIDMOUTH

One of Devon's earliest, and most elegant, of seaside resorts developed in the late C18 and C19s. First patronised by the Prince of Wales (later George 111) who came here to escape his creditors, and childhood home of Queen Victoria, who narrowly escaped being shot by a neighbouring child.

The town is positioned within a narrow valley beset by high, sandstone cliffs, and bisected by the River Sid rising from the hills to the north. A town of distinction and character, with no less than 484 "Listed" buildings. Many of whom belong to the Blue Plaque Scheme.

The town has an open and relaxed air about it. The sun reflects brilliantly on many of the Regency buildings painted in their creams and whites. Often mirrored by the cricketers standing about on the turf laid down in 1820.

Surely one of the country's most attractive town grounds, where I have had the good fortune to play, for The Boffins, these past 30-years.

There are energetic coastal walks to be had, to the west and east, but if architecture holds your attention, then spend a few hours wandering around with the Blue Plaque Guide. I was at a loss to find a guide detailing the entire, 484 "listed" buildings. You may have more luck.

The town comes alive during the Folk Festival in August, and while I was there in November surfers were riding a Slow Break. It has youth in numbers, and unlike nearby Budleigh, it likes to party.  (L7)

## TO VISIT...

**Sid Vale Heritage Centre, Church St**. Local lace, costumes, geology, archaeology, prints, photographs etc. Open Apr-Oct M 1-4, Tu-Sa 10-4. (L6) 01395 516139

**Toy & Model Museum, Chapel St.** A  nostalgic trip down memory lane to revisit ancient and recent memories; Star Wars, Harry Potter, Corgi and Dinky Cars...
sidmouthtoymuseum.com

## EAT...DRINK...RELAX...

**Neil's Restaurant, Radway Place**. Chef Neil Harding has 30+ years experience, so be prepared to be spoilt and indulge yourself in the English Channel's rich larder, for fish is his speciality.  Booking advised. Open Tu-Sa from 6.30pm. Lunch and business parties by arrangement. (L6) 01395 519494 neilsrestaurant.com

**Salty Monk, Church St, Sidford**. Annett and Andy Witheridge have been running this Restaurant With Rooms for an age where they delight in Devon's propitious source of goodies. All the food is prepared on the premises. The accommodation includes mini-spa baths, hydro massage showers and King-size beds. (M5) 01395 513174 saltymonk.co.uk

## EAT...DRINK...SLEEP...

**Hotel Riviera, The Esplanade**. One of the great architectural sights of Sidmouth's seafront. The bow fronted windows hide a hotel that determines convention and old-fashioned hospitality. There is a solid formality that is loved by a diminishing, some might argue discerning market. (L7) 01395 515201 hotelriviera.co.uk

**The Kingswood Hotel, The Esplanade.** If you seek a contemporary hotel with an unfussy style in a great location beside the seafront that's also dog friendly and beside the coastpath and town centre. Here you are. (L7) 08000 481731 kingswoodsidmouth.co.uk

## TOPSHAM

One of South Devon's most attractive little towns, and a popular "Eating Out" destination for Exeter folk. The nearby Darts Farm is a great attraction. The long, narrow High Street is fronted with many old houses in the "Dutch" style dating from the C17 and C18. Take a stroll along the High Street and admire the many Lifestyle shops, the view from the Churchyard, take some refreshment in one or more of the hostelries and you will soon come to the small harbour and antique emporium. The former port of Exeter, hence its evident heritage of past wealth. (C6)

## EAT...DRINK...SLEEP....

**The Salutation Inn, 68 Fore St.** Unless you are already staying here, and are in dire need of refreshment, best to stop here awhile for breakfast, brunch or lunch and head for **The Glasshouse Café.** Dinner is slightly more formal and extravagant with three menus on offer. Your Patron has worked with Caines, Ramsey...This is the hostelry

**1808**  Dartmoor Prison founded at Princetown for French and American prisoners of war. Converted to present use in 1850.

### LIGHT BITES...

As you head towards the Quay drop in to **Circle**, 37 Fore St for their coffee and cake, perhaps a house plant, then arriving at the **Quay**, to your left the **Route 2 Café & Apartments, 1 Monmouth Hill**. This is a café in the former **Steam Packet Inn**. Opens daily at 8 for breakfasts, coffee and more. Cream teas in the afternoons. All set close to the cycle route NCR2 and the **Exe Estuary Trail**. (C6) 01392 875085 route2topsham.co.uk

Next door, **Route 2 Bike shop & hire** 01392 879160 route2bikes.co.uk

If you continue south you will enter a yard and **The Pig & Pallet**. If you are fond of swine and their cuts of meat from bacon to sausages to ribs. Beef burgers and steaks are also served. Devon beers. 01392 668129 pigandpallet.co.uk

to eat, sleep and head to in Topsham. What's New? A fresh fish counter beside reception. (C6) 01392 873060 salutationtopsham.co.uk

### SPECIAL PLACES TO TO TO VISIT...

**Artenax, 32 Fore St.** Nikki, your hostess, has over 100 British designers/makers supplying her with original works, all with a splash of colour. A visit will brighten your day and bring a smile to all. Open daily. 01392 874172 artenax.co.uk

**Pebblebed Vineyard, Darts Farm**. Vineyard and wine tastings tours of producers of Sparkling Rose from May-Sept on Th & Sa. See website for details. (D6) pebblebed.co.uk

**Topsham Museum, 25 The Strand**. Late C17 merchant's house with attractive period rooms, sail loft, gardens. Shipbuilding, maritime trade, the Exe Estuary. Honiton Lace and Vivien Leigh. Teas 2.30-4.30pm. Shop. Open Apr-Oct W-Su (Tu in Aug), 2-5. (C6) 01392 873244 devonmuseums.net

### EAT...DRINK...RLAX...

**Black Horse, Old Honiton Road, Sowton**. Large inn serving all manner of food. Very popular with local businessmen, and the retired with time on their hands. (D3) blackhorseinnexeter.co.uk

**Diggers Rest Inn**. Child friendly pub serves pasta and fishnchips, and free ice cream. Beer garden. Food from 12-2, 7-9.30pm. (F5) 01395 232375

### BEACHES...

**Exmouth**. Wide sandy beach with rocks. Water sports. D/LG/R/WC. Also, a sandy beach at the east end beneath Orcombe Cliffs. (E10)

**Budleigh Salterton**. Steeply shelving with oval pebbles. D/R/WC. (H9)

**Ladram Bay**. Pebble beach with high cliffs. Short walk from P. Café/D/R/WC. (K8)

**Sidmouth**. Sand at low tide. "Jacobs Ladder" leads down to western beach with rock pools, pebbles and shingle. Main beach below promenade has pebbles. Water sports. Surfing is unusual. D/R/WC. (L7)

### COASTAL FOOTPATH...

**Exmouth to Budleigh Salterton**; 6 miles. The first 2 miles are along Exmouth Promenade, followed by an ascent to the 'High Land of Orcombe' (NT). Then a descent to Littleham Cove and a steep climb to 'The Floors,' where the undercliff is noted for birdlife, and a gradual descent into the town.

**Budleigh Salterton to Sidmouth**; 8 miles. A detour is needed to cross the Otter a mile upstream. Returning to the coast the path ascends the red sandstone cliffs and provides a fairly level walk with fine views. Ladram Bay is noted for its curious rock formations and bird life. The final section involves a steep climb over Peak Hill.

*Sidmouth Beach*

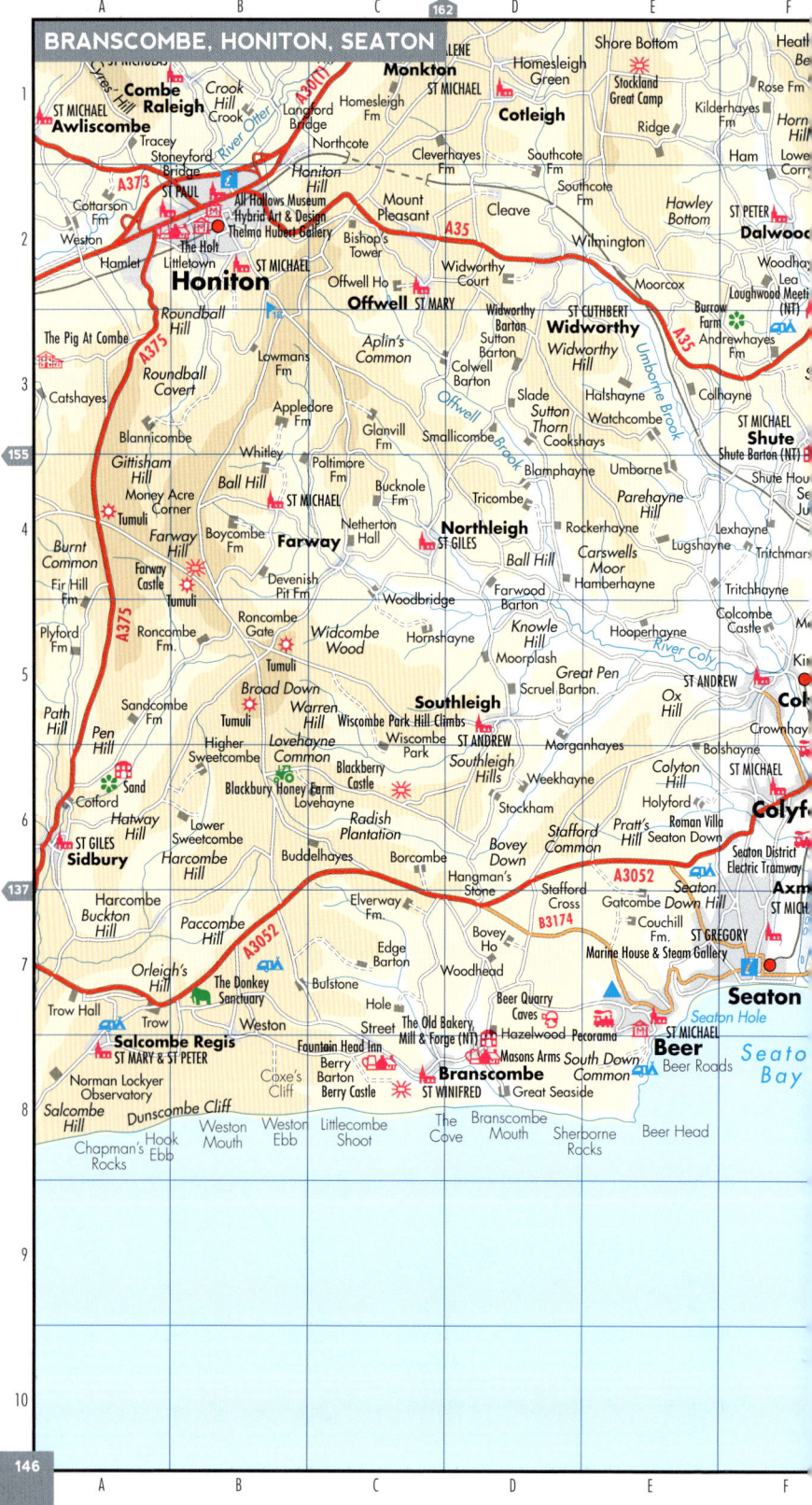

# BRANSCOMBE, HONITON, SEATON

**Row 1:**
ST NICHOLAS · Combe Raleigh · Crook Hill · ...LENE · Monkton · ST MICHAEL · Homesleigh Green · Shore Bottom · Heath · Be... · St Michael · Awliscombe · Crook Hill · A30(T) · Langford Bridge · Homesleigh Fm · Cotleigh · Stockland Great Camp · Rose Fm · Horn Hill · Tracey · Stoneyford Bridge · Northcote · Cleverhayes Fm · Southcote Fm · Ridge · Kilderhayes Fm · Ham · Lowe... Corn...

**Row 2:**
Cottarson Fm · A373 · ST PAUL · Honiton Hill · All Hallows Museum · Hybrid Art & Design · Thelma Hubert Gallery · Mount Pleasant · Cleave · Southcote Fm · Wilmington · A35 · Hawley Bottom · ST PETER · Dalwoo... · Weston · Hamlet · The Holt · Littletown · ST MICHAEL · Bishop's Tower · Widworthy Court · Moorcox · Woodha... Lea · Loughwood Meeti... (NT)

**Row 3:**
Honiton · Offwell · ST MARY · Widworthy Barton · Sutton Barton · ST CUTHBERT · Widworthy · Burrow Farm · Andrewhayes Fm · The Pig At Combe · Roundball Hill · A375 · Aplin's Common · Colwell Barton · Widworthy Hill · Colhayne · Catshayes · Roundball Covert · Lowmans Fm · Slade · Sutton Thorn · Halshayne · Watchcombe · ST MICHAEL · Shute · Blannicombe · Appledore Fm · Glanvill Fm · Smallicombe · Cookshays · Blamphayne · Umborne · Shute Barton (NT) · Shute Hou... Se... Ju...

**Row 4:**
Gittisham Hill · Whitley · Poltimore Fm · Bucknole Fm · Tricombe · Parehayne Hill · Lexhayne · Tritchmar... · Money Acre Corner · Ball Hill · ST MICHAEL · Netherton Hall · Northleigh · ST GILES · Ball Hill · Rockerhayne · Carswells Moor · Lugshayne · Tritchhayne · Tumuli · Farway Hill · Boycombe Fm · Farway · Farwood Barton · Hamberhayne · Colcombe Castle · M... · Burnt Common · Farway Castle · Devenish Pit Fm · Fir Hill Fm · Tumuli

**Row 5:**
Plyford Fm · A375 · Roncombe Fm · Roncombe Gate · Widcombe Wood · Woodbridge · Hornshayne · Knowle Hill · Moorplash · Hooperhayne · River Coly · Ki... · Tumuli · Great Pen Hill · Scruel Barton · Ox Hill · ST ANDREW · Col... · Path Hill · Sandcombe Fm · Broad Down · Tumuli · Warren Hill · Southleigh · Wiscombe Park Hill Climbs · Crownhay... · Pen Hill · Higher Sweetcombe · Lovehayne Common · Wiscombe Park · ST ANDREW · Southleigh Hills · Morganhayes · Bolshayne · Sand · Blackbury Honey Farm · Blackberry Castle · Weekhayne · Colyton Hill · ST MICHAEL

**Row 6:**
Cotford · ST GILES · Sidbury · Hatway Hill · Lower Sweetcombe · Lovehayne · Radish Plantation · Stockham · Holyford · Roman Villa · Colyf... · Harcombe Hill · Buddelhayes · Borcombe · Bovey Down · Pratt's Hill · Seaton Down · Seaton District Electric Tramway · Axm... · Harcombe Buckton Hill · Paccombe Hill · A3052 · Elverway Fm · Hangman's Stone · Stafford Common · Stafford Cross · A3052 · Gatcombe Down Hill · Seaton · ST MICH... · Bovey Ho · B3174 · Couchill Fm · ST GREGORY · Marine House & Steam Gallery

**Row 7:**
Orleigh's Hill · The Donkey Sanctuary · Bulstone · Edge Barton · Woodhead · Beer Quarry Caves · Pecorama · Trow Hall · Trow · Weston · Street · Hole · The Old Bakery, Mill & Forge (NT) · Hazelwood · ST MICHAEL · Seaton

**Row 8:**
Salcombe Regis · ST MARY & ST PETER · Norman Lockyer Observatory · Fountain Head Inn · Berry Barton · Berry Castle · Branscombe · ST WINIFRED · Masons Arms · South Down Common · Great Seaside · Beer · Beer Roads · Seaton Hole · Seato... Bay · Salcombe Hill · Dunscombe Cliff · Weston Mouth · Weston Ebb · Littlecombe Shoot · The Cove · Branscombe Mouth · Sherborne Racks · Beer Head · Chapman's Rocks · Hook Ebb

146

**Rivers & roads:** River Otter · Offwell Brook · Umborne Brook · A35 · A375 · A373 · A3052 · B3174

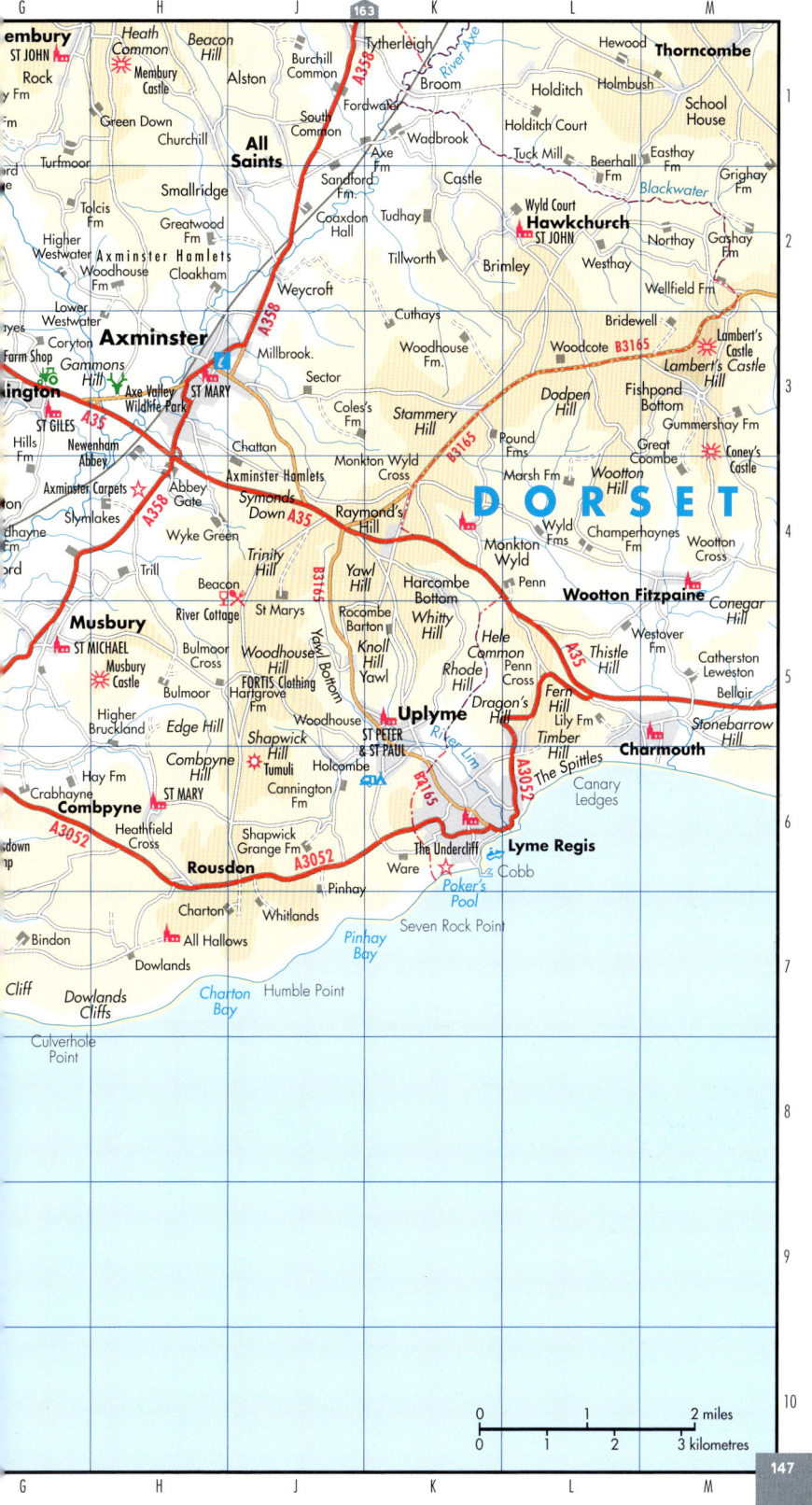

## Axminster

Well situated to be an ancient and quiet market town on a slight contour above the River Axe. The Roman Fosse Way passed close by. King Athelstan, the first King of All England fought a victorious battle against the Danes in 937 nearby on Brunanburgh field and in celebration he founded a College, now completely vanished. The Royalist troops occupied in 1644 during the Siege of Lyme Regis. Later, Axminster Carpets were in business from 1755-1835, later to be revived in 1937 by Harry Dutfield.

Today there's a quiet buzz about the town. Community based projects engineered at the Heritage Centre and from

### LIGHT BITES...

First head to South Street where you will find **Higgler Coffee,** a popular café for the discerning. One of the West Country's best coffee houses and where conversation may be lively. Certain subjects are frowned upon: The EU, medical stuff etc.

In need of ale? Turn L and R at junction toward the **Axminster Inn, Silver St**. It's a friendly ale house serving fresh seafood. 01297 34947 axminsterinn.pub

If perhaps a coffee, a pizza or some pasta is to your liking then just opposite the Churchyard is **Le Pisani**. A charming building of style and comfort. You get the full med experience - Devon style. 01297 631697 lepisani.com (H3)

above the Waffle House are endearing.

### TO VISIT...

**Axe Valley Wildlife Park**. A small zoo home to zebras, antelopes, wallabies, flamingos, owls, otters, snakes, and creepy crawlers. Daily feeding times. Children's play areas. Open daily mid-Feb to Oct from 10. 01297 34472 (H3) axevalleypark.co.uk

**Axminster Carpets, Musbury Rd**. Factory outlet showroom with small museum and video of production from fleece to floor. Seconds, remnants and perfects available here. Open M-F 9-5.30, Sa 10-5. 01297 33993 (H4) axminstershop.co.uk

**Axminster Church, St Mary**. Cruciform in shape with Norman doorway. Fine East window in Chancel, exceptional North & South windows, sedilia and piscina. Effigy of headless priest. Finely carved C17 pulpit. On his travels in 1740 Daniel Defoe saw the Monuments of the Saxon Bishop of Sherburne and two Dukes slain at the Battle of Brunanburgh, yet nothing in evidence today. (H3)

**Axminster Heritage Centre, Silver St**. The story of the town is handsomely told (in a fine building): the Fosse Way, Cistercian Monks, World famous carpet manufacturing, brush factories, agrciculture. Open East-Oct M-F 10-4, Sa 10-1. Nov-East Tu & Th 10-4. (H3) 01297 639884 axminsterheritage.org

**FORTIS Clothing, Trinity Hill.** Craftmanship, custom-made and sustainability determine these products for outdoor pursuits, be it fishing,

riding, shooting, snow, military; jackets, smocks, trousers... tweeds. Open M-F 9-5, Sa 10-4. (J4) 01297 442180 fortisclothing.co.uk

**River Cottage Kitchen & Store, Trinity Hill.** This is where much of their produce is grown. The kitchen café is open 9-5. Breakfast 9-11.30, lunch 12-3. On sale, their products and books. For courses on gardens, foraging, beekeeping see the website. (J4) 01297 630300 rivercottage.net

**Trinity Hill Woods.** An area of open heathland with five trails suitable for mountain biking and various woodland paths. (J4) forestengland.uk

## Axmouth

Before this village silted up in the C17 it held a large harbour. Now the silted mud flats are a haven for birdlife, an ornithologist's delight. Campsite in village centre next to one of the two pubs that failed to impress. (F7)

**Axmouth Church, St Michael.** Norman c. 1140 with additions in 1330. A perpendicular stair-turret tower. Three Italianate wall paintings. (F7)

## Beer

The major coastal attraction in this part of East Devon. An old fishing and smuggling village made notorious by the published diaries of one Jack Rattenbury in 1837 who later lived the life of a gentleman. Lace making was a major occupation; Queen Victoria's wedding dress was woven here, and Beer Stone was quarried here, first in Long Galleries, then as open cast supplying the stone for Exeter Cathedral.

*Branscombe Cottages*

## LIGHT BITES...

If you are in luck and desire breakfast, a crab sandwich and a strong cuppa head to **Ducky's** on the beach opening 8.30 in season. There is also **Chapples Ice Cream** on the beach serving up teas, cakes and savouries. Above the beach is the **Bay View Café & B&B** for breakfast, sarnis, toasties and ice creams. (E7) 01297 20489 bayviewguesthousebeer.com

Perhaps after a day on the beach you need a strong pick-me-up? **Osborne's Cocktail and Wine Bar** will do the trick. Just ascend the street.

---

The fishing boats are shelved on the beach and you can buy fresh fish ( sole, flounders, pollock) from **Beer Fisheries** hut above the beach. A dashing stream runs beside the high street and plunges over a cliff into the pebbles. The coastal path rises 400 feet to Beer Head, the most southerly chalk cliffs in England that run down from Flamborough Head in Yorkshire. Below are cliffs, "riddled with caverns and rent with spires," made useful by smugglers past. (E7)

## TO VISIT...

**Beer Quarry Caves**. A 2,000-year old history of quarrying stone from the Romans until the last century. Tour of awe-inspiring caves like a vast underground cathedral. Also formerly used to hide persecuted Catholics and for storing the contraband of notable smuggler, Jack Rattenbury. Open daily Apr-Oct 10-5. (D7) 01297 680282 beerquarrycaves.co.uk

**Marine House & Steam Gallery, Fore St**. Established gallery representing a fine collection of painters, sculptors, ceramicists and jewellers. Open daily 10-5. (E7) 01297 625257 marinehouseatbeer.co.uk

**Pecorama**. The Beer Heights Light Railway, PECO model railway exhibition, children's safety surfaced activity area, all surrounded by manicured gardens with fine sea views. Restaurant. Open daily 10-5. (E7) 01297 21542 peco-uk.com

## BRANSCOMBE

One of the most romantic and picturesque villages in Devon set amidst a series of deep, narrow, tortuous combes. Three hamlets, or nests of houses make up the village. Notable church, forge (NT) and baker. Many of the cottages (some thatch) and houses are built of local Beer stone. Legend has it that a Spanish galleon foundered here in the C17, whence the sailors wed the local girls, and dark haired and brown eyed folk have "melted into the flaxen-haired Saxon fold." The ladies would sit at their cottage doors with cushion and bobbin darning the lace.

At Branscombe Mouth (parking charge) there is a fine stretch of chalk cliff, broken by landslips and noted for fossils. There's also a café/beach restaurant serving locally caught fish. Shingle beach. (D8)

## TO VISIT...

**Branscombe Church, St Winifred**. Magnificent and stately for a small, isolated village with Norman tower, gallery, 3-decker pulpit and tomb of Joan Tregarthen d. 1583, mother of twenty children, fathered by her two husbands who stand opposite

1814    The Devon prophetess Joanna Southcott claims to be pregnant with Shiloh, the second Messiah.

149

*Day's Catch, Beer*

each other. Turn R out of the entrance descending to a footpath that leads along the valley, zig-zagging to Branscombe Mouth. (C8)

**The Old Bakery, Manor Mill & Forge (NT)**. Now thankfully restored to working order after the closure of the business in 1987. The baking equipment has been preserved and the building is used as a tearoom. The Manor Mill supplied the flour for the bakery, and the forge is open daily, all year, where the blacksmith sells the ironwork he produces, and takes commissions. Old Bakery open in season. Manor Mill Open Apr-Oct Su 2-5. (D8)

### EAT...DRINK...RELAX..

**Masons Arms.** "Here Ye Toil Not" but enjoy the fine ales and food; lobster and crab dishes, a speciality. Fireplaces and exposed walls. Summer beer festival. Restaurant. Bar food. Sit outside and idly watch passes-by. Accommodation. Sadly, it's all gone rather corporate and

### LIGHT BITES...

**Honiton** has a long **High St**, and depending how desperate you are for that cuppa and snack...best park at the West end. It has to be **Toast Café & Patisserie at No. 155**. You'll be met with a warm welcome, and you'll love the rustic, farmyard chic decor, the large garden and food on offer. Open M-Sa 8.30-5, Su 9.30-4. 01404 598067 cafetoast.co.uk.

Across the road (for some ale) is **The Holt (Inn), 178 High St.** This was set up by the local Otter Brewery to provide uncomplicated and popular dishes and ales. Cookery classes on tapas, sauces, knife skills and more. Artworks line the walls. Film nights every second Su. (B2) 01404 47707 theholt-honiton.com

Up the East end is the **Boston Tea Party** housed in a beautiful, Georgian building, a former bookshop, hotel, home, acres to get lost in, and opens for breakfast M-Sa 8-5, Su 9-4. (B2) Then we come to **The Yellow Deli**, 43 High Street. A community-run café with an extravaganza of designs in recycled wood, an experience in itself. The in-house bakery produces tasty bread, a real treat to accompany their soups and delicacies. Open M-F 7am-11pm, Su 12 noon to 11pm. 01404 378023 yellowdeli.uk

lacks character. (D8) 01297 680300 masonsarms.co.uk

**Fountain Head Inn**. On the western (top end) edge of the village. An intimate, popular little C14 pub serving

fresh meals (12-2 & 6.30-9) and real ales (from the local Branscombe Vale Brewery). Popular with CAMRA afficionados. Small seating area outside. 01297 680359 (C8) fountainheadinn.com

## COLYFORD

Former site of Roman villa on the western edge of the **River Axe**, and probable fort beside the **Fosse Way**. Wide water meadows beside the river strike northwards towards **Colyton**. (F6)

## COLYTON

A pretty village noted for its sumptuous church, village square and highly rated Grammar School. In the C15 one of the wealthiest wool towns in Devon that took advantage of exporting its goods through nearby Seaton. Saxon traditions still prevail in the town, for the Town Councillors are still known as Feoffes. Move off in a north west direction and you'll experience the beautiful Umborne Valley with its grassy water meadows and wild flowers. (F5)

## TO VISIT...

**Colyton Church, St Andrew.** Fine, impressive building with central tower. Memorials to Margaret, Countess of Devon, granddaughter of John of Gaunt. Her tomb was smashed up by the Parliamentarian troops in Civil War. Also monuments to Sir John Pole and his wife Elizabeth who lived at nearby, Shute. (F5)

## HONITON

One gets the feeling that Honiton is undergoing a revival of good fortune. New restaurants, new coffee shops and galleries...there's a buzz about the place. The long, wide High Street with Georgian buildings is always busy and bustling. I counted half a dozen antique-bric-a-brac-emporia shops at the west end, and more at the top, east end. At the east end, the earthy **Honeybee**

**Coffee Shop**, and at the west end, next to a wine bar, the **Boston Tea Party** with art gallery and garden.

A deep connection with lace and glove making, as illustrated in the little museum. The almshouse was the former leper hospital, St Margaret's. July Fair, Agricultural show in August, Carnival in September. (B2)

## TO VISIT...

**All Hallows Museum of Lace & Antiquities, High St.** Local history and world famous lace with demos in Honiton's oldest building. Open East-Oct M-F 9.30-4.30, Sa 9.30-1. (B2) 01404 44966 honitonmuseum.co.uk

**Hybrid Gallery, 51 High St.** An attractive and lively art gallery, and shop, selling original and hand-crafted work. Also, a Design Consultancy. Open Tu-Sa 10-5. (B2) 01404 43201 hybrid-devon.co.uk

**Thelma Hulbert Gallery, Dowell St.** East Devon's only public art gallery shows an exciting programme of contemporary art and craft exhibitions. Open Tu-Sa 10-5. (B2) 01404 45006 thelmahulbert.com

## SEATON

A small resort with pebble beach not noted for its architecture like nearby Sidmouth but there are attractive Georgian buildings in the centre of town. The small harbour is of interest, also the coastal path to Downland Cliffs. The cliffs rise to either side of the town affording sweeping views from the coastal footpath. There are precious stones to be found on the beach; jaspers and garnets.

In former times the Romans used the Fosse Way and the harbour here as a conduit to ship out Cotswold and Mendip wool back to their Republic. A Roman pavement was found here in 1921 measuring 16 feet square with a twisted pattern, now in Exeter Museum. Much later in the C19 coal was exported off the beach, sometimes beside patients seeking the calm waters of Seaton Spa! A fact noted in Francis Kilvert's diaries, the Worcester parson. The bridge crossing the Rive Axe was opened in April 1877 and became the first concrete toll in England, until September 1907. Bass are caught off the bridge. The Axe is also known to favour salmon and sea trout. (F7)

*Wiscombe Park Hill Climbs ss*

**1816**  John Heathcoat, inventor of the bobbin machine, sets up lace manufacture in Tiverton.

151

*Shute Barton*

## TO VISIT IN SEATON…

**Seaton Tramway Co., Harbour Rd.** An unforgettable 3-mile ride; Seaton-Colyford-Colyton. Unique open top and enclosed single deck trams giving superb views of the beautiful Axe valley, noted for its wading river birds. Open daily East-Oct. (F6) 01297 20375 tram.co.uk

## TO VISIT…

**Blackbury Camp (Castle) (EH)**. When the bluebells are in bloom this is a magical place. An Iron Age hillfort dating back to the C4. Impressive ramparts and ancient tracks excavated in the 1950s. (C6)

**Blackbury Honey Farm**. Butterflies and bees flourish here, amongst the wild flowers. The Basterfield family have been beekeeping since 1972. They hold courses and display the art of pollination and have a shop selling honey and beeswax products. Open Feb-Dec W-Su 10-4. (B5) 01404 871600 blackburyfarm.co.uk

**Burrow Farm Gardens**. Just celebrated 55-years of colour and form, all within a 13-acre woodland garden; rhododendrons, azaleas, primulas. Planned for a foliage effect. Bog garden. Cream teas. Open daily Apr-Oct 10-6. (F3) 01404 831285 burrowfarmgardens.co.uk

**Church of St Giles, Northleigh**. A fine Norman doorway with intricate carvings of animal heads. C16 fan-vaulted screen with colourful vine leaves, and so it is claimed, the oldest stained glass in Devon; figures of St Peter and St Paul. (C4)

**Hawkesdown Camp**. An oblong earthwork consisting of two banks with a fosse between. (G6)

**Lyme Bay Winery**. A specialist producer of English Wines, Country Wines, ciders, meads and liqueurs, all on sale from M-F 9.30-5, Sa 10-3, Su 11-3. (F4) 01297 551355 lymebaywinery.co.uk

**Miller's Farm Shop, Kilmington**. Established 30+-years ago, it's a successful combination of a French deli (with imports from Miller's Normandy farm) and an English farm shop. Open M-Sa 7.30-5. Teapot café 9-5. (G3) 01297 35390 millersfarmshop.com

**Musical Woods & Wild School**. Chris Holland's forest school has a musical and wild twist. Helping children to connect with nature and each other through music. All set in a magical wood with a shallow stream and heathland. (C6) 07980 601830 wholeand.org.uk

**Shute Barton (NT)**. Impressive entrance to medieval manor house built in 1380 with later additions in the C18. The Pole family lived here until the fire, leaving just the gatehouse and one wing. Open some W/Es May-Nov. Check website for details: nationaltrust.org.uk 01752 346585

**The C13 Church of St Michael**, just up the hill, is cruciform, and has fine memorials of William Pole d.1741, Master of Queen Anne's household. (F3)

**Wiscombe Park Hill Climbs**. Hill climbs have been staged here since 1958. All started over a glass or two of Malt. The two Majors, Richard Chichester and Charles Lambton thought the terrain suitable for such goings-on. The parkland is of great beauty and a wonderful backdrop for racing vintage cars and motorcycles, some reaching speeds of 125mph on what is considered a demanding 'drivers hill'. Events take place from April to September. (C5) 01404 971474 wiscombepark.co.uk

## VILLAGES TO VISIT...

### LYME REGIS

Although just over the border in Dorset, if you are touring this area you can't exclude this fascinating little town from your itinerary. Its literary and film connections are endless; from Jane Austen to John Fowles. Who can forget the *French Lieutenant's Woman* (Meryl Streep) standing isolated on the Cobb, almost being swept away by the crashing waves until rescued by the dashing Jeremy Irons in the film of the same name? There are two parts of the village, the High Street area, and the Cobb (harbour). The High Street has a number of galleries, fossil emporia and places to eat plus the excellent

local museum, to visit. A walk along the promenade connects to the Cobb where you can watch the fishing boats come and go, and sit on the little beach. A small aquarium is open in season, and there are a number of pubs, cafés and gift shops. (L6)

### MUSBURY

Birthplace in 1650 of John Churchill, the first Duke of Marlborough. The Musbury Monument erected in 1611 commemorates the Drake family. A pleasant walk is to be had leading away from the Musbury Castle earthwork, an Iron Age hillfort along the old packhorse route to Combpyne via Higher Bruckland farm. (G5)

### UPLYME

Attractive village to the north west of Lyme Regis just across from the Dorset border. Set amidst quaint, sheltered valleys. An early Saxon and Roman settlement connected to the fort at Seaton. (K5)

## CHURCHES...

**Uplyme Church, St Peter & St Paul.** Pretty little church with Gallery and wagon roof painted with clear blue and embellished with gold stars. (K5)

## COASTAL FOOTPATH...

**Sidmouth to Seaton**
11 miles. One of the toughest sections of the path with cliffs up to 450 ft and intervening valleys. Much of this stretch is National Trust land. The red sandstone gradually changes to chalk and there is some difficult going in places. The path descends to sea level at Branscombe Mouth, and again at Beer.

**Seaton to Lyme Regis**
8 miles. After crossing the Axe there is a steep climb and the path enters the 'Landslip', an area of broken ground caused by a major earth movement in 1839. Here again there is some difficult ground but there is much to interest the naturalist and geologist. Shortly before reaching Lyme, the path crosses into Dorset.

## BEACHES...

**Branscombe**. Steep pebble beach. Interesting rocks at LT. 45-minute walk to Sherborne Rocks. P Charge. R/WC. (D8)

**Beer**. Steep shingle and pebble beach with rocks. Boating pool. Short walk from P. D/R/WC. (E7)

**Seaton**. Shelving pebbles. Sand at LT. D/R/WC. (F7)

*Ammonite, Lyme Regis Fossil Shop ss*

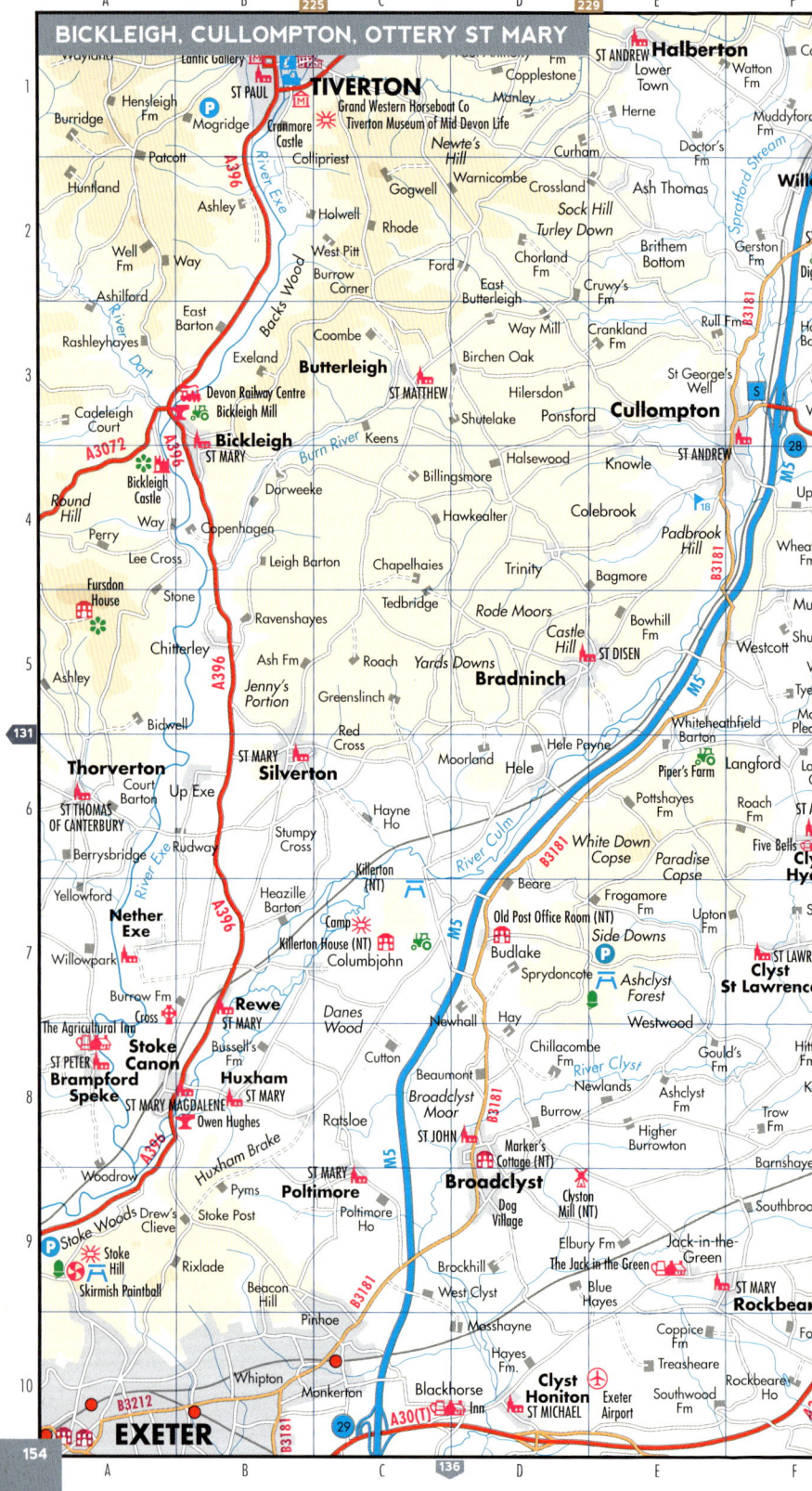

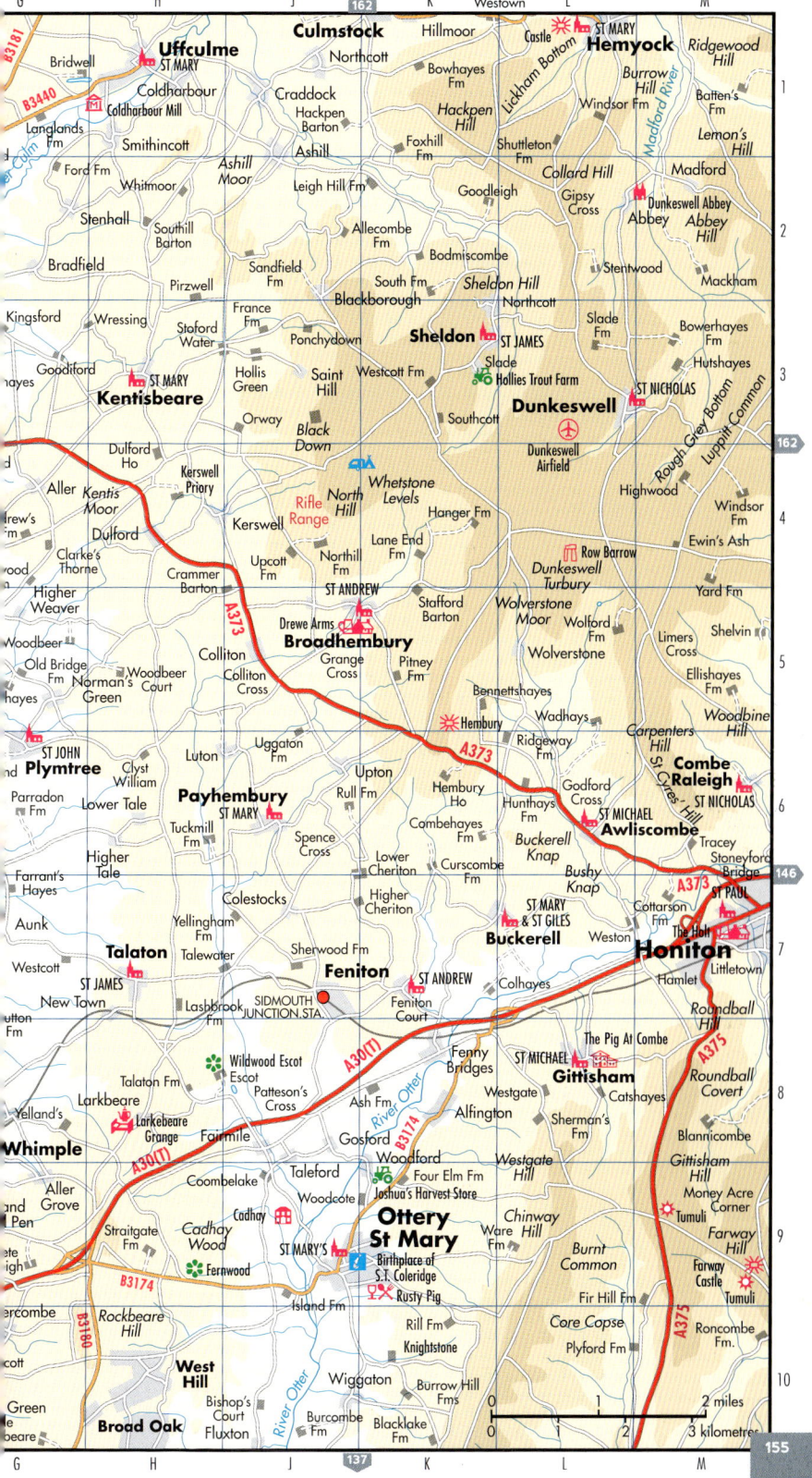

*Cadhay*

## BICKLEIGH

A pretty village beside the River Exe with fine bridge and fisherman's cottages. You can sit in the garden of the Inn and admire the pastoral scene. (B3)

### TO VISIT...

**Bickleigh Castle.** Royalist stronghold spanning 900 years of history. C11 Chapel, Armoury, Guardroom, Great Hall and Tudor bedroom. Picturesque moated garden. Now a Wedding Venue with a number of B&B options. B&B line on 01884 855796. Tours of the Castle by appointment. (A4) 01884 855363 bickleighcastle.com

**Bickleigh Mill.** Extensive shopping with crafts, gallery, ladies' & gentlemen's fashions, interiors, furnishings and the Bistro Restaurant and Bar which is open from 10. Riverside walks in 10-acres of land. Open daily 10-5. (B3) 01884 855419 bickleighmill.com

### Devon Railway Centre.

Train rides on two lines with 10 working model layouts and over 30 trains in motion. Museum. Shop. Café. Open East-Sept & Oct W/Es & half-term 10.30-5. (B3) 01884 855671 devonrailwaycentre.co.uk

## CULLOMPTON

Often used as a drive through to Exeter to avoid the M5. It is certainly worth a visit to the Church. Walk the High Street and be impressed by the surviving buildings of the 1839 fire; the C17 half-timbered **Manor House** and the restored C17 double L-shaped frontage of **The Walronds** used for local events and holiday lets.

**St Andrew's Church.** The great West Tower added in 1545-1549 dominates the town's skyline, and is exceptional. It measures 100 feet and the pinnacles are nearly 20 feet higher. The clock and gargoyles are a memorable sight. One of the great wagon roof and rood screens of Devon. Fan vaulting in the Lane Aisle with stained glass window by Burne-Jones on south side. Carved heraldic shields of the Moore family on the parclose screen. C15 Golgotha carving on west side originally part of the Rood Screen. (F3)

1823    Jul 19. The first cholera case reported in Exeter in an epidemic in which 440 were to die.

## OTTERY ST MARY

Famous as the birthplace in 1772 of Samuel Taylor Coleridge; poet, philosopher, naturalist, and son to the Vicar of the parish. Set in the valley of the River Otter, the town is a friendly and pleasing place to visit. The surrounding pastoral landscape is distinguished by a web of narrow lanes. These join little farms and hamlets. Map reading requires concentration or you can just let the road take you hither and thither and explore the rich, red earthy lanes. The Blackdown Hills rise to the north and to the East, the Jurassic Coast of East Devon. The church is not to be overlooked and is plainly a feast for the churchphile. There is a **Heritage Museum** within the **Old Town Hall**, open as advertised. (K9)

**St Mary's Church.** One of the great churches of Devon. Largely built in the C14 but later modelled on Exeter Cathedral with its fine transeptal towers. The Dorset Aisle from 1520 is an exquisite example of fan faulting perhaps only matched by Gloucester Cathedral. Fine Grandisson tomb. Unusual 600-year old clock. The father of the great Romantic poet,

*St Andrew's, Cullompton*

Samuel Taylor Coleridge was vicar here from 1760-81. A studious and simple man, he read the bible in Hebrew to his parishioners, country folk and farm workers! (J9)

### LIGHT BITES...

Just down from the Church is **The Coffee Bank** who are dedicated in expanding your experience of the coffee bean. Open M-F 8.30-3 (Sa 3.30).

Bearing R into town you will arrive at **The Samosa Lady** where you can buy Indian meals of the Gujarati and Regional variety. Open W & Th 11-3, F 11-5 & Sa 10-2.

### TO VISIT...

**Broadclyst – Marker's Cottage (NT)**. A thatched medieval cob house with an interesting interior containing a screen decorated with "grotesque" work, and a landscape scene of St Andrew. Cob summerhouse in garden. Open Apr-Oct Sa-W 1-5. (D8)

**Budlake – Old Post Office (NT).** A charming thatched cottage in 1950s style that housed the village post office.

Outside the washhouse, double-seated privy, pigsty and chicken house. Half an acre of vegetable garden. Open Apr-Oct Sa-W 1-5. (D7)

**Cadhay**. Built in 1550 on the site of an earlier house to incorporate its Great Hall with a fine, timbered roof. Elizabethan Long Gallery and some Georgian work. Splendid Courtyard with statues of Henry VIII and his children. Maritime paintings and ancient fishponds. House is available to rent for house parties, sleeping up to 22 persons. Tea room. House and gardens open F May-Sept, also BH W/Es 2-5.30. (J9)
cadhay.org.uk

**Clyston Mill (NT)**. C19 water powered grain mill lovingly restored to its former glory, and now producing top quality flour. Set beside the River Clyst surrounded by farmland and orchards, an idyllic spot. Open Apr-Oct Sa-W 1-5. (D9)

**Coldharbour Mill.** 200-year old working woollen mill in continuous production since 1797. You can relive the sights and sounds of the Industrial Revolution and witness the creation of textiles, knitting yarn and hand-woven rugs. Giant water wheel. Special Events; Steam Up Days and Autumn Country Fair. Mill shop and waterside gardens. Picnics. Open daily Apr-Xmas 10-5. (H1) 01884 840960 [coldharbourmill.org.uk](coldharbourmill.org.uk)

**Fursdon House**. The Fursdons have lived here since 1259. The guided tour takes you through the medieval, Jacobean, Georgian and Regency periods. Family portraits, furniture and paintings to view. Costume Museum featuring C18 and C19 clothes. House open Jun-Aug. Open Day Tours at 2.30 & 3.30pm. Gardens and Tea Room open East M-Sept  W Th

| 1827 | Teignmouth to Shaldon bridge built at length of 1671 feet. | 1830 | Plymouth Brethren formed. |

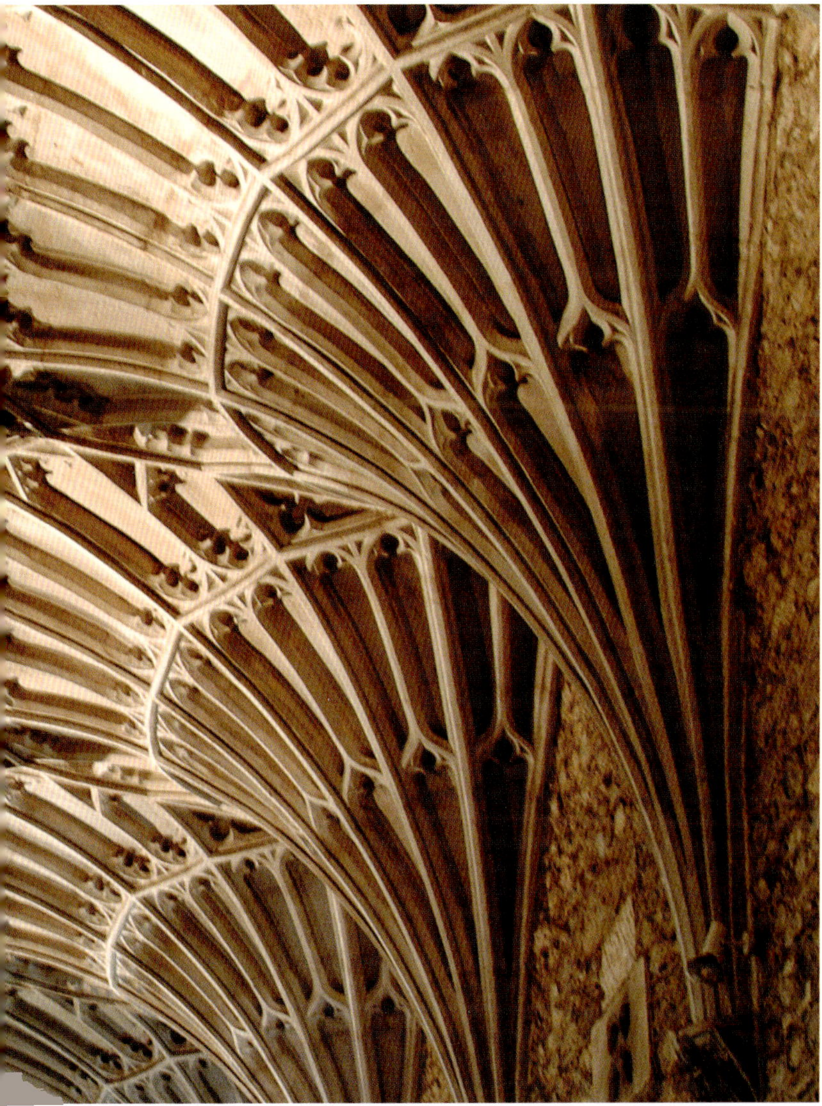

*St Mary's, Ottery St Mary*

& BH Ms. You can stay in one of their holiday cottages. (A5) 01392 860860 fursdon.co.uk

**Killerton House & Garden (NT).** Home of the Acland Family for over three hundred years, and rebuilt in 1778. Downstairs rooms furnished in different periods. Upstairs the Pauline de Bush Costume Collection. 15 acres of superb

1839 Fire destroyed 260 homes in Cullompton.

1839 Dec 25. 8,000,000 tons of soil slipped into the sea near Axmouth.

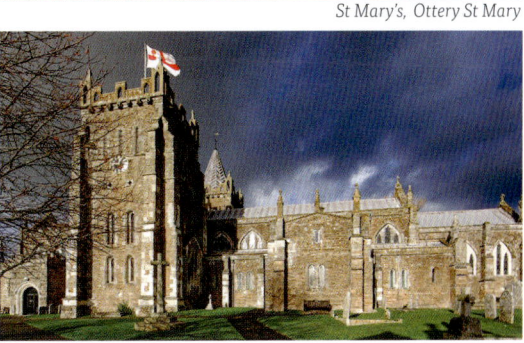

*Killerton Garden*

gardens developed through many generations. Victorian laundry. Ice House. Garden, Park, shop, stables café, plant centre open all year from 10-5.30. House & Restaurant open from early Feb-29 Oct, 25 Nov-31 Dec. Park open all year 8-7. 01392 881345 (C7)

**Skirmish Paintball.** Set in 120 acres of Stoke Woods, close to Exeter city centre. Trenches, bridges, ravines, jungles and swamps. Catering & sheltered rest areas. (A9) 01548 580025 paintballskirmish.co.uk

### COUNTRYSIDE INTERESTS...

**Joshua's Harvest Store, Gosford Rd**. One of the leading specialist food shops in Devon. It celebrates local, fresh, organic and specialist food and drink, and sells gifts and greeting cards. The café serves beautifully presented platters allowing you to sample the food sold in store. Open M-Sa 9-5.30, Su 10.30-4.30. (K9)

01404 815473
joshuasltd.co.uk

**Pipers Farm**. They support a community of local family farms producing red meats, poultry, and sausages and burgers of the highest quality. Visit their shop in Exeter at the Magdelan Road shopping parade. (E6) 01392 881380 pipersfarm.com

**Hollies Trout Farm, Slade Lane**. Supplies many local pubs and restaurants with their award-winning fish. Try catching your own with rod and line. Fly fishing tuition. Log cabins to hire. (K3) 01404 841428 holliestroutfarm.co.uk

### CHURCHES TO VISIT...

**St John the Baptist, Broadclyst**. A magnificent church in the Perpendicular style; the tower is 100 feet and decorated in the style of Somerset tracery with eight pinnacles of Beer stone. This is the fourth church on this site, and forms the second largest parish in Devonshire. The roof was restored with iron tiles by I K Brunel. There are four elaborate tombs and some beautiful, and sad stained glass; the Ellen Acland window commemorates the ten year old killed in a cycling accident. Up high, some fine bosses, the Green Man and the Three Rabbits. In the churchyard, a board remembers the Veitch family of gardeners, of Killerton. (D8)

### EAT... DRINK...RELAX...

**The Agricultural Inn, Brampford Speke**. Centre of village facing a cobbled courtyard. Log fires in winter. Specially brewed Speakeasy Ale and Adnams. Good honest food; casseroles, fillet of Devon beef, confit neckfillet of lamb or seared corn fed chicken breast. (A8) 01392 841591 agriculturalinn.co.uk

**1839**    The ship *Tory* departs Plymouth bound for New Zealand with the first pioneer colonists.

**Drewe Arms, Broadhembury**.
A thatched hostelry with a
warm atmosphere; open fires
for winter night, fresh fish,
quality wines and real ale
(loved by CAMRA) Put simply
- your hosts, Kate, Dan and Viv
are true exponents of their craft
and proud of their hostelry. (K5)
01404 841267
drewearmsinn.co.uk

**Five Bells, Clyston Hydon.**
James and Charlie Garnham,
your host and hostess know
this business inside and out,

and boy does it show. From the
twee thatched roof, to the warm
welcome, to the well-stocked
bar and the ambience of a fine
inn...and top-class food. Open
Tu-Su from 12pm. (F6)
01884 277288 fivebells.uk.com

**The Jack in the Green,
Rockbeare.** One of the first
dining-pubs in Devon started
20+ years ago that has become
more a restaurant than a pub. It
has won countless awards and
accolades from food writers
and built up a loyal clientele.

Seasonal menus. The one
drawback, the large, open
space lacks intimacy. (E9)
01404 822240
jackinthegreen.uk.com

**The Rusty Pig, Yonder
Street, Ottery St Mary**. If
you seek a 'pig out' - yes, their
expression. These guys are
specialist charcuteries, and
are passionate about pigs and
they source the pork from their
smallholding. Feasting House
open W 11-4, Th & F 8-11. (K9)
01404 815580 rustypig.co.uk

ss

**The Pig at Combe, Gittisham, Nr Honiton.** One of the great Country House hotels of England. A Grade 1 Elizabethan manor surrounded by 3,500 acres of parkland. The house has been modernised with large sofas, the old carpets have been removed to reveal stripped floors. The conversion of the stables into a bedroom is a masterstoke of pragmatic design. This could indeed be your Country Retreat for you will have the tranquillity, the blissful comfort and chefs on hand to create cuisine from your massive Kitchen Garden. You, too, can walk in the surrounding parkland and explore Gittisham with its pretty thatched cottages. Non-residents are welcome here and it is a fortuitous stopover for lunch and coffee. (L8) 01404 540400 thepighotel.com

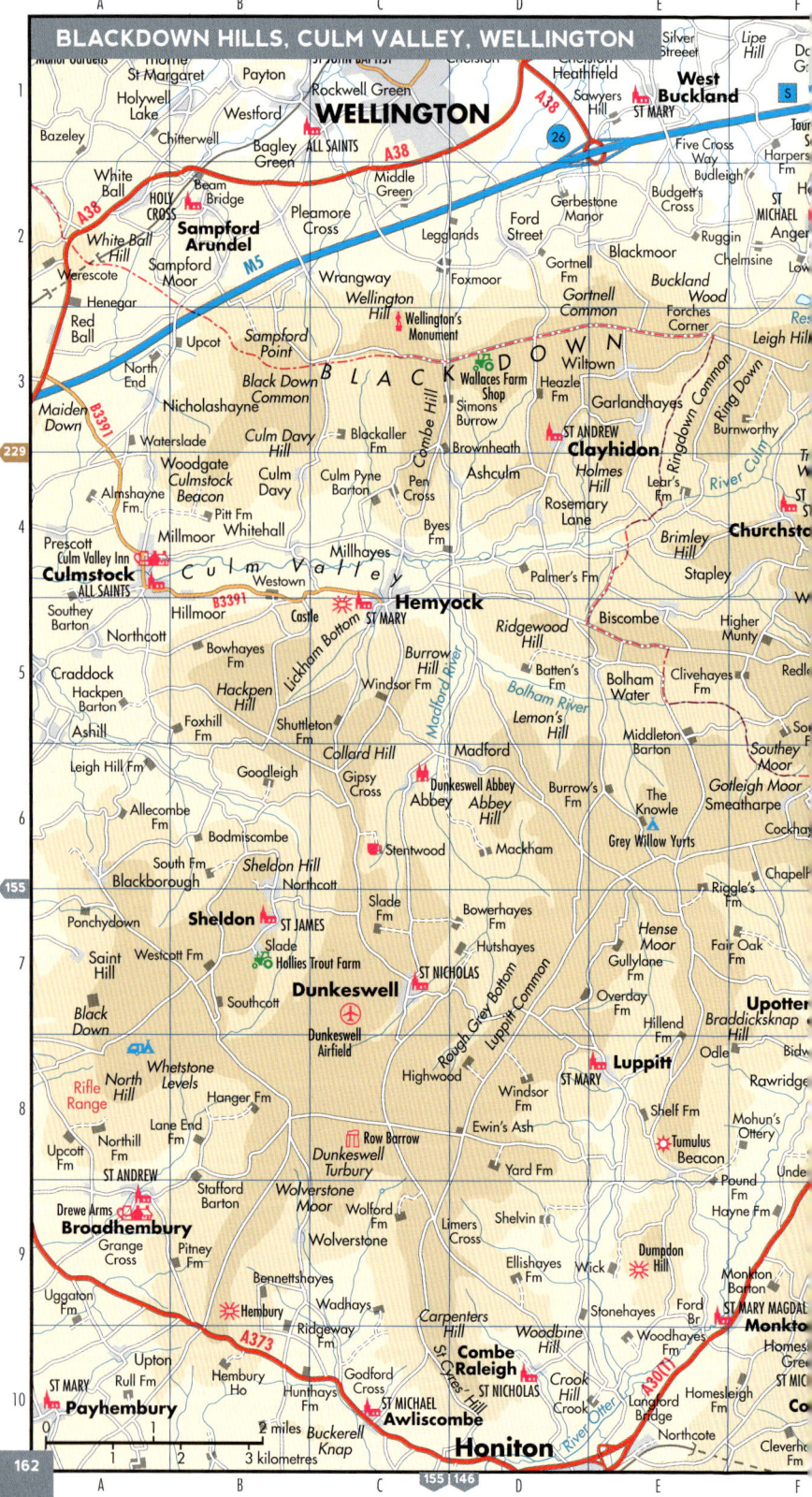

A B C D E F

1

Silver Streeet
Lipe Hill
Do G

Thorne
St Margaret
Payton
ST JOHN BAPTIST
Chelston
Chelston Heathfield
West Buckland

Holywell Lake
Rockwell Green
WELLINGTON
Sawyers Hill
ST MARY

Bazeley
Westford
A38
Five Cross Way
Taur S

Chitterwell
Bagley Green
ALL SAINTS
A38
Budgeigh
Harpers Fm

2

White Ball
Beam Bridge
Middle Green

HOLY CROSS
Gerbestone Manor
ST MICHAEL
Anger

White Ball Hill
Sampford Arundel
Pleamore Cross
Ford Street
Ruggin
Chelmsine
Low

Werescote
Sampford Moor
Legglands
Foxmoor
Blackmoor

Henegar
Wrangway
Gortnell Fm
Buckland Wood

Red Ball
Upcot
Wellington Hill
Gortnell Common
Forches Corner
Leigh Hill

3

Maiden Down
Sampford Point
Wellington's Monument
Wiltown
Ring Down

B3391
BLACKDOWN
Wallaces Farm Shop
Heazle Fm
Garlandhayes
Burnworthy

Nicholashayne
Black Down Common
Simons Burrow
ST ANDREW
Clayhidon
River Culm
Tr

229

Waterslade
Culm Davy Hill
Blackaller
Brownheath
Holmes Hill
Lear's Fm

Woodgate Culmstock Beacon
Culm Davy
Culm Pyne Barton
Pen Cross
Ashculm
Rosemary Lane

Almshayne Fm.
Pitt Fm
Whitehall
Byes Fm
Brimley Hill
Churchsto

4

Prescott
Millmoor
Culm Valley
Millhayes
Palmer's Fm
Stapley

Culm Valley Inn
Culmstock
ALL SAINTS
Westown
ST MARY
Hemyock
Ridgewood Hill
Biscombe
Higher Munty

5

Southey Barton
Northcott
Hillmoor
Castle
Lickham Bottom
Burrow River
Batten's Fm
Clivehayes Fm
Redle

Craddock
Bowhayes Fm
Windsor Fm
Bolham River
Bolham Water
So

Hackpen Barton
Hackpen Hill
Lemon's Hill
Middleton Barton

Ashill
Foxhill Fm
Shuttleton
Southey Moor

6

Leigh Hill Fm
Collard Hill
Madford
Gotleigh Moor

Allecombe Fm
Goodleigh
Gipsy Cross
Dunkeswell Abbey
Abbey Hill
Burrow's Fm
The Knowle
Smeatharpe
Cockha

Bodmiscombe
Abbey
Mackham
Grey Willow Yurts

155

South Fm
Blackborough
Sheldon Hill
Northcott
Riggle's Fm
Chapel

7

Ponchydown
Sheldon
ST JAMES
Slade Fm
Bowerhayes Fm
Hense Moor
Fair Oak Fm

Saint Hill
Westcott Fm
Slade
Hollies Trout Farm
Hutshayes
Gullylane Fm

Black Down
Southcott
Dunkeswell
ST NICHOLAS
Overday Fm
Upotte
Braddicksknap Hill

8

Whetstone Levels
Dunkeswell Airfield
Hillend Fm
Odle

Rifle Range
North Hill
Hanger Fm
Highwood
Windsor Fm
ST MARY
Luppitt
Rawridge

Upcott Fm
Northill Fm
Lane End Fm
Row Barrow
Ewin's Ash
Shelf Fm
Mohun's Ottery

ST ANDREW
Dunkeswell Turbury
Yard Fm
Tumulus Beacon
Unde

9

Drewe Arms
Stafford Barton
Wolverstone Moor
Wolford Fm
Shelvin
Pound Fm
Hayne Fm

Broadhembury
Wolverstone
Limers Cross
Dumpdon Hill
ST MARY MAGDAL

Grange Cross
Pitney Fm
Ellishayes Fm
Wick
Monkto

Uggaton Fm
Bennettshayes
Wadhays
Stonehayes
Ford Br
ST MARY MAGDAL
Monkto

10

Hembury
A373
Ridgeway Fm
Carpenters Hill
Woodbine Hill
Woodhays Fm
Homesle
Gre

Upton
Hembury Ho
Godford Cross
Combe Raleigh
ST NICHOLAS
Crook Hill
ST MIC
Homesleigh Fm

ST MARY
Rull Fm
Hunthays Fm
ST MICHAEL
Awliscombe
Crook
Langford Bridge
Co

Payhembury
Buckerell Knap
Honiton
Northcote
Cleverhe

0 1 2 miles
1 2 3 kilometres

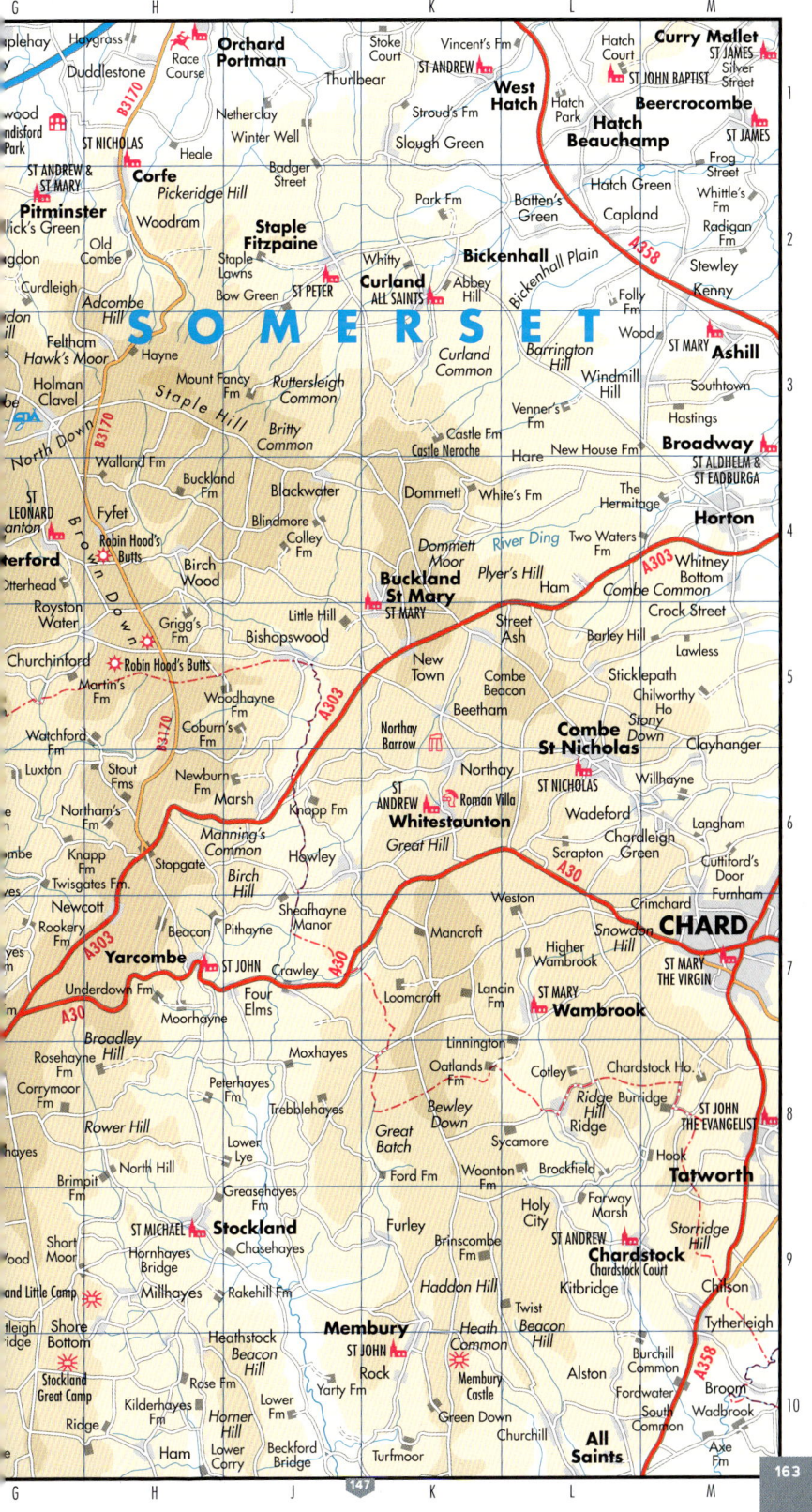

*Wellington Monument*

## BLACKDOWN HILLS

Fine bit of country on the Somerset/Devon border. Get off the A303 and turn right following the B3170, after three miles, take a left at the North Down junction to follow a straight road beneath a tree lined avenue, towards Clayhidon. Follow to Culmstock turn off. Wonderful. (D3)

## CULM VALLEY

An enchanting valley fed by the rivers Culm, Bolham and Madford. Culmstock has a fine pub (described) and Hemyock is an ancient village with castle and church. (C4)

## WELLINGTON

Old established centre of the woollen trade. Fine Georgian houses. The Duke of Wellington took his title from here, and is commemorated in monument on the hilltop three miles south. Small museum. E/C W. (C1)

**Wellington Monument**. A notable landmark, 175 feet high on the Blackdown Hills. The first stone was laid in 1817, and completed in 1892. Arthur Wellesley took his title from Wellington, although it is claimed he only visited the area once in 1819. He did own land hereabouts. Popular dog walking spot. (C3)

## EAT...DRINK...RELAX...

**Culm Valley Inn**. If one has to have favourites then this has been one of mine for many years. When you enter you are rewarded with a warm welcome and a proper old fashioned bar leading off to a chic restaurant with artworks hanging from the walls. Now under new ownership, it is their purpose to maintain the high standards of food and good living. 5-bedrooms to slumber and rest. (A4) 01884 840354 thecaulmvalley.co.uk

**Stentwood Farm Tea Room.** A community run space offering hospitality with fresh bread from their bakery, log fires and a spacious garden. Open Su-F 10-5. (C6) 01823 711038 commonloaf.com/tearoom

**Wallace's Farm Shop, Hill Farm**. Breeds Highland Cattle, Red Deer and Bison. Sells giant pork pies, venison and dry cured bacon. Open daily 9-5. (D3) 01823 680307 welcometowallaces.co.uk

## TO SLEEP...TO STARGAZE...

**Grey Willow Yurts, Knowle Farm**. They call them Yabins. Three solitary Yurts within a 3-acre field that sleep 5-persons. Comfy with wood burner. Dog/family/environmentally friendly. You share a loo and shower. (E6) 07966 617488 greywillowyurts.co.uk

**1841** Construction of Plymouth Breakwater to protect the Fleet from the south-westerlies. Before they would seek safety in Torbay.

*Blackdown Common, Wellington*

| 1841 | The West Country's first factory school built in Tiverton. | 1844 | May 1. The first steam locomotive reaches Exeter from Bristol. |

# NORTH DEVON

North Devon is a rural landscape of small villages, rich pastures, secluded coves and long sandy beaches. The two ancient ports of Barnstaple and Bideford have grown up beside the wide estuary of the Taw and Torridge rivers.

Stretching southwards from these ports is the gentle pastoral countryside known as 'The Land of the Two Rivers' so vividly brought to life in the works of Henry Williamson. The warm equable climate, together with the nature of the countryside provides excellent recreational opportunities, particularly for the walker, fisherman and surfer, and remains a favourite destination for family beach holidays.

The Hartland Peninsula on the western tip is Devon's Land's End, and a place tempered by the punishing seas and dramatic coastline. Often overlooked because of its isolation, a visit should be planned in with its neighbour, Clovelly. The coast is in sharp contrast to the pastoral, inland country that runs in an Easterly direction from Great Torrington to Tiverton.

The Exmoor National Park is largely in Somerset, with a small portion lying in Devon. At times the climate is harsh with mist, cloud and rain, and is reminiscent of Scotland. When the skies clear, the wild, wide beauty is unsurpassed. The landscape is undulating, full of rolling hills, marshland, bracken, heather and gorse, and divided by swift flowing streams which cut through the steep-sided valleys, known as combes.

The rolling moorland provides splendid views seawards across the Bristol Channel to Wales. In places the coast is crowned with high cliffs that fall precipitously to the sea.

The Exmoor sheep and wild ponies are seen everywhere, as are buzzard and raven. The roaming red deer are rarely seen and if startled (although unlikely, for they will hear and smell you coming) they can be a dangerous animal.

Of a somewhat gentler aspect than Dartmoor, and formerly a royal hunting forest. Exmoor is the only highland area of England to overlook the sea. Like Dartmoor, it provides contrasting landscapes of remote moorland and snug villages, but also a fine rugged coastline. It is noted for its ponies, somewhat smaller than the Dartmoor variety, and is the only place in England where red deer can still be seen. Less than half the National Park lies within the Devon boundary, but this includes the towns of Lynton and Lynmouth, the Doone Valley with its romantic associations, the beautiful Heddon Valley and over 20 miles of truly magnificent coastline.

*Hartland*

**LUNDY ISLAND**

North West Point
North East Point
Gannet's Rock
North End
*Gannet's Bay*
Half Wall
Frenchman's Landing
St James's Stone
Brazen Ward
Long House and Farm
Threequarter Wall
(Widows Tenement rems)
Tibbett's Point
*Tibbett's Hill*
*Jenny's Cove*
Halfway Wall
Needle Rock
Quarter Wall
Quarterwall Cottages (rems)
*Beacon Hill* Shop
Old Lighthouse
Milcombe House
Halftide Rock
Jetty
Marisco Tavern
Rat Island
Goat Island
Castle
Surf Point
Shutter Point
Seal's Hole

**ILFRACOMBE (summer only)**
**BIDEFORD**
**CLOVELLY (summer only)**

Baggy Point

Croyde Hoe
*Middleb*
Sandleigh Tea R
*Croyde B*

Downenc

Lund

0    1    2 miles
0  1  2  3 kilometres

### BRAUNTON

A bustling village and one of the oldest in Devon. An early Celtic settlement developed by the legendary St Brannock who arrived by sail in a stone coffin from Brittany! In Devon, considered the West Country's centre for the surf industry due to the proximity of Saunton Sands, Croyde, Putsborough and Woolacombe's Atlantic beaches. Not to be missed, the charming church of St Brannock. Velator is the former shipping centre and harbour for the village. The entrance to Crow Point, a haven of solitude, shipwrecks, glacial sandbanks and the nature reserves of Braunton Marsh and Burrows, and a wide, open space. The village has a number of indistinguished pubs and coffee shops serving light meals. A rush of new builds have hastened the slow pace of traffic through the village which stops at traffic-lights. (J8)

### TO VISIT...

**Braunton & District Museum, Caen Street Car Park**. Super little museum illustrating local life, village crafts, strip-farming and coastal sailing ships. TIC. Open M-Th 10-3, F 10-1. (J8) 01271 816688

**Braunton Burrows**. 2,400 acre National Nature Reserve extending three miles along the estuary and coast. Important for the study of evolution of sand dunes and associated plant ecology (400 species). Abounds in wildlife; foxes, rabbits, hedgehogs, moles, weasels, mink, shrews, lizards and voles. Also butterflies, birds and rare plants. Free public access except for an area sometimes closed for military training. Recently categorised by UNESCO as a Biosphere Reserve to accord it international protection. Nearby is Braunton Great Field (best seen from the hill above), a rare survival of the ancient strip tenure system of farming. Originally divided into one acre strips (on Edward 1's ruling) - the Chief (Lord of the Manor) would have at least 500 acres, the Freeman 100 acres and the

*Saunton Beach Waves*

*Crow Point*

peasants rented strips from their Chief. Families would share their ploughs and oxen. Today, five farmers work this land. (G9)

**Braunton Countryside Centre, Caen St Car Park.** Their mission is to increase the understanding, awareness and enjoyment of coastal and farmed landscapes in and around Braunton, and to appreciate the North Devon Biosphere. Very much worth visiting if the Natural World interests you. Open May-Oct M-Sa 10-4. (J8) 01271 817171 brauntoncountrysidecentre.org

**Braunton Marsh.** Former wild, tidal salt marsh which was tamed into lush pastureland inhabited by cattle, wild flowers and bountiful birdlife. Now no longer protected by the Great Sea Bank stretching from Velator to Broadsands (White House) built in 1808 for this bank was breached 4-years ago and much besides. Horsey Island included, is returning to become a tidal salt marsh, again. (G9)

**Crow Point.** Naturally formed in 1809 which sticks out like a hook. It's 30 feet high in places, topped with (protected) Marram grass. Not as accessible

**LIGHT BITES...**

Visitors to the beaches of North Devon often refer to **Braunton** as the place with the traffic lights. The architecture is uninspiring apart from the **Norman Church of St Brannock** and the cottages on **Church Street**. There are a number of eateries that cater for families. On your left is **Squires** the fish and chip emporium. To your right, **SQ,** their attempt at going up-market. Seek out **Roots** at 1 Exeter Road for their wraps, salad boxes, pies, pastrys, cakes and gelatos where you can prepare for a day on the beach. As you leave on the Croyde Road the last outpost is **Heart Break Hotel**, where the doughnuts send folk into spirals of delight, open W-Su.

as it used to be due to the placement of some hideous lumps of rock, to stop overnight campers. (H10)

**Museum of Surfing, The Yard, Caen St.** The heritage and history of British surfing. The first stop for all experienced, and would-be surfers, where you will get a perspective of this difficult sport, and obsessive life-style.

Open Tu-Su & BHs 10-3. (J8) 01271 815155 museumofbritishsurfing.org.uk

**Saunton Sands.** Extensive 4-mile stretch of compact sands cleansed by the rolling Atlantic waves. Overlooked by the giant rabbit warren, Braunton Burrows. Immortalised in the 1920s works of Henry Williamson: "The Dream of

Fair Women," "The Pathway," "Tarka the Otter" and "Salar the Salmon". Film location in WW11 for Vivien Leigh's Cleopatra, then subsequently mined (Chivenor was an anti U-Boat base), to be later used as a practice venue for the US Normandy Landings of June 1944. Superb situation for water sports; sand-yachting, beach casting, surfing and

## THE TARKA TRAIL

A 180-mile/280km trail follows the route taken by Tarka the Otter on his travels through "The Land of the Two Rivers", the Taw and Torridge, as depicted in Henry Williamson's classic novel 'Tarka the Otter' published in 1928.

The trail can be walked but also offers on and off-road cycling. The trail becomes a dual purpose walkway-cycleway allowing for relatively easy and safe cycling starting at Braunton. The route runs on tarmac beside the Taw Estuary to Barnstaple and can be enjoyed depending on the wind direction. Just hope it follows you. There is, however, abundant birdlife to hold your interest.

From Barnstaple along the south side of the Taw Estuary to Instow with refreshments to be had at Fremington Quay, or **John's Deli** in Instow. The route now becomes more interesting beside the Torridge to the Puffing Billy pub below Great Torrington or across the river to Watergate Bridge.

The trail joins a bridle path and what follows is arguably the most interesting section of the trail. It is cyclable on a hybrid, E-Bike, touring or folding bike all the way to Meeth. Look out for the excellent little café at Yarde, the **Railway summit**. So you have 32 miles (51km) of traffic-free cycling. There is bike hire at Tarka Trail Cycle Hire, Barnstaple Railway Station, Fremington Quay (also bike shop), and the Puffing Billy, Gt Torrington.

1855   Charles Kingsley's novel Westward Ho! Published.

1855   Oct 20. The North Devon Railway opened from Bideford to Barnstaple.

*The Groynes, Crow Point*

windsurfing. Lifeguards in summer. Surf and sea survival school and shops at north end. Beach huts (bungalows) for rent: 01271 892002. **Sands Café Bar** open for food (and drink) only; breakfast, light lunches and dinner. In superb position overlooking the car park (!), and at an excruciating angle for one's neck, the beach. Apparently the local residents blocked the architect's original plans to provide a view. Open from 10 in season. For a really superb view, and a light lunch on the balcony on comfortable sofas, the **Saunton Sands Hotel** is recommended. (G8)

**St Brannock's Church.** Norman tower and recently restored lead spire. Noted for its superb medieval bench ends. (J8)

## VELATOR

Former shipping centre and port to Braunton that traded with South Wales and the Bristol Channel ports in coal, salt, manure and flour. The trade was dictated by tide and weather and eventually proved too difficult after the channels silted up. (J8)

### TO STAY...TO SLEEP...

**Silver Cottage B&B, 14 Silver St.** Two modern double-bedrooms in a quiet backwater close to the beaches of North Devon. 01271 814165 (J8) silvercottagebraunton.co.uk

**Upcott Farm, Upcott.** Two luxurious self-catering cottages beside an old farmhouse in an idyllic valley close to the beaches of North Devon. Blissful comfort with all the mod cons. 01271 816009 (J7) upcottfarm.com

*River Caen, Braunton*

## CROYDE

A popular holiday and surfing centre with pretty thatched cottages, camp-sites, pubs and restaurants. The village can become unduly hectic and rowdy. For the experienced surfer Croyde sets the Bar. They say "If you can surf Croyde, you can surf anywhere." The rips and currents are like no other. The Oyster Fall (just off Downend Point) can be treacherous (see Surfing details). Bracing walks to Baggy Point. A number of fields open for the 2-months of July-August, and become camp sites: Freshwater, Mitchum's and Ocean Pitch and are placed overlooking the sea on the Baggy Point road. (G7)

### TO VISIT...

**Baggy Point.** Given to the National Trust in 1939 by Constance and Florence Hyde. A bracing circular 40-minute walk can be had up to the Point where you may see rock climbers traversing the wall and fishermen aspiring for bass and conger. Inspired Henry Williamson to write many of his nature stories. Note the unusual plaque at entrance. Access possible for wheelchairs but be prepared for a steep push. NT car park (charge). (F6)

### LIGHT BITES...

**Sandleigh Tea Rooms, Moor Lane.** Overlooks the north side of the beach and the entrance to Baggy Point. A great find and an oasis after a long walk or surf. Open daily in season. (F6) 01271 890930

**The Thatch.** A pub patronised by surfers (and hangers-on) and their surf chicks. It can be busy in summer. Real Ales. Variety of lagers. Excellent salads, thick-cut sandwiches and solid fare. 6-rooms for B&B. Next door, **Billy Budds**, more surfy, same ownership. (G7) 01271 890349 thethatchcroyde.com

**New Coast Kitchen.** Next door to the Post Office and a welcome addition to Croyde's eateries. Opens at 9 for brunch, 2 for drinks and 6 for dinner.

### TO STAY...TO SLEEP...

**Bridge Farm B&B.** Located bang in the village centre next to their camp site detailed below. Cottage style comforts of home with new bathrooms. Good value. 01271 890422 (G6)

**The Orchard Village Campsite.** This is for tents and small campers. It's basic, convenient and on an incline and central to Croyde's action. 3-Showers and loos on hand. 07779 371195 (G6) theorchardcampsitecroyde.co.uk

**Combas Farm, Putsborough.** Isolated at the end of a long bridle path but within easy walking distance of Croyde

*Baggy Point*

1859   Brunel's Royal Albert Bridge carries the railway over the Tamar to Cornwall.

and Putsborough. A quaint old-fashioned C17 farmhouse that offers homespun comforts. Large kitchen garden and farm produce delivers fab breakfasts. (G6) 01271 890398
combasfarm.co.uk

**Ocean Pitch Campsite, Moor Lane.** Tents and small vans only. Open in summer months. 07581 024348. (G7)

**Pickwell Manor.** There are ten apartments to rent. From The Chapel (sleeps 2) to Bliss (sleeps 10) and four treehouses all within 6-acres of gardens and grounds a mere 5-minutes drive, or 10-minutes walk to Putsborough Sands. Great for children and weddings. (G6) 01271 890110
pickwellmanor.co.uk

**Ruda.** This is a camp site housing mobile homes and space for large tents. Shop, indoor pool and fish and chips. It hustles and bustles. 0330 2076863 (G7)

## GEORGEHAM

Largely unspoilt village with thatched cottages. Henry Williamson, author of *Tarka the Otter* lived much of his life here settling in Skir Cottage for £5.00 per annum on his return from the First World War. In 1928 he was awarded the Hawthornden Prize for writing Tarka and with the money he bought some land at Ox's Cross and built his Writing Hut. He's buried in the churchyard. Much expansion and building of new homes. Village store and two Inns; **The Rock** (traditional pub) and **The King's Arms** (surfy crowd), both are worthy of your patronage. (H7)

## WHERE TO CAMP...

**Incledon Farm.** A basic laid-back site on a slight slope

ideal for tents and campers. Basic shower block. Dogs (and children) on lead at all times. Walking distance to two pubs. 01271 890200
incledonfarm.co.uk

## ILFRACOMBE

A popular holiday centre developed by the Victorians in the Railway Age. A place of high cliffs and rocky beaches bordered by the sweeping Exmoor hills. Well situated for fine coastal walks and excursions to Exmoor. The ancient harbour is a great attraction and has been refurbished. The loan of Damien Hirst's 66 ft bronze sculpture, Verity (a modern allegory of truth and justice), to the town has brought controversy, publicity and the catalyst for new businesses. The town may have seen better days, but it's on the up and is a popular place to live and property is good value. New restaurants and galleries are opening as are contemporary places to stay. Seek out Fore Street which connects the Harbour to the High Street. Here are new enterprises, new craftie/lifestyle shops and the better eateries. Ilfracombe is close to the beaches of Woolacombe and Croyde and must be considered a place to stay. St Nicholas Chapel and Lighthouse surmount Lantern Hill. Hillsborough Iron Age Fort (a fine walk). Torrs walks. Fishing (mackerel, reef, deep sea), wildlife tours (swim with seals) and sightseeing excursions (Exmoor coast & smugglers caves) from the Harbour's quay. Landmark Theatre. Cinema. Victorian Fair in July. Lundy Island office. E/C Th.(K3)

## TO VISIT...

**Aquarium, The Pier.**
Award-winning, all-weather, family attraction provides a fascinating journey into the aquatic life of North Devon. Follow a unique-zoned journey from an Exmoor stream to Lundy and its marine reserve. Shop and café with outside seating. Open daily Feb-Oct 10-4. (L3) 01271 864533
ilfracombeaquarium.co.uk

**Bristol Channel Cruises.**
On board the paddle steamer Waverley (the last ocean-going paddle steamer in the world) and motor cruiser M.V. Balmoral from Minehead and Ilfracombe July-Oct 1/2 term, timetable from website. (K3) 01446 721221
waverleyexcursions.co.uk

**Chambercombe Manor, Chambercombe Lane.** An attractive small manor with C16-C17 additions. Period furnished rooms, armour and porcelain. Haunted chamber. 4-acres of herb and water garden. Cream Teas. Paranormal Events. Holiday Cottages. Guided Tours. Open East-Oct Su-F. (L3) 01271 862624
chambercombemanor.org.uk

**Coast & Cooking, Fore St.**
Full day and 2-hour courses in all styles of cuisine: Indian, fish, Italian, vegetarian... yummy. (L3) 07771 821740
coastalcoooking.co.uk

**Damien Hirst's Verity, The Harbour.** Damien Hirst, the mega-rich artist has a farm near Combe Martin. He invested in an art gallery and a restaurant which has since closed. I believe he realized that Ilfracombe needed energizing or a heavy kick up the backside. Indeed, the

Burghers who manage the town were quite happy with the Status Quo. How to change things? He has loaned this controversial sculpture to the town until 2032. It shows a heavily pregnant young woman. Her stomach is exposed on one side. Hirst describes its meaning to be "Truth," a modern allegory on truth and justice. It is 66 feet tall and is made of stainless steel and bronze. Some like it, others don't. It invites debate and has placed Ilfracombe firmly on the map. Hence, the new restaurants and boutique B&Bs. (L2)

**Keypits Quads**. Naturally a speciality, as is local Devon quad bikes, karting, paint ball battles, thunderball and 4x4 off-road drives. Open daily. (M3) 0744 6078190
keypitts.com

**Ilfracombe Museum, Wilder Rd.** Fascinating collections of natural history, minerals, Victoriana, maritime and local history. Open daily Apr-Oct 10-5, Nov-Mar Tu-F 10-1. (L3) 01271 863541

**Ilfracombe Princess, The Harbour**. Wildlife and coastal cruises to view seals, porpoises and dolphins, and sea birds. Take binoculars. (L2) 01271 879727
ilfracombeprincess.co.uk

**Hele Corn Mill & Tea Room,** **Watermouth Rd**. Restored C16 watermill with 18ft overshot wheel produces stone ground flour. Cream teas and homemade cakes. Open Easter, W/Es and 1/2 term weeks, daily July-Aug 11-5. (L3) 01271 863185
helecornmill.com

**Osprey Charters, The Quay.** You can charter Skipper Paul Barbeary's boat (a Pro-charter 40) for deep sea fishing, wildlife trips, film work and surveys. 07748 221156. (L2)

**Tunnels Beaches**. Established in 1823; four unique tunnels were handcarved through the rocks to create a stunning, sheltered beach with tidal

1860s. Farm rents are high and farm workers wages are 70% of the national average resulting in a mass exodus of 126,000 folk leaving England.

*Ilfracombe Harbour View*

Good value and close to the coastpath and beaches of North Devon. 01271 867835 oceanbackpackers.co.uk

**Olive Branch Guest House, 56 Fore Street**. An attractive Georgian building close to the harbour provides luxurious double bedrooms of a high standard with fine sea views. 01271 879005 (K3) olivebranchguesthouse.co.uk

**Westwood, Torrs Park**. Helen and John Vowles have transformed a large Victorian house into 6-chic, luxurious ensuite rooms by using contemporary fabrics and furnishings. The bedrooms are spacious and full of the latest mod cons. Open all year. (K3) 01271 867443 west-wood.co.uk

## EAT...DRINK...

**Espresso Café Bar & Grill, 1 St James Place**. An unpretentious and hospitable café serving up freshly caught seafood. A warm welcome is guaranteed. (K3) 01271 855485 seafoodrestaurantilfracombe.co.uk

**Thomas Carr 1873, 63 Fore Street**. North Devon born and a prodigy of Nathan Outlaw and Michael Caines, Carr has the local fish, meat and seasonal vegetables in his blood. Expect imaginative dishes from this Michelin Starred diner. 01271 867831 thomascarrdining.com

## LEE

Set in a sheltered combe known as Fuschia Valley for fuchsias grow wild in the hedgerows and stone banks. The lane leads to Lee Bay, a beach of special marine biological interest overlooked by the empty Lee Bay Hotel, an eyesore in a spectacular position. There are, however, plans afoot to convert the site into luxurious apartments? Low tide provides sand, rock pools, steps to Sandy Cove where dreams are made and memories never forgotten. Beware of getting stranded by the in-rushing tide on left-side beach. Note the special patterns of slate made by the swirling currents. Park

seawater pool. It's ideal family bathing with a swimming and paddling pool. Open daily Apr-Oct 10-5, May-Aug 10-6. Small fee. (K3) 01271 879882 tunnelbeaches.co.uk

## TO STAY...TO SLEEP...

**Habit, 46 Fore St.** A new construct in Ilfracombe with a recent refurbishment to become an 11-bedroom boutique style house and terrace open to rent for house parties. (K3) 01271 863272 habitilfracombe.co.uk

**Ocean Backpackers**. An established independent youth hostel catering for singles, families and groups.

## LIGHT BITES...

**Adele's Café, South Side of Harbour.** Adele's opens at 7.30 for breakfast and for those wishing to build their strength before stepping onto the Balmoral for Lundy. Otherwise, it's toasties, sarnis, paninis, omelettes and more. (L2) 01271 867238 adelescafeilfracombe.com

Now head to **S & P Fish Shop & Café, The Quay**. A hut overlooking the harbour where you can buy fresh fish direct off the local trawlers and/or eat in, quayside. Open daily. 07533 168343. (K3)

In need of a coffee and pastry? It has to be **Stacc** at 13-14 The Promenade for your Hostess is an exceptional pastry chef. Cakes her business, baked and served in house. staccbakes.com

Seeking an alternative? Try **The Cookery** at 28 St James Place for their homemade cakes (Brownies a speciality), soups, panninis and a very warm welcome. Takeaways. Dog friendly. 077907 25933 no28thecookery.co.uk

*Morte Point*

opposite the Church. C14 Grampus Inn/Micro-Brewery for lunch, dinner and Friday music nights. (J3)

### MORTEHOE

A pretty, isolated hilltop village overlooking Woolacombe and Morte Bay. Surrounded by four campsites. Local beaches are either Rockham Bay, reached by a footpath on the North Morte road, or Grunta, below the Old Chapel. There's a lovely circular family walk out to Morte Point and back via the Cemetery. Two uninspiring pubs. (H4)

### TO VISIT…

**Borough Farm.** Working Sheepdog demonstration by TV celebrity, David Kennard and Falconry display by Jonathon Marshall from the North Devon Birds of Prey Centre. Shepherd Experience. (G4) Displays June to early Sept, W 6 pm. 01271 870056 boroughfarm.co.uk

**Morte Point.** Scene of many shipwrecks and loss of life. Beware of the Morte Race, a notorious and treacherous current. In full flow, an amazing site and a humbling and terrifying experience for kayakers who have attempted and failed to cross it. An exhilarating spot on windy days. Look out for the razor-sharp rocks, sculptured by wind, rain and the sea. (G4)

**Mortehoe Museum.** Maritime history, local flora and fauna, farming and country skills.

'Hands on' games and puzzles for children. Tractor and trailer rides in July & Aug, Tu & W. Open East-Oct. except M /F, daily July/Aug. (H4) 01271 870028

**St Mary Magdalene, Mortehoe.** Founded in 1170 by William de Tracey. Superb Norman doorway. 48 magnificent bench ends. (G4)

### TO STAY…TO SLEEP…

**Bull Point Lighthouse.** Built in 1879 to protect shipping from the dangers of Morte Point.

### LIGHT BITES…

**Mor-Shellfish-t-eat, 2 Rockleigh House.** The Huelin family run a Lobster-Crabber boat, The Walrus, out of Ilfracombe, and supply various restaurants in the North Devon area. They have recently opened this café and takeaway, and you won't find fresher lobster or crab anywhere better than this. And, for the beach, they provide Seafood Platters. Open daily East-Sept. (H4) 01271 870633 mortehoefishandchips.co.uk

**Rockleigh Takeaway, Rockleigh House.** It's all cooked on the premises; Thai curry, Moroccan Tagine, Peas mash. Open daily East-Sept at 5.30pm. (H4) 01271 870704.

**1864** Vitifer Mine, near Warren House produces 154 tons of tin, reducing to 22 tons in 1907.

Now an automatic station. 4 self-catering cottages to rent. 01386 597218 (H3) ruralretreats.co.uk

**Town Farmhouse.** Listed building belonging to the National Trust converted into a comfortably furnished and centrally heated B&B close to **Morte Point** and the **Coastal Footpath**. Cream teas in summer. Ample parking. (H4) 01271 870204 thetownfarmhouse.co.uk

**Watersmeet Hotel.** This seaside hotel hangs on a cliff edge overlooking one of Britain's finest beaches (and a family favourite): Combesgate, the Wet Beach. A relaxed, informal atmosphere pervades this bright, colourful boutique hotel. Sea views. Swimming pools. Restaurant (open to non-residents). (G4) 01271 870333 watersmeethotel.co.uk

## WOOLACOMBE

One of the purest beach resorts in the UK, and the World. For the coast is untouched by campsite and bungalow. All about you is National Trust land protecting it from unsavoury development. A busy family holiday village with a two-mile long sandy beach extending to Putsborough Sands. Excellent for swimming, surfing and sandcastles. Invigorating coastal path to Baggy Point (popular with rock climbers) and Ilfracombe. (G5)

## TO STAY...TO SLEEP...

**Woolacombe Bay Hotel.** A family hotel of the old-school run by the Lancaster family for the past 40+ years. Spacious and suitable for children and grandparents of all ages. Squash, tennis and pools. Grounds lead down to beach. Special Autumn and Spring Breaks (2 nights for price of 1). Apartments. (G5) 01271 870388 woolacombe-bay-hotel.co.uk

## TO VISIT...

**Fremington Quay Café.** An exceptionally popular destination café on the Tarka Trail next to the Cycle Hire depot. Coffee, cakes and soups/ lunches featuring exhibitions of this historic quay. Open daily. (K10) 01271 268720

**Marwood Hill Gardens.** A magical 20-acre garden with many rare trees and shrubs. Rock and alpine garden, 3-lakes, large bog garden, famous collection of camellias (largest in country), clematis, Australian plants. Tea Room. Nursery with plant sales. Garden open daily Mar-Sept. (M8) 01271 342528 marwoodhillgarden.co.uk

**Mike Taffinder Woodcrafts, North Buckland.** Wood-framed mirrors and original items crafted from ancient oak by a man with a passion for wood, an eye for the unusual and an eclectic turn of phrase. Best phone before your visit. (J6) 07974 391228 miketaffinderwoodcrafts.com

## LIGHT BITES...

**Beachcomber Café, The Esplanade.** Access through main car park. The view up the beach will provide the heartiest appetite for their burgers, pizzas and stuffed jacket potatoes. (G5) 01271 871644

**Barricane Beach Café.** Sri Lankan curries of varying spiceness (vegan and meat options) served from 5-7pm. Open in summer season, dependent on weather. (G5)

**Meraki Coffee Co, South St.** Tucked away from the holiday hordes a few yards up from the Woolacombe Bay Hotel is this cute café. Open daily from 8.30-3.30 serving breakfast, coffees, hot chocs and vegan options.

**Noel Corston, South St.** This is the Business. If you seek first-rate cuisine from an award-winning chef, look no further. The menus are multi-course, original, seasonal and delicious. Booking essential. (G5) 01271 871187 noelcorston.com

**Red Barn.** With some creative thinking this could be one of the greats. Now under new ownership. One hopes for more imaginative food and cleaner surfaces. However, it will no doubt remain the heart and soul of Woolacombe welcoming surfers and families, alike. Friendly atmosphere, a full range of beers and lagers, and solid food to fill empty tummies but don't expect gastronomic cuisine. Longboards are displayed like Old Masters from the V&A. Live music nights. Open all year. (H5) 01271 870264

**The Porthole, Marine Drive.** It's the location darling! What a truism. Coffee, cakes, bagels, baguettes and sarnis galore. Open daily Apr-Oct, winter closed Tu-Th 07533 33396 theportholewoolacombe.co.uk

## BEACHES...SURFING...

**Rockham Bay.** Sand at low tide. Isolated. Rock pools. Interesting rock formations and wreck remains. 3/4 miles walk from North Morte campsite. (G3)

**Hele Bay.** Shingle and rocks. R/WC/D. (L2)

**Rapparree Cove.** Shingle, sand and rocks. R/D. (L3)

**Lee Bay.** Shingle. Rock pools. A marine biologist's delight. Cut out steps at low tide to **Sandy Cove.** P/WC/Hotel Bistro in summer. (J3)

**Grunta Beach, Mortehoe.** Named after pigs landing. Sand at low tide. Rock pools. Access via coast path. (G4)

**Combesgate, Woolacombe.** New steep steps descend to expansive sandy (wet) beach at low tide. Rock and sand pools. Good surfing with nice peaks at low tide. Protected from north winds. Beware of strong tidal flow/undercurrents. No dogs May-Sept. P on road. (G4)

**Barricane, Woolacombe.** Sand at low tide. Safe family beach. Good for shells and rock pools. Keep an eye out for children. Natural swimming pool at high tide. Asian café (evening meals in summer). Short walk from P. (G4)

**Woolacombe Sands.** Two miles of flat sand. Popular family beach. Water sports all year; surfing, windsurfing, kayaking. Life Savers School. Former Longboard centre - northern end produces Rights at half-tide. Beach casting for bass. R/WC/D/LG/P. (G5)

**Putsborough Sand (Vention).** Superb, flat family beach with spacious sand and dunes. Popular with young families. Water sports. Beach casting for bass. Short walk from P (charge). Dogs allowed on R side. Café/WC/Camping (advised to pre-book). Narrow lanes leading to beach best avoided during bank holidays. (G6)

**Croyde.** Flat sand at LT. Sand dunes and rocks at north and south sides. Surfing for experienced only - can be crowded. Rated as one of England's best beach breaks, especially "Oyster," off Downend. Surf School. R/LG/WC/P. (F7)

**Saunton Sands.** Sand dunes **(Braunton Burrows)**, rocks, water sports, bracing walks. Surf popular with longboarders and beginners - slow breaks. At extreme low tides it's possible to see rock forms that came down from Scotland in the Ice Age. Sands Café Bar/LG/Surf Survival Club/Board hire/P. (G8)

## SAUNTON SURF SCHOOLS...

**Surf South West.** Surf school on Croyde Bay and Saunton Sands. Surf lessons, surf courses and surf holidays. Normal sessions 10.30-12.30 and 1.30-3.30. Open daily mid-Mar to mid-Nov. (F7)
01271 890400
surfsouthwest.com

**Walking On Waves.** Sarah Whiteley's school is based at Saunton Sands and holds individual, group, SUP and family lessons. BSA registered. Also, glamping/luxury camping, bell tent & surf lodge available. (G8)
07496 188692
walkingonwaves.co.uk

## CROYDE SURF SCHOOLS...

**Surfing Croyde Bay, 8 Hobbs Hill.** Courses for all abilities, from two hours, equipment supplied; wetsuits etc. Coasteering. (F7) 01271 891200
surfingcroydebay.co.uk

## COASTAL FOOTPATH...

**Combe Martin to Ilfracombe** (5 miles). Much of this section inevitably follows the main road, but there are interesting diversions around Napps Hill, Widmouth Heath and Rillage Point, and a final climb over Hillsborough with its prehistoric fort and fine views.

**Ilfracombe to Woolacombe** (8 miles). The path ascends through Torrs Walk and continues along an easy level track and down to the village of Lee. From here the going becomes more difficult, keeping close to the cliff edge past Bull Point Lighthouse, and to the promontory of Morte Point, notorious for its wrecks

1872    Kelly College, Tavistock founded by Admiral Kelly.

1869    Closure of the Grand Western Canal.

- then past the shell beach of Barricane and down to the wider sands of Woolacombe.

## Woolacombe to Braunton

(12 miles). From Woolacombe the path traverses 2 miles of sand dunes, though some may prefer the easier going along the beach. From Vention the path rounds Baggy Point, famed for rock climbing and sea birds, and descends to the main road as far as Saunton. From here the path crosses Braunton Burrows Nature Reserve along the Tarka Trail towards Crow Point, then strikes north east beside the estuary to Velator, and follows the old railway line to Barnstaple which has been renamed as the Tarka Trail. It's now possible to follow the Tarka Trail on foot, or by bicycle all the way to Bideford without the encumbrance of the motorcar.

## LUNDY ISLAND (NT)

A romantic and historic island, and one-time fortress and home to pirates. A place of great contrast and beauty, it lies nineteen miles west of Morte Point.

Just three miles long and half a mile wide. Lundy's western cliffs, popular with rock climbers, rise to 400 ft (the Devil's Slide is ever-popular), whilst in the east there are small valleys filled with woodland, bracken, rhododendrons and hydrangeas. The footpath running between these shrubs can be difficult, and it is easy to trip up over their roots. So beware. Soft walking boots or trainers are advised. The small community includes a Victorian church, a pub - the Marisco Tavern, the Marisco Castle and two lighthouses plus a shop. Campsite for 40 people and 23 self-catering properties (landmarktrust.org. uk).A short break or holiday here will contrast sharply with your average city lifestyle. The peace and solitude, the exposure to weather and the lack of cars apart from the farmer's Land Rover will appeal to many. It may take a day or two to get used to the slow pace of life.

Those who find it difficult to adjust may gravitate to the Marisco Tavern. A splendid place; great jollity and friendships to be made here. The home made pies and fine ales are difficult to refuse. Not a bad place to be stuck in foul weather. A return trip on the Oldenburg in a Force 6 is not to be recommended.

Basking sharks can be seen during the months, July to September, puffins May to mid July, and seals all the year, and the best places to see them: Landing Bay, Frenchman's Landing, Gannets Bay, Rat Island and the North End, or always away from rough water.

Visitors can take a day trip aboard the MS Oldenburg from Bideford, or Ilfracombe. Herewith some telephone numbers detailing more information. Sailings: 01237 470422, and accommodation from the Landmark Trust: 01628 825925, or call Lundy on: 01237 431831. Lundy Booking Office: 01271 863636. lundyisland.co.uk

*Woolacombe Bay*

1870s    Plymouth becomes a great liner port with over 500 visits per year.

181

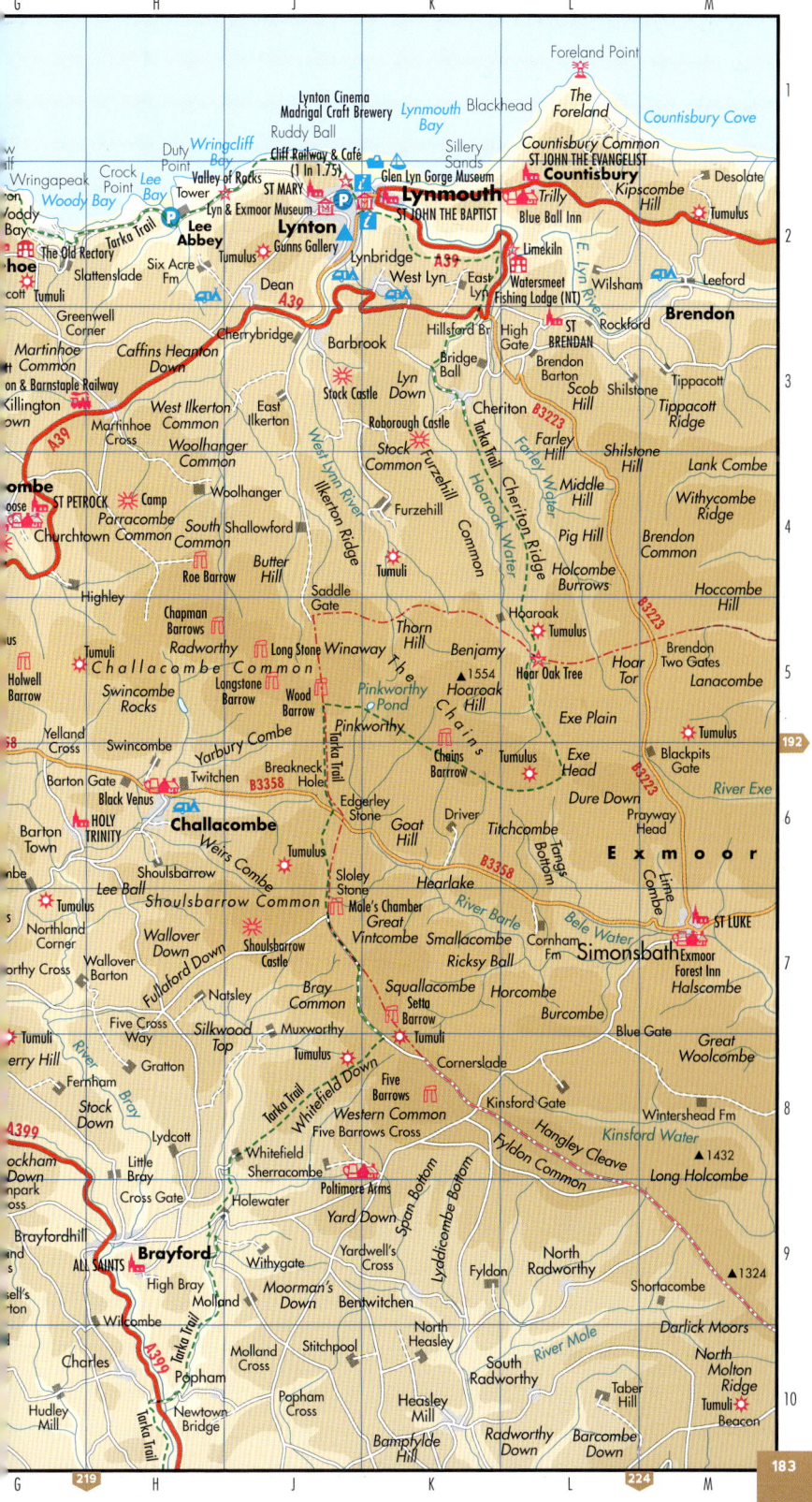

## BARNSTAPLE

The principal town (and former port) of North Devon is undergoing a transformation from sleepy market town to busy route centre. A controversial development on Shapland's warehousing site beside the River Taw has caused grief to many, and the new bridge crossing from Sticklepath to Pottington has eased the bottleneck of traffic. C16 bridge, crook-spired church. Pannier Market (Friday farmer's market). Queen Anne's Walk (C16 colonnaded arcade). Guildhall. Remains of Castle beside Market car park. Cinema. Fair in Sept. Guided Town walks from Museum/TIC. Tarka Tennis & Leisure Centre. E/C W. (B10)

## TO VISIT...

**Butcher's Row & Pannier Market.** No visit to Barnstaple can be made without stepping into the Pannier Market. All sorts of odds and sods on sale, and over the road, Butcher's Row, selling a medley of cheeses, meat, fish and bread. Café. (B10)

**The Museum of Barnstaple and North Devon, The Square.** Victorian gothic building houses this fascinating local museum; history, geology, archaeology, local pottery and the Regimental Collection of the Royal Devon Yeomanry. Tarka Gallery. Undersea World. Teas. Open all year M-Sa 9.30-5. (B10) 01271 346747 barnstaplemuseum.org.uk

## EAT...DRINK...

**Maiden Arch by Robert Bryant, 14 Maiden St**. Rob's a young chef going places and is knocking out succulent dishes galore for Barnstaple's foodies. Seek out his Signatory, Exmoor or Vegetarian Taster options. Lunch from 12.30, Dinner

## LIGHT BITES...

Head for **The Strand** overlooking the River Tamar and beside the Tarka Trail is **Tea By The Taw**. A vintage tea room with an extensive menu. Breakfasts, lunch and tea parties. Popular with families of cyclists. Licensed. (B10) 01271 370032.

The best coffee is at **Artisarni** opposite the Pannier Market on Butchers Row. On the same street is **South West Cheese** for a multiple choice, a little along **East & West Bakery** for sumptuous breads. They also own **Fields Farm Shop & Butchery** on Cross Street where you can stock up for the beach, coast path or a family shop. An alternative is the **Boston Tea Party** overlooking the Market car park. The coffee and cakes, and all-day breakfasts are top notch. Beware of the sinking seats!

*Barnstaple in Winter*

from 6.30. (B10) 01271 523774
maidenarch.co.uk

Near by, the brilliant curry house, **Everest Gurkha Chef** serving authentic Nepalese and Indian dishes. Winners of the prestigious British Curry award. Takeaways, too. 01271 376863
everestgurkha.co.uk

### BERRYNARBOR

A beautiful, ancient village with a history going back to the Bronze Age. The Domesday Book (1085) listed four other manors in the vicinity. St Peter's church, Ye Olde Globe Inn (improving) and tea rooms to visit. A web of footpaths and walks connects the village; see Community Shop and Post Office for details. (B3)
berrynarborvillage.org

### COMBE MARTIN

A long, straggling village bordered by some of the most beautiful countryside in England; rich, undulating pastures that lead down to a small harbour, and beach. Nearby, Trentishoe Downs and the Heddon Valley, and beyond, the wild combes of Exmoor. Former silver mining centre. Fine Parish Church of St Peter ad Vincula. Wildlife Park and Dinosaur Park up the hill, south of the village. Curious C18 inn; 'Pack of Cards'. Aug carnival. E/C W. (C3)

### TO VISIT...

**Combe Martin Museum & Information Point. Cross St.** Illustrates old village industries; silver mining, lime burning, agriculture on three floors. Open as locally advertised. (C3) 01271 889031
combemartinmuseum.co.uk

**St Peter Ad Vincula, Combe Martin.** A magnificent Perpendicular church with fine C12 medieval Tower decorated with pinnacled battlements and a superb collection of gargoyles. It stands at over 100 ft and was built from the wealth of the silver industry. A typical Devon wagon roof, carved English rood screen, medieval

*Barnstaple's New Bridge*

**1874** United Services College founded at Westward Ho! Alma Mater to Rudyard Kipling (and appears in Stalky & Co).

**185**

*Cloudy Waterfalls, East Lyn River*

windows, C14 paintings on the wainscotting and C15 font. Sunday services. (C3)

**Watermouth Family Theme Park & Castle.** C19 castellated house with the accent on family entertainment; mechanical music, 'Granny Kitchen'. Explore the Dungeon Labyrinths and Adventure Land. Open daily Apr-Oct. (A2) 01271 867474
watermouthcastle.com

**Wildlife & Dinosaur Park.** Set in 28 acres of a Sub-tropical paradise. Home to Snow Leopards, Timber Wolves, Sea Lions, Primates and Meerkats, to name a few. Of special interest for children are the many dinosaurs, some are animated and appear to be alive! Open daily Apr to end Oct. (D4) 01271 882486
cmwdp.co.uk

**LYNTON & LYNMOUTH**
Twin villages in a spectacular setting; Lynton on its cliff edge overhangs the small port of Lynmouth. The two are linked by a steep, wooded hill connected by footpath, road and funicular railway powered by water tanks. The rivers East

and West Lyn fall rapidly to the sea through picturesque wooded gorges.

On the night of the 15th August, 1952 a freak cloudburst on Exmoor turned the East and West Lyn rivers into raging torrents destroying all that lay before them; 31 died, 93 houses were destroyed, power lines, bridges, cars and caravans were swept into the sea (similar to Boscastle's recent tragedy). Amazingly the Rhenish Tower c.1860 overlooking the harbour survived.

The area is proud of its literary connections; Percy Bysshe Shelley honeymooned here in 1812, and Samuel Taylor Coleridge conceived the idea of "The Ancient Mariner" whilst on a walking tour with Dorothy and William Wordsworth.

These valleys, and the surrounding country provided the setting for Blackmore's Lorna Doone. Popular walking centre with easy, waymarked trails up to Watersmeet and Countisbury Hill. The steep, coastal road up to Countisbury, and on to Minehead, which overlooks the Bristol Channel

and South Wales, is not to be missed and is arguably one of the most scenic drives in England. (J2)

## TO VISIT…

**Cliff Railway.** Built by the publisher of the Strand Magazine, Sir George Newnes. He wanted to create a little Switzerland, an Alpine-style village in North Devon. This Victorian invention is operated by water ballast tanks and it connects the two villages. You can't visit these two villages without a ride on this extraordinary contraption. Superb sea views and woodland walks. Clifftop Café. Open mid-Feb to early Nov from 10. (J2) 01598 753486
cliffrailwaylynton.co.uk

**Exmoor Coast Boat Trips**. Daily trips from the Quay depending on the tide; to Woody Bay, Valley of Rocks and Lee Abbey. Also, Mackerel drift fishing. (K2) 01598 753207

**Glen Lyn Gorge**. Dramatic ravine that carried much of the flood water during the 1952 disaster. Hydro-Electric plant and exhibition on water-power; Britain's first tidal current turbine. Open daily East-Oct 10-5 (-6 July/Aug). (K2) 01598 753207 theglenlyngorge.co.uk

**Lee Abbey.** Christian Centre for holidays, retreats and conferences. The house was built in 1859 and stands on the site of the old Manor of the de Wichelhalse family. A small natural history museum is open displaying the work of Ursula Kay. There's an Honesty Box toll on the road through the estate leading to the picturesque coastal road to Woody Bay. leeabbey.org.uk

**Lee Abbey Nature Trail**. Passes through the private estate down a wooded valley to cliff girt beaches with rock pools. (H2)

**Lyn & Exmoor Museum, Market Street**. Herewith, the oldest surviving domestic house in Lynton displaying old Exmoor crafts, implements and a way of life. Open East-Oct Tu W Th & Sa 10.30-1.30, 2-5. Su 2-5. (J2) 01598 752225

**Lynton Cinema**. An independent and award-winning cinema adds the personal touch to this art form. (J2) 01598 753397 lyntoncinema.co.uk

**Madrigal Craft Brewery, Lynmouth Manor, Countisbury Hill.** Hear ye, all scholars of yeast and fine ales will be tempted to make a judicious path to this haven of liquid fare. Tours (book) are second W & Saturday every month at 12-6pm. (K2) 07857 560677 madrigalbrewery.co.uk

**Middleham Gardens**. On the site of cottages washed away in the 1952 Flood. A Memorial with a rose and fuchsia garden, Californian redwoods and evergreen oaks. Albeit, somewhat overgrown, but charming. Open daily, all year. (K2)

**Polly Skye Gallery, Castle Hill, Lynton.** If it's colour, form and style you're after then Polly has an artwork for you. Paintings, ceramics, glassware and jewellery all breathe colour and life in this airy gallery with its friendly artist-owner. Open daily. (J2) 01598 753452 pollyskye.co.uk

**Tim Williams Fine Art, 1 Castle Hill.** Acquisitions, Collections and Investments in Fine Art embolden this gallery. Open Tu-Sa 11-5. (J2) 01598 741319 timwilliamnsfine art.com

**Toy Museum & Shop, 29A Lee Rd.** Enthusiasm and a passion for childhood dreams, the toys of one's 1970/80s youth is jam packed here. Open daily.(J2) 01598 752096 lyntontoymuseum.co.uk

**Valley of Rocks.** A place of legend and dramatic scenery tempered by a micro-climate of swirling mists and brazen winds. The geologist will tell you it's a rock-strewn elevated valley created in the Ice Age, a mere collection of massive sandstone outcrops inhabited by Cheviot goats imported from Northumberland. They have become quite an attraction and a talking point in the local press when yet another tourist has her handbag snatched. A great place to scramble on the rocks, the more refined walker will follow the coastal path. Below the rocks, nestling in a bowl, a Cricket Ground, and just along the road, **Mother Meldrum's Tea Gardens** open for brunch, light lunches and cream teas in season. (H2)

**Watersmeet Fishing Lodge (NT)**. Built in 1832 and set in a picturesque valley at the confluence of the East Lyn and Hoar Oak Water. Focal point for many lovely walks. NT shop and tearoom. Open daily mid-March to Oct 10.30-dusk. (L2) 01598 753348

**Watersmeet (NT)**. Five miles of wooded valleys of

---

**LYNTON LIGHT BITES...**

There is no end of choice. My favourite is **Charlie Friday's Coffee Shop**, at the bottom of **Church Steps**. It's fun and friendly for humans (and dogs), and the coffee/hot choc is made with gusto. The decor is all-colour and a little crazy. Open daily from 9. 01598 752032

**Nartnapa Thai Kitchen@The Cottage Inn, Lynbridge**. The locals love the fusion of Thai food, homage to Buddha and the choice of English ales and ciders. 01598 753496 nartnapa.co.uk

**LYNMOUTH LIGHT BITES...**

You are here for the sea (and countryside), and sea views so there is only one choice. **The Pavilion Café** above the **National Park Centre**. A full range of food on offer: breakfasts, burgers, salads, toasties, quiches, vegan and home-made cakes. But, it's the view, darling. Impressive, for you can watch surfers at play through the massive window. Open daily 10-5.

---

**1884** John Babbacombe Lee unsuccessfully hanged three times for the murder of Mrs Keyes.

187

*Valley of Rocks path*

the East Lyn River and its tributary, the Hoar Oak. A spectacular landscape of fast-flowing rivers, ancient woodland and steep-sided hillsides. Waymarked trails with two fine high-level walks up Myrtleberry Cleave and Lyn Cleave (easiest ascent from Hillsford Bridge). Easy riverside walk up from Lynmouth. All dog walkers (and those wearing shorts) beware of tics! (L2) nationaltrust.org.uk

**Woody Bay**. Worth the steep descent off the coastpath to this glorious pebbled (slippery) beach with waterfall and tidal pool. Lime kiln and remains of pier storm damaged in 1902, the dream of bankrupted entrepreneur, Benjamin Lake. (G2)

**Lynton & Barnstaple Railway.** Train rides along the first mile re-opened of Former Woody Bay Station, closed in 1935. Open daily Apr-Oct 11-4, W/Es & Su in winter. Steam W/Es, Sch Hols & Christmas.

(G3) 01598 763487
lynton-rail.co.uk

### EAT...DRINK...

**The Old Bank, Church Steps.** Herewith, an ensemble of enthusiastic youth serving nourishing and creative dishes. The ambience is cosy and friendly. All ingredients for success, no less. (J2)
01598 751487
theoldbanklynton.co.uk

### SLEEP...

**Chough's Nest B&B, North Walk.** Well placed for coastal and country walks. A charming hotel with seven comfortable bedrooms providing fine sea views. WIFI. (J2) 01598 753315
choughsnesthotel.co.uk

**Highcliffe House, Sinai Hill.** This is a new, enthusiastic venture. A classy B&B affording spectacular views of the coast. Stylish beds with intricately carved headboards. No children or dogs. (J2)
01598 752235
highcliffehouse.co.uk

#### SIMONSBATH
Situated in the very heart of Exmoor in a sheltered valley beside the River Barle. Popular angling and walking centre.
**Exmoor Forest Inn** to assuage your thirst following a walk beside the River Barle to Cow Castle. Free parking. (M7)

### TO VISIT...

**Foreland Point, Countisbury & Watersmeet**. 13,000 acres of National Trust land, including the East Lyn River up to Rockford Bridge, and several miles of coast and cliffs to the east of Lynmouth. Many footpaths (details from excellent National Trust leaflets). Foreland Point Lighthouse is open weekday afternoons. Footpaths ascend to Watersmeet from Lynmouth and continue in many directions. (L1)

**Great Hangman.** Imposing hill rising to 1044 feet which drops precipitously to the sea. An impressive coastal landmark. Remote place inhabited by skylark, wheatear, raven and stonechat. On coastal footpath. Named after a sheep rustler who mistakenly hanged himself. (D2)

**Heddon Valley and Mouth**. A beautiful, thickly wooded valley sided by steep hillsides. Arguably one of the most enchanting valleys in England. A path leads from behind the right side of the Inn down a tricky slope to the riverbank and follows the river to Heddon Mouth, a rock strewn beach with a massive old limekiln. The river is only fordable in dry months. The valley has numerous walks in all directions. National Trust shop opposite car park.

**Hoar Oak Tree**. Ancient boundary mark of Exmoor Forest. The present tree was planted in 1917, and is the third in more than three centuries. To reach it, follow the wall westwards from Brendon Two Gates for two miles across rough country. (L5)

**Kevin Green Pottery, Parracombe**. A simplicity of style, individual pieces in stoneware often with unique motifs set Kevin's work apart. Open daily. 01598 763516 (G4) kevingreenpottery.co.uk

**River Barle.** The source begins in the north-west corner of Exmoor beside the man-made Pinkworthy Pond. The Barle winds a diagonal course in a south-easterly direction meeting the River Exe just to the north of Exebridge. A walk beside this river provides a key insight into the magic of Exmoor. (K5)

**Rockford Bridge**. Popular beauty spot on the East Lyn River. (L3)

**Shoulsbarrow Castle**. Iron Age fort on remote moorland. (J7)

**The Chains**. Central area of Exmoor; the source of the rivers Barle, Exe and West Lyn. Remote, desolate and waterlogged. (K5)

**Trentishoe**. A strategic hamlet with farmstead, church and mill overlooking the Heddon Valley. The church mainly dates from 1861, yet there's documentary evidence of Rectors back to 1260! Worth a detour.

**Wistlandpound Reservoir**. Fishing available for natural brown trout and larger rainbows. Season 15 Mar - 12 Oct. Permits from Post Office, Challacombe, The Kingfisher, Barnstaple and Fishing Tackle, Combe Martin. (F6)

## EAT...DRINK...SLEEP...

**Kentisbury Grange**. A Victorian manor house combining country house style with over-the-top luxurious bedrooms. The Coach House restaurant was once a talking point amongst North Devon folk given its opulence and unusual, bling, style. (E5) 01271 882295 kentisburygrange.co.uk

**The Old Rectory Hotel, Martinhoe**. Small C19 Country House hotel set in 3-acres of mature, tranquil gardens. Rooms are cosy and tastefully furnished. Romantic candlelit dinners from local organic produce. In superb walking country. No children under 14. No dogs. Closed Nov to end March. (G2) 01598 763368 oldrectoryhotel.co.uk

## PUBS SERVING FOOD...

**Blue Ball Inn, Countisbury**. In spectacular position with stupendous views to be gained in summer from their outside seating area. Log fires, comfy sofas and a changing selection of dishes. Real Ales. Friendly towards walkers and their dogs. B&B. Start off point for many circular walks. (L2) 01598 741263 blueballinn.com

**Fox & Goose, Parracombe**. Fresh fish in season supplied by local boats, and on the menu the day I visited; bass, fish stew, tiger prawns, red mullet fillets, and game in season.... all the walls are covered in bric-a-brac; lobster pots, badger and fox heads, hunting prints and paraphernalia. A good time feel factor. Local Exmoor brews. Foremost, a dining pub rather than a local inn. B&B. (G4) 01598 7633239 foxandgooseinnexmoor.co.uk

**Hunters Inn, Heddon Valley**. An imposing, Swiss-style, hostelry that is at last being decorated toward the original is set in a valley of great beauty. Heddon Valley is a centre for walking and riding. Home cooked, seasonal fare, and real ales. B&B. Open daily. (F2) 01598 763230 thehuntersinnexmoor.co.uk

**Poltimore Arms, Yarde Down**. Isolated little country pub popular with Exmoor folk. Serves real ales and pub-grub at a fair price. Opens for breakfast at 7am. Beer garden and dogs welcome. Village shop & gallery, next door. (J9) 01598 710381 poltimorearms.co.uk

**Pyne Arms, East Down.** This is a cracking little pub with 3-cracking new bedrooms providing first-rate food. Their Sunday Lunches are the talk of Devonshire and beyond. Husband and wife team, Ellis (chef) and Amie (front of house

1890    Lynton-Lynmouth Cliff Railway opened by Sir George Newnes.

189

and pastry chef), are a great team. Well located for Exmoor, the North Devon beaches and Hartland. 01271 850055 (C6) pynearms.co.uk

**The Exmoor Forest Inn, Simonsbath**. Hostelry caters for walkers and fishermen who may well have flogged the Barle all day, and are in dire need of sustenance. Restaurant/pub food uses local produce. B&B. Dog friendly. (M7) 01643 831341 exmoorforestinn.com

## TO VISIT…

**Arlington Court & The National Trust Carriage Museum (NT)**. Elegant house built in 1822 by Thomas Lee. Home of the Chichester family; the present contents consist largely of the collections of Rosalie Chichester (aunt of Sir Francis), who died in 1949. Fascinating medley of objets d'art, model ships, pewter, costumes and furniture. Watercolours by William Blake. Costume displays. Famous collection of horse carriages (rides available), including Queen Victoria's pony bath chair. Victorian formal garden. Extensive park and nature trail. Garden open daily mid-march to Oct & BHs 10.30-5 (House 11-5) except Sa. Footpaths through park and woodland open all year. NT shop and licensed restaurant. (D6) 01271 850296 nationaltrust.org.uk

**Arlington Court.** Two-mile nature trail through the park. Lakeside and woodland scenery, Shetland ponies, Jacob's sheep, botanical and ornithological interest. Buzzards and ravens. Heronry and bird hide. Open daily 11-6. Small admission charge to Park. (D6) 01271 850296

**Blakewell Fishery**. Trout fishery. Family fun, catch your own trout. Farm shop, tackle room, ornamental fish and water garden. Tea Room/ Café - open 11-5, East/May until September. Fishery and Visitor Centre open daily 9-5. (A8) 01271 344533 blakewell.co.uk

**Broomhill Estate, Muddiford**. One of the great attractions of North Devon: Sculpture Gardens with 300 sculptures, set in 10-acres of gardens in a most glorious valley, an Art Hotel, Restaurant and Zen Room (treatments and massage). Garden open daily July-Sept 9-9, Oct-June 10-5. (B8) 01271 850262 broomhill-estate.com

**Chapman Barrows**. Eleven Bronze Age burial mounds on Challacombe Common. Fine views towards North Devon. (H5

**Exmoor Zoological Park**. Over 12-acres of landscaped gardens on the edge of the National Park with mammals, exotic birds and the Exmoor Beast, a black leopard! Open daily; summer 10-6, winter 10-4. (F6) 01598 763352 exmoorzoo.co.uk

## SHORT WALKS ON EXMOOR…

1. **Lynmouth** to **Countisbury** and **Foreland Point Lighthouse**. (H1)

*Outside Combe Martin*

2. **Lynmouth** to **Watersmeet** via **Lyn Cleave and Myrtleberry Cleave**. (H1)

3. **Watersmeet** to **Rockford Bridge** beside the **East Lyn River**. (H1)

4. **Arlington Court Nature Trail**. (D6)

## BEACHES...

**Lynmouth**. Shingle, sand and rocks. Boating pool. Breaks for experienced surfers only. R/WC/D. (K1)

**Lee Abbey**. Sand and rocks. Short walk from P/R/WC. Toll. (H2)

**Combe Martin**. Pebbles, rocks and pools. Some sand at LT. Boating pool. R/WC/D. (B3)

**Watermouth Castle**. Protected inlet popular for mooring light craft. Sand at LT/P. (A2)

**Two Moors Way.** This is a Long Distance footpath, although not officially designated as one, which runs from Lynton to Ivybridge, linking the Exmoor and Dartmoor National Parks. The Way makes use of footpaths, bridleways and public roads. From Lynton to Watersmeet then southwards along the Cheriton Ridge to Hoar Oak Tree and Exe Head, crossing the B3358 at Cornham Farm. Then striking south-east to meet the River Barle below Pickedstones Farm. Cross country to Withypool, the Way proceeds down-stream beside the Barle to Tarr Steps. Then south towards West Anstey.

## COASTAL FOOTPATH...

**County Gate to Lynmouth.** (8 miles). Follow the path back to Glenthorne House where it continues along the coast towards Foreland Point, above some of the highest cliffs in England. After a steep climb to Countisbury Common there are two alternative routes; one following the coast, with fine seaviews towards Lynmouth, and the longer route crossing over to the wooded valley of the East Lyn.

**Lynmouth to Combe Martin** (13 Miles) The path starts with the beautiful North Walk leading to the Valley of the Rocks. From here to Woody Bay the route runs along a minor road, but there is an alternative way through the woods higher up. From Woody Bay the path follows a level elevated track with fine views, then descends to the River Heddon and zig-zags its way up Heddon Mouth Cleave. The path ascends to Trentishoe Down and follows a course over open grassland, culminating in the ascent of Great Hangman and the final descent past Little Hangman into Combe Martin.

*White Cottage, Woody Bay*

1892    Aug 15. Torquay granted royal charter for incorporation as a municipal borough.

191

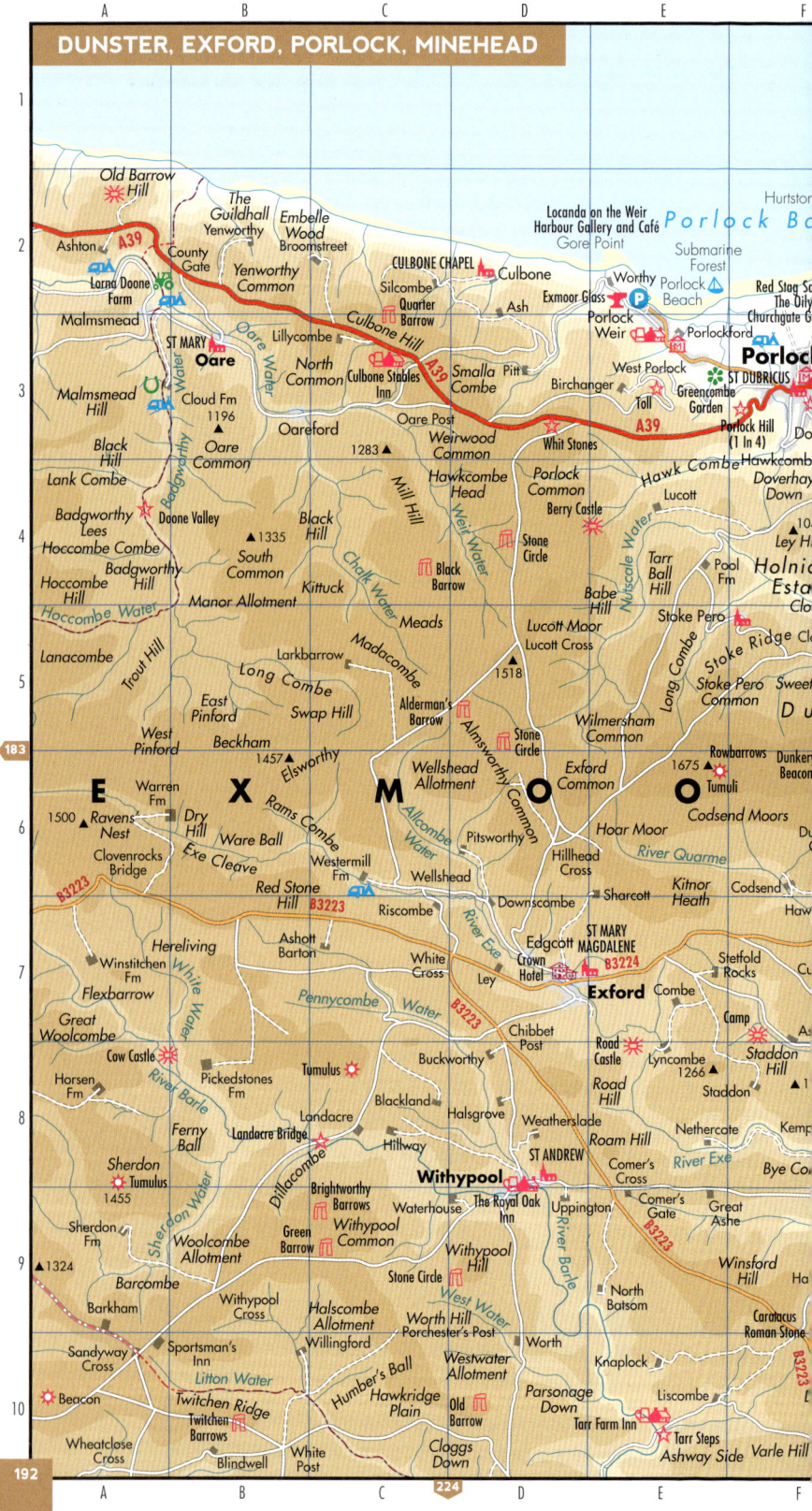

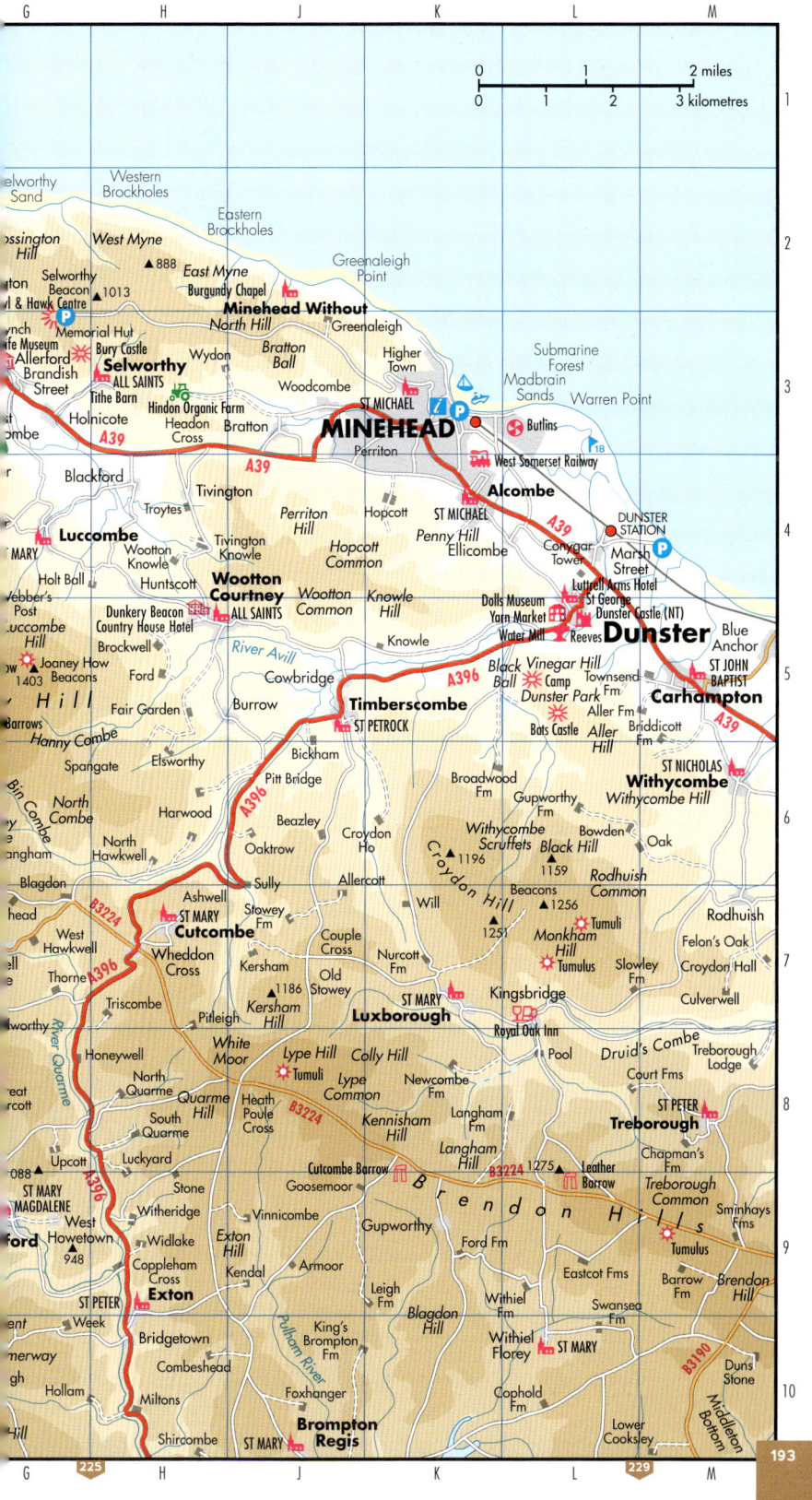

This map page shows an area of Somerset, England including the following places:

**Grid references top:** G H J K L M

**Grid references bottom:** G H J K L M

Scale: 0 to 2 miles / 0 to 3 kilometres

- elworthy Sand
- Western Brockholes
- Eastern Brockholes
- ssington Hill
- West Myne
- Greenaleigh Point
- Submarine Forest
- Madbrain Sands
- Warren Point
- 888 East Myne
- Selworthy Beacon 1013
- Burgundy Chapel
- Minehead Without
- North Hill
- Greenaleigh
- Higher Town
- Memorial Hut
- & Hawk Centre
- Bury Castle
- fe Museum
- Allerford
- Brandish Street
- Selworthy
- ALL SAINTS
- Tithe Barn
- Wydon
- Bratton Ball
- Woodcombe
- ST MICHAEL
- **MINEHEAD**
- Butlins
- West Somerset Railway
- Holnicote
- Hindon Organic Farm
- Headon Cross
- Bratton
- Perriton
- **Alcombe**
- A39
- Blackford
- Tivington
- Troytes
- Perriton Hill
- Hopcott
- ST MICHAEL
- Penny Hill
- DUNSTER STATION
- **Luccombe**
- Wootton Knowle
- Tivington Knowle
- Hopcott Common
- Ellicombe
- Conygar Tower
- Marsh Street
- MARY
- Holt Ball
- Huntscott
- **Wootton Courtney**
- ALL SAINTS
- Wootton Common
- Knowle Hill
- Dolls Museum
- Yarn Market
- Water Mill
- St George
- Dunster Castle (NT)
- **Dunster**
- Blue Anchor
- ebber's Post
- Dunkery Beacon Country House Hotel
- uccombe Hill
- Brockwell
- Ford
- Cowbridge
- River Avill
- Knowle
- Reeves
- ST JOHN BAPTIST
- Joaney How
- 1403 Beacons
- HILL
- Fair Garden
- Burrow
- **Timberscombe**
- ST PETROCK
- Black Vinegar Hill
- Black Ball
- Camp
- Dunster Park
- Townsend
- Aller Farm
- **Carhampton**
- A39
- arrows
- Hanny Combe
- Bickham
- Bats Castle
- Aller Hill
- Briddicott Fm
- ST NICHOLAS
- Bin Combe
- Spangate
- Elsworthy
- Pitt Bridge
- Broadwood Fm
- Gupworthy
- **Withycombe**
- Withycombe Hill
- ye
- North Combe
- Harwood
- Beazley
- Croydon Ho
- Withycombe Scruffets
- Bowden
- Black Hill 1159
- Oak
- angham
- North Hawkwell
- Oaktrow
- Croydon Hill 1196
- Rodhuish Common
- Blagdon
- Sully
- Allercott
- Will
- Beacons 1256
- Rodhuish
- head
- West Hawkwell
- Ashwell
- ST MARY
- Stowey Fm
- 1251
- Tumuli
- Monkham Hill
- Felon's Oak
- **Cutcombe**
- Wheddon Cross
- Kersham
- Couple Cross
- Nurcott Fm
- Tumulus
- Slowley Fm
- Croydon Hall
- Thorne
- A396
- Triscombe
- Pitleigh
- Kersham Hill 1186
- Old Stowey
- ST MARY
- **Luxborough**
- Kingsbridge
- Culverwell
- worthy
- River Quarme
- Honeywell
- White Moor
- Lype Hill
- Colly Hill
- Pool
- Royal Oak Inn
- Druid's Combe
- Treborough Lodge
- reat rcott
- North Quarme
- Tumuli
- Lype Common
- Newcombe Fm
- Court Fms
- ST PETER
- **Treborough**
- 088
- South Quarme
- Quarme Hill
- Heath Poult Cross
- B3224
- Kennisham Hill
- Langham Fm
- Chapman's Fm
- Upcott
- Luckyard
- Langham Hill
- Treborough Common
- Sminhays Fms
- ST MARY MAGDALENE
- West Howetown 948
- Stone
- Witheridge
- Vinnicombe
- Cutcombe Barrow
- Goosemoor
- Gupworthy
- Brendon Hills
- B3224 1275
- Leather Barrow
- Tumulus
- Brendon Hill
- ford
- A396
- Coppleham Cross
- Widlake
- Exton Hill
- Armoor
- Ford Fm
- Eastcot Fms
- Barrow Fm
- B3190
- **Exton**
- Kendal
- Leigh Fm
- Withiel Fm
- Swansea Fm
- Dun's Stone
- ST PETER
- Week
- King's Brompton Fm
- Blagdon Hill
- Withiel Florey
- ST MARY
- Middleton Bottom
- merway
- gh
- Bridgetown
- Cophold Fm
- Hollam
- Combeshead
- Foxhanger
- **Brompton Regis**
- Lower Cooksley
- ill
- Miltons
- Shircombe
- ST MARY

Road numbers: A39, A396, B3224, B3190, 225, 229

**193**

### Dunster

Arguably the most picturesque of Exmoor villages overlooked and dominated by the Castle. You can park on the north and south end of the village or on the High Street next to the C17 Yarn Market. Do explore on foot and visit the Gallox bridge, the Water Mill and admire some of the 200 listed buildings. The beautiful Parish Church is quite outstanding. Always a popular centre from which to explore Exmoor and the coast. Hobby Horse Dance, 1st May. It is becoming a centre for fine cuisine and there are a number of tearooms. Waymarked circular walks lead off into Vinegar Hill, to Bat's Castle, but the more adventurous climb up Knowle Hill which can on a clear day provide expansive views. (L5)

#### TO VISIT…

**Conygar Tower**. A rich man's folly built in 1775 rises to 59ft. It can be walked to through woodland from the Castle in 1.5 mile circuit. (L5)

**Dunster Castle (NT)**. Imposing C13 building with many additions through the years, and major remodelling from 1868-72. Home of the Luttrell family for 600 years. Notable staircase, ceilings, family portraits and stables. Terrace walk with sub-tropical plants. Garden and park open daily Feb-December, from 11 to dusk. Castle open Mar-31 Oct daily 11-5, Dec W/Es 11-4. (L5) 01643 821314
nationaltrust.org.uk

**Dunster Museum & Doll Collection, 17 High St**. Home to over 900 dolls from all over the world. Open daily Easter to Oct 11-3. (L4) 01643 821493
dunstermuseum.co.uk

---

#### LIGHT BITES…AND MORE…

If you have entered from the A39 and are in dire need of coffee, tea and cakes or more, the **Luttrell Arms Hotel** will furnish your needs. Enter via a glass door into a haven of wood panelling, pargetting, log fires and ancient beams. Open all day for food.

Perhaps, after a walk around the village you will have passed the Church and entered West Street. On your right is **Chapel House**, a craft shop and tea room. Comfy chairs and a warm welcome will usher you in to stay to sample their home made cakes and west country cheeses. 01643 822343

A few doors down, **Hathaways**, an Italian restaurant recommended by their peers. All is cooked to order; fish (in season), meat and vegetarian dishes for dinner. 01643 821725
hathawaysofdunster.com

**Reeves, 20-22 High St**. This has gained a well deserved reputation. Cosy and intimate, with a flair for interior design, the food is prepared by Justin who trained in Oxford and at country house hotels in the Cotswolds. Open Tu-Sa for dinner, and lunch weekends 12-2pm. (L5) 01643 821414
reevesrestaurantdunster.co.uk

---

**Dunster Working Waterwheel (NT), Mill Lane**. This is a fully operational C18 mill, a rare example of a double-overshot mill. Oats and stoneground flour produced, and on sale. Riverside tearoom. Open daily Mar-Oct 10-5. (L5)

**Parish Church of St George**. Priory church built in the C14 shared by the monks and parishioners. Bell tower is open on Th evenings during bell ringing practice. (L4)

#### EAT…DRINK… SLEEP……

**The Luttrell Arms Hotel**. Small, C15 hotel used in medieval times as a guesthouse for the Abbots of Cleeve. You can enter via a stylish glass door from where you can sink into a comfortable armchair and relax, unwind and enjoy the log fires and all-day bar snacks or the more formal restaurant with al fresco dining. Or later fall into a 4-poster bed. (L5) 01643 821555
luttrellarms.co.uk

### Minehead

Seaside resort on the Bristol Channel developed in the C19 from an old fishing port sheltered by high cliffs to the west. The sandy beach is extensive at low tide but the grey Bristol Channel does not invite a leisurely bathe, better to drive west to Woolacombe. The town has some fine Georgian houses and the picturesque Old Town with its fine C14 church is not to be missed. The town's situation makes for a convenient centre from which to explore Exmoor, the Quantocks and Brendon Hills. It is possible to walk up to North Hill through the Old Town, and onto Selworthy via the coastal footpath. On May 1st, the Minehead Sailors' Hobby Horse parades through the streets in commemoration of a phantom wreck that

**1896**   New county boundary adds the villages of Stockland, Chardstock and Hawkchurch to Devon.

*Porlock Weir*

entered the harbour without Captain or crew, and has done so for years. (J3)

## TO VISIT…

**Butlins Minehead, Seafront.** Sub-Tropical sunsplash waterworld; funfair, family fun and daytime entertainment, Odeon cinema and bowling alley. Quite an experience now with New Style Chalets! Open daily. (L3) 0330 100 6648
butlins.com

**West Somerset Railway.** One of the major railway preservation schemes - 20 miles from Bishops Lydeard to Minehead. Trains (steam but sometimes diesel) run daily May-Oct, and some days in April. Connecting buses between Bishops Lydeard and Taunton. All trains steam-hauled from mid-July to end Aug & BHs. Ten restored stations along the line. (K4) 01643 704996
westsomersetrailway.vticket.co.uk

## PORLOCK

Picturesque village set back from the coast in a beautiful Exmoor valley protected on three sides by heather covered moors. An abundance of flora and fauna, and pure air plus a temperate climate makes for a relaxing ambience. Fine church

with interesting tombstones. A popular walking centre close to the coastal footpath and many fine Exmoor walks.

## TO VISIT…

**Churchgate Gallery, High St**. Their Mantra is Just Beautiful Art, in all its guises; paintings, ceramics, jewellery and natural history. 01643 862238
churchgategallery.co.uk

**Dovery Manor Museum**. Quaint little museum displaying the history of the locality. Open M-Sa May-Sept. (F3) 01643 863083
doverymanormuseum.org.uk

**Greencombe Gardens**. Enchanting old garden on the edge of woodland overlooking Porlock Bay. Choice rhododendrons, azaleas, camellias, maples, roses, hydrangeas, ferns and small woodland plants. Completely organic with compost heaps on show. Plant sales. No dogs. Open daily. (E3) 01643 862363
greencombe.org

## PORLOCK WEIR

One of the jewels of the Exmoor Coastline. Indeed, a mere hamlet with a charming harbour overlooked by woodland and fishermen's cottages. Much of this area is

owned by the National Trust and the Blathwaite Estate (Owners of Dyrham Park, Bath) who have thankfully retained a continuity of lifestyle by renting cottages and business lets to the same families for many generations. E/C W. (F3)

## TO VISIT…

**Exmoor Adventures.** Here you have the full gamut: E-Mountain Bike Hire, kayaking, Archery, Start-Up Paddle Boarding, Tree Climbing with coaches and in groups. 01643 805001
exmooradventures.co.uk

**Exmoor Glass.** Glassblowers create top quality decanters, goblets, vases and jugs. Regular demos. Gallery open daily 10-5. Studio M-F 9-4. (E3) 01643 863141
exmoorglass.co.uk

**Real Exmoor Studio.** Two artists delight in painting/drawing local wildlife scenes and pet portraits. Commissions undertaken. Open daily. 078910 28250
petportraitdrawings.com

## EAT…DRINK…SLEEP…

**Locanda On The Weir.** Herewith an Italian Restaurant With Rooms. The cuisine is sophisticated, the decor tasteful and imaginative, the four bedrooms luxurious and comfortable. The location, truly a delight. 01643 863300
locandaontheweir.co.uk

**The Cottage B&B, Porlock.** An C18 build offering the full compliment: bedroom with bathrooms, WIFI, bike storage, packed lunches, proximity to coastpath. Open all year. (F3) 01643 862996
cottageporlock.co.uk

## LIGHT BITES... PORLOCK

The **Big Cheese, High St** is just that, with a full panoply of West Country cheeses, hampers, pates, preserves and picnics made up for you. 01643 862773 thebigcheeseporlock.co.uk and Eastwards the **Home Cook Café** for breakfasts, soups of the day, special burgers, homemade cakes and cream teas. Open daily from 10.

## LIGHT BITES... PORLOCK WEIR

Turn Right out of the car park, pass the hotel and soon you come to **The Harbour Gallery & Café**. A healthy concoction of coffee, cakes, ceramics, paintings, smoked fish and shellfish platters in the Porlock Estate's former stables. All with a view and a sea breeze. Open daily Apr-Oct 10-5, Nov-Mar F-Tu 10.30-4. 01643 863514 harbourgalleryandcafe.co.uk

Next door, **Ziangs On The Weir** for Far Eastern street food with Noodle Bar. Open M-Sa 12-7. 01643 863215 Next door, **Porlock Bay Oysters.** Add a slice of lemon and you have the delicacy of Kings.

**The Porlock Weir Hotel.** A stylish place to eat and stay especially if antiques and design is an interest for you. For it was here that Miller of Antique fame displayed his wares. Some, still remain. Sister hotel to the Luttrell Arms, so expect courteous treatment and expertise. 01643 800400 porlockweirhotel.co.uk

## VILLAGES TO VISIT...

**Allerford.** Pretty village noted for the Packhorse Bridge and thatched cottages. Fine walks to Selworthy, Bossington Hill and Porlock Bay. (G3)

**Culbone.** Hamlet with the smallest church in England. Once home to charcoal burners and a leper colony. Reached via car, or the coastal footpath from Porlock Weir, or County Gate. (D2)

**Horner**. Quaint hamlet of thatched cottages and running water. A steep ascent leads off into the woods. Walking centre. Tea shops. (G4)

**Exford.** Bright, attractive village astride the River Exe with a village green, and two sportsmen's inns. Exmoor's fox and stag hunting centre now in decline following the recent hunting ban. (E7)

**Luccombe**. Quiet little village with white-washed thatched cottages which overlook a peaceful churchyard. Amidst superb walking and trekking country. (G4)

**Oare**. Scattered village in steep wooded country. The church was immortalised in R D Blackmore's novel *Lorna Doone* as the setting for Lorna's wedding. (B3)

**Selworthy.** National Trust village with many picture-postcard thatched cottages. Superb views across the Holnicote Estate towards Dunkery Beacon. Fine wagon roof to church. Short, easy waymarked walks lead into the woods. (H3) **Periwinkle Cottage Tea Rooms**. Home-made cakes and soups, light lunches and cream teas. Open daily in season. (H3) 01643 863341

**Winsford.** One of Exmoor's prettiest villages and well known for the thatched **Royal Oak Inn**, and as the birthplace of Ernest Bevin in 1881, the Labour Statesman. (G9)

**Withypool**. Unspoilt village in the centre of Exmoor spanned by a beautiful five-arched bridge. R D Blackmore wrote much of *Lorna Doone* while staying at the Royal Oak Inn. Fine country to the south-west, and riverside walk beside the Barle to Tarr Steps. (D8)

## NATURAL WORLD TO VISIT...

**Badgworthy Water**. A beautiful little valley associated with the Lorna Doone story. Convenient parking at Malmsmead for the easy-going walk, or pony trek beside the riverbank to Badgworthy Wood, an ancient place with tangled oaks, moss and lichen. (A4)

**Brendon Hills**. Rolling hills of patchwork fields and woodland in varying shades of greens and brown. Often overlooked as a place of great beauty because of their close proximity to Exmoor and the Quantocks. The walk across Exmoor through these fields to the Quantock Hills was considered by John Hillaby, the great long distance walker and author, to be "the most beautiful part of England". (K9)

**Caractacus Stone**. Inscribed ancient stone of the Dark Ages set in a shelter on Winsford Hill. (F9)

**Clatworthy Reservoir.** Artificial lake of 130 acres created in 1960. trout fishing. Viewing area and nature trail.

**Coastal Road; Porlock to Lynmouth.** One of the most spectacular and awe-inspiring

*Selworthy*

coastal drives in England. It begins, or ends, with a warning more reminiscent of the "Golden Age of Motoring" when cars were not given to good brakes and trenchant tyres: "Stay in First Gear." It remains a steep, and hazardous ascent (for an under-powered vehicle) up Porlock Hill, a 1 in 4 gradient. There is an alternative route: the toll road through the Blathwaite Estate, a less dramatic route, but blessed with the buzzard and raven, and wild flowers. Once up on the brow of the hill, there are superb views seawards and inland across the rolling patchwork landscape. On a clear day you can spy the South Wales coast all the way to Worms Head on the Gower Peninsula. It is worth turning around and driving back the route you came, for it will look very different.

**Cow Castle.** Iron Age stronghold in commanding position. Fine viewpoint overlooking the River Barle. Reached via a flat, easy walk from Simonsbath running parallel with the Barle. (A8)

**Dunkery Beacon**. Rises to 1,704 feet, and is the highest place on **Exmoor**. Formerly the site of a fire beacon. Wonderful views in all directions. Short-easy walk from road. (F6)

**Holnicote Estate (NT).** Over 12,000 acres given over to the National Trust by Sir Richard Acland. Extends from the coast to the summit of Dunkery Beacon, including the picturesque villages of Allerford, Bossington, Selworthy, Tivington and Luccombe. Three packhorse bridges and several prehistoric sites plus Selworthy Tithe Barn, the Horner Valley, Selworthy Beacon, Hurlstone Point and North Hill. The footpaths criss-cross in all directions and can be quite mind boggling to navigate around. They have crazy names based on Acland's children and grandchildren. Booklets of walks available from the National Park. (F4)

**Horner Wood**. Ancient and secluded woodland below Dunkery Hill. The little stream, the Snorer (Hwrnwr), saxon named because of its gurgling sound, winds its way around the knobbly oaks. Now one of Britain's National Nature Reserves. (G4)

**Landacre Bridge.** Medieval bridge in excellent condition. Popular picnic spot beside the River Barle. Walks beside Barle to Cow Castle, a fine viewpoint. (B8)

**North Hill**. Lovely scenic drive from Minehead to Selworthy Beacon. Nature trail. Campsite. (J3)

**Tarr Steps**. Ancient clapper bridge crossing the River Barle, and one of Exmoor's most visited attractions so beware of large crowds on weekends and bank holidays. Walks up riverbank. It's possible to cross the river in a 4 x 4, or on horseback but not in a saloon car. Car park and toilets in close proximity. Best approached from the B3223 on Winsford Hill. **Tarr Farm Inn** provides teas and refreshments. (E10)

**Webber's Post**. Popular spot below Dunkery Hill with fine views over Stoke Pero Common and Selworthy Beacon. Nature trails and bridleways leadoff in all directions, and can cause havoc with your map reading skills. Paths to Stoke Pero church and Dunkery Beacon. Car park. (G5)

### TO VISIT...

**Exmoor Owl & Hawk Centre, Allerford**. Flying displays; owls to hawks at 2pm. Feed the animals. Hawk walk. Falconry tuition. Shop and tea garden. B&B. Pony trekking across Exmoor. Open Mar-Oct Su-F 10.30-4.30, & BH Sa. (G3) 01643 862816 exmoorowlhawkcentre.co.uk

**Discovery Safaris of Porlock**. This Exmoor safari views the National Park in a specially designed Land Rover Defender to explore the stunning scenery of Exmoor by using off-road routes. Available all year. Trips last 2-3 hours. (K3) 01643 863444 discoverysafaris.com

**Lorna Doone Farm, Malmsmead.** C14 farmhouse known as Plovers Barrow Farm in Blackmore's *Lorna Doone*, the home of John Ridd. Now an artsncrafts and gift shop, next door The Buttery Tea Rooms. Open daily late Mar-Oct 10-6, Nov-Christmas 11-4.30. (A2) 01598 741388

**Red Stag Safari**. In the comfort of a Land Rover Discovery you will be whisked around the delights of Exmoor; wildlife, panoramic viewpoints, fast-flowing rivers, and more. 01643 841831 redstagsafari.co.uk

**West Somerset Rural Life Museum, Allerford**. Victorian schoolroom, laundry and dairy. Craft workers' tools. Croquet lawn. Picnic area. Open Apr-Oct Tu-F 10.30-4, Sa 11-3. (G3) 01643 862529 allerfordmuseum.org.uk

### EAT...DRINK...SLEEP...

**Crown Hotel.** This family-run C17 Coaching Inn and sporting hotel delivers a warm welcome to you, your dogs and horses. Log fires and luxurious bedrooms. Impressive food in Restaurant. Cosy country bar and meals. Shooting Party rates. (D7) 01643 831554 crownhotelexmoor.co.uk

**Dunkery Beacon Hotel.** A small, family-run Country House Hotel with an award-winning restaurant. Add the views, location and professional expertise on hand and you have a winning combination. 01643 841241 dunkerybeacon accommodation.co.uk

**Hindon Organic Farm**. Lovely old creaking farmhouse at the end of a long, long lane. Be prepared to reverse! An organic farm for many years producing fresh organic meats; Aberdeen Angus beef, Gloucester Old Spot pork, Hindon hams, sausages and pies. (H3) 01643 705244 hindonfarm.co.uk

**Royal Oak Inn at Luxborough**. Hidden away in the Brendon Hills, this little cosy, flagstoned pub has built a reputation for good, honest fare and real ales. Luxurious cottage-style accommodation with bathrooms. (L7) 01984 641498 theroyaloakinnluxborough.co.uk

**Tarr Farm Inn.** C16 farm set in its own 40-acres overlooking Tarr Steps, and the River Barle. Modern bedrooms with all mod cons. Restaurant provides meals from local farms. Activities and Events organised. Opens at 12. (E10) 01643 851507 tarrfarm.co.uk

### WALKING ON EXMOOR...

Walking is the most satisfying way to experience Exmoor's

many virtuous delights. Her charms will seduce you into returning again, and again, and whether you are a naturalist, geologist or botanist, fresh air fiend, or just a keen horseman. You will always be in her debt. We are privileged to walk her beautiful paths.

The National Park is dissected by scores of footpaths and bridleways (about 650 miles in total). Most signposted and waymarked. There are many publications available giving detailed plans for walks, including some excellent leaflets published by the Exmoor National Park, the National Trust and local tourist offices. Guided, and special interest walks can also be arranged throughout the season through several Tourist Information Centres. The recommended walks listed below are only a small indication of some of the areas, and routes worthwhile

exploring. All start within easy reach of a car park.

1. **Bossington** to **Selworthy**, either via **Hurlstone Point** or **Selworthy Beacon**. (G2)

2. **North Hill** 3-mile trail. (J3)

3. **Webber's Post** to **Stoke Pero Church** and **Dunkery Beacon**. (G4)

4. **Cloutsham Woodland Trail.** (F5)

5. **Horner** to **Webber's Post** via **Horner Wood**. (G4)

## BEACHES & SURFING...

**Blue Anchor.** Sand and shingle. R/WC/P. (M4)

**Dunster Beach**. Shingle and sand. R/WC/P. (M4)

**Minehead.** Shingly sand. R/P/ WC. (K3)

**Porlock Weir**. Pebbles. HZ swimming. Fast waves for experienced surfers. P/WC/R. (E2)

## COASTAL FOOTPATH...

**Minehead** to **County Gate** (9 miles). The path begins fairly easily from the end of Minehead Quay, passing gently through woodland onto North Hill. For about three miles there is wonderful high level walking towards Selworthy Beacon, a fine viewpoint at 1013 feet, and worth a slight detour. Then down the hill to Bossington, a pretty village, and a short length of road work before following the beach to Porlock Weir, a delightful little harbour overlooked by a row of fishermen's cottages.

The path then climbs up beside Yeanor Wood towards Culbone Church, set secluded in a wooded glade. The path continues with slight elevations to Glenthorne House. From here the path ascends to County Gate where there is a car park and National Park Centre.

*Tarr Steps*

1917    Food rationed and factories taken over for the war effort.

199

# THE HARTLAND PENINSULA

Hartland Point
West Titchberry Farm
Cow & Calf
Blagdon
Titchberry
Upright Cliff
Damehole Point
Blegberry
Dyer's lookout
Markadon
Lavender Farm
Berry
The Warren
Hartland Abbey
Cheristow
Broad Beach
Hartland Quay
ST NECTAN
Hartland Quay Museum
Stoke
2 Harton Manor
St Catherine's Tor
Little Barton
Speke's Mill Mouth
Kernstone
Longpeak
Trellick
Docton Mill
Milford
Lymebridge
Mansley Cliff
Eddistone
Elmscott
Sandhole Cliff
Docton
Nabor Point
Hardisworthy
South Hole
Ramtor Rock
Embury Beach
Embury Beacon
Putshole
Knap Head
Welcombe Mouth
Welcombe
ST NECTAN
Tredown
The Old Smithy
Mead
Darracott
Upcott
Marsland Mouth
Gull Rock
Marsland Cliff
Gooseham Mill
Woolley
Yeol Mouth
Marsland
Gooseham
Henna Cliff
Cornakey Cliff
Westcott
Eastcott
Woolley Barrow
St John Baptist
Tea Rooms
Marwenstow
Bush Inn
Crimp
West Youlstone
Higher Sharpnose Point
Tonacombe
Rule Cross
Shop
Milton
Tumuli
Stanbury
Woodford Cross
Wrasford Moor
Uppacott
Eastaway

# CORNWALL

Stursdon Cross
Stanbury Mouth
Woodford
Stursdon
Lower Sharpnose Point
Hollamoor
Taylor's Cross
Tumuli
Broxwater
Coombe
Coombe Valley Nature Trail
Aldercombe
Darracott
Steeple Point

Eldern Point
Chapman Rock
Shipload Bay
Gawlish Cliff
Fatacott
Exmansworthy Cliff
Beckland Bay
Windbury Point
Blackchurch
Exmansworthy
Mouthmill
Gallant Down
Snacksland
Brownsham
Pitt
Pattard Cross
Norton
Yapham
ALL SAINTS
Clovelly Court
Pattard Restaurant
Hescott
Velly
Wrink Sler
Ballhill
Hartland
Rosedown
Mettaford
Hugglepit
B3248
Natcott
Highford
B3248
Leigh
Farford
Warmleigh
Clovelly Dyk
Philham
B3248
Baxworthy Corner
A39(T)
Staddon
Welsford
High
Tosberry
Burford
Tosberry Moor
Welsford Moor
Seckington
Tumuli
Bursdon Moor
Tumuli
Gorvin
Tumulus
Lutsford
Summerwell
Huddisf
Wembsworthy
Bursdon
Tumuli
Henaford
A39(T)
Tumulus
Biteford
Welcombe Cross
Deptford
Mar
Greadon
Horton Bridge
Meddon
Shorstone
Tumuli
Brimford Bridge
Tumulus
Hor
Hardsworthy
Nor
East Youlstone
Dinworthy
River
Ryall
Berrio
Tumuli
Blatchborough
Stowt
Milton
Tumuli
Upper Tamar Lake
Kimw
Newland
Kilkhampton
Alfardiswo

200
120

**Westward Ho!**

Morans
Café Italia

Rock Nose

*Mermaid's Pool*

Buckleigh

The Pig on the Hill

Cornborough Range   Cornborough

Rickard's
Down

Abbotsham
Court

Greencliff Rock

**Abbotsham**

Greencliff

ST HELEN

Winsford

The Big Sheep   Handy
Cross

Cockington

Bowood

Babbacombe

*Babbacombe Mouth*

A39(T)

Atlantic Village

Abbotsham
Cross

Higher
Rowden

Knotty
Corner

Hotel
entre
Silk
Museum

nt Rock

**ovelly**

*Bight a Doubleyou*

Portledge

Ford

Littleham
Court

*Lower Bight
of Fernham*   The Gore

Gauter
Point

Peppercombe
Castle

Fairy Cross

Winscott

Woodtown

Yeo
Vale

The Hobby

bby Drive
urnstone

Hobby
Lodge

Walland
Cary

Buck's
Mills

Northway

Gilscott

Milky Way
venture Park
ornery

Hoops Inn

Hoops

A39(T)

ST ANDREW

**Alwington**

Slade

Bitworthy

Buck's
Cross

Waytown

Foxdown

Horns
Cross

Goldworthy

Bulland

Kennerland
Cross

Broadparkham

Tuckingmill

Halsbury

West
wn

Cranford

*River Yeo*

Sedborough

Bocombe

ST JAMES

Newhaven

**Parkham**

Stone

ST MARY & ST BENEDICT

**Buckland
Brewer**

**Woolfardisworthy**

Farmer's Arms

Wulfhead Manor

Cabbacott

Coach & Horses

Venn

Ash

Hordland

Bableigh

Alminston
Cross

Melbury

Gorwood

Stroxworthy

*Melbury
Reservoir*

Beara Farmhouse

Thorne

uerdon

Melbury
Bridge

Leworthy

Winslade

▲ *Melbury
Hill*

Bilsford

Craneham

*River Dunty*

lew Cross

Hole

Ashmansworthy

Tumulus

Powler's
Piece

Lower
Twitchen

Rush
Barrow

Eckworthy

Hembury Castle

Ashbury

Hele

*River Torridge*   Dipple

Narracott

Common
Moor

Tumuli

Wrangsworthy
Cross

Collingsdown

Milford

Tythecott

Tumulus

Challash

East Ash

Kismeldon
Bridge

**East
Putford**

Venn

Thornehill
Head

Wonders
Corner

Volehouse

Cory

Mambury

Galsworthy

*Thorne
Moor*

Withecott

Ley

**West
Putford**

Tumulus

Silworthy
Cross

Field
Irish

Hankford

Bower

Stibb
Cross

dworthy
ommon

Silworthy

Colscott

Haytown

ST MICHAEL

*Doves
Moor*

ST JOHN BAPTIST

**Bradworthy**

Wheelers
Cross

Thriverton

Chollaton

**Bulkworthy**

Downmoor

Binworthy

Cleverdon

Roseland Cross

ST JAMES

Abbots
Bickington

Eastbridge

A388

le Ford

Northcott

Brendon

Five
Lanes

Worden

Durpley

orthy Cross

South Lane

Great
Derworthy

Camp
Woodford
Bridge

ST PETROCK

**Newton
St Petrock**

Durpley
Castle

Billhole

ST ANDREW

Matcott

Shop

Forestreet

Instaple

**Sutcombe**

211

*Buck's Mills*

## BUCK'S MILLS

Name derived from the Saxon "Bussac Hewise," meaning homestead. An isolated hamlet of romantic cottages (most are second homes, and are usually empty) at the bottom of a steep combe protected by high cliffs to either side, and from behind, thick woodland. In times gone by, the villagers made a living from fishing; herring, mackerel, lobster and prawn, as well as coastal lime burning needed for the fertilising of inland farms, so as to neutralise the acid soil. The steep, wide road from the beach was built to transport lime shipped in from South Wales. Hence, the massive lime kilns above the beach. As the fishing declined, the villagers sought new employment in the quarries on Lundy, sailing daily to and from work. Bygod, they were tough, in them, thar days. (J4)

## CLOVELLY

A timeless village of cobbled streets and quaint cottages descend steeply to a harbour and backdrop of rich blue sea. Set in a superb position amidst beautiful scenery Clovelly belongs to the Rouse family who take great care to maintain the buildings in traditional materials. It's a former fishing port whose major wealth came from catching mackerel and herring. Today, it's a centre for small fishing trips, and visiting day-trippers.

When the fishing dried up Clovelly men would seek employment digging the quarries on Lundy. Clovelly folk were a hardy breed. It was not just the men who worked their socks off, the women got stuck in, too. With the quarrying, and the making of fishing nets.

Visiting Clovelly is an unforgettable experience and loved by children and folk of all ages. Take sensible shoes, the descent on cobble stones can be slippery. It is also steep, and the unfit or elderly would be wise to either take a ride on a donkey, or seek a lift in the Land Rover to the harbour.

On arrival, park in the parking area provided and enter via the Visitor Centre where there is a charge which helps maintain the village for future generations. Café, Shop & WCs. Open daily. (G4) 01237 431781 clovelly.co.uk

### TO VISIT IN CLOVELLY...

**Clovelly Court Garden.** These gardens have undergone a major restoration programme. A classic example of a Victorian kitchen garden with magnificent greenhouses. The unique maritime microclimate provides exotic flower borders and fruit. Open daily, all year 10-4. (F4) 01237 431781

*Orange Ladder, Clovelly*

In the Courtyard there is **Clovelly Pottery**. Where you can throw a pot and exhibits from different ceramicists. Next door, **Clovelly Soaps**…

**Clovelly Silk.** Scarves, ties, cushions and accessories designed and handprinted onto silks, velvets and fine wools. Commissions and day courses undertaken at workshop. Open Summer, daily 10-5. Winter, M-F 10.30-3.30. (G4) 01237 431033 clovellysilk.com

**Hobby Drive Walk.** Follow the signs from Clovelly. This was laid out between 1811-29 by Sir James Hamlyn Williams, as a celebration of nature. One of the schemes that came to mirror the Romantic Movement of the early C19. The pathway was designed to accommodate carriages, and it features four gently curving bridges. The panoramic views peer down on Clovelly, and westwards towards Lundy and West Wales. They are

*Pebbled Lane, Clovelly*

1921   March. Henry Williamson moves to live in Georgeham, arriving on his 499 cc long-stroke Norton motorcycle and rents Skirr Cottage for £5 a year.

203

unforgettable. There are a number of caves just off this drive that were used to store the C19 smuggler's contraband. But, beware of ghostly forms. (G4)

## HARTLAND PENINSULA

An isolated corner of Devon full of interest. The village of Hartland is a popular centre for the arts and crafts and has a number of pubs and tearooms. The church is strangely two miles westwards at Stoke. A regular location for films and TV. More recently *The Night Manager* and *Rebecca*.

### TO VISIT IN AND AROUND HARTLAND…

**Hartland Abbey & Gardens.** Founded in 1157, the current building has been an historic family home since 1539. Furnished in Queen Anne, Georgian and Regency splendour; pictures, murals, furniture, porcelain. Beautiful informal gardens designed by Gertrude Jekyll with a woodland walk to the Atlantic Ocean. "Special Days & Exhibitions." Cream teas. Open 3 Apr to 3 Oct Su-Th & BHs House 2-5, Gardens & Tea Room 11-5. (C4) 01237 441496 hartlandabbey.com

**Hartland Quay**. A wild and windswept corner of England forever associated with smugglers of contraband, and a favourite landing for Sir Francis Drake and Sir Richard Grenville, Devon men. It's set on a treacherous coastline, and little wonder that the quay was swept away in 1841, 1887 and 1896. The present quay was rebuilt in 1979. The former harbour master's house is now the hotel and inn. A wide road leads down to the slipway built for the transport of lime imported from South Wales. (B4)

**Hartland Quay Shipwreck Museum**. Features four centuries of local shipwrecks, old coastal occupations, shipping, smuggling and fishing. A wonderful introduction to this corner of Britain. Gift shop. Open daily. (B4) 01237 441371

**Sarah Jane Lander, No.39 Pottery, Fore St**. Sarah uses red earthenware clay and stoneware clay to produce decorated domestic ware. Open Sa-Th. (B4) 01237 441883

**Springfield Pottery**. Established in 1979 by Philip Leach, grandson of Bernard Leach. He and his wife, Frannie produce earthenware pottery hand-made from local clays; tiles, garden pots, domestic ware and individual pots. Open by appointment. Commissions undertaken. (D4) 01237 441506 studiopottery.com

1921 Sir Ernest Shackleton's ship, Quest, bound for the south seas on her final voyage, puts in at Plymouth.

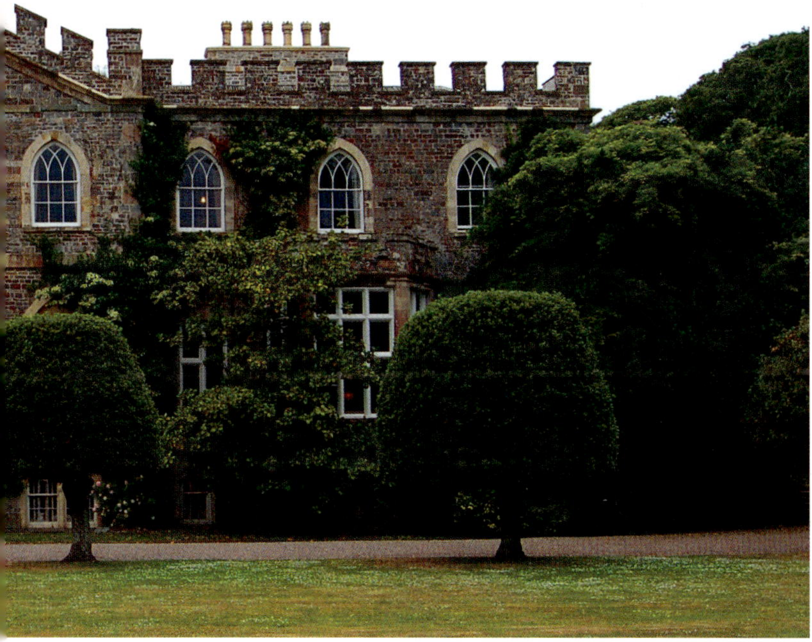

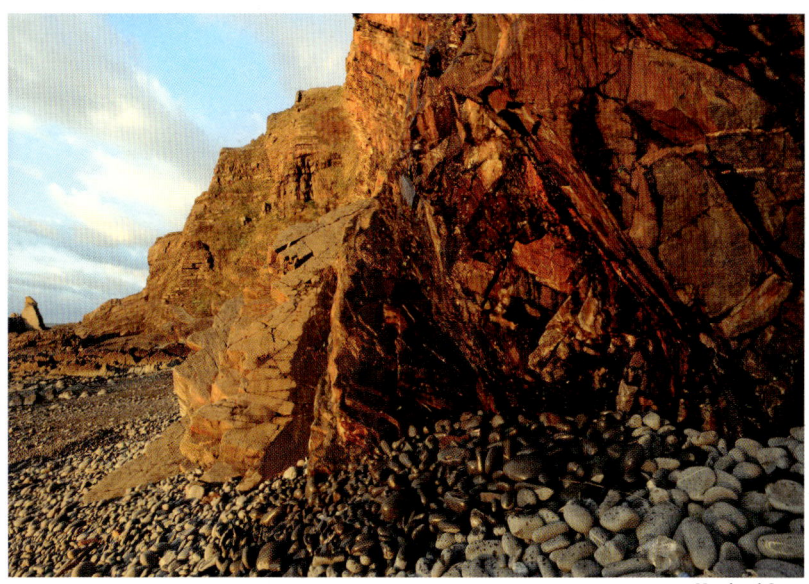

Hartland Abbey ss

**St John's Chapel of Ease, Hartland.** A substantial building in the centre of the village. A former Town Hall and Chapel to St Nectan. Beneficiary of a Town Clock installed in the C17 and one of the oldest working civic clocks in the country. (D4)

**St Nectan's Church, Stoke**. A sailor's landmark for miles around, and one of the finest churches in Devon and the West Country. The 128 foot tower is the tallest in North Devon. Perpendicular, and largely built in the mid C14.

Hartland Quay

1927 October. Henry Williamson's "Tarka the Otter" is published.

1941 Mar 20. The Plymouth blitz at its worst. 336 civilians killed on 20 and 21 March.

The tower is in four stages with buttresses and massive gargoyles. The interior is large and lofty, indeed spacious with Early Jacobean pulpit, C15 Rood Screen, C20 stained glass by Christopher Webb. A simple plaque to Sir Allen Lane, the founder of Penguin Books whose family have a long association with Hartland. There's a little museum with all manner of pieces that gives this church that extra wow factor.

### TO STAY…TO SLEEP…

**2 Harton Manor B & B, The Square.** C16 building set in the heart of the village. Comfortable bedrooms and lounge are decorated with original art. Your hostess, Merlyn Chesterman runs printmaking Woodcut Workshops. Open all year. (D4) 01237 441670
twohartonmanor.co.uk

**Hartland Quay Hotel**. Without doubt one of the most spectacularly sited hotels in Britain. Set on dramatic, rugged cliffs overlooking the Atlantic. Book in when a Force 8 is forecast. Experience some real weather, and if the wind and drama doesn't blow you away, get stuck into some food and beer in the Wrecker's Retreat Bar (and hopefully, you'll sleep through the storm). Simple, pine furniture in bedrooms with bathrooms and stupendous views. (B4) 01237 441218
hartlandquayhotel.co.uk

**Stoke Barton Campsite.** Host to caravans and tents with full facilities. Beach and pub within walking distance. Open Apr-Oct. 01237 441238
westcountry-camping.co.uk

### MORWENSTOW

No visit to this area will be complete without a visit to this historic village. The village is only made up of a few farms and cottages, but it is to the church, pub and tearoom that one is drawn.

**Church of St John the Baptist.** Famous for Richard Stephen Hawker, 1803-75, the eccentric and original vicar-poet, and originator of harvest festivals. A compassionate man, he would stalk the wild coast in beaver hat, fisherman's

1942    May 4. 10,000 incendiary bombs dropped on Exeter killing 161 civilians and destroying 1,500 buildings.

long boots and yellow cloak in search of shipwrecked sailors. Many of those he failed to save, he laid to rest in his churchyard. To stimulate and awaken his congregation he sometimes dressed as a mermaid! His original hut made of driftwood clings to the cliffs. Opposite, the **Rectory Tea Rooms**, open daily in season. (A9)

**The Bush Inn.** C13 freehouse revitalised into a contemporary gastro-pub on the Devon-Cornish border. Cosy, authentic snug bars plus a more spacious, modern dining area. Local fish and steaks, a speciality. B&B/Holiday Let. (A9) 01288 331242 thebushinn-morwenstow.com

### TO VISIT...

**Cheristow Lavender Farm.** Grows over 100 varieties of lavender and many English roses. Soaps and oils. Tearoom. Campsite. Breeders of Devon Red Ruby cattle (Beef on sale). Open Mar-Sept W-Sa 12-5. (C4) 01237 440078 cheristow.co.uk

**Docton Mill Gardens & Tea Room.** Historic site of former flour mill now a flourishing and captivating garden with water features; leat, head weir and tailrace. 8 acres encompass bog garden, orchard and woodland. Walk to coastal waterfall and beach at Spekes Mill Mouth. B & B. Plant sales and award-winning tea room. Open daily Apr to early Oct 10-5. (C6) 01237 441369 doctonmill.co.uk

**Haytown Pottery.** Domestic earthenwares and humorous individual animals made by David Cleverly. Advised to call before visiting. 01409 261476 (K9) david-cleverlyceramics.co.uk

**Milky Way Adventure Park, Nr Clovelly.** Great family fun; rides, large indoor adventure play area, sports hall, narrow gauge railway, collection of farming and agricultural equipment, dodgems and Birds of Prey. Open daily Mar-Nov, W/Es & 1/2 terms Nov-East. (G5) 01237 431255 themilkyway.co.uk

**Woolfardisworthy (Woolsery).** An isolated village with an unpronounceable name. Hence, the shortened version. Now firmly on the map (at least for Gastromomes) for the **Farmer's Arms** has been restored to its former glory. The mission of Americans, Michael and Xochi Birch, founders of Bebo to revitalise the village. His spiritual home where his ancestors lived and where he holidayed as a youth. A fish and chip shop and village shop have added to the village's attractions.

### EAT...DRINK...

**Farmers Arms, Woolsery.** An oasis of chic, cool, style and professional expertise. A country pub that's exploded onto the culinary subconscious of North Devonian gastronomes. Art pervades, craftmanship and comfort. Booking advised. Open W-Su from 11.30. Details: 01237 439328. Further developments are planned: a sparkling country house and spa hotel, **Wulfhead Manor**, is a project to further your culinary and hedonistic senses. (G6) woolsery.com

*Rocks around Hartland Quay*

**Pattard Restaurant, Hartland.** Fine dining using the finest of North Devon seasonal produce cooked by a masterful chef who has learnt his trade here in the UK, Australia and the Far East. Booking advised. Open W-Sa 6-9.30, Su 12-4. 01237 441444 (D4) pattardrestaurant.co.uk

### EAT...DRINK...SLEEEP...

**Beara Farmhouse**. B&B. The Dorsets know a thing or two about the comforts of home, interior design and building skills. Their fabulous home has been converted from a ruin into a rural idyll at the bottom of a rough track. Self-catering cottages, too. (L6) 01237 451666 bearafarmhouse.co.uk

**Red Lion Hotel, Clovelly**. Waking up to the sounds of an ancient harbour is a blissful experience. The rooms are all modern and comfortable with nautical themes, and have superb harbour or sea views. All with bathrooms and mod cons. The restaurant serves fish directly off the local boats. (G4) 01237 431237 redlion-clovelly.co.uk

**West Titchberry Farm B&B**. A traditional farmhouse; clean and comfortable, a little old fashioned. Don't expect "Country Living" decor. All rooms have their own bathroom. Packed lunches and pick-up off the Coast Path can be arranged. Self-catering. (C3) 01237 441287 westtitchberryfarm.co.uk

**Coach & Horses, Buckland Brewer**. Popular "local" providing fine ales and pub-grub; skate, bass, monkfish, and local vegetables in season. Themed nights. 01237 451393 (M6)

**Hoops Inn B&B.** Thatched hostelry dating from the C13. Log fires, real ales and seasonal produce have made this a popular inn down the years. More a Dining Pub with Rooms. Dogs welcome. In former times, a meeting place for smugglers and seafarers.

Sir Richard Grenville, Drake, Raleigh and Hawkins, all met here and planned their adventures. 01237 451222 (J5) hotelsnorthdevon.co.uk

### NATURAL WORLD TO VISIT...

**Coombe Valley Nature Trail.** Start from Combe Cottage and follow a green and peaceful wooded valley rich in oak woods, honeysuckle and birdlife; buzzards, woodpeckers, dippers. Nearby, Stowe Barton, home of Sir Richard Grenville who was immortalised in Tennyson's poem, "The Revenge." (B10)

**Peppercombe.** The section of the coastal path from this hamlet to Buck's Mills is wonderful, and a detour to the beach is worth considering for its geological interest; triassic marl colours in reds, browns and bright yellow. The castle was demolished by fierce storms and eroding cliffs around 1900. (K4)

*Hartland Abbey Gardens*

1944    June 6. American and British troops leave Devon ports for D-Day landings on Normady.

**Shipload Bay.** If you have the legs for it, descend the 260+ steps to a beach of grey shingle, and if your luck is in you can watch Grey seals laze here in early summer. (C3)

## COASTAL FOOTPATH...

**Westward Ho!** to **Clovelly** (12 miles). For the first mile the path makes use of the old railway track beneath the Kipling Tors, but soon becomes more arduous with many ups and downs following the rock coast to the tiny fishing village of Bucks Mills. A few miles further on the path joins the "Hobby Drive," and by an easy twisting route through beautiful woodlands it reaches Clovelly. (M2-G4)

**Clovelly to Hartland Quay** (10 miles). Probably the finest section of the whole path. From Clovelly the route ascends the windswept headland of Gallantry Bower, then drops down to the little rocky cove of Mouth Mill. There follows some 4 miles of fine walking along the cliff tops to Shipload Bay, one of the rare sandy beaches of this coast, and onward to Hartland Point. The coastline now turns sharply to the south and the seascapes increase in magnificence with their fantastically contorted geological formations. There is some hard but rewarding walking over these last few miles to Hartland Quay. (G4)

**Hartland Quay to Marsland Mouth** (6 miles). The spectacular scenery continues with some fairly stiff walking. At Spekes Mill Mouth there is a fine waterfall, from which the path ascends once again to the cliff tops. From here the path maintains a fairly steady altitude until descending to the small beach at Welcombe Mouth. A further half-mile leads the traveller, at last, to the Cornish border. (H4)

**Forest Trails.** The Forestry Commission have organised waymarked trails scattered throughout the county. Most have information centres where detailed booklets can be obtained. Locations include Eggesford, Hartland Forest, Holsworthy, and Melbury in the north west. forestry.gov.uk

## BEACHES ...SURFING...

**Bucks Mills.** Small harbour with sand and rocks. 1/2 mile from P (J4).

**Clovelly**. Shingle and pebbles. Boating pool. R/WC, 1/2 mile walk from P (G4).

**Shipload Bay**. Shingly sand and rocks 1/2 mile from P (C3). Hartland Point. Shingle, rocks, cliffs. Short walk from P. (B3).

**Welcombe Mouth**. Haunt of Cruel Coppinger, an C18 smuggler. Pebbles, rocks and a sandy beach at LT. Short walk from P/R. (A7)

**Marsland Mouth**. Rocky. Not conducive to bathing unless you are a hardy surfer. Poet's hut on north hillside set up by the late Ronald Duncan, playwright and novelist.

*Image from The Hartland Quay Museum ss*

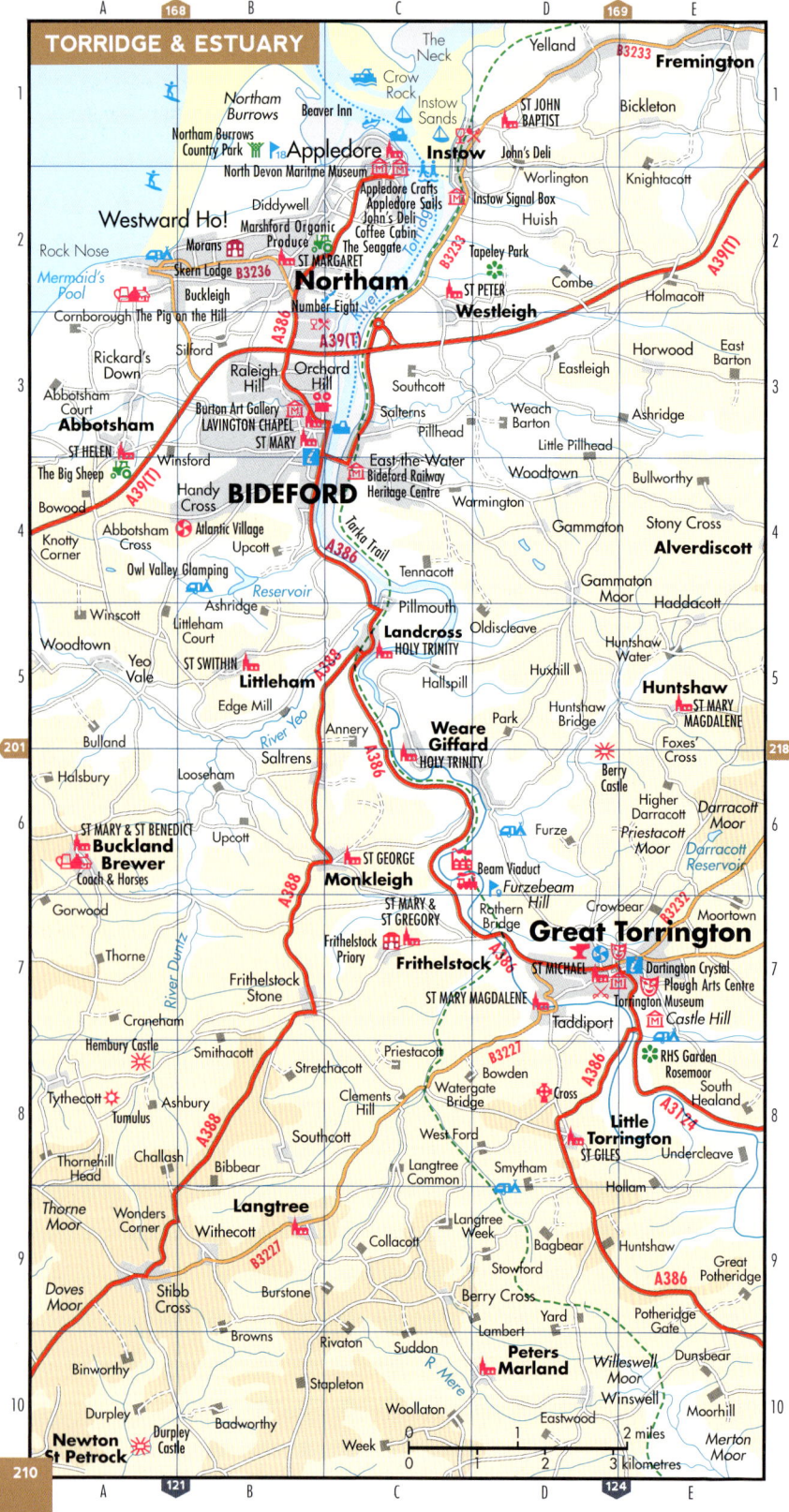

## BIDEFORD

A lively and busy town on the Torridge Estuary, and to this day, cargo ships load and unload on the quay. In the C16 and C17, one of Britain's major seaports, handling cargoes from, and to, the New World. A favourite haunt of Drake, Grenville, Hawkins and Sir Walter Raleigh, who it is claimed brought his first cargo of tobacco to Bideford. Furthermore, in the late C17, local merchants traded wool with Newfoundland sending out more ships than any other apart from London and Topsham.

The fine 24-arch C15 bridge is one of the longest (677 ft) in the country, but now overshadowed by the new bridge down river. New Year's Eve attracts over 20,000 revellers to celebrate the New Year who dress up in all manner of garb. Pannier Market on Tuesdays and Saturdays. Trips to Lundy Island. Regatta in Sept. E/C W. (B4)

### TO VISIT...

**Bideford Railway Heritage Centre, Former Railway Station.** Visitor Centre in restored railway carriage. Refreshments. Hibberd 0-4-0 "Planet" Diesel loco No. 3832 built in 1957. Open East - Oct Su & BHs 2-5. Nov-East Su 2-4. (C4) 01237 423585

**Burton Art Gallery & Museum, Kingsley Rd.** The Museum of Bideford; with three exhibition spaces; museum, craft gallery, shop, workshop and lecture theatre and Café du Parc. TIC. Open M-Sa 10-4, Su 11-4. (B3) 01237 471455 burtonartgallery.co.uk

**Pannier Market.** One is never sure what will turn up here; antiques, works of art, sculptures, home-made bread. Indeed, a fine mix of entrepreneurs and artists. At 15 Butcher's Row is the **Curious Creatures Gallery.** Pieces made from tin, steel and iron cast offs.

### LIGHT BITES...

Start you visit at the **Café du Parc** set within the **Burton Art Gallery**. A little bit of France, for the Patron and the Waiter are both French, and **Les Petit Plats du Maison** will provide you with the energy to wander the streets of **Bideford**. 01237 429317

On leaving with the river on your left hand side walk to the High Street. Just past the bookshop is **King Father Fish and Chips**, for takeaway or sitting in.

Then ascend to **Café Collective**, 9 Grenville Street. Its funky, dog friendly, quirky...gluten free cakes and fresh pizzas. Open 10-4 and summer evenings. 01237 238297 cafecollectivebideford.co.uk

*The Old & New Bridges, Bideford*

*Appledore*

## TO STAY...TO SLEEP...

**Owl Valley Glamping, Bideford**. Two cabins, a Bell Tent and a Geodome set in a secluded valley amongst wild animals, birds and flowers. Environmentally friendly with compost loo and eco shower. 01237 721535 (B4) owl-valley.co.uk

## EAT...DRINK...

**Number 8, 8A Allhalland St., Bideford.** If you managed to bag a table. A rarity - Congratulations! British seasonal food of supreme quality, and good manners provide a winning combination. Opens W-Sa from 6.30pm. 01237 237589 (B3) onebideford.co.uk

## APPLEDORE

One of the most attractive villages in North Devon. It's set on the Torridge Estuary, and has ancient inter-connecting streets with rows of colour-washed cottages reminiscent of the Greek, Cycladean islands. A thriving fishing and trading village since the C14. Many of the fishermen's cottages date back to the Elizabethan period. The centuries old shipbuilding tradition has had a precarious existence. Many pubs, craft shops, and home to many artists. The view out to sea from the RNLI Station & Museum is memorable. It is worth exploring the little streets and watching the boats come and go. Like a lot of holiday places the cottages are often sadly empty but for a few months of the year. Instow Ferry. (C2)

## TO VISIT...

**Appledore Crafts Co, 5 Bude St**. Co-operative gallery founded by local craftsmen who produce fine furniture, lighting, paintings, ceramics, glass, textiles and jewellery. Open: Jan-Mar W/Es 10-4, Apr-Oct daily 11-5, Nov-Dec W-Su 10-4. (C2) 01237 423547 appledorecraftscompany.co.uk

**Appledore Sails, 1 The Quay.** Charter a two-mastered 15ft lug boat with skipper and sail the Torridge-Taw Estuary, and beyond if

## LIGHT BITES...

As you enter the village, on your left is **John's Deli & Café** where you can refresh yourself with a coffee, pastry and perhaps prepare a picnic hamper.

Moving north you come to **The Coffee Cabin**, another pleasant venue for a coffee and homemade cakes.

Perhaps, you require steak and chips, a pint of ale, a comfy chair and a bed for the night, **The Seagate** overlooking the **Quay**. 012137 472589 theseagate.co.uk

There are two fish and chip takeaways; **The Royal Plaice** and **Sylvesters**.

Untainted by time, untouched by tide or no man stands the **Beaver Inn** on **Irsha Street**. A popular, unpretentious Freehouse that provides seafood and meat dishes. And, has up its sleeve superb panoramic views of the Estuary. Jazz nights. Dogs welcome. (C2) 01237 474822 beaverinn.co.uk

desired. For 4-persons and dog. (C1) 01237 423163 appledoresails.co.uk

**North Devon Maritime Museum, Odun Rd.** North Devon's nautical history displayed with paintings, models, tools and photos. Shipbuilding through the ages. Wrecks and rescues. World War 11. Fishing and navigational exhibits. Open daily Apr-Oct 10.30-5. (C2) 01237 422064

**Skern Lodge**. Adventure activities for all ages and abilities. Climbing, powerboats, abseiling, surfing, archery, rafting, canoeing and tunnels. (B2) 01237 475992 skernlodge.co.uk

### INSTOW

A popular holiday village with sandy beach, pedestrian ferry to Appledore and fine views of the Torridge Estuary.

**Sailing Club**. Unique thatched cricket score box and pavilion. Stopping off point for riding the Tarka Trail. **The Commodore Hotel** is a civilised destination, popular with golfers and the retired. (C2)

### TO VISIT...

**Instow Signal Box, Level Crossing.** Built in 1873, now restored to its former glory with levers, gate wheel and instruments. Open East-Oct Su & BHs 2-5, Nov-East Su 2-4. (D2) 01237 423585

### LIGHT BITES...

You won't go hungry or thirsty in **Instow**. At the top (north) end of the village, a cluster of inns, **The Wayfarers**, **Instow Arms** and eatery **The Boathouse**. It's a question of your style and choice, not much in it...

Further down the seafront you come to **John's Deli and Café**. They have everything you need, a coffee, pastry, cheeses and now meals, breakfast, brunch and lunch. Fill you knapsacks if cycling the Tarka Trail. And, Bon Voyage!

*Instow*

### Great Torrington

An ancient hilltop town set in a strategic position overlooking the River Torridge and rolling, green countryside. The English Civil War's Battle of Torrington in 1646 ended the Royalists' resistance to the Parliamentarian cause in the West Country. The TV series "Down To Earth" was shot around the town and vicinity. Note the fine Market Square with Town Hall and other interesting buildings. Twenty miles of footpaths on The Commons, a public area of 365-acres with flora and fauna. The town is the centre for many Sealed Knot re-enactments of the Civil War. Pannier Market on Friday and Saturdays. May Fair, first Th. (E7)

**Dartington Crystal.** Handmade lead crystal ware. Viewing galleries and guided tours. Historic glass exhibition. Family Activity Centre. Open daily. Tours M-F 9-3.15, Shop/Restaurant daily from 10. (D7)
01805 626221
dartington.co.uk

**Great Torrington Museum**. Collection of local historic interest including the Coronation Coronets and robes of the last Earl and Countess Orford of Torrington. Open May-Sept M-F 11-4, Sa 11-1. (E7)
01805 938008
torringtonmuseum.org.uk

### LIGHT BITES...

Park in the large space (charge) beside **Torrington 1646** (closed) overlooking fabulous country, and great for exercising your dogs.

For a full English breakfast it has to be the **Café** in 1646. On the other end of town is the Café in **The Plough Arts Centre, 9-11 Fore St**. A loyal following stop here for their toasties and savouries. Relaxing before or after intellectual stimulae.

To the north-west of the town is the **Puffing Billy** beside the **Tarka Trail**, open from 9-5 (10-4 winter) for breakfast. The homemade food is basic pub-grub sourced from local suppliers; soups, quiches, jacket potatoes. Railway afficionados will feel at home here. 01805 623050 puffingbilly.co.uk

Next door, **Torrington Cycle Hire, Station Yard.** 01805 622633 (D7)
torringtoncyclehire.com

**The Plough Arts Centre, 9-11 Fore St.**, Lively centre with special workshops, galleries, live events, film shows and more. Café. Open daily. (E7) 01805 624624 theploughartscentre.org.uk

## TO VISIT…

**Frithelstock Priory.** Commanding ruin of C13 Augustinian priory with adjoining church. (C7)

**Kenwith Nursery.** Specialists in dwarf and rare conifers. Mail order. Tu-Sa 10-4.30. (E8) 01805 603274 kenwithconifernursery.co.uk

**Marshford Organic Produce, Churchill Way.** For the past 30-years they have specialised in varieties of mixed salads and greens; oakleaf, spinach and rocket, plus little gems, caesars and more. Open daily. 01237 477160 (C2) marshford.co.uk

**Northam Burrows Country Park.** 253 hectares of grassy plain, saltmarsh, dunes and a notable pebble ridge. Access to two miles of safe, sandy beach. Walks and trails. Burrows Centre has exhibitions and displays. Shop. Toilets for disabled. Centre open daily East to Oct 10-5. Park open all year. (B2) 01237 479708 torridge.gov.uk/ northamburrows

**RHS Garden Rosemoor, Nr Great Torrington**. An enchanting 65-acres of gardens and woodland, including 2,000 roses in 200 different varieties, colour theme gardens, herb garden and potager, stream and bog garden, cottage garden, fruit and vegetable garden, and semi-tropical areas. Plant Centre, Restaurant and Shop. Picnic area. Open daily Apr-Sept 10-6 (-5 Oct-Mar). (E7) 01805 624067 rhs.org.uk/gardens/rosemoor

**Tapeley Park Gardens, Nr Instow.** With magnificent views out to sea, these fascinating gardens offer a variety of exciting terrains; wooded lakes, pleasure grounds, new Organic Permaculture garden, traditional walled kitchen garden, and beside the unique Italian terraces rare plants flourish in the warm Devon climate. Home since 1700 to the Christie family who built the Opera House at Glyndebourne. Also, pigs and pets, pug's graves, ilex tunnel, grotto, croquet, bowls, plant

*The View from Torrington*

sales, lunches and cream teas in the Queen Anne Dairy. Health & Harmony Festive Weekends. Open daily late Mar to early Nov Su-F 10-5. (D2)
01271 860897
christieestates.co.uk

**The Big Sheep.** Sheep in all shapes, sizes and disguises, combining to create the bizarre, the entertaining and the unexpected. Sheep dairy and sheep milking. Mountain Boarding. Open daily Apr-Oct & winter W/Es & school hols, 10-6. (M3) 01237 472366
thebigsheep.co.uk

## Westward Ho!

Unusually, a seaside resort named after a book - it was established in 1863 in recognition of Charles Kingsley. Rudyard Kipling was educated at United Services College (some buildings survive as guest houses), and set 'Stalky & Co' in the hills to the south, now named 'Kipling Tors'. Interesting pebble beach to north. A quieter beach (but can be muddy) to surf becoming increasingly popular, away from the hordes of Croyde and Saunton. Of late, increasing building developments in the shape of apartments overlooking the sea, and a luxury hotel is in the planning stages. Fine bass fishing, and excellent fishing tackle shop. Major tennis club in North Devon. E/C W. (B2)

## BEACHES & SURFING...

**Westward Ho!** Wide expanse of sand. Pebble ridge behind. Water sports. R/WC/LG. (B2)

**Instow**. Flat, estuary sand, fine for sun bathing and ball games, but not conducive for bathing. R/P. (C1)

### LIGHT BITES...

Just off the Green is **Morans**, a restaurant and bar fusing Thai cuisine with English country fare, add a spectacular Cocktail, its a recipe for success. Opens at 11.30 M-F, Sa 10.30, Su 12.00 til late. 01237 472070 moransrestaurant.co.uk

A little distance away (by car) is **The Pig On The Hill.** This is a popular pub in a pastoral location. The food is pub-grub. On site, three self-catering cedar cabins. (B3) 01237 459222 pigonthehillwestwardho.co.uk

1966  Francis Chichester sets sail in Gypsy Moth IV on a solo one-stop global navigation, to be knighted the following year at Greenwich.

*Across the Estuary from Westward Ho!*

*Across the Estuary from Instow*

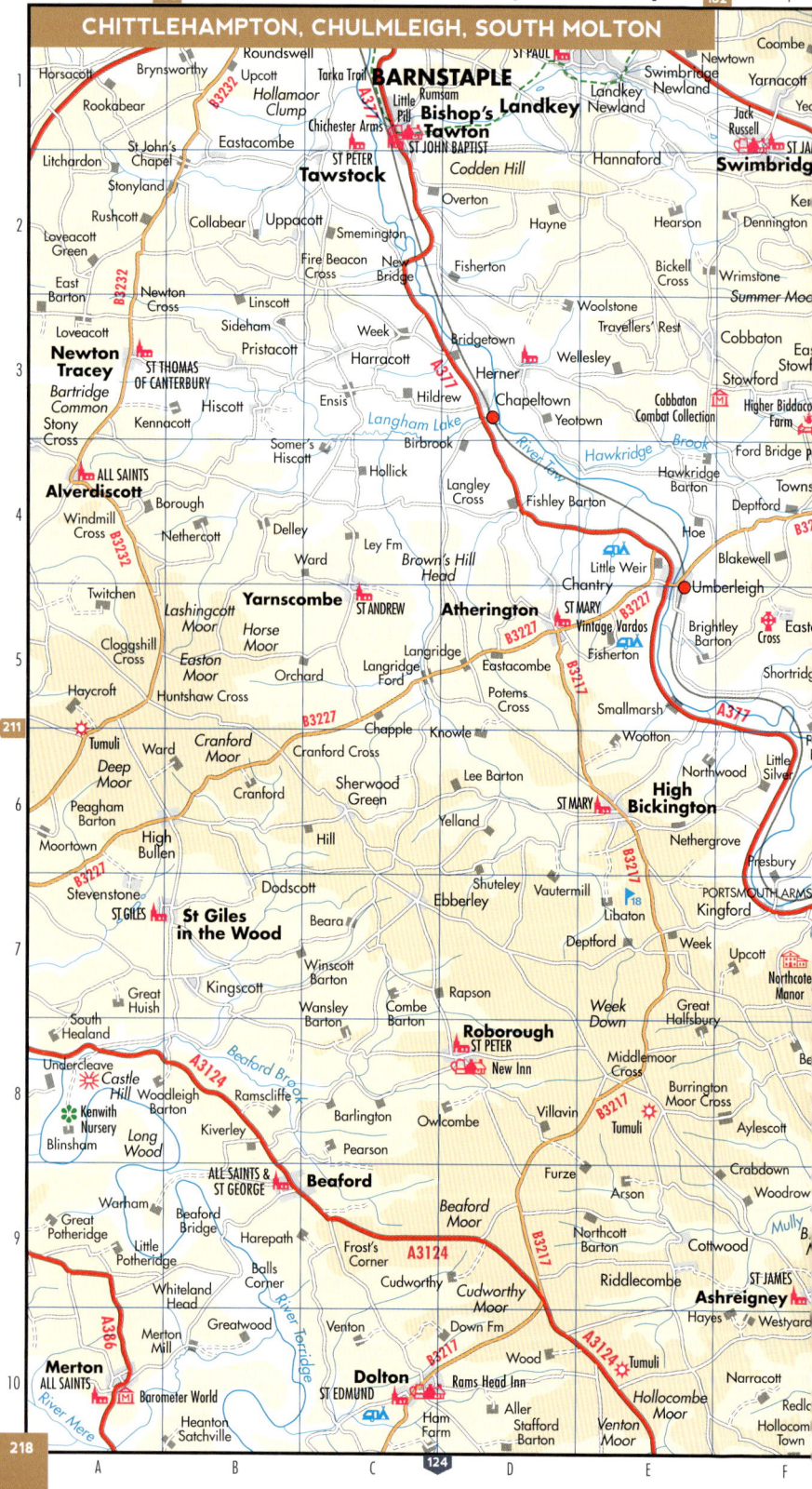

Horsacott • Brynsworthy • Roundswell • Upcott
169
182
Coombe
Newtown • Yarnacott
Rookabear
Hollamoor Clump
Tarka Trail
BARNSTAPLE
ST PAUL
Swimbridge Newland
Jack Russell
ST
Litchardon • St John's Chapel
Eastacombe
Chichester Arms
Little Pill
Rumsam
Bishop's
Landkey
Landkey Newland
Hannaford
Swimbridg
Stonyland
ST PETER
ST JOHN BAPTIST
Tawton
Codden Hill
Tawstock
Loveacott Green • Rushcott • Collabear • Uppacott • Smemington • Overton • Hayne • Hearson • Dennington
East Barton
B3232
Fire Beacon Cross
New Bridge
Fisherton
Bickell Cross
Wrimstone
Summer Moc
Loveacott
Newton Cross • Linscott
Woolstone
Travellers' Rest
Cobbaton
Eas Stowf

Newton Tracey
ST THOMAS OF CANTERBURY
Sideham • Pristacott • Week • Harracott
Bridgetown
Wellesley
Herner
Stowford
Higher Biddaco Farm
Bartridge Common
Hiscott • Ensis • Hildrew
Chapeltown
Yeotown
Cobbaton Combat Collection
Ford Bridge p
Stony Cross • Kennacott
Somer's Hiscatt
Birbrook
Langham Lake
River Taw
Hawkridge
Hawkridge Barton
Towns
ALL SAINTS
Hollick
Langley Cross
Fishley Barton
Hoe
Deptford
Alverdiscott
Borough • Delley
Ley Fm
Brown's Hill Head
Little Weir
Chantry
Blakewell
B37
Windmill Cross • Nethercott • Ward
Yarnscombe
ST ANDREW
Atherington
ST MARY
Vintage Vardos
B3227
Brightley Barton
Easte Cross
Twitchen • Lashingcott Moor • Horse Moor
Langridge
Eastacombe
Fisherton
Umberleigh
Shortridg
Haycroft • Cloggshill Cross • Easton Moor • Huntshaw Cross • Orchard
Langridge Ford
Potems Cross
B3217
A377
B3227
Chapple
Knowle
Smallmarsh
Wootton
Littl Silver
Tumuli • Ward • Cranford Moor • Cranford Cross
Sherwood Green
Lee Barton
Northwood
Deep Moor • Cranford
Hill
Yelland
ST MARY
High Bickington
Nethergrove
Presbury
Peagham Barton • Moortown • High Bullen
Dodscott
Shuteley
Vautermill
B3217
PORTSMOUTH ARMS
Stevenstone
ST GILES
St Giles in the Wood
Beara
Ebberley
18
Libaton
Kingford
Great Huish • Kingscott • Winscott Barton • Wansley Barton • Rapson
Deptford
Week
Upcott
Northcote Manor
South Healand • Undercleave
Castle Hill
Woodleigh Barton
Ramscliffe
Combe Barton
Week Down
Great Halfsbury
Kenwith Nursery
Kiverley
Barlington
Owlcombe
Villavin
Middlemoor Cross
Burrington Moor Cross
Crabdown
Woodrow
Blinsham
Long Wood
Pearson
Furze
Arson
B3217
Tumuli
Aylescott
Warham
ALL SAINTS & ST GEORGE
Beaford
Beaford Moor
Northcott Barton
Cottwood
Mully B
Great Potheridge • Beaford Bridge • Harepath
Frost's Corner
A3124
B3217
Riddlecombe
ST JAMES
Ashreigney
Little Potheridge • Balls Corner • Cudworthy
Cudworthy Moor
A386
Whiteland Head
Greatwood
Venton
Down Fm
Hayes
Westyard
Merton
ALL SAINTS
Merton Mill
River Torridge
B3217
Wood
A3124
Tumuli
Narracott
Barometer World
Dolton
ST EDMUND
Rams Head Inn
Venton Moor
Hollocombe Moor
Redl
Heanton Satchville
Ham Farm
Aller Stafford Barton
Hollocom Town

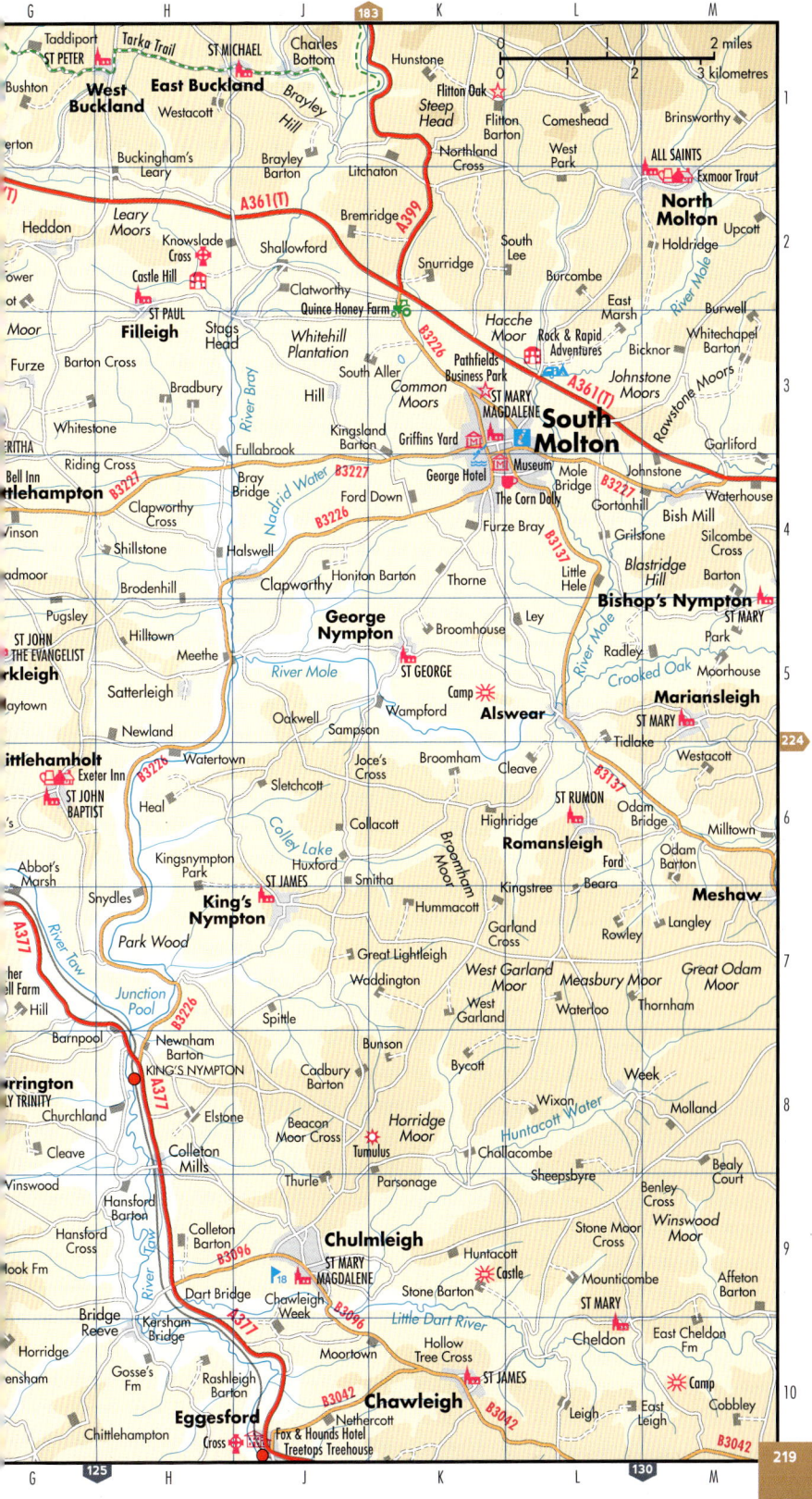

*Treeetops Treehouse, Eggesford*

### SOUTH MOLTON

Busy Market town for North East Devon, and route centre for Exmoor. Wide main street. C18 Guildhall and Museum. As the town's prosperity grew from the wool and cloth trade in the C17, and as several of the mills were powered by the River Mole, processing wool and corn, the town became an important thoroughfare for merchants, gaining a riotous reputation employing some 500 Ladies of Ill Repute (see Museum). Sheep Fair - end Aug. E/C W. (L3)

#### TO VISIT IN TOWN...

**Quince Honey Farm, Aller Cross.** Britain's largest and

*Quince Honey Farm, South Molton ss*

1998    Local government re-organisation.
Plymouth and Torbay become unitary authorities.

## LIGHT BITES...

**Corn Dolly, 115a East St.** Real tea shop providing breakfast, light lunches and cream teas. Home baked fare. Gifts. Open daily. (K4)

**Griffin's Yard, North St.** An organic and natural foods emporium, as well as a Café serving lunch, teas and coffees. 01769 572372 Also, KK Design, a personal service creating curtains, clothing and soft funishings. 01769 572299. Open M-Sa from 9am. (K3) griffinsyard.co.uk

most innovative honey farm, and home to millions of bees with a unique exhibition of observation hives. You can wander around the beautiful Nectar Gardens to view the bees up close. Honey and beeswax products for sale. Open daily 9.30-5. (K3) 01769 572401 quincehoneyfarm.co.uk

**South Molton Museum, The Guidhall.** Glimpses into the domestic life, trades, industry, mining and farming of the town and district's

past. Open late Mar to early Nov M & Tu 10.30-4. Th & Sa 10.30-1. (L3) 01769 572951 southmoltonmuseum.org

## TO VISIT...

**Castle Hill.** Grade 1 Palladian mansion built in 1730 by Hugh Fortescue, Lord Clinton, as his family home is set in 5,500 acres of prime agricultural land. Home of the late Sir John Fortescue, historian and the Queen's Librarian at Windsor Castle and good friend to Henry Williamson who lived for seven years at Shallowford where he wrote Salar the Salmon and raised many children. Now the home of the Earl and Countess of Arran. House open by appointment only, Gardens all year M-F from 11am. An impressive sight from the road. Public access is permitted along two paths from Feb-Sept inclusive, starting from Filleigh Village Hall (3/4 hour) and Filleigh Sawmill (1/2 hour). (H2) 01598 760421 castlehilldevon.co.uk

**Cobbaton Combat Collection.** British and Canadian fighting vehicles of World War 11. Field guns, radios and other equipment. Home Front section, Women's Land Army. Children's play area. Militaria shop. Open Su-F Apr-Oct & Su July-Aug, Nov-Mar M-F 10-5. (E3) 01769 540740 cobbatoncombat.co.uk

## EAT...DRINK...SLEEP...

**Fox & Hounds Hotel, Eggesford.** Former Victorian Coaching Inn set amidst the beautiful Taw Valley. Roaring fires and comfy leather sofas will relax you. The bedrooms have been refurbished. Fishing rights on five beats; Ghillie services and fly fishing tuition available. Day tickets available to non-residents. Bar foods and restaurant. The **Treetops Treehouse** set within a 250-year old oak tree may be more your thing. It's over-the-top (sic) luxury. No dogs. All set within the North Devon Biosphere Reserve and the River Taw, below. (J10) 01769 580345 foxandhoundshotel.co.uk

*Shallowford Bridge*

**Higher Biddacott Farm, Chittlehampton**. B&B in C12 farm house. Large bedroom with 1680 pargetted ceiling by the famous Abbot Brothers. Jonathan Waterer is a Devon-style Horse Whisperer, training Heavy and Light Horses. Wagon tours. Pre-arranged Dinner available. Also, a Self-catering cottage and a Wildlife Trail. (F3) 01769 540222
heavyhorsesnet.wordpress.com

**Northcote Manor, Nr Burrington**. C18 manor house set in 20-acres of mature woodland with outstanding views overlooking the Taw Valley. Classic English Country House hotel provides luxury and comfort at a relaxed pace. Great bathrooms and big beds. Boasts one of North Devon's finest restaurants (open to non-residents for lunch and dinner). If your conversation is at a loss then admire the Murals of monks past. Worth visiting for Afternoon Teas. (F7) 01769 560501
northcotemanor.co.uk

**Vintage Vardos, Fisherton Farm.** Ever wished to really get away from it all? To immerse yourself in nature; the sound of birdsong, waving trees, running water and a firepit to cook and eat like Kings and Queens. Fresh lamb and beef supplied from this farm. Groups of up to 14 to share 4 Gypsy Wagons. (E5) 07977 535233
fishertonfarm.com

## ARTS & CRAFTS...

**Chittlehampton Pottery**. Roger Cockram creates handmade pots and jars based on a Natural World theme. Open M-F 10-1, 2.15-5 (F4) 01769 540420
rogercockramceramics.co.uk

**2006    December.** Sgt (sniper) Steve Ross of the 1st Battalion Grenadier Guards from Barnstaple is awarded the Military Cross at the Battle of Al Amarah, Iraq, June 11.

## COUNTRYSIDE INTERESTS…

**Higher Hacknell Organic Farm.** An award-winning food supplier farming organically since 1985; South Devon beef, Lleyn and Lenx Texel lamb, pork sausages. Food Boxes (and Ready Meals) to satisfy all carnivores. (F7) 01769 560909
higherhacknell.co.uk

**Rock and Rapid Adventures South Molton.** Indoor climbing wall and outdoor activities galore; rock climbing, coasteering, swimming, caving, jumping, survival training and more, all with qualified instructors. Café. Outdoor gear/hire shop. Open daily 10 til late. (L3) 01769 309003
rockandrapidadventures.co.uk

## EAT… DRINK…RELAX…

**The Grove Inn, Kings Nympton.** Gracious and friendly hospitality awaits you in this traditional country pub serving fine Devon cuisine and real ales. No wonder we keep hearing encouraging reports about this dining pub. (J7) 01769 580406
thegroveinn.co.uk

**The New Inn, Roborough.** A traditional C16 thatched Inn bestows a warm hospitality and a snug ambience. Good, wholesome pub-grub. (D8) 01805 603247

**The Rams Head Inn, Dolton.** This is a welcome new hostelry on the North Devon stage. Their young chef was trained by a Michelin-starred chef, and the food is an exponent of this. The decor is a kaleidoscope of form. The B&B is luxurious. (A10) 01805 804255
ramsheadinn.co.uk

*Brayford Trees*

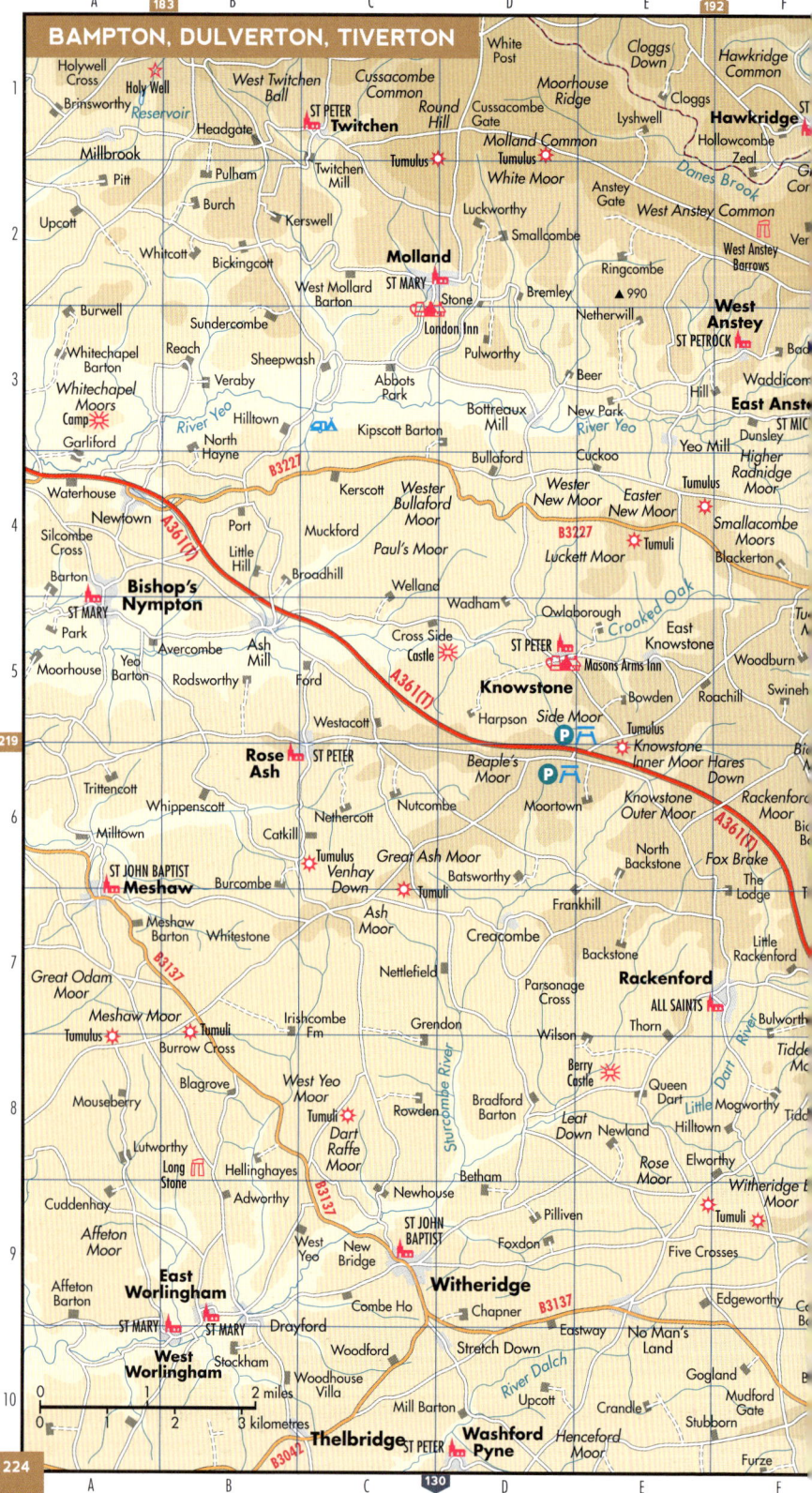

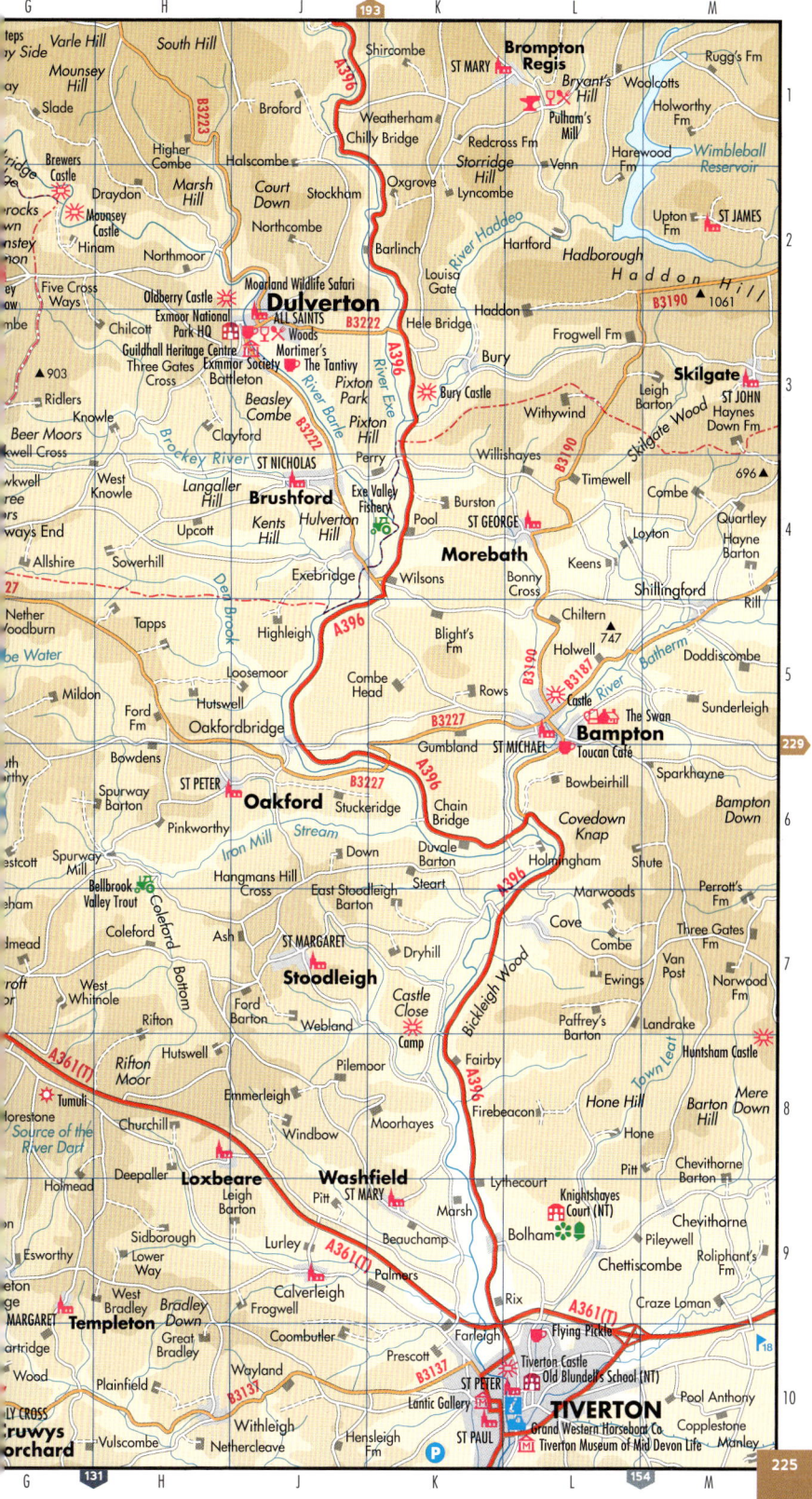

G H J K L M

1

Varle Hill
South Hill
Shircombe
**Brompton Regis**
ST MARY
Rugg's Fm
Mounsey Hill
Slade
Broford
Weatherham
Chilly Bridge
Bryant's Hill
Woolcotts
Pulham's Mill
Holworthy Fm
Wimbleball Reservoir

2

Brewers Castle
Draydon
Higher Combe
Marsh Hill
Halscombe
Court Down
Stockham
Oxgrove
Storridge Hill
Redcross Fm
Venn
Harewood Fm
Upton Fm
ST JAMES
Mounsey Castle
Hinam
Northmoor
Northcombe
Barlinch
River Haddeo
Hartford
Haddon Hill
1061

3

Five Cross Ways
Oldberry Castle
Moorland Wildlife Safari
**Dulverton**
ALL SAINTS
Louisa Gate
Hele Bridge
Haddon
Frogwell Fm
Hadborough
Skilgate
ST JOHN
Chilcott
Exmoor National Park HQ
Woods
Mortimer's
Bury
Leigh Barton
Skilgate Wood
Haynes Down Fm
Three Gates Cross
Guildhall Heritage Centre
Exmoor Society
The Tantivy
Pixton Park
Bury Castle
Withywind
696
Ridlers
Knowle
Battleton
Beasley Combe
Clayford
Pixton Hill
Willishayes
Timewell
Combe
Quartley
Beer Moors
West Knowle
Langaller Hill
Perry
ST NICHOLAS
St Nicholas
Exe Valley Fishery
Burston
ST GEORGE
Loyton
Hayne Barton

4

Allshire
Sowerhill
**Brushford**
Kents Hill
Hulverton Hill
Pool
**Morebath**
Keens
Shillingford
Rill
Upcott
Exebridge
Wilsons
Bonny Cross
Nether Woodburn
Tapps
Highleigh
Blight's Fm
Chiltern
Holwell
747
Doddiscombe

5

be Water
Mildon
Loosemoor
Combe Head
Rows
Castle
The Swan
Sunderleigh
Ford Fm
Hutswell
Oakfordbridge
Gumbland
ST MICHAEL
**Bampton**
Toucan Café
229

6

Bowdens
Spurway Barton
ST PETER
**Oakford**
Stuckeridge
Chain Bridge
Bowbeirhill
Sparkhayne
Bampton Down
Pinkworthy
Down
Duvale Barton
Covedown Knap
Spurway Mill
Hangmans Hill Cross
East Stoodleigh Barton
Steart
Holmingham
Shute
Perrott's Fm
Bellbrook Valley Trout
Coleford
Ash
ST MARGARET
Dryhill
Marwoods
Cove
Combe
Three Gates Fm
Van Post
Norwood Fm

7

West Whitnole
Rifton
Ford Barton
**Stoodleigh**
Webland
Castle Close
Ewings
Landrake
Huntsham Castle
Rifton Moor
Hutswell
Pilemoor
Camp
Bickleigh Wood
Paffrey's Barton
Fairby
Hone Hill
Barton Down
Mere Down

8

Tumuli
Churchill
Emmerleigh
Moorhayes
Firebeacon
Hone
Horestone
Source of the River Dart
Windbow
Pitt
Chevithorne Barton
Holmead
Deepaller
**Loxbeare**
Leigh Barton
Pitt
**Washfield**
ST MARY
Marsh
Lythecourt
Knightshayes Court (NT)
Chevithorne
Pileywell

9

Esworthy
Sidborough
Lower Way
Lurley
Beauchamp
Bolham
Chettiscombe
Roliphant's Fm
West Bradley
Calverleigh
Palmers
Rix
Craze Loman
ST MARGARET
**Templeton**
Bradley Down
Frogwell
Coombutler
Prescott
Farleigh
Flying Pickle
A361(T)
18

10

Great Bradley
Wayland
Plainfield
Withleigh
Hensleigh Fm
Prescott
ST PETER
Old Blundell's School (NT)
**Tiverton**
Pool Anthony
Copplestone
Manley
LY CROSS
ruwys orchard
Vulscombe
Nethercleave
Lantic Gallery
ST PAUL
Grand Western Horseboat Co
Tiverton Museum of Mid Devon Life

G 131 H J K L 154 M

## Bampton

A natural route centre set in a sheltered wooded valley. Fine C13 and C16 church and Heritage Centre (that should be your first stop-off) with Saxon Cross. A thriving wool centre in the C18 and by the 1800s the largest sheepfair in the South West, for over 14,000 sheep were sold at Bampton Fair. Today, the town is famous for the annual October Fair, on the last Thursday. In the 1880s it became, for the next one hundred years, the famous Bampton Pony Fair trading in Exmoor ponies. The locality is rich in wildlife encouraged by the conservation policy in the town.

### LIGHT BITES... SERIOUS BITES...

The **Toucan Café Bistro** on pretty **Brook Street** has had a loyal following for many years. Open daily from 9 for breakfast and light lunches. 01398 331777 toucanrestaurant.co.uk

I am not impressed by awards for best pub or best café but **The Swan B&B** behind the **Churchyard** has been in the news as a Pub of the Year. It has a mixed clientele; rustic artisans pop in for an after work drink, or two followed by a more refined crowd in search of fine dining and good-value pub-grub. Bampton has been crying out for such a venue. 01398 332248 theswan.co

Seeking out a treat? Head to **Spelt**, 42 Brook Street. A cute, youthful little restaurant inspired by trips to Barcelona and the flavours issued, hitherto, to Bampton. (L5) 01398 31044 speltbampton.co.uk

## Dulverton

Often described as the gateway to southern Exmoor but it is much more than that. It's a thriving community with all sorts of buildings and interesting shops, plus antiques, galleries, tearooms, pubs and restaurants. An old-fashioned country town happy with its lot. The National Park have their HQ here, and there are easy riverside walks beside the River Barle.  It has the best shooting and fishing on Exmoor, the Barle is well stocked with Brown Trout and Salmon. The church tower dates from the C12, and inside are memorials to the colourful Sydenham family, and stained glass provided by the founder of the YMCA, George Williams. Nearby is Pixton Park, former home of the Herbert family (Earls of Carnarvon) whom the Catholic novelist and travel writer Evelyn Waugh married into, and the Aclands of Killerton Park and Selworthy. (J3)

### Guildhall Heritage & Arts Centre, Off Fore St.

Exhibitions of local artists and craftsmen, plus Touring Exhibitions. Open daily East-Oct 10-4.30. (J3) 07969 243887

### The Exmoor Society, 34 High St.

Their purpose is to protect and fight to maintain Exmoor's heaths, grass moors, ancient woodlands, tranquil landscapes and uncluttered skylines. They organise walks, talks, field visits and more. Independent of the National Park. Open daily. (J3) 01398 323335 exmoorsociety.com

## ARTS & CRAFTS ...

**Lantic Gallery, 38 Gold Street.** Gallery displaying a variety of artists and craftsmen;

### LIGHT BITES...

**Dulverton** is awash with pubs and tearooms. If in need of lunch and ale I always head for **Woods Bar & Restaurant, 4 Bank Square**. Genial, cosy and a relaxed ambience pervades this pub decorated with old prints. A log fire, British cooking with a French bias is all-enticing. (J3) 01398 324007 woodsdulverton. co.uk Looking for coffee, cake and a newspaper, or walking map to tramp **Exmoor's** paths, you better start at **The Tantivy**. Breakfast is from 9. If a Welsh Rarebit is your salvation head down the **High Street** to **Mortimer's** where you can get a cream tea, and ice cream for your dog, no less. 01398 323850 mortimersfood.co.uk

John Maltby, Les Grimshaw... and constantly changing exhibs. Open M-Sa 9.30-5. (L10) 01884 259888 lanticgallery.co.uk

**Pulhams Mill, Nr Brompton Regis.** Solid timber furniture in English hardwoods, and hand painted English china and tiles with rural scenes. Tuition on-hand. Tea room and gardens. Barn Shop a showcase of British arts and crafts. Open daily.  (L1) 01398 371366 pulhamsmill.co.uk

### COUNTRYSIDE INTERESTS...

**Bellbrook Valley Trout Fishery.** If you seek peace, wildlife and are of a mind to catch trout then visit this isolated haven. There are 7 lakes fed from 2 streams in a 40-acre valley. Fly fishing for Rainbows. Day fishing. Tuition

available. Open all year. (H6)
01398 351292
bellbrookfishery.co.uk

**Exe Valley Fishery, Exebridge**.
Rainbow Trout are reared here
where you will find a farm shop
and fly fishing lakes. Fly fishing
courses. Open daily 8-6. (K4)
01398 323008
exevalleyfishery.net

**Wimbleball Lake.** A 370-acre
reservoir housing the Outdoor
& Activity Centre that organises
fishing, dinghy sailing,
camping, waymarked walks,
windsurfing, a nature reserve
and trail. Circular cycle route
with cycle hire. Café. Open daily,
all year. Not accessible by public
transport. (M1)
01398 371460

## EAT...DRINK...

**London Inn, Molland**.
Now thankfully back under
new ownership. The tell-tale
signs are positive and the
Sunday lunches a treat. How
a country pub in a rural idyll
should be. 01769 550269
londoninnmolland.co.uk

**Masons Arms Inn,
Knowstone**. A thatched village
inn with a small, cosy bar leading
to the restaurant. Mark Dodson's
cuisine has been lauded with
awards. It will empty your
pockets of change, and arrest
your bank balance. The Dining
Room extension has interesting
murals on the ceilings and fine
countryside views. Masterclasses
organized. Food Station.
Booking advised. Just off the
Two Moors Way. Open Tu-Sa 12-
2.30, 6-11 pm. (E5) 01398 341231
masonsarmsdevon.co.uk

## TO STAY...TO SLEEP...

**Bulworthy Project,
Rackenford.** Stay in an off-
the-grid cabin and experiment
with low impact living. Forage
for wild food and listen out for
badgers, foxes and owls. No
mains electricity. (G8)
07594569441
bulworthyproject.org.uk

**Rosemary Cottage B&B.**
Ideally situated for footsore
folk in need of rest after a long
trek. Two bedrooms. Book in
advance. (E5) 01398 341510
rosemary-cottage.co.uk

## TIVERTON

The Market Town for the
Exe Valley and main centre
for the north-east corner of
Devon. The major attractions
being the imposing Castle,
Old Blundell's School and the
notable Parish Church next
to the Castle. There is a Town
Trail leading you to the most
interesting aspects of this
small, industrial town. The
major employer, the Heathcoat
lace factory, in operation since
1816 has a store selling all
manner of lace and fabrics.
The Luddites had forced John
Heathcoat, inventor of the
bobbinet lace machine, to leave
Loughborough, so he headed
south to friendly Devonshire.
The Railway Station at Tiverton
Parkway is a conduit for all
rail travellers heading out into
North/Mid-Devon and Exmoor.

## TO VISIT...

**Cothay Manor Gardens**
This is a magical garden of
12-acres laid out in the 1920s,
which was redesigned and
replanted within the original
framework of the yew hedges.
The Manor was built in 1480
and has remained virtually
untouched. No dogs. Open
for "Open Days," as locally
advertised. (E6) 01823 672283
cothaymanor.co.uk

*St Peter's, Tiverton*

### LIGHT BITES...

Park opposite the **Tiverton Museum** and bear R to **The Duck & Bean**, a friendly civilised eatery on 5 Fore Street with back garden. Breakfast to Supper and Evening Cocktails. 01884 798330
theduckandbean.co.uk

Enter the High Street, R at fork into Gold Street. Soon to reach **LIZNOJAN Books & Coffee** translated to Road to Enlightenment or Wisdom. An Independent Bookshop with Café serving gluten free and plant based coffee, teas, cakes, lunches and cocktails 9-4 M-Sa. 01884 250183
liznojanbooks.co.uk

Alternatively walk down to **The Flying Pickle** at 40 Gold Street where you can have a splendid repast, a deli and café of impressive heights. 01884 242661
flyingpickledeli.co.uk

Further down the street towards Tesco, on the corner opposite the ancient build that was Blundells, a Vietnamese noodle bar, **Pho Nam** opens 11-2.30, 6-9. (L10) phonam.co.uk

**Grand Western Canal Country Park, Canal Hill**. The canal meanders through eleven miles of beautiful Devon countryside. On either side a rich diversity of wildlife; wildflowers, plants, hedgerows, fields and small woodland. The towpath provides easy walking with good car parking and picnic sites available. The Canal today (Tiverton-Lowdeswells) is a remnant section of the intended route between Bristol and the English Channel. Work began in 1810, was completed in 1814, with the northern section completed in 1838. However, it was unprofitable and closed in 1869. (L10) 01884 254072

**Grand Western Horseboat Co., The Wharf**. The enchantment and tranquility of travel, at a slow pace; a painted barge pulled by heavy horses mingles with nature. Boat hire. Café-Bar. Picnics. Open Tu-Su & BHS Apr/East to end Oct. Reservations advised: (L10) 01884 253345
tivertoncanal.co.uk

**Knightshayes Court (NT)**. Victorian Gothic house designed by two contrasting architects. Richly decorated interior. Paintings. Garden of interest at all seasons; specimen trees, formal terraces, unique topiary, rare shrubs, 'Garden in the Wood'. Plant sales. Restaurant and NT shop. Parkland open all year, dawn to dusk. House/Garden open daily from 10. (L9) 01884 254665
nationaltrust.org.uk

**Parish Church of St Peter.** A grand building built from the proceeds of the wool trade. The intricate detail of sailing ships cut into the white limestone of the South Porch was the gift of the wool merchant, John Greenway in 1517. Inside, Tomb Memorials to the rich burghers of the town; George Slee and John Waldron. (L10)

**Tiverton Castle.** Historic fortress of Henry 1 built in 1106. Fine medieval gatehouse and tower. Romantic ruins of chapel, solar and curtain walls. Fine Civil War armoury, old wall and new gardens. Open East Su to end Oct, Su, Th & BH Ms, 2.30-5.30. Other times for parties of 12 or more. (L10) 01884 253200
tivertoncastle.com

**Tiverton Museum of Mid Devon Life, Beck's Square**. An award-winning museum that depicts local industries, a railway gallery, Victorian laundry, Great Western Canal relics, wartime history and model aircraft. TIC: 01884 230878. Open Feb-Dec 21 M-F 10.30-4.30, Sa 10-1. Winter W-Sa 11-4. (L10) 01884 256295
tivertonmuseum.org.uk

### VILLAGES TO VISIT...

**Sampford Peverell.** Fine church built by Sir Hugh Peverell, Lord of the Manor from 1241 to 1296. His monument lies on the north side of the Chancel. Restored in the mid C19.

### EAT...DRINK...

**Globe Inn, Appley.** Hidden away down narrow Somerset lanes is this popular C16 Freehouse with cosy, little rooms. Superb prints of ships. No dogs. Open W-Su. (D6) 01823 673147

*St Peter's, Tiverton*

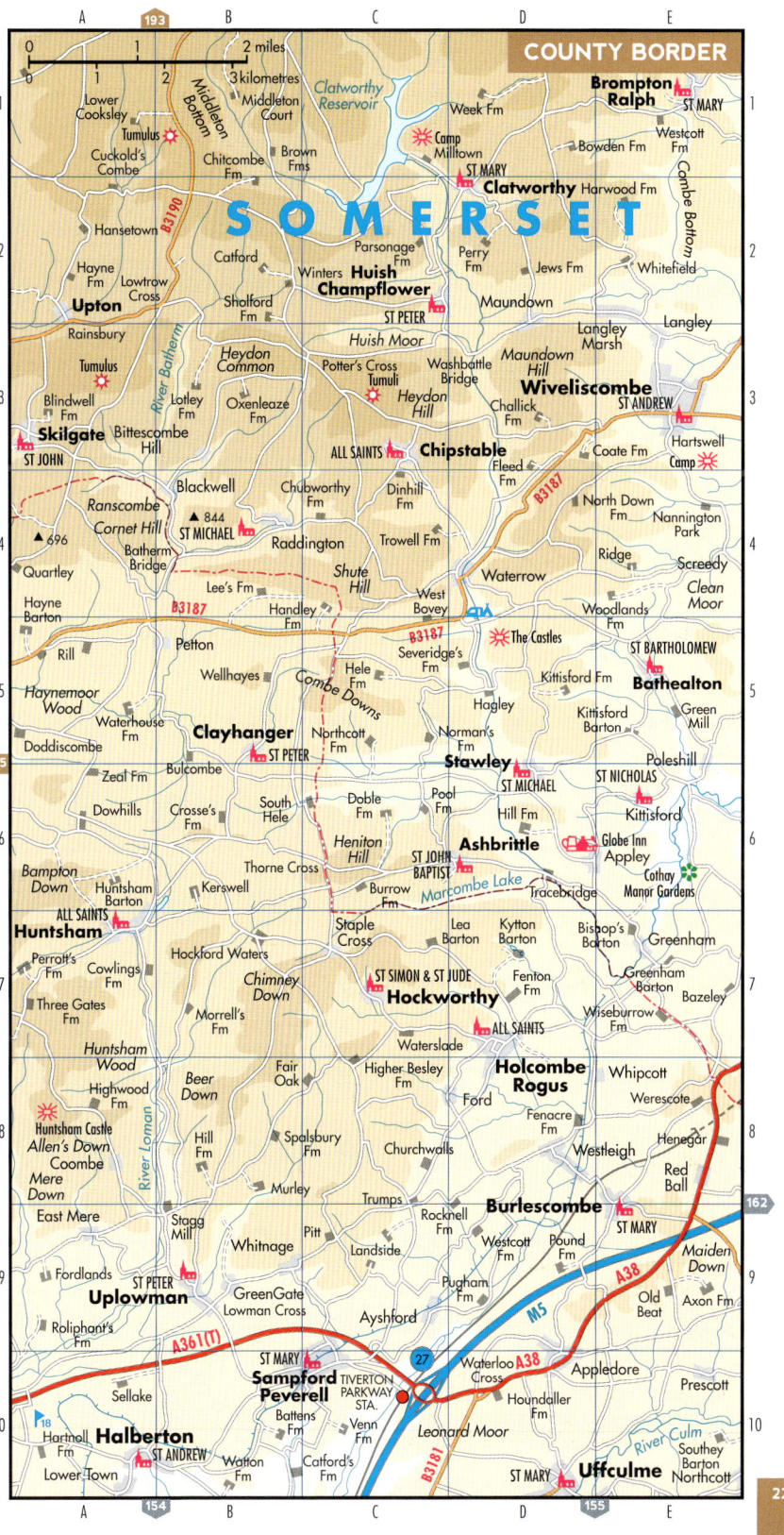

**SOMERSET**

Brompton
Ralph
ST MARY

Lower
Cooksley
Tumulus
Cuckold's
Combe
Week Fm
Camp
Milltown
ST MARY
Clatworthy
Bowden Fm
Westcott
Fm
Combe Bottom

Middleton
Bottom
Middleton
Court
Chitcombe
Fm
Brown
Fms
Clatworthy
Reservoir
Harwood Fm

Hansetown
Hayne
Fm
Lowtrow
Cross
Upton
Rainsbury
Catford
Sholford
Fm
Parsonage
Fm
Huish
Champflower
ST PETER
Winters
Perry
Fm
Maundown
Jews Fm
Whitefield
Langley
Marsh
Langley

Tumulus
Blindwell
Skilgate
ST JOHN
Lotley
Fm
Oxenleaze
Fm
Bittescombe
Hill
Heydon
Common
Huish Moor
Potter's Cross
Tumuli
Heydon
Hill
Washbattle
Bridge
Challick
Maundown
Hill
Wiveliscombe
ST ANDREW
Hartswell
Camp
Coate Fm

Blackwell
Ranscombe
696
Cornet Hill
844
ST MICHAEL
Raddington
Batherm
Bridge
Chubworthy
Fm
Dinhill
Fm
Trowell Fm
ALL SAINTS
Chipstable
Fleed
Fm
North Down
Fm
Nannington
Park
Ridge
Screedy
Clean
Moor

Quartley
Hayne
Barton
Rill
Lee's Fm
Handley
Fm
Shute
Hill
West
Bovey
Waterrow
B3187
B3187
Woodlands
ST BARTHOLOMEW
Bathealton
Green
Mill

Petton
Haynemoor
Wood
Waterhouse
Fm
Doddiscombe
Clayhanger
ST PETER
Wellhayes
Hele
Fm
Severidge's
Fm
The Castles
Hagley
Kittisford Fm
Kittisford
Barton
Poleshill

Zeal Fm
Dowhills
Bulcombe
Crosse's
Fm
South
Hele
Northcott
Fm
Norman's
Fm
Stawley
ST MICHAEL
ST NICHOLAS
Kittisford

Bampton
Down
Huntsham
Barton
Kerswell
Thorne Cross
Doble
Fm
Heniton
Hill
Pool
Fm
Hill Fm
Ashbrittle
ST JOHN
BAPTIST
Globe Inn
Appley
Cothay
Manor Gardens

ALL SAINTS
Huntsham
Perrott's
Fm
Cowlings
Fm
Three Gates
Fm
Hockford Waters
Chimney
Down
Morrell's
Fm
Burrow
Fm
Staple
Cross
Lea
Barton
Kytton
Barton
ST SIMON & ST JUDE
Hockworthy
ALL SAINTS
Fenton
Fm
Bishop's
Barton
Greenham
Greenham
Barton
Bazeley
Wiseburrow
Fm
Tracebridge
Marcombe Lake

Huntsham
Wood
Highwood
Fm
Huntsham Castle
Allen's Down
Coombe
Mere
Down
Beer
Down
Hill
Fm
Spalsbury
Fm
Murley
Fair
Oak
Higher Besley
Fm
Waterslade
Churchwalls
Ford
Holcombe
Rogus
Fenacre
Fm
Westleigh
Whipcott
Werescote
Henegar
Red
Ball

East Mere
Fordlands
Roliphant's
Fm
Stagg
Mill
Whitnage
Pitt
Landside
Trumps
Rocknell
Fm
Westcott
Fm
Pound
Fm
Burlescombe
ST MARY
Maiden
Down

Uplowman
ST PETER
GreenGate
Lowman Cross
Ayshford
Pugham
Fm
Waterloo
Cross
A38
Houndaller
Fm
Appledore
Prescott
Old
Beat
Axon Fm
A38

Sellake
Halberton
ST ANDREW
Lower Town
Hartnoll
Fm
Battens
Fm
Watton
Fm
Catford's
Fm
ST MARY
Sampford
Peverell
TIVERTON
PARKWAY
STA.
Venn
Fm
Leonard Moor
Uffculme
ST MARY
River Culm
Southey
Barton
Northcott

River Batherm
River Loman
Combe Downs

Devon history starts with the discovery of Early Man in the caves of Torquay (Kent's Cavern) and Brixham. He lived off reindeer and hunted with weapons sharpened from flint. Their successors, the long-headed Iberians settled on Dartmoor living in circular stone huts topped with thatch.

At first they buried their dead in the crouch position. They later burnt them to store their ashes in clay pots. A stone chest was erected around the body or pot and covered with earth. At around 2,500 BC bronze was discovered and Dartmoor streams were washed for tin. In 1,000 BC a Celtic invasion from Ireland subdued the Iberians. With a second Celtic invasion around 500 BC came the knowledge of Iron and a new language with the Brythons. Some words continue in use to this day:- dun – hill, dur – water, combe – hill side valley, pen – head or end, and avon – river.  The Celts later gave way to the Romans. But, it is important to understand the countless Neolithic and Bronze Age terms and their original uses.

## BURIAL CHAMBERS (Dolmens/Cromlech)

Originally built as family mausoleums made up of several large stones with a capstone, or two across the top. Inside, the unburned body was placed, then filled over with earth.  The finest example is "Spinster Rock" at Shilstone Farm, Drewsteignton. You can park beside the road and walk into the field where it remains in fine condition. A more sophisticated development of this design, the chambered tumulus, is to be found at Carnac, Brittany, Belas Knap, Gloucestershire and in Wiltshire.  Small burial chambers (Kistvaens) were scattered all over Dartmoor. There is little evidence of these today, all desecrated long ago.  You would have seen a heap of stones with ashes placed in a pot. The normal construction would take a surround of stone circles. Examples to be seen at Merrivale Bridge, Postbridge or Lake Head Hill, Hound Tor

## STONE CIRCLES.

These are to be found all over Dartmoor. The stones were set upright in a diameter of between 60-100 feet but often larger. Marked with a small stone (burial chamber) in the centre. A ditch or bank may border the site. The best examples to be seen at Scorhill near Chagford, Greywethers near Fernworthy, and at Langstone Moor near Peter Tavy.  Their original purpose is not clear. Some scholars believe they were used for tribal meetings; judicial, religious, sepulchral. Large charcoal remains in the centre

suggest great fires or rituals; sacrificial burials, or mass burials following disease or pestilence.

## STONE ROWS OR STONE AVENUES (single or double rows).

These have long been associated with funeral rites. At the head of the row, a tumulus or burial chamber and at the end, a blocking stone. Each stone would have represented a household, or family of the tribe, and would have been placed in honour of their chief. Fifty plus such sites have been counted on Dartmoor. The best are to be seen at Drizzlecombe,  Down Tor, Merrivale Bridge and Watern Hill.

## STANDING STONES (Monoliths/Menhirs)

These are prehistoric memorials, remnants of stone that have survived the elements; wind and rain, and archaeological interference. The Christian Celts sculpted crosses out of the granite blocks, and more recently the Romans and others drew inscriptions. The finest survivors, Caratacus Stone, Winsford Hill and Toreus Stone in Yealmpton churchyard.

## ANCIENT VILLAGES (Hut Circles)

There are literally hundreds of these scattered across Dartmoor. The original smallholding, a basic hut with enclosure to protect their animals from preying beasts. Occupied by late Neolithic and Bronze Age Man. The village would be located in a dry, well drained position close to pure water stocked with abundant fish, and on open ground, easily protected against wild beasts and away from the hostile valleys and wild swamps. As time moved on into the Bronze Age, Man learnt to exploit the streams working for tin, later to trade and export to the Continent through the mouths of the rivers Otter, Axe, Dart and Exe. Early trade routes have been traced from Wray Barton in Moretonhampstead, by Berry Road to Merripit, via Postbridge and on to Mis Tor. A Roman route runs south from Okehampton from 100 BC to 100AD.

## THE ROMAN PERIOD.

The Romans didn't venture much beyond their garrison at Exeter beside the River Exe although satellite warning forts have been discovered at Countisbury on the North Coast and they would have reached this remote spot via sea, sailing down from Gloucester (Glevum). Evidence of the Roman Occupation has been excavated at Seaton and Uplyme. A Roman road through Honiton and south to Axminster (and Axmouth) connects the Fosse Way.

**THE CELTIC PERIOD.** Once the Romans left, Britain was ripe for invasion. In the early C5 the Irish Celts invaded North Devon and Cornwall, and the west became the Kingdom of Dumnovia, to be Christianised by Irish missionaries. They gave firm resistance to the Saxon invaders. Later in the C6 and C7 the mystical King Arthur was born. In the C9 and C10, Kings Egbert and Athelstan pushed to forge a united Kingdom. Thereafter the Saxons settled into the valleys within their enclosures to raise their crops and domestic animals. Peace was interrupted by the invading Danes in the C9 who ravaged the coast. It was not until the Norman Conquest of the C11 that life took on a modicum of stability for the Saxon peasant.

**WILLIAM I**. William divided the Saxon lands amongst his favourite Norman knights. The great Lords of Devon became the Earl of Mortain, Earl Hugo, Baldwin the Sherrif, Judhael de Totnes, William de Mohun and Ralph de Pomeroy. Many of the Saxon manors were passed to the churches (Abbeys) in Normandy. Exeter Castle was put to siege and most of the county barring Dartmoor and Exmoor was disafforested and given over to agriculture.

**THE TUDOR MONARCHS**. With Henry V11, Henry V111 and Edward V1, life in Devon was full of strife and difficulty. In 1497, the men of Devon and Cornwall rose up against the burden of taxation, and took to arms under Lord Audley. They were defeated at Blackheath. Later that year the Pretender Perkin Warbeck collected followers from Devon and Cornwall and besieged Exeter to be beaten back by the Earl of Devon. The Dissolution of the Monasteries under Henry V111 kept unrest on the boil. But, things took a turn for the worse under Edward V1 when he introduced changes to the Common Book of Prayer (the following turn of events incomprehensible today). A rebellion started at Sampford Courtenay, and quickly spread. Headed by Sir Thomas Pomeroy, they marched to Exeter, occupied the town and set up fortifications at St Mary Clyst. To be soundly defeated by German mercenaries under the command of Lord Russell. The ringleaders were summarily executed; hung, drawn and quartered. So ended the Devon Rebellion.

**ELIZABETH I**. Devon men took patriotism (and self-interest) to all corners of the globe. Under a galaxy of famous sea captains; Raleigh, Drake, Gilbert and the Hawkins. Their devotion to England and her cause (or Queen) could not be questioned.

**THE CIVIL WAR**. The gentry and countryside were Royalist, whilst the towns largely followed the Parliamentarians (Cromwell). The Queen, Henrietta Maria, inspected Prince Rupert's army at Crediton. Plymouth and Dartmouth withstood sieges, and Exeter was garrisoned by the Parliamentarians. Tavistock became a Royalist stronghold in 1643. Tiverton changed hands many times. Torrington was the scene of one of the bloodiest battles when Fairfax defeated the Royalists under Lord Hopton in 1646. The irony was that the Parliamentarian General Monk, a Torrington man, became the main force behind the Restoration (return of Charles 11).

**AGRICULTURE**. The Devon man was soon to become shaped by his social and economic circumstances. Those living beside, or close to, the sea made a living from it, either as sailors in the Navy, or as fishermen. Devon had long held a tradition of trade well before the Roman Occupation. The development of shipbuilding in the ports of Bideford and Barnstaple, Brixham, Dartmouth and Plymouth, enlivened the entrepreneurial skills of merchants who took to trading on a global scale. The landscape was shaped by the Devon peasant. The small fields, or enclosures were cleared of rock and stones, to shape either drystone walls evident on Dartmoor, or the tall, thick hedges that look soft and inviting as you drive past in the summer but beware they have an underbelly of rock and solid earth. The same earth, mixed with straw and stones, made the mixture known as cob, the vernacular building material to be topped with thatch. The substance of the soil moulded the variations in Agriculture. The rich, red soil of South Hams encouraged cream and cider production, the district of Holsworthy was noted for horses, today it's the Ruby Red Devon cattle. The Tamar Valley took to strawberries. Dartmoor was overlooked for cereal production but the ruggedness suited sheep farming. The North Devon soil produced clay.

**INDUSTRY**. The major industry of the time was developed from the metals, tin and copper. The two western counties, Devon and Cornwall were the sole suppliers of tin up until about 1700. Obtained either as stream-tin or mined-tin (from alluvial deposits). The governance of tin came under the auspices of the Courts of Stannary set up under a Charter by Edward 1.

# DEVON HISTORY

The Court was held at Crockern Tor, an isolated location in the middle of Dartmoor Forest, often attended by 300 gentlemen on horseback. They fixed the price and production.

The purchase and distribution of tin was organised through the four Stannary towns; Ashburton, Tavistock, Plympton and Chagford. The manufacture of woollen cloth was an important Devon industry through the Middle Ages and up to the C19. Crediton and later Exeter were the centres, second to only Leeds in the C18. Tiverton and Cullompton were also centres. But by 1825 the trade had declined. Lace production in the towns of Honiton, Bampton, Uffculme, Cullompton, Ottery St Mary compensated for the loss of the woollen industry and the outlying villages were responsible for much of the labour but this was short-lived. The construction of the Grand Western Canal was a hoped-for saviour to connect Topsham with the River Tone at Taunton.

Exeter however continued to grow as a City. The Napoleonic Wars restricted European travel so the gentry were forced to seek out new places to relax. Exmouth became the first watering-place, soon followed by Sidmouth, Budleigh Salterton, Teignmouth and Torquay. So began the great tourist industry. New roads made the sojourn easier, and so the transformation from horse-borne to horse-drawn began along the new road from London to Exeter via Amesbury (A303 today). Later the Golden Age of the Railways brought much needed affluence, and the development of more coastal towns; Ilfracombe, Minehead, Dawlish and Totnes.

The C20 brought prosperity to the county through the increase in tourism. Small companies moved to the region to provide a higher standard of living for their employees, and the ever-present pensioner looked to the South West Coast as a pleasing place to end their days. The great naval dockyard at Devonport flourished in the two World Wars, and continues to this day, maintaining our fleet of nuclear submarines. The fishing fleets of Brixham and Plymouth provide seafood for the many restaurants of the Southwest, and beyond. Shipbuilding has had a similarly precarious time of it. It is difficult to keep up to date with their news.

The results of a recent poll in a national newspaper concluded that Devon would be the first choice county to live in the UK. It is host to the same number of visitors as Cornwall per year.

# DEVON CELEBRITIES

### Sir John Hawkins (1532-1595)
Adventurer, Privateer, Slave Trader. Son of Plymouth privateer William Hawkins. He was one of the first to capture slaves in Sierra Leone and to sell them on to the Spanish settlers in the Caribbean. Voyages backed by Elizabeth 1 and the Earls of Leicester and Pembroke. Knighted for his role in defeating the Spanish Armada. Later made Treasurer of the Navy. Foiled plot to assassinate Queen Elizabeth 1.

### Sir Humphrey Gilbert (1539-1583)
Explorer, MP, Navigator, Soldier. Born at Greenway, lived at Compton Castle. Educated at Eton and Oxford where he studied Navigation and the Art of War. Later called to the Bar at the Inns of Chancery. Half-brother to Sir Walter Raleigh. Military career in Ireland and the Netherlands. Obsessed with the Elizabethan Quest to find the North West Passage. He sailed to America and discovered Newfoundland in 1583, but generally his sea voyages achieved very little and ended disastrously.

### Sir Francis Drake (1541-1596)
Explorer, Pirate, Privateer, Slave Trader and the Queen's Favourite. Beckoned to the sea aged 13, to learn his trade in the North Sea. Later, aged 23, he made his first voyage to the New World as a slave trader (first started by the Spanish). His dislike of the Spanish endeared him to Queen Elizabeth who encouraged his raiding of Spanish and Portugese shipping. His successful circumnavigation of the world between 1577-1580 on the Golden Hind was his greatest achievement. He was second-in-command during the Armada campaign and Mayor of Plymouth. He died of dysentery off the coast of Panama.

### John Davis (1550-1606)
Arctic Explorer, Cartographer, Inventor, Scientist. Writer on Seamanship. Born at Sandridge Park near Stoke Gabriel beside the River Dart. He made three unsuccessful voyages in search of the North West Passage. He did, however, map the coastlines of Greenland, Baffin Island and Labrador. The Davis Strait was named after him. He identified the cod fishing banks off Newfoundland, and his famous "Traverse Book" became a model for the ships' log books. Inventor of the navigational

device, the backstaff and double quadrant (Davis Quadrant). Commanded the Black Dog against the Spanish Armada. Discovered the Falkland Islands in 1592 aboard the Desire, having earlier failed to pass through the Straits of Magellan. His crew killed 14,000 penguins for homeward bound food, but the meat went foul on reaching the Tropics, and only 14 out of a crew of 76 men survived. Assassinated by Japanese pirates off the coast of Malaysia.

## SIR WALTER RALEIGH (1554-1618)

Explorer, Seafarer, Pirate, Poet and Politician (who came to a sticky end – beheaded for Treason on James 1's ruling). Born at Hayes Barton, East Budleigh. His exploits at sea came to the notice of Queen Elizabeth 1 where he became one of her favourites. Posted to the Captain of the Guard, he foiled the "Babington" plot whose purpose was to replace Elizabeth with Mary, Queen of Scots. His trips to the New World, and discovery of tobacco, originally thought of as a cure for coughing, brought him great wealth. He later built Sherborne Castle in Dorset.

## SIR RICHARD HAWKINS (1562-1622)

Adventurer, Seafarer, Mayor of Plymouth. Son of Sir John Hawkins. Sailed with Drake in 1585 to the Caribbean, to attack Spanish shipping. Later, distinguishing himself commanding The Swallow against the Spanish Armada. Sailed through the Straits of Magellan, attacked Valparaiso (Chile), to be held captive by the Spanish for ten years. Vice Admiral of Devon. Knighted in 1603 by James 1.

## ROBERT HERRICK (1591-1674)

Cavalier Poet, Country Parson. Born in Cheapside, London. Apprenticed to a Goldsmith. Educated at St John's College, Cambridge. He was a friend of the poets Dryden and Marvel, and one of the "Sons of Ben", the Cavalier Poets who idolized Ben Jonson, meeting regularly in the London tavern, the Devil's Head.  In 1629, he was appointed by Charles 1 to be Vicar of Dean Prior. At first, country life bored him. Country people misunderstood him. He was to write his greatest poems in "dull Devonshire". Still hankering for the fleshpots of London. The puritans sent him packing back to London in 1647. In 1648, Hesperides was published, a mighty tome of 1,200 poems. He continued to live well, patronised by the Earls of Buckingham,

Pembroke and Westmorland where his poems were read at Court. The Restoration of Charles 11 in 1660 returned him to Devon where he died a bachelor dreaming of fair Julia and Dianeme.

*Gather ye rosebuds while ye may,*
*Old time is still a flying*
*And this same flower that smiles today*
*Tomorrow will be dying"*
*To the Virgins to make Much of Time*

## JOHN CHURCHILL, 1ST DUKE OF MARLBOROUGH (1650-1722)

Soldier, Statesman. Born Ashe. The greatest European General of his generation. Served with distinction in Ireland and Flanders, later during The War of the Spanish Succession, 1701-1714 where on the fields of Blenheim (Hochstadt), Ramillies and Oudenarde, his place in history was assured. His wife, Sarah Jennings, was a confidant and friend to Queen Anne whose gift was Blenheim Palace after his victory over Louis XIV at Blenheim halted Louis ambitions to capture Vienna, and dominate Europe.

## THOMAS NEWCOMEN (1663-1729)

Inventor. "Father of the Industrial Revolution". Born in Dartmouth. A humble, Ironmonger by profession and Baptist Lay Preacher. He invented the Atmospheric Steam Engine around 1710, and with the help of Thomas Savery, and his patents, one hundred engines were operating in Britain and Europe by the time of his death. His designs were later improved by James Watt who arranged for the steam to be condensed in a separate condenser.

## JOHN LETHBRIDGE (1675-1759)

Inventor. Wool Merchant. Based in Newton Abbot, and as a father of seventeen children he sort wealth to feed them. He invented the one-man, enclosed diving suit with glass porthole for viewing and two watertight armholes with sleeves. The suit was made up of reinforced leather over an airtight oak barrel. His salvage work brought him great wealth.

## JOHN GAY (1685-1732)

Countryman, Dramatist, Journalist, Poet, Satirist, Wit. Born in Barnstaple, and educated at the local Grammar School. Apprenticed to a London silk merchant. He was friend to Pope and Swift, and William Congreve. His patrons were the Duke and Duchess of Queensberry, and the Earl of Burlington. This man loved to party, he loved good food, good company and blue ribbons. He was an early chronicler of country life. His breakthrough came with the play The Beggar's Opera in 1728, a satirical play about highwayman and the corrupt governing class. The two main characters, Captain Macheath and Polly Peacham, have entered the Hall of Fame. The basis for Kurt Weil and Bertolt Brecht's Threepenny Opera. Financially ruined by the South Sea Bubble. He lies in Poets' Corner, Westminster Abbey. On his tombstone, Pope wrote this epitaph: "Life is a jest, and all things show it, I thought so once, and now I know it".

## SIR JOSHUA REYNOLDS (1723-1792)

English Painter. Born in Plympton and son of a clergyman. Studied in Rome 1749-52. The most influential of C18 English Painters specialising in portraits and promoting the "Grand Style". First President of the Royal Academy. Friend to Dr Johnson, Oliver Goldsmith, Edmund Burke and David Garrett. In his lifetime, 3,000 portraits commissioned. Buried in St Paul's Cathedral.

## SAMUEL TAYLOR COLERIDGE (1772-1834)

Poet, Philosopher and Womaniser. Born in Ottery St Mary and educated at Jesus College, Cambridge. He's considered one of the great Romantic poets (and philosophers). Shakespeare scholar, and friend to the Wordsworths, Southey and Lord Byron. He and Southey married the Fricker sisters of Clevedon. His poem The Rhyme of the Ancient Mariner is listed on many school syllabuses.

## CHARLES BABBAGE (1792-1871)

Computer Genius, Inventor, Mathematician. Born in London, moved to Devon, aged 8. Educated in Totnes and at Cambridge where he founded the Analytical Society in 1872 to combat poor learning methods. Designed the first mechanical computer, later the Analytic Engine, a complex machine, and the first mathematical machine to use punch cards (previously used on textile machines).

## THE REVEREND JOHN RUSSELL (1795-1883)

Dog Breeder, Huntsman, "The Sporting Parson". Born in Dartmouth. Educated at Blundell's and Oxford where he spotted a terrier bitch called Trump owned by the local milkman. His ambition was to develop a hardy breed of terrier that could flush out the fox. He became a founder member of the Kennel Club, and friend

of King Edward VII, who as the Prince of Wales, commissioned a portrait of Trump. Buried in Swimbridge churchyard, opposite the Jack Russell Inn.

## CHARLES KINGSLEY (1819-1875)

Chartist, Clergyman, Novelist, Poet, Political Activist, Social Reformer, Wit, Writer. Born at Holne. Educated at Kings College, London and Magdalene College, Cambridge. Brought up around Clovelly. He has the unique legacy of having a town named after his novel, Westward Ho! which in due course inspired the construction of the Appledore-Bideford Railway. Witnessing the Bristol Riots of 1831 formed his social and political outlook. His parish was Eversley in Hampshire.

## SIR RICHARD BURTON (1821-1890)

Adventurer, Diplomat, Explorer, Fencer, Linguist, Orientalist, Soldier, Translator. Born in Torquay. He was thrown out of Oxford and continued to undermine authority for much of his life. He had a natural empathy with languages and as a master of disguise managed to enter the Forbidden Cities of Harar, Mecca and Medina. He co-discovered Lake Tanganyika searching for the source of the Nile. He translated the Arabian Nights, and the Kama Sutra, and introduced the words Pyjama and Safari to the English language. Served in India. Diplomat in Equatorial Guinea, and Brazil. Knighted by Queen Victoria. He died in Trieste.

## R. D. BLACKMORE (1825-1900)

Classicist, Horticulturalist, Literary Pioneer, Naturalist, Poet. Born in Oxfordshire, but his roots and ancestry lay in Devon. Educated at Blundell's and Oxford. His early life was spent at Culmstock and Ashford, then later on Exmoor beside Badgworthy Water. The setting for much of his classic novel, Lorna Doone. Called to the Bar in 1852, he was later advised by his Doctor (on account of his epilepsy) to live a calmer life. So he settled for teaching Classics in Teddington, Middlesex. By all accounts a lovely man, reclusive after his adoring wife's death. He started a Market Garden specialising in fruit. Fellow of the RHS.

## SABINE BARING-GOULD (1834-1924)

Hymn-Writer, Novelist, Scholar, Squire & Parson. Born in Exeter, lived for 40 years at Lewtrenchard

Manor where he fathered 15 children with Grace, a Yorkshire mill girl, and his wife for 48 years, who on meeting and then marrying her sent her off to be educated for two years. Wrote Onward Christian Soldiers and 200 published works. His output was immense, not least his enthusiasm for West Country folk songs resulting in the collection "Songs of the West".

## CAPTAIN ROBERT FALCON SCOTT (1868-1912)

Antarctic Explorer, Royal Naval Officer and father of Peter Scott; Founder of the Wildfowl and Wetlands Trust, and the World Wide Fund for Nature. Born at Outlands, Stoke Damerel. He led two expeditions backed by the Royal Geographical Society; The Discovery Expedition of 1901-1904 was the first attempt at reaching the South Pole. They turned back 450 miles from their objective. This included Ernest Shackleton in the party. The second, and final attempt, the Terra Nova Expedition of 1910-1913, "The Race to the South Pole" failed. Beaten by the Norwegian, Raold Amundsen, by a month. On their return journey to base camp all four of his party died of exposure and hunger eleven miles from their fuel and food depot.

## AGATHA CHRISTIE (1890-1976)

Born and brought up in Torquay, later to live with her archaeologist husband, Max Mallowan, at Greenway on the banks of the River Dart. Known as the Queen of Crime, and inventor of crime's two famous sleuths; Hercule Poirot and Miss Marple. Two billion copies of her books have been sold world-wide.

## HENRY WILLIAMSON (1895-1977)

Broadcaster, Farmer, Naturalist, Soldier, Writer. Born in Brockley, South London. He fought on the Western Front during the First World War, at the Battles of the Somme, and Passchendale. Wounded, he returned home to speak out against the horrors of the trenches. Belittled, ignored, he found solace in the writings of Richard Jeffries, WH Hudson, Francis Thompson and the music of Delius, and Richard Wagner. On the publication of his first book, The Beautiful Years, he was thrown out of home, so rode his Norton 500 Motorcycle down to his beloved North Devon, and Skir Cottage, Georgeham. Remembered for the magnificent Tarka the Otter, Winner of the Hawthornden Prize in 1928, Salar the Salmon, and his tetrology The Flax of Dreams, and his fifteen-book work of Edwardian life, The Chronicle of Ancient Sunlight. He was largely ignored, shunned, ostracised by the British establishment due to his misguided dalliance with Mosleyism in the 1930s. His death coincided, to the day, with David Cobham's filming of Tarka's death scene in the film of the book.

## SIR FRANCIS CHICHESTER (1901-1972)

Aviator, Navigator, Solo Sailor, Map Publisher and Writer. Born in Barnstaple, emigrated to New Zealand aged 18 where he set up a lumber and property business. An interest in flying fostered a passion for navigation. He was to write the official Navigation Manual for the Air Ministry. Best remembered for his epic single-handed circumnavigation of the globe in 1966, from West to East, with one stop in Sydney. Knighted by Queen Elizabeth 11 using Sir Francis Drake's sword.

## TED HUGHES (1930-1998)

Children's Author, Farmer, Fly Fisherman, Naturalist, OM, Poet Laureate. Born in Mytholmroyd, West Yorkshire and raised on the surrounding farms. He entered Pembroke College, Cambridge to read English but switched to Archaeology and Anthropology. He married the American poet and feminist, Sylvia Plath 1956-63, who committed suicide, aged 30. His second great love, Assia Wevill, gassed herself and their four- year old daughter, Shura six years after Plath's death. He lived at Court Green, North Tawton and fished the River Torridge being a great encourager to fellow children's author, Michael Morpurgo. His last marriage to Carol Orchard, nurse, lasted until his early death from cancer.

## MICHAEL MORPURGO (BORN 1943)

Children's Author and Laureate, Countryman, Farmer, Fly Fisherman. Born in St Albans, he has lived in Mid Devon for thirty years. Good friend of Ted Hughes, who offered kind encouragement in his early days as a writer. With his wife, he founded the charity, Farms for City Children, in 1976. At the last count, more than 50,000 children have spent at least a week staying in one of their three farms. He has written over 90 books winning countless awards. Now a father and grandfather. He is the current Children's Laureate.

# INDEX

# INDEX

# ABOUT THE AUTHOR & PHOTOGRAPHER

William Fricker was born in Somerset and educated at Stonyhurst College, Lancashire, and in various places of learning in Austria and Germany. He has worked in publishing for many years.

William first worked with William Collins (now Harper Collins) in London where he became a Creative Director in their paperback division before taking a sabbatical to make a 6,000 km trek across Europe (France-The Alps-Italy, to Greece) along the old mule tracks, footpaths and pilgrim's routes. Inspired by Patrick Leigh Fermor's A Time of Gifts, and Laurie Lee's As I Walked Out One Midsummer Morning. On reaching Greece, his original plan was to then head south and walk up the Nile, but he believes his better judgement prevailed and returned on a bicycle via North Africa, Spain and France amassing 5,000 km. He would like to record he found walking a lot easier. For the past thirty plus years he has built up Goldeneye compiling the research, editorial and photography for more than two hundred UK travel guides and books on cycling, touring and walking. More recently, he has been re-developing his Guidebooks to The Cotswolds, Cornwall, Devon and the Lake District. He lives with his wife Caroline and their youngest child in the West Country.

## FURTHER READING

The finest guidebook to have been written about Devon was W G Hoskin's Devon in 1954 published by William Collins. All books written since that date, refer or nod in appreciation to this great work. Also, published by William Collins, Shirley Toulson's Companion Guide to Devon is a fine piece of work.

Crossing's Guide to Dartmoor, 1909
Worth's Dartmoor, 1953
Bell's Pocket Guide to Devon, Winbolt & Ward, 1929
Goldeneye's Exmoor and Dartmoor Touring Map & Travel Guides since 2004.

Church Pamphlets. These can be bought for a small sum at the back of the church and rarely credit the author. They are invaluable tools as they often combine the history of the church with the village and its famous (past) inhabitants.

## ACKNOWLEDGMENTS

I would like to thank my wife Caroline for her continued support and love in these difficult times of 24-hour care for our youngest daughter, Alice, to whom this book is dedicated. Thank you Izy for your added research and editorial skills. Not to be forgotten, all my friends and colleagues who provide me with leads and knowledge about new venues, existing ones and their ever-changing skills.

Goldeneye would like to thank the following for allowing us to photograph their property or for providing us with an image or two:- Mark Harold & Liz Luck of the National Trust (Devon and Cornwall Regional Office), Lady Arran of Castle Hill, Lady Stucley of Hartland Abbey, Ingrid Oram of Powderham Castle, Rupert Thistlethwayte of Cadhay, Visitor Services at Exeter Cathedral, John Rouse of Clovelly Estates. And, to Marwood Hill Gardens, Lympstone Manor, Boringdon Hall, The Pig at Combe, North Morte Camping, Arundel Arms Hotel, Culm Valley Inn, Home Farm Café, Thomas Carr, Salutation Inn, Noel Corston, Gidleigh Park, Mor shellfish, Broomhill Estate, Poltimore Arms, Hartland Quay Museum, Hotel Endsleigh, Plymouth Aquarium, Bovey Tracey Church, Ottery St Mary Church, Wiscombe Park hill climbs, Dart Valley Railway, Shoreham Vineyard. For this, the Third Edition, thank you to the Old Exeter Inn, Burgh Island Hotel, Vigilance Trustees, Luttrell Arms Hotel, Elephant Restaurant, Dartmoor Inn, Ainscough Gallery, Mayne Gallery, Harberton Church, Imperial Hotel, Moretonhampstead Motor Museum, Phil Butcher, Museum of Dartmoor Life, Bicton Park and Quince Honey Farm,

Thank you to all the attractions, places to stay and eat, for showing me around their establishments and either allowing us to photograph them or for providing an image for use in this book.

The bare bones of the Timeline originated from the Devon Regional Library at Exeter.

William Fricker, May 2022, Penryn